STOKVIS STUDIES IN
HISTORICAL CHRONOLOGY
AND THOUGHT
ISSN 0270-5338
Number One

W9-CRN-316

Lords Temporal
and
Lords Spiritual

*A Chronological Checklist of the Popes, Patriarchs,
Katholikoi, and Independent Archbishops and Metropolitans
of the Autocephalous and Autonomous Monarchical
Churches of the Christian East and West*

SECOND EDITION
Revised and Expanded

by

Michael Burgess

California State University, San Bernardino

R . REGINALD
The Borgo Press
San Bernardino, California ▫ MCMXCV

THE BORGO PRESS

Twentieth Anniversary, 1975-1995
Post Office Box 2845
San Bernardino, CA 92406
United States of America

*   *   *   *   *   *   *   *

Copyright © 1985, 1995 by Michael Burgess

Library of Congress Cataloging-in-Publication Data

Burgess, Michael, 1948-
  Lords temporal and lords spiritual : a chronological checklist of the
popes, patriarchs, katholikoi, and independent archbishops and metropolitans of the autocephalous and autonomous monarchical churches of the
Christian East and West / by Michael Burgess. — 2nd ed., rev. and
expanded.
    p. cm. (Stokvis studies in historical chronology and thought, ISSN
0270-5338 ; no. 1)
  Includes bibliographical references and index.
  ISBN 0-89370-326-5 (cloth). — ISBN 0-89370-426-1 (pbk.)
  1. Patriarchs and patriarchate—Registers. 2. Patriarchs and patriarchate
(Catholic Oriental)—Registers. I. Title. II. Series: Stokvis studies in
historical chronology & thought ; no. 1.
BX100.8.B87 1995   87-6319
280'.2—dc19   CIP

SECOND EDITION

CONTENTS

3

INTRODUCTION

PRIMUS INTER PARES

Lords Temporal and Lords Spiritual is the second and much expanded edition of a chronological checklist of the patriarchs and other heads of the Eastern churches and their western counterparts.

The goal of this new edition remains as before: to record as authoritatively as possible the leaders and brief histories of every Eastern church that claims autocephaly (and, in this second edition, autonomy), and which has some reasonable historical or national claim to recognition as an independent church group; or, while lacking such universal recognition from other groups, nonetheless possesses a significant body of communicants. Several small splinter groups that claim ecclesiastical descent from the various attempts between the wars to erect national American churches have been dropped in this edition; however, fifteen new ecclesiastical jurisdictions have been added, including the autonomous churches of Crete, Finland, Japan, and the ex-Soviet Bloc states, as well as the Church of Macedonia, whose claims of autocephaly are recognized by few groups outside of itself, but which meets all the other criteria. Also included are those Latin Churches which correspond to the ancient Eastern sees, even though most became no more than titular honors following the departure of the crusaders who had erected them; but such Western patriarchates as Venice, Lisbon, and the East and West Indies have been omitted, since they have never followed the pattern of the other churches.

Other new features include: expanded histories of each church, source citations, a comprehensive index to primates, and a completely reformatted and reset text, including diacritical marks to distinguish the Greek letters *éta* and *ómega* from *epsilon* and *omicron*. Finally, each list has been reverified by mailing copies of the new versions of each to the heads of the ecclesiastical bodies; I have once again been gratified by the generous level of response.

In both editions the officially sanctioned list of each church has been regarded as final. Where two or more churches claim the same basic patriarchal list prior to a certain date, but differ on exact names and dates, each list has been run separately, without any attempt to sort out claims and counterclaims, and without making any effort to rectify the lists one against another. I have never actually found any two such lists that completely agreed with one another; also, in every case where

5

I received an "official" list from a church, its records disagreed with all the others in my possession, sometimes widely.

The reasons for adopting such guidelines are obvious. The official lists determine the postnominal numbering of both past and future church leaders; to vary from them, even slightly, is to invite ever-increasing discrepancies, in a world where such variations are already pervasive. Historians may quibble over the reality or even the name of this or that patriarch, as they do with certain rulers of secular states; in the end, however, we must agree to call Louis XVIII of France by that name, and not Louis XVII (who never reigned), in order to establish some common ground for discussion. This book is my attempt at finding that common ground. Only in the case of the Ethiopian Orthodox Church, where the "official" list varies so widely from the known historical record, have I felt compelled to provide two lists, the second derived from independent research.

Finally, the patriarchs' names have been transliterated as closely and consistently as possible from the languages actually used in each of the churches today. It was A. M. H. J. Stokvis who, in his monumental work, *Manuel d'Histoire, de Généalogie, et de Chronologie de Touts les États du Globe*, first established the principle of reproducing the names of rulers in the forms approximating as closely as possible those actually used in the vernaculars of their countries. Although the Eastern churches are, as a group, often referred to as "Greek Orthodox" by the uninformed, many of the churches that once used Greek as their official tongue now employ Arabic or some other native language. The transliterations are based on the systems established by the Library of Congress and the American Library Association for the romanization of non-English alphabets (see the Library of Congress's *Cataloging Bulletin*, nos. 118 and following), with occasional minor variations to standardize usage between similar languages. Since there is, as yet, no universally accepted method of transliterating the Syriac language into English, the system used by Arthur John MacLean in his *A Dictionary of the Dialects of Vernacular Syriac* (Oxford, 1901) has been followed, with some minor exceptions.

In those instances where there is some legitimate question as to which language is considered official by a particular church, in every case the language in common use among the people covered by its jurisdiction has been chosen first, with alternate versions where known. For example, the Coptic Church uses both Coptic and Arabic for official purposes; however, Coptic has long since ceased to be spoken except for liturgical purposes, and so the Arabic versions of the patriarchs' names are listed first, followed by the Coptic versions in parentheses. Similarly Arabic has been preferred over Syriac for the two Syrian patriarchates of Antioch.

The primary source for each church's history and leadership is, finally, the church itself. In compiling the first edition I contacted each of these bodies directly, and sent them copies of the lists and histories I had already compiled, requesting facsimile copies of their official records in the languages used by them for everyday church purposes. Eighty percent of the churches responded to my queries, either by providing copies of their official lists, or by referring me to published records they accepted as accurate and authoritative. A handful accepted the lists I sent them as genuine. All of the lists were buttressed by further research in the sources cited at the bottom of the history of each church, plus other research. These citations are not intended to be exhaustive, but merely reflect those books or periodical articles I personally found most useful.

On the subject of doctrine I remain mute. My purpose here is to record the chronology of each church as it perceives itself; I make no judgments about the correctness or legitimacy of any jurisdictional or theological beliefs or claims or counterclaims. The fragmentation of the churches of Eastern Christendom is a fact of history which cannot be denied by the impartial observer; however, the reasons behind the balkanization of Orthodoxy are complex and not easily understood, having more perhaps to do with the cultural and historical backgrounds of each region than with any real or perceived differences in doctrine. These frequent feuds and jealousies have resulted, for example, in five different churches claiming the title of Patriarch of Antioch, three of them acknowledging the supremacy of the Pope of Rome.

To avoid this maze I have included here any established Eastern church that claims autocephaly (complete canonical independence from its brothers) or autonomy (complete self-governance except for the consecration of its primate), that elects a patriarch or an equivalent monarchical figure as its primate, and that possesses at least a patina of ecclesiastical legitimacy (a structure recognized by other autocephalous churches, or one that corresponds to a national boundary, or one that possesses a certain size and organizational structure). Also included are those uniate Eastern churches that correspond to one of the ancient patriarchal sees but acknowledge the supremacy of the Roman Church; plus the Church of Rome itself, since it was one of the original patriarchates of early christianity. The autocephaly of some of these churches is not recognized by others, and the mere inclusion of a church, however large or small, should not be regarded as an endorsement of the claims it makes for itself. For those few churches that did not respond to my queries, I have produced as accurate an amalgamation of current scholarly opinion as possible, taking into account the known chronology of recent patriarchs to standardize their numbering.

The churches are arranged in alphabetical order by their chief sees or national boundaries. Each entry includes a brief summary of the church's history, some indication of the location and size and language of its flock, the official title of the primate, the chief see of the church, a note on the language used in each church, and a chronological checklist of its primates. The second section of the book provides a selected bibliography, a comparative table showing the differing forms of each Christian name, language by language, and a complete primate index. Additions and corrections are welcome, and should be sent to the author c/o Borgo Press.

I wish to thank each of the churches and churchmen who responded to my many letters of inquiry, and also those other individuals who assisted in various ways, particularly (in alphabetical order):

E. Alexandra Amrine and her staff in the Interlibrary Loan Department of the Cal State Library, who obtained many rare books for me; Mary Burgess; Araxie Charukian, library assistant at the Tomás Rivera Library and cousin of Armenian Catholicos Garegin I; Dr. Jeffrey M. Elliot; Father Gareth M. Evans; Kenneth A. Gakus; Chakir al-Hamwi; Dr. Robert H. Hewsen; Rev. Demetrius J. King; Father Patrick McReynolds; Rev. Nenos S. Michael; Dr. Fran J. Polek; the late Archbishop Andrew Prazsky; Bishop Karl Prüter; Bishop Thomas Mar Makarios; Rev. Father Alexey Young. Thanks also to my predecessors in compilation, Anthony Stokvis, the Assemanis, Bertold Spuler, Otto Meinardus, Michel Le Quien, and others, whose pioneering efforts to record accurately the facts of both secular and religious chronology provided much inspiration to an aspiring young student.

Thanks also to the following libraries and organizations who provided varying levels of assistance: Le Centre Orthodoxe de Patriarcat Oecuménique, Chambésy, Genève, Switzerland; The Crosby Library, Gonzaga University, Spokane; The Doheny Library, University of Southern California, Los Angeles; Dr. Elizabeth Briere and the Fellowship of St. Alban and St. Sergius; The Library of Congress; The John M. Pfau Library, California State University, San Bernardino; The Tomás Rivera Library, University of California, Riverside; the Libraries of the University of California at Los Angeles; the LaVerne University Library.

Finally, as before, this book is dedicated to my childhood friend, Dick Marchand, who saw the beginnings of this work, but who died of a brain tumor at the age of thirty-two before it was completed; and to my dear colleague and fellow editor, Ted Dikty, a kind and gentle man whom I miss dearly. *Requiescant in pace*, old friends.

—Michael Burgess
California State University, San Bernardino
11 February 1985-11 February 1995

GLOSSARY

Surnames are listed for primates when known, in italics following their reign name. Alternate names are sometimes given in parentheses for primates when the official appelation in use today appears to vary from the language in use at the time the primate actually reigned.

"ANTI-PATRIARCH" or "ANTI-POPE" or "ANTI-ARCHBISHOP"—that is, a primate considered by the current succession to have been elected or appointed uncanonically, although he may have commanded a considerable (even a majority) following in his time.

"COADJUTOR" or "SUFFRAGAN" signifies a prelate elected or appointed to assist the primate—he may or may not have succeeded in his own right, and may or may not be numbered with the rest of his church's leaders.

"INTERREGNUM" in theory designates any intermediate period, however brief, between the death, resignation, or deposition of one primate, and the succession of another. For the purposes of this book I have abitrarily chosen to note only those interregna which have lasted three years or longer, on the grounds that these represent a significant interruption in the normal sequence of governance.

"LOCUM TENENS" designates a prelate who may never have served as primate, but who acted as chief administrator of the primatial office until a new primate could be elected. I have added in this Second Edition the *Locum Tenentes* for twentieth-century interregna, when known.

"PRIMATE," the elected, appointed, or hereditary leader of a church, who may bear the title of patriarch, pope, catholicos, metropolitan, metran, archbishop, exarch, bishop, or some variation thereof.

"2ND TIME," "3rd TIME," etc., indicates the second, third, etc., reign of a particular primate.

"UNCONSECRATED" notes a primate who was properly elected but never actually consecrated, and therefore may or may not be included on the official list of primates of that church.

In Memoriam

Anthony Marinus Hendrik Johan Stokvis
(23 September 1855-17 November 1924)

Richard Bruce Marchand, S.J.
(17 September 1946-10 March 1979)

Thaddeus Maxim Eugene Dikty
(16 June 1920-11 October 1991)

In Lætitiam

Bishop Karl Prüter

Abbess Katherine Kurtz

Patriarch Maximos V Hakim

"Serint arbores quae alteri seculo prosint"

I.

THE CHURCH OF AGHT'AMAR

The Armenian Catholicate of Aght'amar was founded in 1113, the result of a schism with the mother church that was not mended until
1409. Aght'amar was essentially a local church, located on an island
in, and on the shores around, Lake Van, in what is now Eastern
Turkey, southwest of Armenia proper. Although able to maintain itself
for many centuries as a separate and autonomous church, it became increasingly dependent on Echmiadzin for clergy and support.

The terrible massacres of Armenians conducted by the Turks
between 1890-1915, and the subsequent explusion from Turkey of most
the survivors, decimated the Aght'amar Church; when the last Catholicos died in 1895, in the middle of the upheaval, a successor could not
be elected; by the time the situation had stabilized, after World War I,
so few Armenians remained in Eastern Turkey that restoration of the
Catholicos was impractical. Aght'amar was then reduced in status to a
diocese under the direct control of the Church at Echmiadzin.

SOURCES: *The Church of Armenia* (Ormanian); *Dictionnaire
d'Histoire et de Géographie Ecclésiastique*; *The History of the Armenian People* (Morgan).

CATHOLICOS-PATRIARCHS OF AGT'AMAR

1.	Dawit' I *T'ornikian*	1113-1165?
	Grigor [coadjutor?]	1140?
	Hovhannês [coadjutor?]	1155?
2.	Step'anos I	1165?-1185?
	INTERREGNUM	
3.	Step'anos II	-1272
4.	Step'anos III *Sefedinian*	1272-1296?
	Khach'atur [coadjutor?]	1287?
	Step'anos (IV) *Tghay* [anti-catholicos?]	1288-1292
	Eghishê [anti-catholicos?]	1292-1300
5.	Zak'aria I *Sefedinian*	1296-1336
	Nersês [coadjutor]	1312
	Dawit' *Sefedinian* [coadjutor?]	1326?
6.	Step'anos IV *Ardzruni*	1336?-1346

7.	Dawit' II *Sefedinian*	1346-1368?
	Nersês *Bolat* [anti-catholicos]	1368?-1369?
8.	Zak'aria II *Nahatak*	1369-1393
	Nersês [anti-catholicos]	1393?
9.	Dawit' III	1393-1433
10.	Zak'aria III	1434-1464
11.	Step'anos V *Kurdjibeguyan*	1464-1489
	Nersês *Kurdjibeguyan* [anti-catholicos]	1489?
12.	Zak'aria IV	1489-1496
13.	Atom	1496-1510
14.	Hovhannês I	1510-1512
15.	Grigoris I	1512-1544?
16.	Grigoris II	1544?-1586?
17.	Grigoris III	1586?-1612?
	Step'anos (VI) [anti-catholicos]	1612?
	Baghdasar [anti-catholicos]	1630?
	INTERREGNUM	
18.	Martiros *Gurji*	1660-1662
	Karapet *Krdshadz* [anti-catholicos]	1661?
19.	Petros I	1662?-1670
20.	Step'anos VI	1671?
21.	P'ilippos	1671?
22.	Karapet I	1677-1679?
23.	Hovhannês II *T'iwt'iwnji*	1679-1681?
24.	T'ovma I *Toghlabeghian*	1681-1698
25.	Awetis	1697
26.	Sahak *Artskets'i*	1698
27.	Hovhannês III *Kêtsuk*	1699-1704
28.	Hayrapet *P'aykhets'i*	1705-1707
29.	Grigor IV *Gawahets'i*	1707-1711
	INTERREGNUM	
30.	Hovhannês IV *Hayots'-Zobets'i*	1720
	T'ovma [locum tenens]	1722?
	Ghazar [locum tenens]	1723?
31.	Grigor V *Hizants'i*	1725
32.	Baghdasar	1735?-1736
	Sahak (II) [anti-catholicos]	1736
	Hakob [anti-catholicos]	1736
33.	Nikoghayos	1736-1751
34.	Grigor VI	1751-1761
35.	T'ovma II	1761-1783
36.	Karapet II	1783-1787
37.	Markos	1788-1791
	Hovhannês (V) [anti-catholicos]	1791?
38.	T'êodoros	1792-1794
39.	Mik'ayêl	1796-1810

40.	Karapet III	1810?-1813?
41.	Khach'atur I	1813-1814
42.	Karapet IV	1814?-1816?
43.	Harut'iwn	1816?-1823
44.	Hovhannês V *Shatakhets'i*	1823-1843
45.	Khach'atur II *Mokats'i*	1844-1851
46.	Gabriêl *Shiroyan*	1851-1857
47.	Petros II *Pilpilian*	1858-1864
48.	Khach'atur III *Shiroyan*	1864-1895

THE CATHOLICOSATE DISCONTINUED

II.

THE CHURCH OF AGHUNIE
(CAUCASIAN ALBANIA)

Located on the western shores of the Caspian Sea, directly east of Armenia, the Armenian state of Albania was an independent Armenian principality which bordered on both Armenia proper and on the Kingdom of Georgia. As with Georgia, Aghunie (the Armenian name) soon developed its own Church, independent of Armenia by the fifth century, if not sooner.. For more than a thousand years the Albanian Church maintained a semi-autonomous existence, sometimes acting as an autocephalous body, on other occasions depending upon the Church of Armenia to supply new patriarchs or bishops. With the disappearance of the secular state of Albania, circa 1100, the Catholicosate gradually lost its separate status. The last patriarch, who bore the title of Catholicos of Aghunie, Lpink, and Choga, was deposed in 1815, and died in 1828, the Church thereupon being demoted to the status of a diocese under Echmiadzin.

SOURCES: "The Albanian Chronicle of Mxit'ar Gos" (Dowsett); *Dictionnaire d'Histoire et de Géographie Ecclésiastique*; *The History of the Armenian People* (Morgan); *A History of the Caucasian Albanians* (Movsês); "A Neglected Passage in the History of the Caucasian Albanians" (Dowsett); *O Literature Kavkazskoi Albanii* (Mnatsakanian).

CATHOLICOS-PATRIARCHS OF CAUCASIAN ALBANIA

1.	Eghishê	-79
	INTERREGNUM	
2.	name unknown	302-325
	INTERREGNUM	
3.	Grigoris I	340-342
4.	Matt'êos I	342-
5.	Sahak I	
6.	Movsês I	
7.	Pant	
8.	Ghazar	
9.	Zak'aria I	

10.	Dawit' I	-399
11.	Hovhan(nes) I	400-
	INTERREGNUM	
12.	Shup'aghishoy	500-
13.	Eremia I	-552
14.	Abas	552-596
15.	Viroy	596-630
16.	Zak'aria II	630-646
17.	Hovhan(nes) II	646-670
18.	Ukhtanês	670-681?
19.	Eghiazar	681?-687?
20.	Nersês I	687?-704
21.	Simêon I	704-706
22.	Mik'ayêl	706-741
23.	Anastas	741-745
24.	Hovsêp' I	745-762
25.	Dawit' II	762-766
26.	Dawit' III	766-775
27.	Matt'ê (or Matt'êos) II	775-777
28.	Movsês II	777-779
29.	Aharon	779-781
30.	Soghomon I	782
31.	T'êodoros	782-786
32.	Soghomon II	786-797
33.	Hovhannês III	797-822
34.	Movsês III	822
35.	Dawit' IV	822-849
36.	Hovsêp' II	849-874
37.	Samuêl	874-891
38.	Hovhan IV	892-901
39.	Simêon II	902-923
40.	Dawit' V	923-929
41.	Sahak II	929-947
42.	Gagik I	947-961
43.	Dawit' VI	961-968
44.	Dawit' VII	968-974
45.	Petros I	974-992
46.	Movsês IV	992-997
47.	Markos I	997-
48.	Hovsêp' III	1038?
49.	Markos II	-1077
50.	Step'anos I	1077-1103
51.	Hovhannês V	1103-1130
52.	Step'anos II	1130-1132
	INTERREGNUM	
53.	Grigoris II (or Gagik II)	1139-

54.	Babkên	1147?
55.	Step'anos III	1155?-1195
56.	Nersês II [coadjutor?]	1171?
57.	Hovhannês VI	1195-1235
58.	Nersês III	1235-1262
59.	Step'anos IV	1262-1323
60.	Suk'ias	1323
61.	Petros II	1323-
62.	Hovhannês VII	
63.	Hovhannês VIII	
64.	Petros III	-1406
65.	Karapet	1406-1411
66.	Dawit' VIII	1411
67.	Matt'êos III	1412-1440
68.	At'anasios	1440-1441
69.	Grigor III	1441-
70.	Hovhannês IX	-1470
71.	Matt'êos IV	1470-
72.	Aristakês I	-1478
73.	Nersês IV	1478-1481
74.	Chmavon I	1481-
75.	T'ovma	-1495
76.	Arakel	1495-1511
77.	Aristakês II	1511-1521
78.	Sargis I	1521-1555
79.	Grigor IV	1556-1563
80.	P'ilippos	1563-
81.	Dawit' IX	1573-1574
82.	Hovhannês X	-1586
83.	Chmavon II	1586-1611
84.	Aristakês III	1588-1593
85.	Melk'iset'	1593-1596
86.	Simêon III	1596-
87.	Hovhannês XI	1633-1634
88.	Grigor V	1634-1653
89.	Petros IV	1653-1675
	Simêon IV [anti-catholicos]	1675-1701
90.	Eremia II	1676-1700
91.	Esayi	1701-1727
	Nersês V [anti-catholicos]	1706-1727
92.	Nersês V	1727-1763
	Israyêl [anti-catholicos]	1763-1765
93.	Hovhannês XII	1763-1786
94.	Simêon V	1794-1810
95.	Sargis II *Hassan-Jalaliants'*	1794-1815

THE CATHOLICOSATE DISCONTINUED

III.

THE CHURCH OF ALBANIA

Albania was placed under the ecclesiastical jurisdiction of the Patriarchate of Pec in 1346. With the abolition of the Serbian patriarchate in 1766, the administration of the Church was transferred to the Ecumenical Patriarch in Constantinople. During the centuries of Ottoman occupation, most of the population converted to Islam, approximately one-fourth remaining Christian; two-thirds of the latter are Orthodox, the rest being Catholic or other denominations.

When Albania became independent in 1914, the Orthodox Church there asserted itself, unilaterally declaring its autocephaly in September 1922. In January 1924, three priests—Teofan "Fan" Noli, an Albanian-American, Hierotheos, a Greek, and Chrysostomos, also Greek—were consecrated as bishops of the new church, and formed themselves into a Synod, with Hierotheos being named first Archbishop of Albania. Questions were raised by other Orthodox churches over these consecrations, and the Ecumenical Patriarch refused his recognition. Five years later, Vissarion Xhuvani (Besarione Giovanni) gained the recognition of the government of King Zog I, and was consecrated Archbishop on 12 February 1929; he reconstituted the Synod and reasserted Albanian autocephaly on 18 February.

Constantinople still withheld recognition, until an agreement was reached with Kristofor Kissi, a member of the Albanian Synod, on 12 April 1937. Vissarion was deposed, and Kissi installed as Metropolitan Archbishop. The Communist regime deposed Kissi in 1949, installing Païsi Voditsa, and putting great pressure on the Church during the next two decades. The government finally abolished the practice of religion altogether in 1967; every place of worship was closed, public and private worship being forbidden. Archbishop Damian was arrested after serving less than a year; he died in prison in 1973.

In late 1990 and early 1991, under pressures both internal and external, the Communist government agreed to allow free elections, and restored freedom of religion to the population; mass was openly celebrated in an Orthodox church for the first time in twenty-three years. The Ecumenical Patriarch promptly announced a program of assistance to re-establish the Albanian Church, appointing (at the end of 1990) a

Greek Exarch, Anastasios Gannoulatos (Anastas Xhanulatos in Albanian) to ordain new clergy and reconstitute the shattered Church finances and physical resources. Xhanulatos was promoted to Archbishop on 2 August 1992, amid protests from some of his communicants, who felt that the post ought to go to an Albanian. By 1994 dissident members had formed a protest group lobbying for restoration of autocephalous status to the Church of Albania and banishment of all foreign nationals from the hierarchy.

The head of the Albanian Church bears the title Metropolitan of Tiranë and Durresi, Archbishop of All Albania. The official language is Albanian. There were roughly 160,000 communicants in Albania (according to *Eastern Christianity and Politics*) prior to 1967; the number of those who have returned to the church in the 1990s is unknown.

An American branch of the Church, originally organized in 1912 by Fan Noli, split into two groups, one joining the Orthodox Church in America in 1971, the other (larger) body placing itself at the same time under the Greek Orthodox Archdiocese of North and South America of the Ecumenical Patriarchate. A third faction, the Independent Albanian Orthodox Church of St. Paul, was founded about 1958 by Archbishop Kristofor Rado; when he died in 1974, one part of his church joined the Orthodox Church in America, the other becoming part of the Vasiloupolis Church.

SOURCES: *Eastern Christianity and Politics in the Twentieth Century* (Ramet, ed.); *Échos d'Orient*; *Episkepsis*; *Europa World Yearbook*; *Gegenwartslage der Ostkirchen* (Spuler); *History of the Church* (Jedin, ed.); *Orthodoxia*; *Profiles in Belief* (Piepkorn).

METROPOLITAN ARCHBISHOPS OF ALBANIA

1.	Hierotheos	1924-1929
2.	Vissarion *Xhuvani*	1929-1937
3.	Kristofor *Kissi(s)*	1937-1949
4.	Païsi *Vodica*	1949-1966
5.	Damian *Kokonesi*	1966-1973
	Sofron *Borova* [locum tenens]	1967-1973
	INTERREGNUM	
	Anastas *Xhanulatos* [exarch]	1990-1992
6.	Anastas *Xhanulatos*	1992-

IV.

THE COPTIC CHURCH OF ALEXANDRIA

The ancient Patriarchate of Alexandria was one of the original seats of early Christianity, having been founded, according to legend, by St. Mark the Evangelist. Although renowned as an early center of monasticism, the Egyptian Church was also plagued with schisms and controversy from its earliest centuries. The supporters of Arianism erected a separate patriarchate in the year 336; it survived, with breaks, until 378. Less than a century later, the patriarch Dioskoros (or Di[u]squrus) I embraced monophysitism, precipitating a major doctrinal struggle at the Council of Chalcedon in 451. Dioskoros was subsequently declared a heretic, deposed, and banished, with the full support of Eastern Emperor Markianos. The Greek ruling class of Egypt elected Proterios to fill the now-vacant see; the native population, however, most of whom spoke Coptic (a degenerate form of ancient Egyptian), rallied around Dioskoros, sending him a delegation to assure him of their loyalty. He died in 454, before he could return from exile.

Thus began the great split in the Alexandrian Church. At the death of Dioskoros, the populace demanded a new patriarch, but the government refused; when the Emperor died, however, an Egyptian mob murdered Proterios, and installed their own leader, Timotheos Ailouros ("The Cat") in his place. Constantinople was unable to reestablish civil control over Egypt for three years, at which point Timotheos was exiled, and a supporter of Chalcedon, Timotheos Salophakiolos ("Wobbling Hat"—in other words, vacillating), was put in his place. Ailouros was restored by the Emperor Basiliskos in 475, deposed again in 476, and died in 477. The Emperor Zénón, determined to put an end to the civil and religious strife in Egypt, banished the Greek patriarch in 489, leaving the Coptic line without rivals for fifty years. In 536, the Copts split again, one faction following Gaïanos; the Roman pope used the occasion to establish Paulos as Melkite Patriarch of Egypt. Despite periods of success, the Copts were never really secure from the depredations of the Greeks until the Arab conquest of 642; from this point forward, except for a seventy-six year gap between 651-727, there are two separate lines of patriarchs.

The Coptic line, representing the common people, has always been by far the larger church, encompassing perhaps 80% of the Chris-

19

tian population in Egypt. Coptic is the official language of the Church, but Arabic is used for everyday purposes (and the patriarchs below are listed with the Arabic versions of their names). A month before his assassination in 1981, Egyptian President Anwar al-Sadat tried to placate Muslim extremists by exiling Coptic Pope Shanudah III to a monastery in the Egyptian desert. He was kept there under house arrest until 1 January 1985, when President Hosni Mubarak restored him to his position.

The primate bears the title "Pope and Patriarch of the Great City of Alexandria and of All the Land of Egypt, of Jerusalem the Holy City, of Nubia, Abyssinia, and Pentapolis, and All the Preaching of St. Mark." Although the chief see of the Church is technically Alexandria, its administrative offices are actually located in Cairo. Eight to ten million communicants are spread throughout Northern Africa (particularly Egypt), with strong overseas populations in the United States and other countries.

SOURCES: *Christian Egypt Ancient and Modern* (Meinardus); *Die Christlich-Koptische Agypten Einst und Heute* (Cramer); *Coptic Egypt* (Kamil); *The Coptic Encyclopedia* (Atiya); *Dictionnaire d'Histoire et de Géographie Ecclésiastiques*; *Episkepsis*; *Gegenwartslage der Ostkirchen* (Spuler); *Histoire de L'Église Copte* (Roncaglia); *Historia tés Ekklésias Alexandreias (62-1934)* (Papadopoulos); *History of the Church* (Jedin, ed.); *The History of the Coptic Church* (Yuhanna); *A History of the Patriarchs of the Egyptian Church* (Atiya; regarded as official by the church); *A History of the Patriarchs of the See of Alexandria* (Tawudrus); *A Lonely Minority: The Middle East and North Africa*; *The Modern Story of Egypt's Copts* (Wakin); *Monks and Monasteries of the Egyptian Desert* (Meinardus); *Die Morgenlandischen Kirchen* (Spuler); *Mujaz Tarikh Batarikat al-Iskandariyah* (Nabib); *Oriens Christianus* (Le Quien); *Orthodoxia*; personal communication; *Précis de L'Histoire d'Egypte* (Munier); *Profiles in Belief* (Piepkorn); *Qissat al-Khanisah al-Qibtiyah* (al-Misri).

COPTIC POPES AND PATRIARCHS OF ALEXANDRIA
(Coptic forms of the names are given in parentheses)

1.	Murqus I (Markos)	43?-68
2.	Aniyanus (Anianos)	68-85
3.	Miliyus (Milios)	83-98
4.	Kurdunus (Kerdón)	98-109
5.	Abrimus (Primos)	109-122
6.	Yustus (Ioustos)	122-130
7.	Awminiyus (Eumenios)	130-142
8.	Markiyanus (Markianos)	143-154
	INTERREGNUM	
9.	Kallawtiyanus (Kallauthianos)	157-167

10.	Aghribbinus (Agrippinos)	167-180
11.	Yuliyanus (Ioulianos)	180-189
12.	Dimitriyus I (Démétrios)	189-231
13.	Yaraklas (Hieraklas)	231-247
14.	Diyunisiyus (Dionysios)	247-264
15.	Maksimus (Maximos)	264-282
16.	Thawna (Theónas)	282-300
17.	Butrus I (Petros)	300-311
18.	Arshalawus (Archelaos or Achillas)	311-312
19.	Aliksandarus I (Alexandros)	312-326
20.	Athanasiyus I (Athanasios)	326-373
21.	Butrus II (Petros)	373-380
22.	Timuthawus I (Timotheos) [brother of #21]	380-385
23.	T(h)awfilus (Theophilos)	385-412
24.	Kirillus I (Kyrillos) [nephew of #23]	412-444
25.	Disqurus I (Dioskoros)	444-458
26.	Timuthawus II (Timotheos) *Ailouros* "The Cat"	458-460?
	Timuthawus *Salophakialos* [anti-pope]	460-475
	Timuthawus II (Timotheos) [2nd time]	475-480
27.	Butrus III (Petros) *Mongos*	480-488
28.	Athanasiyus II (Athanasios)	488-494
29.	Yuhannis I (Ióannés) *Hemula*	495-503
30.	Yuhannis II (Ióannés) *Nikiotés*	503-515
31.	Disqurus II (Dioskoros) [nephew of #26]	515-517
32.	Timuthawus III (Timotheos)	517-535
33.	Thawdusiyus I (Theodosios)	535-567
34.	Butrus IV (Petros)	567-569
35.	Damiyanus (Damianos)	569-605
36.	Anastasiyus (Anastasios)	605-616
37.	Andruniqus (Andronikos)	616-622
38.	Banyamin I (Beniamin)	622-661
39.	Aghathu(n) (Agathón)	661-677
40.	Yuhannis III (Ióannés)	677-686
41.	Isaaq (Isaak)	686-689
42.	Simawun I (Symeón)	689-701
	INTERREGNUM	
43.	Aliksandarus II (Alexandros)	705-730
44.	Qusma(n) I (Kosmas)	730-731
45.	Thawdurus (Theodóros)	731-743
46.	Kha'il (or Mikha'il) I (Chaél)	744-767
47.	Mina I (Minas)	767-774
48.	Yuhannis IV (Ióannés)	775-799
49.	Murqus II (Markos)	799-819
50.	Ya'qub (Iakóbos)	819-830
51.	Simawun II (Symeón)	830
52.	Yusab I (Ióséph)	830-849

53.	Kha'il (or Mikha'il) II (Chaél)	849-851
54.	Qusma(n) II (Kosmas)	851-858
55.	Sanutiyus (or Shanudah) I (Senouthios)	858-880
56.	Mikha'il III (Michaél)	880-907
57.	Ghubriyal I (Gabriél)	909-920
58.	Qusma(n) III (or Quzman) (Kosmas)	920-932
59.	Makariyus I (Makarios)	932-952
60.	Thawfaniyus (Theophanios or Theophanés)	952-956
61.	Mina II (Minas)	956-974
62.	Abram (or Afram) *ibn Zar'ah* (Abraam)	975-978
63.	Filut(h)awus (Philotheos)	979-1003
64.	Zakhariya(s) (Zakharias)	1004-1032
65.	Sanutiyus (or Shanudah) II (Senouthios)	1032-1046
66.	Akhristudulus (Christodoulos)	1047-1077
67.	Kirillus II (Kyrillos)	1078-1092
68.	Mikha'il IV (Michaél)	1092-1102
69.	Makariyus II (Makarios)	1102-1128
	INTERREGNUM	
70.	Ghubriyal II *ibn Turaik* (Gabriél)	1131-1145
71.	Mikha'il V (Michaél)	1145-1146
72.	Yuhannis V *ibn Abi'l-Fath* (Ióannés)	1147-1167
73.	Murqus III *ibn Zur'a* (Markos)	1167-1189
74.	Yuhannis VI *ibn Abi Ghali* (Ióannés)	1189-1216
	INTERREGNUM	
75.	Kirillus III *Dawud ibn Laqlaq* (Kyrillos)	1235-1243
	INTERREGNUM	
76.	Athanasiyus III *ibn Kalil* (Athanasios)	1250-1261
77.	Yuhannis VII *ibn Abi Sa'id* (Ióannés)	1262-1268
78.	Ghubriyal III (Gabriél)	1268-1271
	Yuhannis VII [2nd time]	1271-1293
79.	Thawdusiyus II (Theodosios)	1294-1300
80.	Yuhannis VIII (Ióannés)	1300-1320
81.	Yuhannis IX (Ióannés)	1320-1327
82.	Banyamin II (Beniamin)	1327-1339
83.	Butrus V (Petros)	1340-1348
84.	Murqus IV (Markos)	1349-1363
85.	Yuhannis X *al-Mu'taman* (Ióannés)	1363-1369
86.	Ghubriyal IV (Gabriél)	1370-1378
87.	Mattawus (or Matta) I (Mattheos)	1378-1409
88.	Ghubriyal V (Gabriél)	1409-1427
89.	Yuhannis XI *Abu'l-Farag* (Ióannés)	1427-1452
90.	Mattawus II (Mattheos)	1452-1465
91.	Ghubriyal (or Ghabrial) VI (Gabriél)	1466-1475
92.	Mikha'il VI (Michaél)	1476-1478
93.	Yuhannis XII (Ióannés)	1479-1482
94.	Yuhannis XIII (Ióannés)	1484-1524

95. Ghubriyal VII (Gabriél)	1525-1568
96. Yuhannis XIV *al-Manfaluti* (Ióannés)	1570-1585
97. Ghubriyal VIII (Gabriél)	1586-1601
98. Murqus V (Markos)	1602-1618
99. Yuhannis XV (Ióannés)	1619-1634
100. Mattawus III (Mattheos)	1634-1649
101. Murqus VI (Markos)	1650-1660
102. Mattawus IV *al-Miri* (Mattheos)	1660-1675
103. Yuhannis XVI *al-Maghribi* (Ióannés)	1676-1718
104. Butrus VI (Petros)	1718-1726
105. Yuhannis XVII *al-Malawi* (Ióannés)	1726-1745
106. Murqus VII (Markos)	1745-1769
107. Yuhannis XVIII *al-Fayumi* (Ióannés)	1769-1796
108. Murqus VIII (Markos)	1796-1809
109. Butrus VII *al-Gawli* (Petros)	1809-1852
110. Kirillus IV *Dawud Tuma Bashut* (Kyrillos)	1854-1861
111. Dimitriyus II (Démétrios)	1862-1870
INTERREGNUM	
Murqus [locum tenens]	1870-1874
112. Kirillus V *ibn Ibrahim Sa'ad Matar al-Nasikh* (Kyrillos)	1874-1927
113. Yuhannis XIX (Ióannés)	1928-1942
Yusab *Filibbus* [locum tenens]	1942-1944
114. Makariyus III (Makarios)	1944-1945
Athanasiyus [locum tenens]	1945-1946
115. Yusab II *Filibbus* (Ióséph)	1946-1954
INTERREGNUM	
Athanasiyus [locum tenens]	1954-1959
116. Kirillus VI *Azir Yusuf 'Ata* (Kyrillos)	1959-1971
117. Shanudah III *Gayid Rafail* (Senouthios)	1971-

GAIANITE PATRIARCHS OF ALEXANDRIA
(Not considered valid by the Coptic Church)

33. Gaïanos (Gaïnas or Kayanus)	536-565
34. Elpidios	565-567
35. Dórotheos	567-
36. Ióannes (III) [anti-pope]	567-
INTERREGNUM	
37. Theodóros	700?

V.

THE COPTIC CATHOLIC CHURCH OF ALEXANDRIA

The Church of Rome regarded Patriarch Dioskoros (Disqurus) and his successors as heretics; and although attempts were made by both churches at various times to resolve their differences, these had ceased by the middle ages. In 1675 Catholic missionaries entered Egypt, and gradually managed to convert some of the Coptic population during the ensuing sixty-six years. In 1741, when the Coptic Bishop Athanasiyus of Jerusalem recognized the supremacy of Rome, he was made Apostolic Administrator of the Catholic Copts, and was confirmed in his rank by the Pope. A Coptic Patriarchate was established by Pope Leo XII in 1824, but no patriarch was appointed until 1899, in the person of Kirillus Makariyus. Kirillus was forced to resign in 1908, when he rejoined the original Coptic Church; thereafter, the patriarchal office remained vacant until 1947.

The primate bears the title "Patriarch of Alexandria of the Copts and of All the Preaching of St. Mark." The official language of this small church is Coptic, but Arabic is used on most occasions (and the patriarchs listed below are given in the Arabic versions of their names). Administrative offices are located at Cairo. There are some 150,000-200,000 communicants in Egypt, with a few churches in the United States.

SOURCES: *The Catholic Eastern Churches* (Attwater); *Catholic Encyclopedia*; *The Christian Churches of the East* (Attwater); *Dictionnaire d'Histoire et de Géographie Ecclésiastiques*; *Gegenwartslage der Ostkirchen* (Spuler); *The Middle East and North Africa*; *Die Morgenlandischen Kirchen* (Spuler); *New Catholic Encyclopedia*; "Pope Calls for Broad Mideast Peace" (Montalbano).

COPTIC CATHOLIC PATRIARCHS OF ALEXANDRIA
(Patriarchs of the Old Church Recognized As Legitimate)

1.	Murqus I (Markos)	50?-68
2.	Aniyanus (Anianos)	68-83
3.	Abiliyus (or Miliyus) (Abilios)	83-95
4.	Kurdunus (Kerdón)	95-106

5.	Abrimus (Primos)	106-118
6.	Yustus (Ioustos)	118-129
7.	Awminiyus (Eumenés)	129-141
8.	Markiyanus (Markianos)	141-152
9.	Kallawtiyanus (Keladión)	152-166
10.	Aghribbinus (Agrippinos)	166-178
11.	Yuliyanus (Ioulianos)	178-188
12.	Dimitriyus (Démétrios)	188-230
13.	Yaraklas (Héraklas)	230-246
14.	Diyunisiyus (Dionysios)	246-264
15.	Maksimus (I) (Maximos)	264-282
16.	Thawna (Theónas)	282-300
17.	Butrus I (Petros)	300-310
18.	Arshalawus (Archelaos)	310-311
19.	Aliksandarus (Alexandros)	312-328
20.	Athanasiyus (I) (Athanasios)	328-373
21.	Butrus II (Petros)	373-378
22.	Timuthawus (Timotheos)	378-384
23.	Thawfilus (Theophilos)	384-412
24.	Kirillus I (Kyrillos) [nephew of #23]	412-444

THE CATHOLIC PATRIARCHATE RESTORED
(Apostolic Administrators 1741-1899, 1908-1947)

25.	Athanasiyus (II) (Athanasios)	1741-1781
26.	Yuhannis *Faragi* (Ióannés)	1781-1788
27.	Mattawus *Righat* (Mattheos)	1788-1822
28.	Maksimus (II) *Jayid* (Maximos)	1824-1831
29.	Thawdurus *Abu Karim* (Theodóros)	1832-1854
30.	Athanasiyus (III) *Khuzam* (Athanasios)	1854-1864
31.	Aghabiyus *Bishai* (Agapios)	1866-1887
	INTERREGNUM	
32.	Kirillus II *Makariyus* (Kyrillos)	1895-1908
33.	Maksimus (III) *Sidfawi* (Maximos)	1908-1926
34.	Murqus II *Khuzam* (Markos)	1926-1958
35.	Istifanus I *Sidarus* (Stephanos)	1958-1986
36.	Istifanus II *Ghattas* (Stephanos)	1986-

VI.

THE GREEK CHURCH OF ALEXANDRIA

Greek was the *lingua franca* of the ancient world, so it was only natural that the educated class, including the hierarchies of the early Christian churches, usually wrote and spoke in Greek. Before the Arab conquests of the seventh century, Egypt was ruled from Byzantium; court and governmental officials also spoke Greek, reinforcing the pattern. The people, however, spoke a degenerate form of old Egyptian called Coptic. The split between these two classes became evident during the reign of Patriarch Dioskoros, who embraced monophysitism, thereby causing a permanent split in the Alexandrian Church.

Dioskoros was replaced by a Greek-speaking, government-sponsored candidate, Proterios, who had acceded to the mandates of the Council of Chalcedon. The Melkite patriarchate was supplanted by the Emperor Zénón in 489, and not restored until 537; it again lapsed between 651-727, in the aftermath of the Arab invasion. The Greek Church has always been much smaller than its Coptic brother, essentially serving only the Greek-speaking populations of North Africa, which have declined dramatically in the last century. In recent decades efforts have been made to establish missionary colonies south of the Sahara, with some success.

The official language of the Church is Greek. The primate bears the title (recognized in 325) of "Pope and Patriarch of Alexandria and All Africa," and ranks first in primacy behind the Ecumenical Patriarch. The Church has approximately 350,000 members, 20,000 in Egypt, the rest located in Africa south of the Sahara and overseas.

SOURCES: *Dictionnaire d'Histoire et de Géographie Ecclésiastiques*; *Échos d'Orient*; *Episkepsis*; *Gegenwartslage der Ostkirchen* (Spuler); *Historia tés Ekklésias Alexandreias (62-1934)* (Papadopoulos; regarded as official by the Church); *History of the Church* (Jedin, ed.); *Jahrbuch der Orthodoxie* (Proc); *The Middle East and North Africa*; *Die Morgenlandischen Kirchen* (Spuler); *Oriens Christianus* (Le Quien); "Pinakes Patriarchón"; *Profiles in Belief* (Piepkorn).

POPES AND PATRIARCHS OF ALEXANDRIA

1.   Markos I *Euangelistés*   -61

2.	Anianos	61-82
3.	Abilios	83-95
4.	Kerdón	96-106
5.	Primos	106-118
6.	Ioustos	118-129
7.	Eumenés (or Hymenaios)	129-141
8.	Markos II (or Markianos)	142-152
9.	Keladión	152-166
10.	Agrippinos	166-178
11.	Ioulianos	178-189
12.	Démétrios	189-232
13.	Héraklas	232-248
14.	Dionysios	248-264
15.	Maximos	265-282
	Paphnytios [anti-pope]	282-
16.	Theónas	282-300
17.	Petros I	300-311
18.	Achillas	312-313
19.	Alexandros I	313-328
20.	Athanasios I	328-373
21.	Petros II [brother of #22]	373-381
22.	Timotheos I *Aktémón* [brother of #21]	381-385
23.	Theophilos I	385-412
24.	Kyrillos I [nephew of #23]	412-444
	Dioskoros [anti-pope]	444-451
25.	Proterios	451-457
	Timotheos *Ailouros* [anti-pope]	457-460
26.	Timotheos II *Salophakialos*	460-475
	Timotheos *Ailouros* [2nd time]	475-477
	Timotheos II *Salophakialos* [2nd time]	477-482
27.	Ióannés I *Talaïas*	482-489

INTERREGNUM

28.	Paulos	537-542
29.	Zóïlos (or Zoïlos)	542-551
30.	Apollinarios	551-569
31.	Ióannés II *Theopeithés*	569-579
32.	Eulogios I	581-608
33.	Theodóros *Skribón*	608-610
34.	Ióannés III *Eleémón*	610-621
35.	Geórgios I	621-630
36.	Petros III	631-641
37.	Kyros *of Phasis*	642-651

INTERREGNUM

38.	Kosmas I *"The Needle-Maker"*	727-768
39.	Politianos	768-813
40.	Eustathios	813-817

41.	Christophoros I	817-841
42.	Sóphronios I	841-860
43.	Michaél I	860-870
44.	Michaél II	870-907
45.	Christodoulos	907-932
46.	Eutychios	933-940
47.	Sóphronios II	941
48.	Isaak	941-954
49.	Iób (or Iakóbos I)	954-960
50.	Élias I	963-1000
51.	Arsenios	1000-1010
52.	Theophilos II	1010-1020
53.	Geórgios II	1021-1052
54.	Leontios	1052-1059
55.	Alexandros II	1059-1062
56.	Ióannés IV *Kódónatos*	1062-1100
57.	Theodosios	1100?-
58.	Kyrillos II	1110?
59.	Sab(b)as	1117?
60.	Eulogios II	1130?
61.	Sóphronios III	1137-1171
62.	Élias II *Alphtheras*	1171-1175
63.	Eleutherios	1175-1180
64.	Markos III	1180-1209
65.	Nikolaos I	1210-1243
66.	Grégorios I	1243-1263
67.	Nikolaos II	1263-1276
68.	Athanasios II	1276-1316
69.	Grégorios II	1316-1354
70.	Grégorios III	1354-1366
71.	Néphón	1366-1385
72.	Markos IV	1385-1389
73.	Nikolaos III	1389-1398
74.	Grégorios IV	1398-1412
75.	Nikolaos IV	1412-1417
76.	Athanasios III	1417-1425
77.	Markos V	1425-1435
78.	Philotheos I	1435-1459
79.	Markos VI	1459-1484
80.	Grégorios V	1484-1486
81.	Athanasios IV	1500?
82.	Philotheos II	1523-
83.	Ióakeim I *"Panu"*	-1567
84.	Silbestros	1569-1590
85.	Meletios I *Pégas* [#184 of Constantinople]	1590-1601
86.	Kyrillos III *Loukaris* [#187 of Constantinople]	1601-1621

87.	Gerasimos I *Spartaliótés Krés*	1621-1636
88.	Métrophanés *Kritopoulos*	1636-1639
89.	Niképhoros *Klarontzanés*	1639-1645
90.	Íoannikios *Diodios ho Berrhoias*	1645-1664
91.	Íoakeim II *Kós*	1665?-1671
92.	Païsios	1671-1678
93.	Parthenios I *Prochoros*	1678-1688
94.	Gerasimos II *Palidas*	1688-1710
95.	Samouél *Kapasoulés*	1710-1723
96.	Kosmas II *Byzantios* [#218 of Constantinople; #60 of Sinai]	1723-1736
97.	Kosmas III *Kalokagathos*	1737-1746
98.	Matthaios *Psaltés*	1746-1766
99.	Kyprianos [ex-anti-Archbishop of Cyprus]	1766-1783
100.	Gerasimos III *Gémarés* (*Kaliklas*)	1783-1788
101.	Parthenios II *Pankóstas*	1788-1805
102.	Theophilos III *Pankóstas*	1805-1825
103.	Hierotheos I	1825-1845
104.	Artemios	1845-1847
105.	Hierotheos II *Staphylopatés*	1847-1858
106.	Kallinikos *Olympios*	1858-1861
107.	Iakóbos II *Pankóstas*	1861-1865
108.	Nikanór	1866-1869
109.	Sóphronios IV [#254 of Constantinople]	1870-1899
110.	Phótios	1900-1925
111.	Meletios II *Metaxakés* [#262 of Constantinople; #114 of Greece]	1926-1935
112.	Nikolaos V *Euangelidés*	1936-1939
113.	Christophoros II *Daniélidés*	1939-1966
	Kónstantinos *Katsarakés* [locum tenens]	1966-1968
114.	Nikolaos VI *Barelopoulos*	1968-1986
115.	Parthenios III *Koinidés*	1987-

ARIAN PATRIARCHS OF ALEXANDRIA
(Not considered valid by the Greek Church)

21.	Pistos	336-338?
22.	Grégorios	339-341
	INTERREGNUM	
	Grégorios [2nd time]	344-348
	INTERREGNUM	
23.	Geórgios	357-361
	INTERREGNUM	
24.	Loukas	365-378

VII.

THE LATIN CHURCH OF ALEXANDRIA

The Latin Patriarchate of Alexandria was established in the year 1215 by Pope Innocent III, being one of four such creations made during the time of the crusades to correspond to the patriarchates of the ancient world, and to provide rival jurisdictions to the Greek churches and primates already established at each see. The Alexandrian Church survived in actuality for a brief period only, no more than one hundred years, after which time it became a purely titular honor, with the patriarchs being based in Rome. The list of primates is probably incomplete. The title was abolished by Pope Pius XII about 1953.

SOURCES: *The Catholic Encyclopedia*; *De Patriarchis Alexandrinis* (Sollerius); *Dictionnaire d'Histoire et de Géographie Ecclésiastiques*; *The New Catholic Encyclopedia*; *Oriens Christianus* (Le Quien).

LATIN PATRIARCHS OF ALEXANDRIA

1.	Athanasius *de Clermont*	1219-
2.	Ægidius *de Ferrare*	1295-1310
3.	Otto *de Sala*	1322-1323
4.	Ioannes I *de Aragón*	1328-1334
5.	Guillelmus *de Chanac*	1342-1348
6.	Humbertus *de Vienne*	1351-1355
7.	Arnaldus Bernardus *du Pouget*	1361?-1369
8.	Ioannes II *de Cardaillac*	1372-
9.	Petrus I *Amiel de Brenac*	1388?-
10.	Simon *de Cramaud*	1391?
11.	Leonardus *Delfino*	1401-1402?
12.	Ugo *de Robertis*	1402-
13.	Petrus II *Amaury de Lordat*	1409?
14.	Ioannes III *Vitelleschi*	1435?
15.	Marcus *Condolmer*	1445?
16.	Ioannes IV *d'Harcourt*	1451?
17.	Bernardinus *Caraffa*	1505?
18.	Alphonsus *de Fonseca*	1506?
19.	Christophorus *del Monte*	1550?
20.	Ferdinandus *de Loazes* [#31 of Antioch]	1566?

21.	Alexander I *Riario*	1570?
22.	Henricus *Cajétan*	1585?
23.	Michael *Bonelli*	1587?
24.	Seraphinus Oliverus *Razalio*	1602?
25.	Fredericus *Borromée* [#60 of Constantinople]	1655?
26.	Alexander II *Crescenzi* [#36 of Antioch]	1675?
27.	Carolus Ambrosius *Mezzabarba*	1719?
28.	Hieronymus *Crispi*	1740?
29.	Iosephus Antonius *Davanzati*	1746?
30.	Paulus I Augustus *Foscolo*	1847-1867
31.	Paulus II *Ballerini*	1867-1897
32.	Dominicus *Marinangeli*	1898-1912+
33.	Paulus III *de Huyn*	1921-1945+
34.	Lucas Ermenegildus *Pasetto*	1950-1953?

VIII.

THE CHURCHES OF AMERICA

In the twentieth century, America has become the refuge of last resort for churches exiled from their original jurisdictions. Each of the major national churches has established separate branches in North America. Only one of these, the Orthodox Church in America, has officially been granted autocephaly by the Russian Orthodox Church, and even this grant of independence is not universally acknowledged by the rest of Orthodoxy. Other churchmen have attempted to erect independent Orthodox jurisdictions to provide blanket havens for all of their Orthodox brethren, of whatever nationality or ethnic background. The lists below are by no means complete, including only those bodies with significant histories and/or congregations.

SOURCES: *Bishops Extraordinary* (Prüter); *Directory of Autocephalous Bishops* (Prüter); *Eastern Christianity and Politics in the Twentieth Century* (Ramet, ed.); *The Encyclopedia of American Religions* (Melton); *Europa World Yearbook*; *History of the Church* (Jedin, ed.); *Gegenwartslage der Ostkirchen* (Spuler); *Jahrbuch der Orthodoxie* (Proc); *The Old Catholic Sourcebook* (Prüter & Melton); *Orthodox America: 1794-1976* (Tarasar); *Profiles in Belief* (Piepkorn); *Year Book and Church Directory of the Orthodox Church in America* (many years); *Year Book of the Greek Orthodox Diocese of North and South America* (many years).

THE GREEK ORTHODOX DIOCESE OF
NORTH AND SOUTH AMERICA (ECUMENICAL PATRIARCHATE)

In 1924, following the republican revolution in Greece, Archbishop Basileios Kompopoulos, the royalist Metropolitan of Chaldeia, proclaimed an independent American church on 18 March; at a synod held 26 November 1924, the delegates ratified his decision, calling the new body the Autocephalous Greek Orthodox Church of America. Basileios was subsequently elected Metropolitan of American and Canada, in opposition to Archbishop Alexandros. The schism was not healed for six years, until the appointment by the Ecumenical Patriarch Phótios II of Archbishop Athénagoras as Archbishop. Basileios returned to Turkey on 20 June 1930, abandoning his claims of ecclesiastical independence.

Athénagoras, perhaps the most remarkable Orthodox churchman of the twentieth century, was a personal friend of President Harry S. Truman; he resigned his position early in 1949 to accept election as Ecumenical Patriarch, and later become known for his efforts to bridge the differences between Eastern Orthodoxy and Roman Catholicism.

The Archdiocese is the largest Orthodox body in the Americas, comprising two and one-half million communicants, under the jurisdiction of a primate who operates virtually independently, but acknowledges the Patriarch of Constantinople as his superior. The head of the church bears the title Archbishop of North and South America. The official Church language is Greek, although English (and other languages) are also used in some parishes. In recent decades several other American branches or groups of parishes of national churches have put themselves under the administration of the Archbishop, including Ukrainian and Albanian dioceses.

ARCHBISHOPS OF NORTH AND SOUTH AMERICA
(Under the Ecumenical Patriarch)

1.	Alexandros	1922-1930?
2.	Athénagoras *Spyrou* [#269 of Constantinople]	1930-1949
3.	Timotheos *Euangelidés*	1949
4.	Michaél *Kónstantinidés*	1949-1958
5.	Iakóbos *Kykysés*	1958-

METROPOLITANS OF AMERICA AND CANADA

1.	Basileios *Kompopoulos*	1924-1930

THE ORTHODOX CHURCH IN AMERICA

The Orthodox Church in America originated as the Alaskan diocese of the Russian Orthodox Church; it later expanded its mission to the continental United States. The chaos of the Russian Revolution hindered communications between the mother church and its overseas branches, causing a split in loyalties. Some believers adhered to the Soviet-dominated Russian Patriarchate which emerged from World War I; others favored the Russian Orthodox Church Outside Russia. The American branch of the Russian Orthodox Church resisted attempts by both churches to re-establish control, finally asserting its independence in 1919 by electing its own leader, Archbishop Alexander.

In 1924 the Fourth Sobor of the Church met in Detroit, declaring "temporary autonomy," and naming Archbishop Platon "Metropolitan of All America and Canada." Two years later Platon rejected the claims of the Russian Orthodox Church Outside Russia, and in 1931 further rejected attempts by the Patriarchate of Russia to reassert direct control, although Moscow was acknowledged as theoretically paramount. The name of the Church was changed in 1955 to the Russian Orthodox Greek Catholic Church in America.

The parent church finally accepted the inevitable, and granted the Americans autocephaly on 10 April 1970; a year later, the church was renamed The Orthodox Church in America. Several other Orthodox denominations, including Albanians and Romanians, joined the new church as semi-autonomous dioceses. The Church is the second largest Orthodox ecclesiastical body in America, comprising some one million communicants. The head of the Church bears the title Archbishop of Washington, Metropolitan of All America and Canada. The church claims one million communicants in North America. The official Church language is English, although some parishes continue to use Russian (and other national languages).

METROPOLITAN ARCHBISHOPS OF THE
ORTHODOX CHURCH IN AMERICA
(Bishops 1798, Archbishops 1905, Metropolitans 1924)

1.	Ioasaf	1798-1799
	INTERREGNUM	
2.	Innokentiî *Veniaminov* [#30 of Russia]	1840-1858
3.	Petr	1859-1867
4.	Pavel	1867-1870
5.	Ioann	1870-1876
6.	Nestor	1879-1882
	INTERREGNUM	
7.	Vladimir	1888-1891
8.	Nikolaî	1891-1898
9.	Tikhon *Belavin* [#11 of Russia]	1899-1907
10.	Platon *Rozhdestvenskiî*	1907-1914
11.	Evdokim *Meshcherskiî*	1914-1917
12.	Aleksandr *Nemolovskiî* (or *Kukelevskiî*)	1919-1922
	Platon [2nd time]	1922-1934
13.	Theophilus (Feofil) *Pashkovskiî*	1934-1950
14.	Leonty (Leontiî) *Turkevich*	1950-1965
15.	Ireney (Ireneî) *Bekish* [#5 of Japan]	1965-1977
16.	Theodosius (Feodosiî) *Lazor*	1977-

THE AMERICAN ORTHODOX CATHOLIC CHURCH

In 1905 Russian Archbishop (later Patriarch) Tikhon Belavin recommended that a separate exarchate be created for "the National Orthodox Churches with their own bishops." Subsequently, several foreign bishops were ordained, but no separate church structure was organized until 2 February 1927, when Metropolitan Platon erected the Holy Eastern

Orthodox Catholic Apostolic Church as an autonomous body under the Russian Orthodox Church in America; Archbishop Aftimios, head of the Syrian diocese of New York, was named Primate. The name of the church was changed to the American Orthodox Catholic Church on 1 December 1927. Disagreements between the two primates appeared almost immediately. In October 1929 Aftimios denounced Platon, causing a permanent split. He retired on 19 April 1933, and died on 24 July 1966.

Following his departure, the structure of the Church rapidly began disintegrating. One of his four bishops returned to Platon's jurisdiction, and two died in 1934, leaving only Ignatius Nichols. Nichols divided the Church into Eastern and Western rites, retaining the latter for himself, and naming Bishop Sophronius Bishara head of the Eastern rite. He also ordained new bishops, the first of which was consecrated alone, in violation of canon law, due to lack of higher clergy. By this time, however, most of his congregations had fallen away, and the ensuing history of this church is one of continued splintering. Therefore, only Archbishop Aftimios is listed below.

PRIMATES OF THE AMERICAN
ORTHODOX CATHOLIC CHURCH

1. Aftimios   1927-1933

IX.

THE GREEK CHURCH OF ANTIOCH

The ancient Church of Antioch ranks third in primacy among the original patriarchal sees of the Near East, behind Constantinople and Alexandria. Founded by St. Peter, the Church grew rapidly in the third greatest city of the Roman Empire, led by a series of learned and illustrious primates. However, like the Church of Alexandria, Antioch was to be plagued by a series of heresies, controversies, and misfortunes. The Patriarch Sebéros espoused monophysitism, under the protection of Byzantine Emperor Anastasius. When the Emperor died in 518, his successor, Justin I, forced Sebéros to flee to Alexandria, although the Bishop maintained his position in exile. At Antioch, Paul was consecrated as Sebéros's successor, thereby creating a dual patriarchate similar to that of Alexandria. Each party maintained it was the rightful heir to the patriarchal throne, but neither was able to overthrow the other. The Melkite faction, so-called because it had the support of the Empire, catered mainly to the Greek population; the Jacobite faction, as it came to be known, had the support of a majority of the common people. This disparity only increased after the Muslim invasion of the seventh century.

Unlike its brother churches of Alexandria and Jerusalem, however, the Orthodox Patriarchate of Antioch gradually moved away from its Greek origins, ordaining its first native-speaking clergy in the sixteenth century. The process was accelerated by a further split in the Church that occurred in 1724. At the death of Patriarch Athanasiyus, two factions emerged: one group of bishops elected Kirillus, who acknowledged the supremacy of the Pope of Rome, the other chose Silfistrus, who claimed autocephaly. Since then there have been two separate churches, the Catholic faction being called Melkite, the other group Orthodox. The former continued to appoint native priests and bishops; the price paid by the Orthodox faction for having their candidate consecrated primate by the Ecumenical Patriarch was 180 years of interference by Constantinople in Antioch's patriarchal elections; only previously-approved Greeks were allowed to succeed. The election of the first native-born patriarch in two hundred years was engineered by a faction of the Holy Synod in 1898, who chose Malatiyus II; he in turn replaced the last of the Greek clergy with Syrians, thereby insuring native successions in the future.

A third schism took place when Orthodox Patriarch Ghrighuriyus died in 1928. A majority of the Synod elected Arsaniyus as his replacement, on 7 February 1931; a minority faction elected Aliksandarus. The breach was not healed until the death of Arsaniyus on 9 January 1933. In recent decades the Church has consistently supported the right of the Palestinians to their own state; the funeral of Ilyas IV in 1979 was attended by high-ranking officials of the Syrian government, in an unusual display of solidarity between Christians and Muslims.

The primate of the Orthodox Church bears the title Patriarch of Great Antioch and of all the East. His chief see is located at Damascus, Syria. The official Church language is Arabic. Roughly 65,000 communicants are scattered throughout the Middle East (primarily in Southern Syria and Lebanon), plus a thriving overseas community in North and South America and in Australia.

SOURCES: *Dictionnaire d'Histoire et de Géographie Ecclésiastiques*; *Échos d'Orient*; *Episkepsis*; *Gegenwartslage der Ostkirchen* (Spuler); *History of the Church* (Jedin, ed.); *Jahrbuch der Orthodoxie* (Proc); *Die Morgenlandischen Kirchen* (Spuler); *Oriens Christianus* (Le Quien); *Orthodoxia*; "Pinakes Patriarchón"; *Profiles in Belief* (Piepkorn); *Syrian Christians in Muslim Society* (Haddad).

GREEK PATRIARCHS OF ANTIOCH

1.	Butrus I (Petros) *Apostolos* [#1 of Rome]	36-53
2.	Afudiyus (Euodios)	53-68
3.	Ighnatiyus I (Ignatios)	68-104
4.	Hirus I (Hérós)	104-126
5.	Kurniliyus (Kornélios)	126-151
6.	Hirus II (Hérós)	151-169
7.	Thiyufilus (Theophilos)	169-188
8.	Maksiminus (Maximinos)	188-191
9.	Sirabiyun (Serapión)	191-212
10.	Asqlibiyadhis (Asklépiadés)	212-218
11.	Filitus (Philétos)	218-231
12.	Zibinus (Zebinos)	231-238
13.	Babilas (Babylas)	238-250
14.	Fabiyus (Phabios)	250-252
15.	Dimitriyanus (Démétrianos)	252-260
16.	Bulus I (Paulos) *Samosateus*	260-268
17.	Dumnus I (Domnos)	268-271
18.	Timayus (Timaios)	271-279
19.	Kirillus I (Kyrillos)	279-303
20.	Tiranus (Tyrannos)	304-314
21.	Fitaliyus (Bitalis)	314-319

22.	Filughunus (Philogonios)	319-324
23.	Afstatiyus (Eustathios)	325-330
24.	Baflinus (Paulinos) *of Tyre*	330-331
25.	Aflaliyus (Eulalios)	332
26.	Afruniyus (Euphronios)	332-333
27.	Flakilus (Phlakilos)	333-342
28.	Istifanus I (Stephanos)	342-344
29.	Lawndiyus (Leontios) *"The Eunuch"*	344-358
30.	Afdhuksiyus (Eudoxios) [#31 of Constantinople]	358-359
31.	Aniyanus (Annias)	359
32.	Malatiyus I (Meletios)	360-361
33.	Afzuyus (Euzóïos)	361-376
	Malatiyus I [2nd time]	378-381
34.	Flafiyanus I (Phlabianos)	381-404
35.	Burfirus (Porphyrios)	404-414
36.	Aliksandarus I (Alexandros)	414-424
37.	Thiyudutus (Theodotos)	424-428
38.	Yuhanna I (Ióannés)	428-441
39.	Dumnus II (Domnos)	441-449
40.	Maksimus (Maximos)	451-455
41.	Basiliyus I (Basileios)	457-458
42.	Akakiyus (Akakios)	458-459
43.	Martiriyus (Martyrios)	459-471
44.	Butrus II (Petros) *Knapeus ("The Fuller")*	464-467
45.	Yuliyanus (Ioulianos)	471
	INTERREGNUM	
	Butrus II [2nd time]	475-476
46.	Yuhanna II (Ióannés) *Kódónatos*	477
47.	Istifanus II (Stephanos)	477-481
48.	Kalandhiyun (Kallandión)	481-485
	Butrus II [3rd time]	485-490
49.	Baladhiyus (Palladios)	490-498
50.	Flafiyanus II (Phlabianos)	498-512
51.	Subrus (Sebéros) *al-Antakhah*	512-518
52.	Bulus II (Paulos) *Xénodokos*	519-521
53.	Afrasiyus *ibn Malaha*	521-526
54.	Afram *of Amida*	527-545
55.	Dhumniyunus (Domnianos)	545-559
56.	Anastasiyus I (Anastasios) *al-Sinaïtah*	559-570
57.	Ghrighuriyus I (Grégorios) *al-Sinaïtah*	570-593
	Anastasiyus I [2nd time]	593-598
58.	Anastasiyus II (Anastasios) *al-Sinaïtah*	599-609
59.	Ghrighuriyus II (Grégorios)	610-620
60.	Anastasiyus III (Anastasios)	620-628
61.	Maqiduniyus (Makedonios)	628-631
62.	Athanasiyus I (Athanasios) *al-Jama'il*	631

	Maqiduniyus [2nd time]	632-640
63.	Jawrjiyus I (Geórgios)	640-655
64.	Makariyus I (Makarios)	656-681
65.	Thiyufanis (Theophanés)	681-687
66.	Istifanus III (or Sibastianus) (Stephanos)	687-690
67.	Jawrjiyus II (Geórgios)	690-695
68.	Aliksandarus II (Alexandros)	695-702
	INTERREGNUM	
69.	Istifanus IV (Stephanos)	742-748
70.	Thiyufilaktus *ibn Qanbara*	748-
71.	Thiyudhurus I (Theodóros)	767-787
	INTERREGNUM	
72.	Yuhanna III (Ióannés)	798-811
73.	Ayyub I (Iób)	811-826
74.	Niqulawus I (Nikolaos)	826-834
75.	Sim'an I (Symeón)	834-840
76.	Ilyas I (Élias)	840-852
77.	Thiyudusiyus I (Theodosios)	852-860
78.	Niqulawus II (Nikolaos)	860-871
79.	Istifanus V (Stephanos)	871
	Niqulawus II [2nd time]	871-879
80.	Mikha'il I (Michaél)	879-890
81.	Zakhariya (Zacharias)	890
	INTERREGNUM	
82.	Jawrjiyus III (Geórgios)	902-917
83.	Ayyub II (Iób)	917-939
84.	Afstratiyus (Eustratios)	939-960
85.	Khristufurus I (Christophoros)	960-966
86.	Thiyudhurus II (Theodóros)	966-977
87.	Aghabiyus (Agapios)	977-995
88.	Yuhanna IV (Ióannés) *Polités*	995-1022
	INTERREGNUM	
89.	Niqulawus III (Nikolaos) *Stoudités*	1025-1031
90.	Ilyas II (Élias)	1032-1033
91.	Jawrjiyus IV (Geórgios) *Laskaris* (or Thiyudhurus [Theodóros] III)	1034-1042
92.	Basiliyus II (Basileios)	1042-1052
93.	Butrus III (Petros)	1052-1056
94.	Yuhanna V (Ióannés)	1057-1062
95.	Amiliyanus (Aimilianos)	1062-1075
96.	Thiyudusiyus II (Theodosios) *Chrysobergés*	1075-1084
97.	Niqifurus (Niképhoros) *"The Black"*	1084-1088
98.	Yuhanna VI (Ióannés) *Oxeités*	1088-1106
99.	Yuhanna VII (Ióannés)	1106-1137
100.	Luqa (Loukas)	1137-1155
101.	Yuhanna VIII (Ióannés)	1155-1159

102.	Aftimiyus I (Euthymios)	1159-1164
103.	Makariyus II (Makarios)	1164-1166
104.	Athanasiyus II (Athanasios)	1166-1180
105.	Thiyudusiyus III (Theodosios)	1180-1182
106.	Ilyas III (Élias)	1182-1184
107.	Khristufurus II (Christophoros)	1184-1185
108.	Thiyudhurus IV (Theodóros) *Balsamón*	1185-1199
109.	Yuwakim I (Ióakeim)	1199-1219
110.	Duruthiyus I (Dórotheos)	1219-1245
111.	Sim'an II *ibn Abu Sa'ib*	1245-1260
112.	Aftimiyus II (Euthymios)	1260-1269
113.	Thiyudusiyus IV (Theodosios)	1269-1276
114.	Thiyudusiyus V (Théodose) *de Villehardouin*	1276-1285
115.	Arsaniyus I (Arsenios)	1285-1293
	Kirillus II (Kyrillos) [anti-patriarch]	1287-1308?
116.	Dhiyunisiyus (Dionysios)	1293-1308
117.	Murqus I (Markos)	1308-1342
118.	Ighnatiyus II (Ignatios)	1342-1353
119.	Mikha'il II (Michaél)	1353-1376
120.	Bakhumiyus I (Pachomios)	1376-1393
121.	Nilus (Neilos)	1393-1401
122.	Mikha'il III (Michaél)	1401-1410
123.	Bakhumiyus II *al-Hawrani*	1410-1411
124.	Yuwakim II (Ióakeim)	1411-1426
125.	Murqus II (Markos)	1426-1436
126.	Dhuruthiyus II *ibn al-Sabbuni*	1436-1454
127.	Mikha'il IV *ibn al-Mawardi*	1454-1462
128.	Murqus III (Markos)	1462-1476
129.	Yuwakim III (Ióakeim)	1476-1483
130.	Ghrighuriyus III (Grégorios)	1483-1497
131.	Dhuruthiyus III *ibn al-Sabbuni*	1497-1523
132.	Mikha'il V *ibn al-Mawardi*	1523-1541
133.	Duruthiyus IV (Dórotheos)	1541-1543
134.	Yuwakim IV *ibn Jumma*	1543-1576
135.	Mikha'il VI *al-Hamawi*	1577-1581
136.	Yuwakim V *ibn Daww*	1581-1592
137.	Yuwakim VI *Ziyada*	1593-1604
138.	Duruthiyus V *ibn al-Ahmar*	1604-1611
139.	Athanasiyus III *al-Dabbas*	1611-1619
140.	Ighnatiyus III *'Atiyah*	1619-1634
141.	Aftimiyus III *al-Karmah*	1635-1636
142.	Aftimiyus IV (Euthymios) *apo Chiou*	1636-1648
143.	Makariyus III *al-Za'im*	1648-1672
144.	Niyufutus (Neophytos) *apo Chiou*	1674-1684
145.	Athanasiyus IV *al-Dabbas* [#45 of Cyprus]	1686-1694
146.	Kirillus III *al-Za'im* [grandson of #143]	1694-1720

	Athanasiyus IV [2nd time]	1720-1724
	Yuwakim VII [anti-patriarch]	1724
147.	Silfistrus (Silbestros) *apo Kyprou*	1724-1766
148.	Filimun (Philémón) *apo Aleppo*	1766-1767
149.	Daniyal (Daniél) *apo Chiou*	1767-1791
150.	Antimiyus (Anthemios) *of Helenopolis*	1792-1813
151.	Sirafim (Serapheim) *apo Kónstantinopoleós*	1813-1823
152.	Mithudiyus (Methodios) *apo Naxou*	1823-1850
153.	Ayruthiyus (Hierotheos) *Hagiotaphités*	1850-1885
154.	Jirasimus (Gerasimos) *Propapas* [#135 of Jerusalem]	1885-1891
155.	Asbiridun (Spiridón) *apo Kyprou*	1892-1898
156.	Malatiyus II *Dumani*	1899-1906
157.	Ghrighuriyus IV *Haddad*	1906-1928
158.	Arsaniyus II *Haddad*	1930-1931
159.	Aliksandarus III *Tah(h)an*	1931-1958
	Arsaniyus II *Haddad* [anti-patriarch]	1931-1933
	Apifaniyus [anti-patriarch]	1935-
160.	Thiyudusiyus VI *Abu Rajaili*	1958-1970
161.	Ilyas IV *Muawad*	1970-1979
162.	Ighnatiyus IV *Hazim*	1979-

X.

THE GREEK MELKITE CATHOLIC
CHURCH OF ANTIOCH

The history of the Melkite Church of Antioch is closely tied to that of the Greek Orthodox Church. A number of patriarchs during the Middle Ages made formal professions of allegiance to Rome, or sent other ambassadors to the Popes; within the Melkite Church itself, two factions gradually emerged, one favoring continued contacts with Rome, the other preferring complete autocephaly. The controversy came to a head in 1724, when each of the factions elected its own Patriarch. A part of the synod chose Kirillus Tanas, an advocate of autonomy under the Pope, as their new primate; a smaller faction simultaneously elected as rival patriarch one Silbestros, a Greek bishop who favored autocephaly under the tutelage of the Ecumenical Patriarch.

The primates of this Church have long been known for their erudition and learning, and have been native Syrians from before the beginning of the split. Both Maksimus IV Sa'igh and Maksimus V Hakim, the two most recent Patriarchs, have also been prominent in ecumenical efforts.

The primate bears the title Patriarch of Antioch and all the East, of Alexandria and of Jerusalem (the latter two cities being added to his title under Maksimus III); his jurisdiction includes all Greek Melkite uniates in the Near East and the Americas, totalling roughly one million communicants. The Patriarch alternates his residence between the cities of Cairo and Beirut, spending six months in each. The official Church language is Arabic. Although the term "Melkite" was applied in ancient times to all of the Chalcedonian Greek Orthodox churches, the word has now come to refer only to the Greek Catholic Church of Antioch.

SOURCES: *The Almanac of the Melkite Greek Catholic Church 1986* (regarded as official); *The Catholic Eastern Churches* (Attwater); *Catholic Encyclopedia*; *The Christian Churches of the East* (Attwater); *Chronologie des Patriarches Melchites d'Antioche de 1250 à 1500* (Nasrallah); *Dictionnaire d'Histoire et de Géographie Ecclésiastiques*; *Gegenwartslage der Ostkirchen* (Spuler); *The Middle East and North Africa*; *Die Morgenlandischen Kirchen* (Spuler); *New Catholic Encyclopedia*; *Notes et Documents pour Servir a L'Histoire du Patriarchat*

THE GREEK MELKITE CATHOLIC CHURCH OF ANTIOCH

Melchite d'Antioche (Nasrallah); *Oriens Christianus* (Le Quien); "Pope Calls for Broad Mideast Peace" (Montalbano); *Sa Beatitude Maximos IV et La Succession Apostolique du Siège d'Antioche* (Nasrallah); *Syrian Christians in Muslim Society* (Haddad); *Vie de la Chrétiente Melkite sous la Domination Turque* (Nasrallah).

GREEK MELKITE CATHOLIC PATRIARCHS OF ANTIOCH

1.	Butrus I (Petros) *Apostolos* [#1 of Rome]	36-43
2.	Afudiyus (Euodios)	43-70?
3.	Ighnatiyus I (Ignatios)	70?-107
4.	Hirun (Hérón)	107?-130?
5.	Kurniliyus (Kornélios)	130?-150?
6.	Hirus (Heros)	150?-170?
7.	Thiyufilus (Theophilos)	170?-182
8.	Maksimiyanus (Maximianos)	182-191
9.	Sirabiyun (Serapión)	191-212
10.	Asqlibiyadhis (Asklépiadés)	212-218
11.	Filitus (Philétos)	218-231
12.	Zibinus (Zebinos)	231-240?
13.	Babilas (Babylas)	240-250
14.	Fabiyus (Phabios)	250-253
15.	Dimitriyanus (Démétrianos)	253
16.	Bulus I (Paulos) *Samosateus*	253-260
17.	Dumnus I (Domnos)	260-266
18.	Timayus (Timaios)	266-271
19.	Kirillus I (Kyrillos)	271-306
20.	Tiranus (Tyrannos)	306-314
21.	Fitalis (Bitalis)	306-314
22.	Filughunus (Philogonios)	320-325
23.	Afstatiyus (Eustathios)	325-331
24.	Baflinus (Paulinos) *of Tyre*	331
25.	Aflaliyus (Eulalios)	331-333
26.	Afruniyus (Euphronios)	333-334
27.	Flakilus (Phlakilos)	334-343
28.	Istifanus I (Stephanos)	343-344
29.	Lawndiyus (Leontios) *"The Eunuch"*	344-358
	Aniyas (Annias) [anti-patriarch]	357-360
30.	Afdhuksiyus (Eudoxios) [#31 of Constantinople]	358-359
31.	Malatiyus (Meletios)	359?-381
	Afzuyus (Euzóïos) [anti-patriarch]	360-370
	Duruthiyus (Dórotheos) [anti-patriarch]	370-371
	Baflinus (Paulinos) II [anti-patriarch]	371-376
32.	Flafiyanus I (Phlabianos)	381-404
33.	Burfirus (Porphyrios)	404-416
34.	Aliksandarus (Alexandros)	416-417

35.	Thiyudutus (Theodotos)	417-429?
36.	Yuhanna I (Ióannés)	429?-442?
37.	Dumnus II (Domnos)	442?-449
38.	Maksimus I (Maximos)	449?-455
39.	Basiliyus I (Basileios)	456-458
40.	Akakiyus (Akakios)	458-459
41.	Martiriyus (Martyrios)	459-470?
42.	Butrus II (Petros) *Knapeus "The Fuller"*	470?-471?
43.	Yuliyanus (Ioulianos)	471-476?
	Butrus II [2nd time]	476?-477?
44.	Yuhanna II (Ióannés) *Kódónatos*	477?-478?
45.	Istifanus II (Stephanos)	478-481
46.	Kalandhiyun (Kallandión)	481-485
	Butrus II [3rd time]	485-488
47.	Baladus (Palladios)	488?-498
48.	Flafiyanus II (Phlabianos)	498-512
49.	Subrus (Sebéros) *al-Antakhah*	512-518
50.	Bulus II (Paulos) *Xénodokos*	519-521
51.	Afrasiyus (Euphrasión) *ibn Malaha*	521-526
52.	Afram (Ephraim) *of Amida*	526-545
53.	Dumnus III (Domnos)	545-559
54.	Anastasiyus I (Anastasios) *al-Sinaïtah*	559-570
55.	Ghrighuriyus I (Grégorios) *al-Sinaïtah*	570-593
	Anastasiyus I [2nd time]	593-598
56.	Anastasiyus II (Anastasios) *al-Sinaïtah*	599-609
	INTERREGNUM	
57.	Maqiduniyus (Makedonios)	639?-649?
58.	Jawrjiyus I (Geórgios)	649?-660?
59.	Makariyus I (Makarios)	660?-681
60.	Thiyufanis (Theophanés)	681-683?
61.	Tuma (Thómas)	683?-685?
62.	Jawrjiyus II (Geórgios)	685?-702?
	Sabastiyanus (Sebastianos) [anti-patriarch]	687-690
	INTERREGNUM	
63.	Istifanus III (Stephanos)	742?-745?
64.	Thiyufilaktus *ibn Qanbara*	745?-768?
65.	Thiyuduritus (Theodóritos)	787?
66.	Ayyub (Iób)	813?-845?
67.	Niqulawus I (Nikolaos)	847-866?
68.	Istifanus IV (Stephanos)	866-870
69.	Thiyudusiyus I (Theodosios)	870-890
70.	Sim'an I *ibn Zarnaq*	892-907
71.	Ilyas I (Élias)	907-934
72.	Thiyudusiyus II (Theodosios)	936-943
73.	Thiyukharistus (Theocharistos)	944-948
	INTERREGNUM	

74.	Khristufurus (Christophoros)	960-969
75.	Thiyudurus I (Theodóros)	970-976
76.	Aghabiyus I (Agapios)	978-996
77.	Yuhanna III (Ióannés) *Polités*	997-1022
78.	Niqulawus II (Nikolaos) *Stoudités*	1022-1030
79.	Ilyas II (Élias)	1031-1032
80.	Thiyudurus II (Theodóros) *Laskaris*	1033-1041
81.	Basiliyus II (Basileios)	1041?-1051?
82.	Butrus III (Petros)	1052-1057
83.	Thiyudusiyus III (Theodosios) *Chrysobergés*	1057-
84.	Amiliyanus (Aimilianos)	1074?-1090?
85.	Niqifurus (Niképhoros) *"The Black"*	1090-
86.	Yuhanna IV (Ióannés) *Oxeités*	1098-1100
	INTERREGNUM	
87.	name unknown	1137-1155
88.	Athanasiyus I (Athananios)	1157?-1171
	INTERREGNUM	
89.	Thiyudurus III (Theodóros) *Balsamón*	1185?-1195?
	INTERREGNUM	
90.	Sim'an II *ibn Abi Sa'ib*	1206?-1235?
	INTERREGNUM	
91.	Dawud (Dabid)	1242?-1247?
	INTERREGNUM	
92.	Aftimiyus I (Euthymios)	1258?-1273?
93.	Thiyudusiyus IV (Théodose) *de Villehardouin*	1275-1284?
94.	Arsaniyus (Arsenios)	1284?-1290?
95.	Kirillus II (Kyrillos)	1290?-1308?
96.	Diyunisiyus I (Dionysios)	1308?-1316?
97.	Kirillus III (Kyrillos)	1316-
98.	Diyunisiyus II (Dionysios)	1325?
99.	Sufruniyus (Sóphronios)	1335?
100.	Ighnatiyus II (Ignatios)	1344?-1359?
101.	Bakhumiyus I (Pachomios)	1359?-1368
102.	Mikha'il I (Michaél)	1368-1375
	Bakhumiyus I [2nd time]	1375-1377
103.	Murqus I (Markos)	1377-1378
	Bakhumiyus I [3rd time]	1378-1386
104.	Niqun (Nikón)	1387?-1395
105.	Mikha'il II (Michaél)	1395-1412
106.	Bakhumiyus II *al-Hawrani*	1412
107.	Yuwakim I (Ióakeim)	1412?-1425?
108.	Murqus II (Markos)	1425?-1434?
109.	Duruthiyus I *ibn al-Sabbuni*	1434?-1451
110.	Mikha'il III *ibn al-Mawardi*	1451?-1456?
111.	Murqus III (Markos)	1456?-1458?
112.	Yuwakim II (Ióakeim)	1458?-1459?

45

	INTERREGNUM	
113.	Mikha'il IV (Michaél)	1470?-1484?
114.	Duruthiyus II *ibn al-Sabbuni*	1484?-1500?
	INTERREGNUM	
115.	Mikha'il V *ibn al-Mawardi*	1523?-1529
	Yuwakim III [anti-patriarch]	1527
116.	Duruthiyus III (Dórotheos)	1529?-1531
117.	Yuwakim III (Ióakeim) [2nd time]	1531-1534?
118.	Mikha'il VI *Sabbagh*	1534-1543
	Yuwakim IV *ibn Jumma* [anti-patriarch]	1540
119.	Yuwakim IV *ibn Jumma* [2nd time]	1543?-1575
	Makariyus II *ibn Khilal* [anti-patriarch]	1543?-1550?
120.	Mikha'il VII *al-Hamawi*	1576-1593
	Yuwakim V *ibn Daww* [anti-patriarch]	1581-1592
121.	Yuwakim VI *Ziyada*	1593-1604
122.	Duruthiyus IV *ibn al-Ahmar*	1604-1612
123.	Athanasiyus II *al-Dabbas*	1612-1620
124.	Ighnatiyus III *'Atiyah*	1620-1634
	Kirillus IV *al-Dabbas* [anti-patriarch]	1620-1627
125.	Aftimiyus II *al-Karmah*	1634
126.	Aftimiyus III (Euthymios) *apo Chiou*	1634-1647
127.	Makariyus III *al-Za'im*	1647-1672
128.	Kirillus V *al-Za'im* [grandson of #127]	1672
129.	Niyufutus (Neophytos) *apo Chiou*	1672-1682
	Kirillus V [2nd time]	1682-1720
	Athanasiyus III *al-Dabbas* [anti-patriarch]	1685-1694
130.	Athanasiyus III [2nd time] [#45 of Cyprus]	1720-1724
	Yuwakim VII [anti-patriarch]	1724
131.	Kirillus VI *al-Tanas*	1724-1759
132.	Athanasiyus IV *Jawhar* [great-nephew]	1759-1760
133.	Maksimus II *Hakim*	1760-1761
134.	Thiyudusiyus V *Dahan*	1761-1788
	Athanasiyus IV [anti-patriarch]	1765-1768
	Athanasiyus IV [3rd time]	1788-1794
135.	Kirillus VII *Siyaj*	1794-1796
136.	Aghabiyus II *Matar*	1796-1812
137.	Ighnatiyus IV *Sarruf*	1812
138.	Athanasiyus V *Matar*	1813-1814
139.	Makariyus IV *Tawil*	1814-1815
140.	Ighnatiyus V *Qattan*	1816-1833
141.	Maksimus III *Mazlum*	1833-1855
142.	Aklimandus *Bahuth*	1856-1864
143.	Ghrighuriyus II *Yusuf-Sayur*	1864-1897
144.	Butrus IV *Jirayjiri*	1898-1902
145.	Kirillus VIII *Jiha*	1902-1916
	INTERREGNUM	

146. Dimitriyus *Qadi*	1919-1925
147. Kirillus IX *Mughabghab*	1925-1947
148. Maksimus IV *al-Sa'igh*	1947-1967
149. Maksimus V *Hakim*	1967-

XI.

THE LATIN CHURCH OF ANTIOCH

The Latin Patriarchate of Antioch was established in the year 1100 at the time of the first crusade, shortly after the conquest of Jerusalem. This was one of four such creations made during the period of the crusades to correspond to the patriarchates of the ancient world, and to provide rival jurisdictions to the Greek churches and prelates. The Antiochian Church survived until the fall of Acre in 1291, after which time it became a purely titular honor, with the patriarchs being based in Rome. During the renaissance the rank of "patriarch" in the Latin church became a kind of intermediate level between archbishop and cardinal, many patriarchs relinquishing their titles when promoted to the College of Cardinals. The title was abolished by Pope Pius XII about 1953. SOURCES: *The Catholic Encyclopedia; Dictionnaire d'Histoire et de Géographie Ecclésiastiques; The New Catholic Encyclopedia; Oriens Christianus* (Le Quien).

LATIN PATRIARCHS OF ANTIOCH

1.	Bernardus	1100-1134
2.	Radulphus I	1136-1139
	INTERREGNUM	
3.	Aymericus *de Limoges*	1142-1187
4.	Radulphus II	1187-1201
5.	Petrus I *d'Angoulême*	1201-1208
6.	Petrus II *d'Amalfi*	1209-1217
7.	Petrus III *Capoue* [nephew of #6]	1219
8.	Raynerius *de Tuscia*	1219-1225
9.	Albertus I *de Robertis*	1226-1246
10.	Elias	1246?-1250
	INTERREGNUM	
11.	Opizio I	1254-1255
12.	Christianus	1256-1268
13.	Opizio II *Fieschi*	1270?-1292
	INTERREGNUM	
14.	Isnardus *Tacconi*	1311-1329
	INTERREGNUM	

15.	Geraldus Odo *de Camboulit*	1342-1348
	INTERREGNUM	
16.	Raymundus *de Saigues*	1364-1374
17.	Petrus IV *Clasquerin*	1375-
18.	Ioannes I *de Maguellone*	1408-
19.	Ioannes II *de Vico*	1410?
20.	Venceslaus *Králik*	1410?-1416
	INTERREGNUM	
21.	Dionysius *du Moulin*	1439-1447
22.	Iacobus Juvenalis *des Ursins*	1449-1457
23.	Guillelmus I *de La Tour*	1457?-1470
24.	Guillelmus II	1471
25.	Gerardus *de Crussol*	1471-1472
26.	Laurentius I *Zane*	1473-1485
27.	Iordanus *de' Caetani*	1485-
28.	Sebastianus	1495?
29.	Alphonsus I *Carafa*	1504-
30.	Alphonsus II	-1529
	INTERREGNUM	
31.	Ferdinandus *de Loazes* [#20 of Alexandria]	1566-1568
32.	Ioannes III *de Ribera*	1568-1611
	INTERREGNUM	
33.	Ludovicus I Caetanus *di Sermoneta*	1622-1626?
34.	Ioannes IV Baptistus *Pamfili* [#234 of Rome]	1626?-1629
35.	Cæsar *Monti*	1629?-1650
	INTERREGNUM	
36.	Alexander *Crescenzi* [#26 of Alexandria]	1675?-1688
	INTERREGNUM	
37.	Michael Angelus *Mattei*	1693-
38.	Carolus I Thomas *Maillard de Tournon*	1701-1710
39.	Gilbertus *Borromeo*	1711-1717
	INTERREGNUM	
40.	Philippus *Anastasi*	1724-1735
41.	Ioaquim Ferdinandus *Puerto Carrero*	1735-1743
42.	Antonius I Maria *Pallavicino*	1743-1749
43.	Ludovicus II *Calini*	1751-1766
44.	Domenicus *Giordani*	1766-1780
45.	Carolus II *Camuzio*	1781-
46.	Iulius Maria *della Somaglia*	1788-1795
47.	Ioannes V Franciscus Guidus *di Bagno dei Talenti*	1795-1796
48.	Antonius II *Despuig y Dameto*	1799-1810
	INTERREGNUM	
49.	Laurentius II *Mattei*	1822-1833
50.	Antonius III *Piatti*	1837-1841
51.	Nicolaus *Tanara*	1845-1853
52.	Albertus II *Barbolani*	1856-1857

53.	Iosephus Melchiades *Ferlisi* [#78 of Constantinople]	1858-1860
54.	Carolus III *Belgrado*	1862-1866
55.	Paulus *Brunoni*	1869-1877
56.	Petrus V *Villanova Castellacci*	1879-1881
57.	Placidus *Ralli*	1882-1884
58.	Vincentius *Tizzani*	1886-1892
59.	Franciscus de Pauli *Cassetta*	1895-1899
60.	Carolus IV Antonius *Nocella* [#84 of Constantinople]	1899-1901
61.	Laurentius III *Passerini*	1901-1915
62.	Ladislaus Michael *Zaleski*	1916-1925?
63.	Robertus *Vicentini*	1925-1953?

THE PATRIARCHATE DISCONTINUED

XII.

THE MARONITE CHURCH OF ANTIOCH

The Maronite Church is unique among the uniate Eastern churches in having a history unmarred by significant internal schism. Its origins can be traced to the monastery of Bait-Marun, built around the shrine of St. Marun (or Maro) on the bank of the Orontes River. The abbey was closely allied with the Byzantine Emperors, and when the Emperor Heraclius professed monothelitism, Bait-Marun followed suit. In 681, according to unconfirmed tradition, during a period when the Greek Patriarchs of Antioch were living in exile in Constantinople, the monks elected their first primate, whose successors eventually began calling themselves Patriarchs of Antioch; the first documented use of the title was a grant by Pope Alexander IV in 1268. Maronite history claims that this first Patriarch was Yuhanna Marun (or John Maro; he is not, however, the same man as the earlier saint of the same name); in reality, however, the early history of the Maronites before 1100 is almost totally veiled in obscurity, and no verifiable list of its early patriarchs can now be compiled. Most scholars now regard the traditional list of primates between Maro and Yusuf al-Jirjisi as semi-mythical.

When the original monastery was destroyed about the year 900, the monks and their flock moved *en masse* into the protection of the Lebanese mountains, where they remained virtually impregnable against the Muslim hordes. The West first made contact with the Maronites about the year 1100, shortly after their conquest of Jerusalem during the First Crusade. The Maronites acknowledged the ecclesiastical supremacy of the Pope of Rome's about 1182, and have remained a part of the Catholic Church ever since, becoming increasingly Latinized as the centuries have passed. In 1860 the Druze began massacring the unarmed Maronites, provoking conflicts between Christian and Muslim that have continued to this day. As the strongest Christian faction in Lebanon, the Maronites have traditionally held the balance of political and economic power there; an article of the Lebanese Constitution provides that the office of the presidency can only be occupied by a Maronite. In recent decades the Lebanese Civil War has served to isolate even further the Maronites from their Muslim neighbors, and to question their long-term viability.

The primate bears the title Patriarch of Antioch (of the Maronites) and All the East; he resides at Bkerkeh and Dimaneh. Although there are some two to five million Maronites living within Lebanon (estimates vary), there are also a significant number of adherents dwelling in neighboring Middle Eastern countries, as well as in the Americas. The official Church language is Arabic. For several centuries, the Patriarchs of the Maronites have traditionally taken the second name "Butrus" (Peter) in honor of the apostle who, according to legend, founded the Patriarchate of Antioch.

SOURCES: *The Catholic Eastern Churches* (Attwater); *Catholic Encyclopedia*; *The Christian Churches of the East* (Attwater); *L'Église Maronite* (Dib; regarded as official by the Church); *Gegenwartslage der Ostkirchen* (Spuler); *Histoire de l'Église Syriaque Maronite d'Antioch* (Ghabra'il); "Les Listes Patriarcales de L'Église Maronite: Étude Critique et Historique" (Chabot); *The Maronites in History* (Moosa); *The Middle East and North Africa*; *Die Morgenlandischen Kirchen* (Spuler); *Murder, Mayhem, Pillage, and Plunder* (Mishaqa); *Politics and Change in a Traditional Society: Lebanon, 1711-1845* (Harik); *Politics in Lebanon* (Binder); *New Catholic Encyclopedia*; *Oriens Christianus* (Le Quien); "Pope Calls for Broad Mideast Peace" (Montalbano); *Series Chronologica Patriarchum Antiochiae* (Assemani); *Who's Who in Lebanon*.

MARONITE PATRIARCHS OF ANTIOCH

1.	Yuhanna I *Marun*	681-707
2.	Kurush [nephew of #1]	707-
3.	Jibra'il I	
4.	Yuhanna II *Marun*	
5.	Yuhanna III	
6.	Ghrighuriyus I	
7.	Istifanus I	
8.	Murqus	
9.	Awsabiyus	
10.	Yuhanna IV	
11.	Ishu' I	
12.	Dawud I	
13.	Ghrighuriyus II	
14.	Tiyufilaqtus	
15.	Ishu' II	
16.	Dumitiyus	
17.	Ishaq	
18.	Yuhanna V	
19.	Sim'an I	
20.	Aramiya I	
21.	Yuhanna VI	

22.	Sim'an II	
23.	Sim'an III	
24.	Yusuf I *al-Jirjisi*	1100?
25.	Butrus I	1121?
26.	Ghrighuriyus III *of Halat*	1130?-1141
27.	Ya'qub I *Butrus of Ramat*	1141?-1154
28.	Yuhanna VII *of Lahfad*	1160?
29.	Butrus II	1179?
30.	Butrus III	1188?
31.	Butrus IV	1199?
32.	Aramiya II (or Irmiya) *al-Amshiti*	1209?-1230
33.	Danil I *Biblesis*	1230-1236
34.	Yuhanna VIII *Butrus of Giag*	1239?
35.	Sim'an IV	1244?-1268?
36.	Ya'qub II	1268?-
37.	Butrus V	1269?
38.	Danil II *al-Amshiti*	1270?-1272?
39.	Aramiya III *al-Dimlisawi*	1272-1297
40.	Luqa *al-Banhrani* [rival patriarch]	1272-1300
41.	Sim'an V	1300?-1322?
42.	Yuhanna IX	1322?-1357?
43.	Jibra'il II (or Jabra'il) *al-Hajjula*	1357?-1367?
44.	Dawud II *Yuhanna*	1367?-1402
45.	Yuhanna X *al-Jaji*	1404-1445
46.	Ya'qub III *ibn Hid al-Hadathi*	1445-1458
47.	Butrus VI *ibn Yusuf al-Hadathi* [brother of #46]	1458-1492
48.	Sim'an VI (or Shim'un) *ibn Dawud al-Hadathi* [nephew of #47]	1492-1524
49.	Musi (or Musa) *ibn Sa'adi al-'Aquri* (or *Akari*)	1524-1567
50.	Mikha'il I *ibn Yuhanna al-Ruzzi*	1567-1581
51.	Sarkis *ibn Yuhanna al-Ruzzi* [brother of #50]	1581-1596
	INTERREGNUM	
52.	Yusuf II *ibn Musa al-Ruzzi* [nephew of #51]	1599-1608
53.	Yuhanna XI *ibn Makhluf*	1608-1633
54.	Jirjis I *ibn 'Amayrah* (or *Amira*)	1633-1644
55.	Yusuf III *ibn Halib al-'Aquri*	1644-1647
56.	Yuhanna XII *al-Safrawi*	1648-1656
57.	Jirjis II *Habakuk al-Bashalani*	1657-1670
58.	Istifan(us) II *ibn Mikha'il al-Duwayhi*	1670-1704
59.	Jibra'il III *al-Blawzawi*	1704-1705
60.	Ya'qub IV Butrus *Awwad*	1705-1733
61.	Yusuf IV Butrus *Dirgham al-Khazin*	1733-1742
	Tubiyya Butrus *al-Khazin* [anti-patriarch]	1733
62.	Sim'an VII Butrus *Awwad*	1743-1756
63.	Tubiyya Butrus *al-Khazin* [2nd time]	1756-1766
64.	Yusuf V Butrus *Istifan*	1766-1793

65.	Mikha'il II Butrus *Fadl*	1793-1795
66.	Filibbus Butrus *al-Jumayyil*	1795-1796
67.	Yusuf VI Butrus *al-Tiyyan*	1796-1808
68.	Yuhanna XIII Butrus *al-Hilu*	1809-1823
69.	Yusuf VII Butrus *Hubaysh*	1823-1845
70.	Yusuf VIII Butrus *al-Khazin*	1846-1854
71.	Bulus I Butrus *Mas'ad al-Tarsi*	1854-1890
72.	Yuhanna XIV Butrus *Hajj*	1890-1899
73.	Ilyas Butrus *al-Huwayyik*	1899-1931
74.	Antun I Butrus *'Aridah*	1932-1955
75.	Bulus II Butrus *al-Ma'ushi*	1955-1975
76.	Antun(iyus) II Butrus *Khuraish* (or *Khraish*)	1975-1986
77.	Nasr Allah Butrus *Sufayr* (or *Sfayr* or *Sfair*)	1986-

XIII.

SYRIAN CATHOLIC CHURCH OF ANTIOCH

The history of the Syrian Catholic Patriarchate of Antioch is directly tied to that of the Jacobite Church. Catholic missionaries were sent to Syria as early as 1552, seeking to convert both the people and their prelates. About 1650, their efforts resulted in the conversion of one 'Abd al-Ghal Akhijan, who was sent to the Maronites for instruction. The Maronite Patriarch of Antioch consecrated him Syrian Catholic Bishop of Aleppo in 1656, under the name Andrawus. He was able to build a following, and to use his influence to capture the patriarchal throne in the election of 1661. This created a split in the Syrian Church, when a dissident faction elected their own patriarch, with both claiming to be the legitimate primate. Andrawus was followed by Butrus, who was imprisoned in 1701, thereby ending the schism.

In 1783 the reigning Syrian patriarch named as his successor Mar Mikha'il Jarwah, who had recently converted to Catholicism. A dissident faction immediately elected a non-Catholic patriarch, thereby creating a permanent split in the West Syrian Church, one faction acknowledging the supremacy of the Pope of Rome, the other claiming complete autocephaly.

The primate bears the title Patriarch of Antioch of the Syrians. The Church uses both Syriac and Arabic as official languages, but the latter is in common use. The chief see of the Church is Beirut (since 1899), although the roughly 150,000 communicants are spread throughout the Middle East (particularly Syria and Lebanon) and the Americas. Like his Jacobite counterpart, the Patriarch always takes the name Ighnatiyus as his first name, in honor of the saint who served as third Patriarch of Antioch; to this he adds a second saint's name.

SOURCES: *The Catholic Eastern Churches* (Attwater); *Catholic Encyclopedia*; *The Christian Churches of the East* (Attwater); *Chronique de Michel le Syrien* (Michael I); *Eastern Christianity and Politics in the Twentieth Century* (Ramet, ed.); *Europa World Yearbook*; *Gegenwartslage der Ostkirchen* (Spuler); *The Middle East and North Africa*; *Die Morgenlandischen Kirchen* (Spuler); *New Catholic Encyclopedia*; *Oriens Christianus* (Le Quien); "Pope Calls for Broad Mideast Peace" (Montalbano); *Al-Salasil al-Tarikhiyah fi Asaqifat al Abrashiyat al-Suryaniyah* (Tarrazi; regarded as official by the Church);

A Short History of Syriac Christianity to the Rise of Islam (McCullough); Syrian Christians in Muslim Society (Haddad).

SYRIAN CATHOLIC PATRIARCHS OF ANTHIOCH

1.	Butrus I (Petros) [#1 of Rome]	35-42
2.	Awdiyus (Euodios)	42-68
3.	Ighnatiyus I (Ignatios)	68-107
4.	Irun (Hérón)	107-127
5.	Qurnil (Kornélios)	127-154
6.	Irus (Erós)	154-170
7.	Thiyufilus (Theophilos)	170-172
8.	Maksimus I (Maximos)	172-190
9.	Sirabiyun (Serapión)	190-211
10.	Asqlibiyad (Asklépiadés)	211-223
11.	Filitus (Philétos)	223-226
12.	Azibina (Zebinos)	226-236
13.	Babula (Babylas)	236-244
14.	Fabiyus (Phabios)	244-255
15.	Dimitriyus (Démétrios)	255-263
16.	Bulus I (Paulos) *ho Samosateus*	263-271
17.	Dumnus I (Domnos)	271-274
18.	Timathiyus (Timotheos)	274-283
19.	Qurillus (Kyrillos)	283-299
20.	Turanus (Tyrannos)	299-313
21.	Bitalis (Bitalis)	313-315
22.	Bilujin (Philogonos)	315-320
23.	Awstathiyus (Eustathios)	320-332
24.	Fulin (Paulinos) *of Tyre*	332-337
25.	Awlaliyus (Eulalios)	337-338
26.	Afrun (Euphronios)	338-342
27.	Filaqas (Phlakilos)	342-346
28.	Istifan I (Stephanos)	346-351
29.	Aluntiyus (Leontios) *"The Eunuch"*	351-357
30.	Awduksiyus (Eudoxios) [#31 of Constantinople]	357-360
31.	Aniyanus (Anianos)	360-362
32.	Malatiyus (Meletios)	362-381
33.	Flabiyanus I (Phlabianos)	381-404
34.	Awghris (Euagrios)	404
35.	Burfuriyus (Porphyrios)	404-414
36.	Iskandar (Alexandros)	414-424
37.	Thiyudut (Theodotos)	424-427
38.	Yuhanna I (Ióannés)	427-440
39.	Dumnus II (Domnos)	440-449
40.	Maksimus II (Maximos)	449-456
41.	Basiliyus I (Basileios)	456-458

42.	Aqaq (Akakios)	458-460
43.	Martur (Martyrios)	460-470
44.	Butrus II (Petros) *Knapheus*	470-471
	Martur [2nd time]	471-473
45.	Yulyan I (Ioulianos)	473-477
	Butrus II [2nd time]	477-480
46.	Yuhanna II (Ióannés) *Kódónatos*	480
47.	Istifan II (Stephanos)	480-481
48.	Istifan III (Stephanos)	481-482
49.	Qalandun (Kallandión)	482-483
	Butrus II [3rd time]	483-484
	Yuhanna II [2nd time]	484-485
	Butrus II [4th time]	485-488
50.	Baladiyus (Palladios)	488-495
51.	Flabiyanus II (Phlabianos)	495-512
52.	Sawira I (Sebéros) *al-Antakhah*	512-518
53.	Bulus II (Paulos) *Xénodokos*	518-521
54.	Afrasiyus *ibn Malaha*	521-528
55.	Afram I *of Amida*	528-546
56.	Sirkis *of Tella*	539-541
57.	Bulus III *"The Black"*	541-571
58.	Butrus III *of Kallinikos*	571-591
59.	Yulyan II	592-595
60.	Athanasiyus I *Gammala*	595-631
61.	Yuhanna III	631-649
62.	Thiyudur	649-667
63.	Sawira II *ibn Mashqa*	667-680
	INTERREGNUM	
64.	Athanasiyus II *of Baladh*	684-688
65.	Yulyan III *"The Roman"*	688-709
66.	Ayliya	709-723
67.	Athanasiyus III	724-740
68.	Yuhanna IV	740-755
69.	Ishaq I	755-756
70.	Athanasiyus IV *Sandaliyus*	756-758
71.	Jirjis I	758-790
	Yuhanna [anti-patriarch]	758-763?
	Dawud [anti-patriarch]	763-
72.	Yusuf	790-792
73.	Quriyaqus	793-817
74.	Diyunisiyus I *of Tell Mahar*	818-845
75.	Yuhanna V	847-874
	INTERREGNUM	
76.	Ighnatiyus II	878-883
	INTERREGNUM	
77.	Thiyudusiyus	887-895

78.	Diyunisiyus II	896-909
79.	Yuhanna VI	910-922
80.	Basiliyus II	923-935
81.	Yuhanna VII	936-953
82.	Yuhanna VIII	954-957
83.	Diyunisiyus III	958-961
84.	Ibrahim I	962-963
85.	Yuhanna IX *Sarighta*	965-986
86.	Athanasiyus V *Salikha*	987-1003
87.	Yuhanna X *of Abhdun*	1004-1030
88.	Diyunisiyus IV *Khihi*	1032-1042
89.	Yuhanna XI [nephew of #87]	1042-1057
90.	Athanasiyus VI *Khayya*	1058-1063
91.	Yuhanna XII *Ishu' ibn Shushan*	1063-1073
92.	Basiliyus III *Sinnadus*	1074-1075
93.	Yuhanna XIII *Shinudah*	1075-1077
94.	Diyunisiyus V *Lazarus*	1077-1079
95.	Yuhanna XIV	1079-1087
96.	Diyunisiyus VI	1088-1090
97.	Athanasiyus VII *Abu'l-Faraj*	1091-1129
98.	Yuhanna XV *Mawdyani*	1129-1137
99.	Athanasiyus VIII *Ishu' ibn Qatrah*	1139-1166
100.	Mikha'il I *al-Kabir*	1167-1200
101.	Athanasiyus IX *Saliba Qarakha*	1200-1207
102.	Mikha'il II *Ishu' Siftana*	1207-1208
103.	Yuhanna XVI *Ishu'*	1208-1220
104.	Ighnatiyus III *Dawud*	1222-1252
105.	Diyunisiyus VII *Aharon Angur*	1252-1253
106.	Yuhanna XVII *ibn Ma'dani*	1253-1263
107.	Ighnatiyus IV *Ishu'*	1264-1283
108.	(Ighnatiyus) Filuksinus *Nimrud*	1283-1292
109.	Ighnatiyus V *ibn Wahib ibn Zakha*	1293-1333
110.	Ighnatiyus Ismil *Yuhanna*	1333-1366
111.	Ighnatiyus Shihab	1366-1381
112.	Ighnatiyus Ibrahim II *ibn Gharib*	1381-1412
113.	Ighnatiyus Bihnam I *Hajlaya*	1412-1455
114.	Ighnatiyus Khalaf	1455-1484
115.	Ighnatiyus Yuhanna XVIII *Akhsinaya Bar Shilla*	1484-1494
116.	Ighnatiyus Nuh [#77 of India]	1494-1509
117.	Ighnatiyus Ishu' I	1509-1510
118.	Ighnatiyus Ya'qub	1510-1519
119.	Ighnatiyus Dawud	1519-1520
120.	Ighnatiyus 'Abd Allah	1520-1557
121.	Ighnatiyus Ni'mat Allah	1557-1576
122.	Ighnatiyus Butrus IV Dawud	1577-1591
123.	Ighnatiyus Bilatus	1591-1597

124.	Ighnatiyus 'Abd al-Ghani	1597-1598
125.	Ighnatiyus Butrus V	1598-1639
126.	Ighnatiyus Shukr Allah I	1640-
127.	Ighnatiyus Shim'un I *of Tur-Abdin* [rival]	1640-1659
128.	Ighnatiyus Ishu' II *Qamah*	1655-1661
129.	Ighnatiyus Andrawus *Akhijan Murabbi*	1662-1677
	Ighnatiyus Habib *al-Mazziyati* [anti-patriarch]	1674-1686
130.	Ighnatiyus Butrus VI *Shahbadin*	1677-1702
131.	Ighnatiyus Jirjis II	1690-1709
132.	Ighnatiyus Ishaq II	1709-1723
133.	Ighnatiyus Shukr Allah II	1723-1745
134.	Ighnatiyus Jirjis III	1746-1768
135.	Ighnatiyus Jirjis IV	1768-1781
136.	Ighnatiyus Mikha'il III *Jarwah*	1782-1800
137.	Ighnatiyus Mikha'il IV *Dahir*	1802-1810
	INTERREGNUM	
138.	Ighnatiyus Sim'an II *Hindi Zora*	1814-1818
139.	Ighnatiyus Butrus VII *Jarwah*	1820-1851
140.	Ighnatiyus Antun I *Samhiri*	1853-1864
141.	Ighnatiyus Filibbus *Arkus*	1866-1874
142.	Ighnatiyus Jirjis V *Shilhut*	1874-1891
143.	Ighnatiyus Bihnam II *Banni*	1893-1897
144.	Ighnatiyus Afram II *Rahmani*	1898-1929
145.	Ighnatiyus Jibra'il *Tabbuni*	1929-1968
146.	Ighnatiyus Antun II *Huwayyik* (or *Hayek*)	1968-

XIV.

THE SYRIAN ORTHODOX "JACOBITE" CHURCH OF ANTIOCH

When the Antiochian Patriarch, Sebéros, embraced monophysitism, certain members of his Church dissented, finally forcing him into exile at Alexandria in 518. The split, as with the Copts in Egypt, had more to do with temporal politics than spiritual values, the opponents of Sebéros supporting the Greek power structure. When he died in 538, his followers elected Sergios as his successor, thereby perpetuating a dual patriarchate. In 542 Ya'qub al-Barda'i (Jacob Baradæus), a Syrian priest, began a thirty-six-year-long series of travels throughout the Near East, during which time he ordained thousands of priests, and everywhere extolled the virtues of monophysitism. His efforts solidified the Church's support among the people, and left such a lasting impression that his followers are still called "Jacobites" even today.

The "Jacobites" flourished under the early centuries of Muslim rule, but later entered a long decline. In 1313 and again in 1364 the Patriarchate split into several factions. Since that time the Syrian prelates of Antioch have taken the name Ighnatiyus as their prename, in honor of St. Ignatius, the third Patriarch of Antioch; to this is added a second saint's name and numeral. In 1662 the Church split again, as several uniate factions rallied to Patriarch Andrawus. This schism was put down, but a second Catholic break took place in 1783; and since this time there have been two Syrian Patriarchs.

The primate bears the title Patriarch of Antioch and of All the Domain of the Apostolic Throne. He has resided at Homs in Syria (since the 1930s), with administrative offices in Damascus. The official languages of the Church are Syriac and Arabic, but the latter is in common use. Roughly three million adherents of the Church are spread throughout the Middle East, Asia, and the Americas, about half of them in India (Malabar).

SOURCES: "Christian Sect Slips Toward Extinction" (Pope); *Chronique de Michel le Syrien* (Michael I); *Episkepsis*; *Europa World Yearbook*; *Gegenwartslage der Ostkirchen* (Spuler); *History of the Church* (Jedin, ed.); *The Middle East and North Africa*; *Die Morgenlandischen Kirchen* (Spuler); *Oriens Christianus* (Le Quien); *Orthodoxia*; *Profiles in Belief* (Piepkorn); *A Short History of Syriac Chris-*

tianity to the Rise of Islam (McCullough); *Syrian Christians in Muslim Society* (Haddad).

SYRIAN PATRIARCHS OF ANTIOCH

1.	Butrus I (Petros) [#1 of Rome]	37-50
2.	Afudiyus (Euodios)	50-68
3.	Ighnatiyus I (Ignatios)	68-107
4.	Hirun (or Hirus) (Hérón or Hérós)	107-127
5.	Qurniliyus (Kornélios)	127-154
6.	Awrus (or Ayrus) (Erós)	154-169
7.	Thawfilus (Theophilos)	169-182
8.	Maksimiyanus (Maximianos)	182-190
9.	Sirabiyun (Serapión)	190-211
10.	Asqlibiyadis (Asklépiadés)	211-220
11.	Filitus (Philétos)	220-231
12.	Zabina (Zebinos)	231-237
13.	Babula (Babylas)	237-251
14.	Fabiyus (Phabios)	251-254
15.	Dimitriyanus (Démétrianos)	254-260
16.	Bulus I (Paulos) *ho Samosateus*	260-268
17.	Dumnus I (Domnos)	268-273
18.	Timiyus (Timaios)	273-282
19.	Qurillus (Kyrillos)	283-303
20.	Turanniyus (Tyrannios)	304-313
21.	Fitaliyus (Bitalios)	313-319
22.	Filujuniyus (Philogonios)	319-323
23.	Bulinus I (Paulinos) *of Tyre*	323
24.	Awstathiyus (Eustathios)	323-330
25.	Awlaliyus (Eulalios)	331-333
26.	Awfruniyus (Euphronios)	332-333
27.	Filaqilus (Phlakilos)	333-343
28.	Istifanus I (Stephanos)	343-344
29.	Lawntiyus (Leontios) *"The Eunuch"*	344-358
30.	Awduksiyus (Eudoxios) [#31 of Constantinople]	358-359
31.	Aniyanus (Anianos)	359
32.	Militus (Meletios)	360-381
33.	Bulinus II (Paulinos)	362-388
34.	Flabiyanus I (Phlabianos)	381-404
35.	Awighriyus (Euagrios)	388-393
36.	Burfuriyus (Porphyrios)	404-412
37.	Aliksandarus (Alexandros)	413-417?
38.	Thawdutus (Theodotos)	417?-428
39.	Yuhanna I (Ióannés)	428-442
40.	Dumnus II (Domnos)	442-449
41.	Maksimus (Maximos)	449-455

42.	Basiliyus I (Basileios)	456-458
43.	Aqaq (Akakios)	458-459
44.	Marturiyus (Martyrios)	459-468
45.	Butrus II (Petros) *Knapheus*	468-471
46.	Yuliyanus I (Ioulianos)	471-476
	Butrus II [2nd time]	476
47.	Yuhanna II (Ióannés) *Kódónatos*	476-478
48.	Istifanus II (Stephanos)	478-481
49.	Istifanus III (Stephanos)	481-482
50.	Qalandiyun (Kallandión)	482-485
	Butrus II [3rd time]	485-488
51.	Baladiyun (Palladión)	488-498
52.	Flabiyanus II (Phlabianos)	498-512
53.	Sawiriyus I (Sebéros) *al-Antakhah*	512-538
	INTERREGNUM	
54.	Sirjiyus (Sergios) *of Tella*	544-547
	INTERREGNUM	
55.	Bulus II *"The Black"*	552-578?
	INTERREGNUM	
56.	Butrus III *of Kallinikos*	581-591
57.	Yulyan II	591-595
58.	Athanasiyus I *Gammala*	595-631
59.	Yuhanna III	631-648
60.	Thiyudusiyus	649-667
61.	Sawiriyus II *ibn Mashqa*	667-683
62.	Athanasiyus II *of Baladh*	684-687
63.	Yulyan III (Julianus) *"The Roman"*	687-708
64.	Ayliya I	709-723
65.	Athanasiyus III *Sandaliyus*	724-740
66.	Iyunnis I	740-754
	Isaaq [anti-patriarch]	755-756
	INTERREGNUM	
67.	Jawrji I	758-790
	Yuhanna [anti-patriarch]	758-763?
	Dawud [anti-patriarch]	763-
68.	Yusuf	791-792
69.	Quriyaqus	793-817
70.	Diyunisiyus I *of Tell Mahar*	818-845
	INTERREGNUM	
71.	Yuhanna IV	849-873
	INTERREGNUM	
72.	Ighnatiyus II	878-883
	INTERREGNUM	
73.	Thawdusiyus (or Rumanus)	887-896
74.	Diyunisiyus II	896-909
75.	Yuhanna V	910-922

76.	Basiliyus II	923-935
77.	Yuhanna VI	936-956
78.	Iyunnis II	956-958
79.	Diyunisiyus III	958-961
80.	Ibrahim I	962-963
81.	Yuhanna VII *Sarighta al-Ma'tuk*	965-985
82.	Athanasiyus IV *Salikha*	986-1002
83.	Yuhanna VIII *ibn Abhduni*	1004-1033
84.	Diyunisiyus IV *Khihi*	1033-1044
85.	Yuhanna IX [nephew of #83]	1044-1057
86.	Athanasiyus V *Hajji*	1057-1063
87.	Yuhanna X *Ishu' ibn Shushan*	1063-1072
88.	Basiliyus III *Sinnadus*	1074-1075
89.	Diyunisiyus V *Lazarus*	1077-1078?
90.	Iyunnis III	1080-1082

INTERREGNUM

91.	Diyunisiyus VI	1088-1090
92.	Athanasiyus VI *Abu'l-Faraj*	1090-1129
93.	Yuhanna XI *Mawdyani*	1129-1137
94.	Athanasiyus VII *Ishu' ibn Qatrah*	1137-1166
95.	Mikha'il I *al-Kabir "The Great"*	1166-1199
96.	Athanasiyus VIII *Saliba Qarakha*	1199-1207
97.	Yuhanna XII *Ishu'*	1208-1220
98.	Ighnatiyus III *Dawud*	1222-1252
99.	Diyunisiyus VII *Aharon Angur*	1252-1261
100.	Yuhanna XIII *ibn al-Ma'dani*	1261-1263
101.	Ighnatiyus IV *Ishu'*	1264-1283
102.	Filuksinus I *Nimrud*	1283-1292
103.	Mikha'il II *ibn Sawma*	1292-1312
	Qustantinus (I) [anti-patriarch]	1292-
105.	Ighnatiyus V *ibn Wahib ibn Zakha*	1313-1333
106.	Ighnatiyus Isma'il *Yuhanna*	1333-1365
108.	Ighnatiyus Shihab	1365-1381
109.	Ighnatiyus Ibrahim II *ibn Gharib*	1381-1412
111.	Ighnatiyus Bihnam *Hajlaya*	1412-1454
113.	Ighnatiyus Khalaf	1455-1483
114.	Ighnatiyus Yuhanna XIV *Akhsinaya Bar Shilla*	1483-1493
115.	Ighnatiyus Nuh [#77 of India]	1493-1509
116.	Ighnatiyus Ishu' I	1509-1512
117.	Ighnatiyus Ya'qub I	1512-1517
118.	Ighnatiyus Dawud I	1517-1519
119.	Ighnatiyus 'Abd Allah I	1520-1556
120.	Ighnatiyus Ni'mat Allah	1557-1576
121.	Ighnatiyus Dawud Shah II *Butrus ibn Nur ad-Din*	1576-1591
122.	Ighnatiyus Bilatus	1591-1597
123.	Ighnatiyus Hidayat Allah	1597-1639

124.	Ighnatiyus Shim'un *of Tur-Abdin*	1640-1659
125.	Ighnatiyus Ishu' II *Qamah*	1659-1662
126.	Ighnatiyus 'Abd al-Masih I *al-Rawhi*	1662-1686
	Ighnatiyus Habib *al-Mazziyati* [anti-patriarch]	1674-1686
127.	Ighnatiyus Jirjis II	1687-1708
128.	Ighnatiyus Ishaq	1709-1723
129.	Ighnatiyus Shukr Allah	1723-1745
130.	Ighnatiyus Jirjis III	1745-1768
131.	Ighnatiyus Jirjis IV	1768-1781
132.	Ighnatiyus Matiyus *ibn 'Abd Allah*	1782-1817
133.	Ighnatiyus Yunan	1817-1819
134.	Ighnatiyus Jirjis V *Sayyar*	1819-1836
135.	Ighnatiyus Ilyas II *Ankaz*	1838-1847
136.	Ighnatiyus Ya'qub II	1847-1871
137.	Ighnatiyus Butrus IV *al-Ma'usili*	1872-1894
138.	Ighnatiyus 'Abd al-Masih II	1895-1905
139.	Ighnatiyus 'Abd Allah II *al-Saddi* (*Sattuf*)	1906-1915
140.	Ighnatiyus Ilyas III *Shakar*	1917-1932
141.	Ighnatiyus Afram *Barsum*	1933-1957
142.	Ighnatiyus Ya'qub III *Tuma*	1957-1980
143.	Ighnatiyus Zakka *'Iwas*	1980-

SYRIAN PATRIARCHS OF ANTIOCH AT SIS (CILICIA)
(Recognized as valid by the Church)

104.	Mikha'il III *Ishu' ibn Shushan*	1312-1349
	Ighnatiyus Qustantinus (II) [anti-patriarch]	1312-1313
107.	Basiliyus IV *Ghubriyal*	1349-1382
110.	Filuksinus II *"The Scribe"*	1382-1421
112.	Basiliyus V *Shim'un Man'Amaya*	1421-1444

SYRIAN PATRIARCHS OF ANTIOCH AT TUR ABHDIN
(Not recognized as valid by the Church)

106.	Ighnatiyus Sabbas *ibn Wahib*	1364-1389
107.	Ighnatiyus Ishu' I *ibn Muta*	1390-1418?
108.	Ighnatiyus Mas'ud I *Slakhaya*	1418-1420
109.	Ighnatiyus Hinukh *Inwardaya*	1421-1445
110.	Ighnatiyus Quma *ibn Gafil*	1446-1455
111.	Ighnatiyus Ishu' II *Inwardaya*	1455-1466
112.	Ighnatiyus 'Aziz *ibn Shabhta*	1466-1488
113.	Ighnatiyus Yuhanna XV *ibn Qufar*	1488-1493
	Ighnatiyus Shaba *Arbaya* [anti-patriarch]	1488-
114.	Ighnatiyus Mas'ud II	1490?-1495

XV.

THE CHURCH OF ARMENIA

Although the Armenian Church claims to have been founded by the apostles Thaddeus and Bartholomew, most traditions point to St. Gregory as the original organizer of the Church, about the year 300. Gregory was made Bishop of Armenia shortly thereafter. The political isolation of the Armenian kingdom quickly led to its ecclesiastical isolation as well; this was reinforced by the Church's decision (circa 500) to repudiate the Council of Chalcedon, and embrace monophysitism. The Patriarch of Armenia was the first to use the title "Catholicos" (Greek "Katholikos") a distinction which has since been adopted by many neighboring churches in the Near East. About the year 1100, the Patriarch moved his residence from Ashtishat in Armenia to the city of Sis, in Cilicia, then the center of a thriving Armenian/Latin monarchy. After the fall of the kingdom in 1375, the chief see of the Church was moved to Echmiadzin (1441), in Armenia proper, where it remains to this day. Several subsidiary Armenian patriarchates gradually emerged over the centuries. These included Aght'amar (the result of a schism in 1113), Jerusalem (1311), Caucasian Albania (semi-independent from earliest times), Sis (1441), Constantinople (1461), and the Catholic Patriarchate of Cilicia (1742). Two of these, Aght'amar and Albania, have lapsed; of the others, all but Sis and Cilicia acknowledge Echmiadzin as first among equals of the Armenian primates; the churches at Constantinople and Jerusalem accept some guidance in their affairs from the mother church.

The Turkish massacres of Armenian nationals in 1890-1915 decimated the Armenian population in Eastern Turkey, resulting in the abandonment of the Aght'amarian Patriarchate, and changing the balance of power in the Armenian Church. The Catholicosate of Sis moved south into Lebanon, where it found renewed strength; at the same time, Echmiadzin withdrew behind the borders of Armenia proper, which became a Soviet republic in 1921. The Soviet invasion resulted in suppression of the Church during the two decades between the wars; at the death of Patriarch Khorên, in 1938, no election was allowed for a successor. The *Locum Tenens*, Georg, greatly aided the Soviet war effort during World War II, organizing and financing an Armenian regiment; in return, Stalin permitted new patriarchal elections in 1945. Most overseas members of the Armenian Church are governed by bishops appointed from Echmiadzin, although both the Jerusalem and Cilician patriarchates are represented in America.

The primate bears the title Patriarch and Catholicos of All the Armenians. The official Church language is Armenian. Roughly four million communicants are located in Armenia, the Middle East, and the new world.

SOURCES: *Armenia: The Survival of a Nation* (Walker); *The Church of Armenia* (Ormanian); *Dictionnaire de Théologie Catholique*; *Dictionnaire d'Histoire et de Géographie Ecclésiastique*; *Eastern Christianity and Politics in the Twentieth Century* (Ramet, ed.); *Europa World Yearbook*; *Gegenwartslage der Ostkirchen* (Spuler); *The History of the Armenian People* (Morgan); *History of the Church* (Jedin, ed.); *Die Morgenlandischen Kirchen* (Spuler); *Orthodoxia*; *Profiles in Belief* (Piepkorn); *Religion in the Soviet Union* (Kolarz).

TRADITIONAL PATRIARCHS OF THE OLD CHURCH

1.	T'adêos	43-66
2.	Bart'oghimêos	60-68
3.	Zak'aria	68-72
4.	Zementos	72-76
5.	Atrnerseh	77-92
6.	Mushê I	93-123
7.	Shahên	124-150
8.	Shawarsh	151-171
9.	Ghewondios	172-190
	INTERREGNUM	
10.	Mehruzhan	240-270
	INTERREGNUM	

CATHOLICOSES OF ARMENIA

11.	Grigor I "The Illuminator" *Lusaworich'*	302-325
12.	Aristakês I *Parte'* [son of #11]	325-333
13.	Vrt'anês *Part'e* [brother of #12]	333-341
14.	Husik I *Part'e* [son of #13]	341-347
	Daniêl [unconsecrated]	347
15.	P'arhên of *Ashtishat* [cousin of #14]	348-352
	Shahak [locum tenens]	352-353
16.	Nersês I "The Great" [grandson of #14]	353-373
	Shahak [locum tenens]	359-363
17.	Shahak (or Husik II)	373-377
18.	Zawên [cousin of #17]	377-381
19.	Aspurakês [brother of #18]	381-386
20.	Sahak I "The Great" *Part'e*	387-436

	Surmak [anti-catholicos]	428-429
	Brguisho [anti-catholicos]	429-432
	Shmuel [anti-catholicos]	432-437
	Surmak [2nd time]	437-444
	Mesrop [locum tenens]	439-440
	Hovsêp' I [locum tenens]	440-444
21.	Hovsêp' I	444-452
22.	Melitê	452-456
23.	Movsês I	456-461
24.	Giwt	461-478
	Kristap'or *Ardzruni* [anti-catholicos]	478
25.	Hovhannês I *Mandakuni*	478-490
26.	Babkên	490-516
27.	Samuêl	516-526
28.	Mushê II	526-534
29.	Sahak II	534-539
30.	K'ristap'or I	539-545
31.	Ghewond	545-548
32.	Nersês II	548-557
33.	Hovhannês II	557-574
34.	Movsês II	574-604

INTERREGNUM

	Hovhannês [anti-catholicos]	590-611
	Vrt'anês *Kert'ogh* [locum tenens]	604-607
35.	Abraham I	607-615
36.	Komitas	615-628
37.	K'ristap'or II	628-630
38.	Ezr	630-641
39.	Nersês III *Shinogh*	641-661
40.	Anastas	661-667
41.	Israyêl	667-677
42.	Sahak III	677-703
43.	Eghia	703-717
44.	Hovhannês III *Imastaser*	717-728
45.	Dawit' I	728-741
46.	Trdat I	741-764
47.	Trdat II	764-767
48.	Sion	767-775
49.	Esayi	775-788
50.	Step'anos I	788-790
51.	Hovab	790-791
52.	Soghomon	791-792
53.	Gêorg I *Hailorbuk*	792-795
54.	Hovsêp' II *Karidj*	795-806
55.	Dawit' II	806-833
56.	Hovhannês IV	833-855

57.	Zak'aria I	855-876
58.	Gêorg II	877-897
59.	Mashtots'	897-898
60.	Hovhannês V "The Historian" *Patmaban*	898-929
61.	Step'anos II *Rshtuni*	929-930
62.	T'êodoros I *Rshtuni*	930-941
63.	Eghishê *Rshtuni*	941-946
64.	Anania	946-968
65.	Vahan *Siuni*	968-969
66.	Step'anos III	969-972
67.	Khach'ik I *Arsharuni*	973-992
68.	Sargis I	992-1019
69.	Petros *Getadardz*	1019-1058
	Dioskoros [anti-catholicos]	1036-1038
70.	Khach'ik II [coadjutor 1049]	1058-1065
71.	Grigor II *Vkayasêr*	1066-1105
	Gêorg [coadjutor]	1067-1072
	Sargis [anti-catholicos]	1076-1077
	T'êodoros *Alakhosik* [anti-catholicos]	1077-1090
	Poghos [anti-catholicos]	1086-1087
72.	Barsegh [coadjutor 1081]	1105-1113
73.	Grigor III *Pahlawuni*	1113-1166
	Dawit' *T'ornikian* [anti-catholicos]	1114-
74.	Nersês IV *Shnorhali*	1166-1173
75.	Grigor IV *Tghay*	1173-1193
76.	Grigor V *K'aravêzh*	1193-1194
77.	Grigor VI *Apirat*	1194-1203
	Barsegh [anti-catholicos]	1195-1206?
78.	Hovhannês VI *Medzabaro*	1203-1221
	Anania [anti-catholicos]	1204-1208?
	Dawit' [coadjutor]	1204-1207
79.	Kostandin I	1221-1267
80.	Hakob I *Guitnakan*	1268-1286
81.	Kostandin II *Pronogordz*	1286-1289
82.	Step'anos IV	1290-1293
83.	Grigor VII	1293-1307
84.	Kostandin III	1307-1322
85.	Kostandin IV	1323-1326
86.	Hakob II	1327-1341
87.	Mkhit'ar	1341-1355
	Hakob II [2nd time]	1355-1359
88.	Mesrop	1359-1372
89.	Kostandin V	1372-1374
90.	Poghos I	1374-1382
91.	T'êodoros II	1382-1392
92.	Karapet I *Bobik*	1392-1404

93.	Hakob III	1404-1411
94.	Grigor VIII *K'antsoghat*	1411-1418
95.	Poghos II	1418-1430
96.	Kostandin VI	1430-1439
	Hovsêp' [anti-catholicos]	1430?
97.	Grigor IX *Musabêgiants'* [#1 of Cilicia]	1439-1441
98.	Kirakos	1441-1443
99.	Gêorg III *Jalalbêgiants'*	1443-1465
	Karapet [anti-catholicos]	1446-
	Zak'aria [anti-catholicos]	1461-1462
100.	Aristakês II *At'orakal* [coadjutor 1448]	1465-1469
101.	Sargis II *Ajatar* [coadjutor 1462]	1469-1474
102.	Hovhannês VII *Ajakir* [coadjutor 1470]	1474-1484
103.	Sargis III *Miwsayl* [coadjutor 1474]	1484-1515
	Aristakês [coadjutor]	1484-1499
	T'adêos [coadjutor]	1499-1504
	Eghishê [coadjutor]	1504-1505
	Hovhannês [coadjutor]	1505-1506
	Nersês [coadjutor]	1506-1507
104.	Zak'aria II [coadjutor 1507]	1515-1520
105.	Sargis IV [coadjutor 1515]	1520-1536
106.	Grigor X	1536-1545
107.	Step'anos V	1545-1567
	Barsegh [coadjutor]	1549-1552
	Aristakês [coadjutor]	1555-
108.	Mik'ayêl [coadjutor 1545]	1567-1576
	Step'anos [coadjutor]	1567-
109.	Grigor XI [coadjutor 1552]	1576-1590
	T'adêos [coadjutor]	1577-
	Arakel [coadjutor]	1577-
110.	Dawit' III [coadjutor 1579]	1590-1629
	Melk'isedek [coadjutor]	1593-1603
	Grigor *Serapion* [coadjutor]	1603-1624
	Sahak [coadjutor]	1624-1629?
111.	Movsês III	1629-1632
112.	P'ilippos	1632-1655
113.	Hakob IV	1655-1680
	Eghiazar [anti-catholicos]	1663-1682
114.	Eghiazar	1682-1691
115.	Nahapet	1691-1705
116.	Aghek'sandr I	1706-1714
117.	Astuatsatur	1715-1725
118.	Karapet II	1726-1729
119.	Abraham II	1730-1734
120.	Abraham III	1734-1737
121.	Ghazar	1737-1748

	Hovhannês [anti-catholicos]	1740-
	Petros *Kutur* [locum tenens]	1748
	Ghazar [2nd time]	1748-1751
122.	Minas	1751-1753
123.	Aghek'sandr II *Karakashian*	1753-1755
	Sahak *Ahagwin* [unconsecrated]	1755-1760
124.	Hakob V	1759-1763
125.	Simêon	1763-1780
126.	Ghukas	1780-1799
	Hovsêp' *Arghutian* [unconsecrated]	1800-1801
127.	Dawit' IV *Gorghanian*	1801-1807
128.	Daniêl [elected 1801]	1807-1808
129.	Ep'rem	1809-1830
130.	Hovhannês VIII	1831-1842
131.	Nersês V *Ashtaraketsi*	1843-1857
132.	Matt'êos I *Ch'ukhachian* [#66 of Constantinople]	1858-1865
133.	Gêorg IV *K'êrêst'êchian* [#67 of Constantinople]	1866-1882
	INTERREGNUM	
	Nersês *Vartsapetian* [unconsecrated; #72 of Constantinople]	1884
134.	Makar *Ter-Petrosian*	1885-1891
135.	Mkrtich' *Khrimian* [#71 of Constantinople]	1892-1907
136.	Matt'êos II *Izmirlian* [#75 of Constantinople]	1908-1910
137.	Gêorg V *Surenian(ts')*	1911-1930
	Khorên *Muradbêgian* [locum tenens]	1930-1932
138.	Khorên *Muradbêgian*	1932-1938
	INTERREGNUM	
	Gêorg *Ch'êôrêk'chian* [locum tenens]	1938-1945
139.	Gêorg VI *Ch'êôrêk'chian*	1945-1954
	Vahan *Kostanian* [locum tenens]	1954-1955
140.	Vazgên *Palchian*	1955-1994
	T'orgom *Manugian* [locum tenens] [#87 of Jerusalem]	1994-1995
141.	Garegin *Sargisian* [#42 of Cilicia]	1995-

XVI.

THE CHURCH OF ASSYRIA (OF THE EAST)

The Church of Assyria, also called the Church of the East and (erroneously) the Nestorian Church, traces its history to a small Christian community founded by the apostles in the kingdom of Edessa, during the first century after Christ. The list of bishops (with their years of rule) claimed by the Church during these early years cannot be verified; its tradition of apostolic succession has never been challenged, however. About the year 280 Mar Papa organized the Church into a Metropolitanate centered around the city of Seleucia, about thirty miles from the modern city of Baghdad. The title of Catholicos was assumed in 410 A.D. The Church grew rapidly, reaching its peak of cultural development and influence during the reign of Catholicos Yabhalaha III. By this time, Assyrian missionaries had established major branches of the Church throughout China and the Far East, and seem destined to make the Assyrian Church the sole source of Christian instruction for the oriental world. The rise of the Mongols slowed this missionary effort, and nearly destroyed the Church itself.

By the mid-fifteenth century, the remnants of the Assyrian Church had sought refuge in the mountains of Kurdistan. The widespread destruction of churches and the wholesale slaughter of Church leaders led to the election (with Shim'un V [or VI]) of the nephew of the previous patriarch; the new patriarch had been raised in his uncle's house, and trained from birth for the high position which he now occupied. Thus the patriarchate became heredity in the bar Mama family, with succession from uncle to nephew or sometimes brother. When the crisis subsided, a hundred years later, a significant faction of bishops and secular leaders attempted to restore the ancient electoral process on the death of Ishu'yabh Shim'un VII (or VIII) in 1551. They chose as patriarch a monk, Sa'ud bar Dani'il, who took the religious name of Yukhannan Shim'un IX Sulaqa (one of the churches inserts an extra "Shim'un" into their official list of patriarchs, hence the discrepancy in numbering). Dinkha Shim'un VIII bar Mama was named by his family as successor to his uncle, Ishu'yabh, thereby splitting the Church into two factions. To complicate matters, Sulaqa immediately sought the backing of Rome to legitimize his position; the Pope confirmed Sulaqa's election and named him Patriarch. Yukhannan Shim'un IX was arrested and then executed by his rival, Dinkha Shim'un VIII bar Mama, in 1555, and was immediately succeeded by Marun 'Abdishu' IV.

The history of the next ten years is obscure. Dinkha Shim'un VIII bar Mama died in 1558, and was succeeded by his relative, Iliya VI. Marun 'Abdishu' V died in 1567 (or 1571), and was succeeded after some delay by Yabhalaha IV (also called Shim'un X). A third faction, headed by the Metropolitan of Gelu, Dinkha Shim'un (XI), rejected the authority of the bar Mama family, and submitted to Catholicos Yabhalaha; on the latter's death in 1580, Dinkha Shim'un XI was elected his successor, the first patriarch of the Shim'un family. Thus was established a second hereditary line of patriarchs, in opposition to the bar Mama family.

Throughout the next three hundred years, the Catholicoses of the Shim'un family remained isolated in the mountains of Kurdistan, gradually losing contact with Rome. The last hereditary Catholicos, Ishai Shim'un XXIII, succeeded his uncle in 1920 at the age of twelve. In 1933, after returning to Iraq from his British school, he attempted to restore the old civil authority of the Patriarch. His supporters then took up arms, and were massacred by Iraqi government soldiers. Shim'un spent the rest of his life in exile, much of it in San Francisco. He resigned his office in 1973, without any obvious successor, immediately throwing his Church into turmoil. Church leaders from Iraq pleaded with the Patriarch to withdraw his resignation, at least until some provision could be made for the succession; Shim'un agreed to return for a six-month period, at which point a Synod of three bishops was appointed to govern the Church during the interregnum. When Shim'un was murdered in November 1975, the bishops restored the ancient electoral process, and a new patriarch, Mar Dinkha IV, was chosen in October 1976. Dinkha and Pope John Paul II issued a joint declaration of faith on 11 November 1994, stating that their accord represented "a fundamental step on the way to full communion."

The official language of the Church is Syriac. The primate, who uses the title "Catholicos-Patriarch of the Church of the East," resides in Chicago and Baghdad. The roughly 400,000 communicants reside largely in the United States, with a few communities remaining in Iraq and Iran.

SOURCES: *The Catholic Eastern Churches* (Attwater); *Catholic Encyclopedia*; *The Christian Churches of the East* (Attwater); *De Catholicis seu Patriarchis Chaldæorum et Nestorianorum* (Assemani); *Dictionnaire de Théologie Catholique*; *Europa World Yearbook*; *Gegenwartslage der Ostkirchen* (Spuler); *Historia tés Assyriachés Nestorianikés Ekklésias* (Arbanités); *History of the Church* (Jedin, ed.); *The Middle East and North Africa*; *Die Morgenlandischen Kirchen* (Spuler); *New Catholic Encyclopedia*; *Oriens Christianus* (Le Quien); *Orthodoxia*; *Profiles in Belief* (Piepkorn); Rev. Nenos Michael.

CATHOLICOS-PATRIARCHS OF ASSYRIA

1.	Shim'un I *Kipa*	33
2.	T'uma I *Shlikha*	33
3.	Bar T'ulmai	33
4.	Addai (or T'addai) I *Shlikha*	33-45
5.	Agai	45-48
6.	Mari I	48-81
	INTERREGNUM	
7.	Abris	90-107
	INTERREGNUM	
8.	Abraham I	130-152
	INTERREGNUM	
9.	Ya'qub I	172-190
10.	Abad *M'shikha*	191-203
11.	Akha *d'Awuhi*	205-220
	INTERREGNUM	
12.	Shakhlupa *of Kashkar*	224-244
	INTERREGNUM	
13.	Papa *bar Gaggai*	247-326
14.	Shim'un II *bar Sabba'i*	328-341
	INTERREGNUM	
15.	Shahdust	345-347
	INTERREGNUM	
16.	Bar Ba'shmin	350-358
	INTERREGNUM	
17.	T'umarsa	383-393
18.	Qayuma	393-399
19.	Iskhaq	399-411
20.	Akhkhi	411-415
21.	Yabhalaha I	415-420
22.	Ma'na	420
23.	Qarabukt	421
24.	Dadishu'	421-456
25.	Babai (or Babwi) I	457-484
26.	Aqaq	484-496
27.	Babai II	496-502
28.	Shila	505-523
29.	Narsai [rival catholicos]	524-535
30.	Ilisha' [rival catholicos]	524-538
31.	Pulus	539-540
32.	Mari Aba I *Raba*	540-552
33.	Yusip	552-567
	INTERREGNUM	
34.	Khazqi'il	570-581

35.	Ishu'yabh I *Arzunaya*	581-595
36.	Sabrishu' I *Garmaqaya*	596-604
37.	Grigur *Partaya*	605-608
	INTERREGNUM	
38.	Ishu'yabh II *Gdalaya*	628-644
	INTERREGNUM	
39.	Mari Immih	647-650
40.	Ishu'yabh III *Khdayabaya*	650-660
41.	Giwargis I	661-680
42.	Yukhannan I *bar Marta*	680-682
	INTERREGNUM	
43.	Khnanishu' I *"The Lame"*	686-693
44.	Yukhannan II *Garba "The Leper"*	693-694
	INTERREGNUM	
45.	Slibazka	714-728
	INTERREGNUM	
46.	Pit'iun	731-740
47.	Mari Aba II	741-751
48.	Surin	752-754
49.	Ya'qub II	754-773
50.	Khnanishu' II	774-778
51.	Timat'ius I	780-820
52.	Ishu' *bar Nun*	820-824
53.	Giwargis II	825-832
54.	Sabrishu' II	832-836
55.	Abraham II *d'Margaa*	837-850
56.	T'iyadusis I (or T'iyaduris)	850-852
	INTERREGNUM	
57.	Sargis *Subaya*	860-872
58.	Anush *d'Bit' Garmai*	873-884
59.	Yukhannan III *bar Narsai*	884-892
60.	Yukhannan IV *bar Akhiha*	892-898
61.	Yukhannan V *bar Agbara* (or *Bar'aysa*)	900-905
62.	Abraham III *Abraza*	906-937
63.	'Ummanu'il	937-949
	INTERREGNUM	
64.	Israyil *Karkaya* [unconsecrated]	961-962
65.	'Abdishu' I *Garmaqaya*	963-986
66.	Mari II *bar Tubi At'uraya*	987-1000
67.	Yukhannan VI *bar Ishu'*	1001-1012
68.	Yukhannan VII *Nazuk*	1013-1022
69.	Ishu'yabh IV *bar Khazqi'il*	1023-1027
70.	Iliya I	1028-1049
71.	Yukhannan VIII *bar Targali*	1049-1057
72.	Sabrishu' III *bar Zanbur*	1057-1072
73.	'Abdishu' II *bar Arus Anraya*	1072-1090

74.	Makkikha I *bar Shlimun*	1092-1109
75.	Iliya II *bar Mulki*	1111-1132
76.	Bar Suma *d'Subi*	1133-1135
77.	Bar Gabbara	1135-1136
78.	'Abdishu' III *bar Mulki* [nephew of #75]	1138-1147
79.	Ishu'yabh V *Baladaya*	1148-1175
80.	Iliya III *Abu Khalim*	1176-1190
81.	Yabhalaha II *bar Qayyuma*	1191-1222
82.	Sabrishu' IV *bar Qayyuma*	1222-1226
83.	Sabrishu' V *bar Masikh*	1226-1256
84.	Makkikha II (or T'iyadusis II)	1257-1265
85.	Dinkha I *Arbilaya*	1265-1281
86.	Yabhalaha III *bar Turkaya*	1281-1318
87.	Timat'ius II	1318-1328
88.	Dinkha II	1329-1359
89.	Dinkha III	1359-1368
90.	Shim'un III	1369-1392

INTERREGNUM

91.	Shim'un IV	1403-1407
92.	Iliya IV	1407-1420
93.	Shim'un V	1420-1447
94.	Shim'un VI *d'Bat' Sadi*	1448-1490
95.	Iliya V	1491-1504
96.	Shim'un VII	1505-1538
97.	Ishu'yabh Shim'un VIII *bar Mama* [brother of #96]	1538-1551
98.	Dinkha Shim'un IX *bar Mama* [nephew of #97]	1552-1558
99.	Yabhalaha IV Shim'un X	1558-1580
100.	Dinkha Shim'un XI	1580-1600
101.	Iliya Shim'un XII	1600-1653
102.	Ishu'yabh Shim'un XIII	1653-1690
103.	Yabhalaha Shim'un XIV	1690-1692
104.	Dinkha Shim'un XV	1692-1700
105.	Shlimun Shim'un XVI [nephew of #104?]	1700-1740?
106.	Mikha'il Shim'un XVII *Mukhatas* [nephew?]	1740?-1780?
107.	Yunan Shim'un XVIII [nephew?]	1780?-1820?
108.	Abraham Shim'un XIX [nephew?]	1820?-1860
109.	Rubil Shim'un XX [nephew?]	1860-1903
110.	Binyamin Shim'un XXI [nephew of #109]	1903-1918
111.	Pulus Shim'un XXII [brother of #110]	1918-1920
112.	Ishai Shim'un XXIII [nephew of #111]	1920-1975
113.	Dinkha IV *Khnanishu'*	1976-

ANCIENT APOSTOLIC AND CATHOLIC CHURCH OF THE EAST

On 25 September 1968, Mar Thoma Darmo, Metropolitan of the Chaldean Syrian Church of India, and a longtime opponent of the hereditary patriarchate, was elected Catholicos-Patriarch of the newly-organized Ancient Apostolic and Catholic Church of the East, with its seat at Baghdad. The dissidents, including both laity and clergy, were able to persuade the Iraqi government to cede them many of the churches and properties previously owned by the followers of Shim'un XXIII. When Darmo died a year later, he was succeeded by Mar Addai II on 20 February 1972. Efforts by the two rival patriarchs to unite the churches, or to agree on mutually-recognized eastern and western patriarchates, have thus far failed. A major liturgical different between the two denominations is the use of the Julian Calendar by the Old Apostolic Church (its rival uses the Gregorian calendar). Roughly 30,000 communicants reside in Iraq, with another 40,000 located in Kerala, India and the United States. **SOURCES:** news reports; *Orthodoxia*.

CATHOLICOS-PATRIARCHS OF THE CHURCH OF THE EAST

112. T'uma II *Darmu*		1968-1969
	INTERREGNUM	
113. Addai II *Giwargis*		1972-

76

XVII.

THE CHURCHES OF AUSTRIA-HUNGARY
(CERNOVCI, KARLOVCI, SIBIU)

The Church of Sremski Karlovci (or Srijemski Karlovac) was autonomous from at least 1690, when the Holy Roman Emperors granted former Serbian Patriarch Arsenije III and thousands of his followers refuge from Turkish depredations. The archdiocese of Karlovci was located in the southern part of the Kingdom of Hungary (then part of the Holy Roman Empire, later an autonomous section of the Austrian-Hungarian Empire). The Austrians deliberately used the Orthodox denominations within the boundaries of their expanding state to bolster their political and economic claims on southeastern Europe, and to provide ecclesiastical counterpoints against the rising tide of nationalism in the Balkans.

Thus, among the many consequences of the two Austrian revolutions of 1848 were the naming of a new and vigorous Emperor, Franz Josef I, the erection of the Hungarian half of his realm into a second cultural and political center of the Empire, and the unilateral granting of the title "Patriarch" to Josif Rajacic, then Metropolitan of Sremski Karlovci, on 15 December 1848. Although the Ecumenical Patriarch protested this non-ecclesiastical lifting of Karlovci into the patriarchal ranks (and the assumption of autocephaly that went with it), the title remained in use until 1918. This creation of a newly independent rival church just forty miles up the Danube from Belgrade (Beograd), the capital of the rising state of Serbia, was no accident, since it supported the government policy of stopping Serbian expansionism at any cost.

Similarly, the Church of Sibiu was taken from Karlovci, and erected on 24 December 1864 into an autonomous (or autocephalous) church to service the Romanians in northeastern Hungary, and to act as a direct challenge to the newly independent state of Romania and its soon-to-be-proclaimed autocephalous church. The third church, Cernovtci (now Chernovtsy in the independent ex-Soviet state of Ukraine), was made autonomous (or autocephalous) on 23 January 1873 in the northeastern section of the Empire.

All three churches were under the direct supervision of the Austro-Hungarian government, which interferred blatantly in more than one ecclesiastical "election," all higher-level appointments requiring confirmation from the Emperor before the prelates could be consecrated. In 1908, for example, the leading candidate for Patriarch of Karlovci, Gavrilo Zmajevich, although elected, was never consecrated due to government opposition, and a second nominated candidate then declined election when it became obvious that the Emperor would not agree. Finally, the government-sponsored prelate, Bogdanovic, was forced upon the assemblage; in a bizarre twist, he apparently committed suicide five years later by driving his car off a cliff. The see remained vacant until the end of World War I. Unusually, many of the primates of this church were better known under their surnames (e.g., Patriarch Rajacic) than their given names.

The Church of Karlovci, which had some 800,000 communicants prior to World War I, merged into the new Serbian Patriarchate in the aftermath of World War I (during 1919 and 1920), the Serbian leader subsuming the title of Metropolitan of Karlovci. The Church of Sibiu, which included roughly 220,000 members, became a metropolitanate in the Church of Romania in 1918. The Church of Cernovci (or Cernauti or Chernovtsy) in Bukovina, with some half million communicants, became part of the Church of Romania in 1918, some parishes being given to Poland and Russia. When the Soviets occupied the city in 1940, the Church was transferred to Russia, and with the disintegration of the Soviet Union, it now falls under the jurisdiction of Ukraine.

SOURCES: *Biographisches Lexikon zur Geschichte Südosteuropas* (Bernath & Nehring); *Dictionnaire de Théologie Catholique*; *Échos d'Orient*; *The Hapsburg Empire, 1790-1918* (Macartney); *A History of Modern Serbia, 1804-1918* (Petrovich); *History of the Church* (Jedin, ed.); *Istoria Bisericii Ortodoxe Române*; *Karlovacko Vladicanstvo* (Grbic).

METROPOLITAN ARCHBISHOPS OF CERNOVCI (BUKOVINA)

1.	Nicolae	
2.	Stefan I	
3.	Iosif	
4.	Meletie	
5.	Lavrentie I	
6.	Grigorie	
7.	Sava I	
8.	Ghelasie	
9.	Ioanichie	1472-1504
10.	Pahomie	1504-1522
	INTERREGNUM	
11.	Teofan I	1528-1530
12.	Teodosie I	1530-1550?

13.	Mitrofan	1550?-1552
14.	Gheorghe I	1552-1558
15.	Eftimie	1558-1561?
16.	Dimitrie	1561?-1564?
17.	Isaia I	1564?-1577
18.	Gheorghe II *Moghila* (or *Movila*)	1577-1588
19.	Ghedeon I	1588-1591?
20.	Mardarie	1591?-1595
21.	Amfilohie	1595-1598
22.	Teodosie II *Barbovschi*	1598-1600
23.	Anastasie I *Crimca*	1600
	Teodosie II [2nd time]	1600-1605
24.	Ioan	1605-1608
25.	Efrem	1608-1613
26.	Atanasie II	1613-1616?
	Efrem [2nd time]	1616?-1623?
27.	Evloghie	1623-1627
28.	Dionisie	1627-1629
	Evloghie [2nd time]	1628-1639?
29.	Anastasie III	1639?-1644?
30.	Stefan II	1644?-1646?
31.	Teofan II	1646?-1651
32.	Iorest	1651?-1656
33.	Sava II	1656-1658
34.	Teofan III	1658-1666
35.	Serafim	1667-1669
36.	Teodosie III	1669?-1671
	Serafim [2nd time]	1671-1685?
37.	Misail I	1685?-1689
38.	Lavrentie II	1689-1702
	Nicolae *Vasilevic(i)* [anti-Archbishop]	1691-
39.	Ghedeon II	1701?-1708
40.	Calistru	1708-1728
41.	Antonie	1728-1729
42.	Misail II	1729-1735
43.	Varlaam	1735-1745
44.	Iacob *Putneanul*	1745-1750
45.	Dosoftei *Herescu*	1750-1789
46.	Daniil *Vlahovic(i)*	1789-1822
47.	Isaia II *Balosescu*	1823-1834
48.	Eugenie (or Evghenie) *Hacman*	1835-1873
49.	Teofil *Bendela*	1873-1875
50.	Teoctist *Blajevic(i)*	1877-1879
51.	Silvestru *Moraru-Andrievic(i)*	1880-1895
52.	Arcadie *Ciupercovic(i)*	1896-1902
53.	Vladimir *Repta*	1902-1924

54.	Nectarie *Cotlarciuc*	1924-1935
55.	Visarion *Puiu*	1935-1940
56.	Tit *Simedrea*	1940-1945
	Emilian *Antal Tîrgovisteanul* [locum tenens]	1945-1948
57.	Sebastian *Rusan* [titular archbishop]	1948-1950

THE ROMANIAN METROPOLITANATE DISCONTINUED

PATRIARCHS OF SREMSKI KARLOVCI
(Metropolitans 1690, Patriarchs 1848)

1.	Arsenije I *Crnojevic* (or *Carnojevic*) [#43 of Serbia]	1690-1706
2.	Isaija I *D(i)jakovic*	1708
3.	Stevan I *Metohijac*	1708-1709
4.	Sofronije *Podgoricanin*	1710-1711
	Atanasije *Ljubojevic* [locum tenens]	1711-1712
5.	Vicentije I *Popovic*	1713-1725
6.	Mojsej(e) I *Petrovic*	1726-1730
	Nikolaj *Dmitrijevic* [locum tenens]	1730-1731
7.	Vicentije II *Jovanovic*	1731-1737
	INTERREGNUM	
8.	Arsenije II *Jovanovic Shakabent* [#47 of Serbia]	1741-1748
9.	Isaija II *Antonovic*	1748-1749
10.	Pavle *Nenadovic*	1749-1768
	Jovan *Djordjevic* [locum tenens]	1768-1769
11.	Jovan *Djordjevic* [#32 of Sibiu]	1769-1773
12.	Vicentije III *Jovanovic-Vidak*	1774-1780
13.	Mojsej II *Putnik*	1781-1790
14.	Stevan II (or Stefan) *Stratimirovic*	1790-1836
15.	Stevan III *Stankovic*	1837-1841
	Georgije (I) *Hranislav* [locum tenens]	1841-1842
16.	Josif *Rajacic*	1842-1861
	INTERREGNUM	
	Samuïlo *Mashirevic* [locum tenens]	1861-1864
17.	Samuïlo *Mashirevic*	1864-1870
	INTERREGNUM	
	Arsenije (III) *Stojkovic* [locum tenens]	1870-1872
	Nikanor *Gryjic* [locum tenens]	1872-1874
	Arsenije (III) *Stojkovic* [unconsecrated]	1874
18.	Prokopije *Ivachkovic* [#38 of Sibiu]	1874-1880
	Teofan *Zhivkovic* [locum tenens]	1880
	German *Andjelic* [locum tenens]	1880-1882
	Arsenije (III) *Stojkovic* [unconsecrated]	1881
	Teofan *Zhivkovic* [unconsecrated]	1881
19.	German *Andjelic*	1882-1888
20.	Georgije (II) *Brankovic*	1890-1907
	Lukijan *Bogdanovic* [locum tenens]	1907-1908

	Gavrilo *Zmajevic* [unconsecrated]	1908
	Mitrofan *Sevic* [refused election]	1908
21.	Lukijan *Bogdanovic*	1908-1913
	INTERREGNUM	
	Mihaïlo *Gryjic* [locum tenens]	1913-1914
	Miron *Nikolic* [locum tenens]	1914-1919
	Georgije (III) *Letic* [locum tenens]	1919-1920
	MERGED INTO THE CHURCH OF SERBIA	

METROPOLITAN ARCHBISHOPS OF SIBIU
(now Ardealului)

1.	Ghelasie	1376?
2.	Ioan I	1456?
3.	Ioanichie	1479?
4.	Daniil I	1488-1500?
	INTERREGNUM	
5.	Marcu	1516-
6.	Danciu (Stefan?)	1516-1534
	INTERREGNUM	
7.	Petru	1538-1550
	INTERREGNUM	
8.	Ioan II	1553-1557?
9.	Hristofor I	1557-1559?
10.	Sava I	1559-
11.	Gheorghe	1561?-1562
	Sava I [2nd time]	1562-1570
12.	Eftimie	1571?-1574
13.	Hristofor II	1574-1579
14.	Ghenadie I	1579-1585
15.	Ioan III	1585-1605?
16.	Teoctist	1606-1622
17.	Dosoftei	1624-1627
18.	Ghenadie II	1627-1640
19.	Ilie *Iorest*	1640-1643
20.	Simion *Stefan*	1643-1656
21.	Sava II *Brancovic(i)*	1656
22.	Ghenadie III	1659-1660
23.	Daniil II	1660?-1662
	Sava II [2nd time]	1662-1680
24.	Iosif *Budal*	1680-1682
25.	Ioasaf	1682-1683
26.	Sava III	1684-1685
27.	Varlaam	1685-1692
28.	Teofil	1692-1697
29.	Atanasie *Anghel*	1697-1701

	INTERREGNUM	
30.	Iov *Tirca* (or Ioan)	1706?-1707
	INTERREGNUM	
31.	Dionisie *Novacovic(i)*	1761-1767
32.	Ioan IV *Gheorghievic(i)* [#11 of Carlovci]	1768-1769
33.	Sofronie *Chirilovic(i)*	1769-1774
	INTERREGNUM	
	Ioan *Popovic(i)* [locum tenens]	1774-1784
34.	Ghedeon *Nichitic(i)*	1783-1788
	Ioan *Popovic(i)* [locum tenens]	1788-1789
35.	Gherasim *Adamovic(i)*	1789-1796
	INTERREGNUM	
	Ioan *Popovic(i)* [locum tenens]	1796-1805
	Nicolae *Hutovic(i)* [locum tenens]	1805-1811
36.	Vasile I *Moga*	1810-1845
	Andrei *Saguna* [locum tenens]	1846-1847
37.	Andrei *Saguna*	1847-1873
38.	Procopie *Ivascovic(i)* [#18 of Carlovci]	1873-1874
	Ioan *Popasu* [unconsecrated]	1874
39.	Miron *Romanul*	1874-1898
40.	Ioan V *Metianu*	1898-1916
41.	Vasile II *Mangra*	1916-1918
	Ioan *Papp* [locum tenens]	1918-1920
42.	Nicolae I *Balan*	1920-1955
	Justinian *Marina* [#57 of Romania; locum tenens]	1955-1956
43.	Iustin *Moïsescu* [#58 of Romania]	1956-1957
44.	Nicolae II *Colan*	1957-1967
	Nicolae *Corneanu* [locum tenens]	1967
45.	Nicolae III *Mladin*	1967-1981
	Teoctist *Arapas(u)* [#59 of Romania; locum tenens]	1980-1982
46.	Antonie *Plamadeala*	1982-

XVIII.

THE CHALDEAN CHURCH OF BABYLON

The history of the Chaldean Church through 1551, when the great schism occurred, has been given in the chapter on Assyria. Yukhannan Sulaqa, the nominee of the anti-Mama faction, was sent to Rome, where his election was ratified by Pope Julius III. Sulaqa was given the official title of "Patriarch of the Chaldeans." When he returned to Iraq, Sulaqa's rival had him arrested and executed, thereby thinking to end the division. But Sulaqa's supporters elected 'Abdishu' IV as his successor, and then Yabhalaha IV when 'Abdishu' died. Yabhalaha was succeeded in 1580 by the Metropolitan of Gehu, Dinkha Shim'un XI, who founded a second hereditary patriarchate to oppose the bar Mama faction.

 Ironically, the doctrinal positions of the two factions, once so clearly defined, slowly blurred with the centuries. The Shim'uns were forced through political pressure to move their see to the mountains of Kurdistan, thereby isolating their church from outside contact. By the year 1670 their contact with Rome had dwindled to nothing. The bar Mamas, on the other hand, had begun exchanging letters with the Roman Popes in 1586, and formally submitted to papal authority in 1616 at Dyarbekir, although this profession had lapsed by 1669. Subsequently, the Metropolitan of Dyarbekir, Yusip (II), withdrew his allegiance from both parties in 1672, fleeing to Rome by 1675. Pope Innocent XI granted him the title of Patriarch in 1681, thereby creating a third Assyrian patriarchate. Yusip's successor, Yusip III (or II), was erroneously named Patriarch of Babylon in 1701, apparently the result of confusion in Rome over the identity of the city of Baghdad. On the death of Yusip V in 1779, his nephew, Yusip Agustinus Khindi, succeeded his uncle only as Apostolic Administrator and Metropolitan of Dyarbekir; he was never able to obtain official recognition from Rome as the new patriarch.

 Iliya XIII bar Mama, the last hereditary catholicos of his family, died in 1804. His Catholic cousin, Yukhannan (VIII) Khurmiz, claimed the title, and again sought official recognition from the pope. With two Catholic rivals to the patriarchal throne, the Roman Church declined to recognize either claimant until the death of Yusip Khindi in 1828. Khurmiz was thereupon acknowledged as patriarch in 1830. To forestall the possibility of a new hereditary patriarchate, a coadjutor Patriarch with the right of succession was appointed in 1838. The Chaldean Church nearly broke with Rome again in 1869 over the imposition by the Pope of the Bull *Reversurus*, which deprived the patriarch of his prerogative to ordain Chaldean bishops, and which caused similar unrest in Armenian Cilicia. Yusip VI was threatened with excommunication in 1876, but managed to smooth over his difficulties with Rome, dying two years later.

The official language of the Church is Syriac. The primate, who bears the title Patriarch of Babylon of the Chaldeans, resides at Baghdad, Iraq. The roughly 560,000 communicants are scattered throughout the Middle East, particularly in Iraq and Iran, with a strong (50,000-member) overseas contingent in North America, centered largely in Detroit and Chicago.

SOURCES: *The Catholic Eastern Churches* (Attwater); *Catholic Encyclopedia*; *The Christian Churches of the East* (Attwater); *De Catholicis seu Patriarchis Chaldæorum et Nestorianorum* (Assemani); *Dictionnaire de Théologie Catholique*; *Eastern Christianity and Politics in the Twentieth Century* (Ramet, ed.); *Gegenwartslage der Ostkirchen* (Spuler); *The Middle East and North Africa*; *Die Morgenlandischen Kirchen* (Spuler); *New Catholic Encyclopedia*; "Pope Calls for Broad Mideast Peace" (Montalbano); *Oriens Christianus* (Le Quien).

CHALDEAN PATRIARCHS OF ASSYRIA

1.	T'uma *Shlikha*	-33
2.	Addai *Shlikha*	33-
3.	Agai	
4.	Mari I	
5.	Abris	
6.	Abraham I	
7.	Ya'qub I	
8.	Akha *d'Awuhi*	
9.	Shakhlupa *of Kashkar*	
10.	Papa *bar Gaggai*	300?
11.	Shim'un I *bar Sabbai*	-341
12.	Shahdust	341?-342
13.	Bar Ba'shmin	342?-348
	INTERREGNUM	
14.	T'umarsa	388?-
15.	Qayuma	-399
16.	Iskhaq	399-410
17.	Akhkhi	411-414
18.	Yabhalaha I	415-420
19.	Ma'na	420

20.	Qarabukt	420
21.	Dadishu'	421?-456
22.	Babwi	457-484
23.	Aqaq	485-496?
24.	Babai	497-503?
25.	Shila	505-522?
26.	Narsai	524-537?
27.	Ilisha'	524-537?
28.	Pulus I	537?-539?
29.	Aba I *Raba*	540-552
30.	Yusip I	551-567?
31.	Khazqi'il	567-581
32.	Ishu'yabh I *Arzunaya*	582-595
33.	Sabrishu' I *Garmaqaya*	596-604
34.	Grigur *Partaya*	605-609
	INTERREGNUM	
35.	Ishu'yabh II *Gdalaya*	628-646?
36.	Mari Immih	647-650
37.	Ishu'yabh III *Khdayabaya*	650-658?
	INTERREGNUM	
38.	Giwargis I	661-681?
39.	Yukhannan I *bar Marta*	681?-683
40.	Khnanishu' I *"The Lame"*	685?-700?
	Yukhannan (II) *Garba "The Leper"* [anti-Catholicos]	691-693?
	INTERREGNUM	
41.	Slibazka	714-728
	INTERREGNUM	
42.	Pit'iun	731-740
43.	Aba II	741-751
	INTERREGNUM	
44.	Surin	754
45.	Ya'qub II	754-773
46.	Khnanishu' II	773-780
47.	Timat'ius I	780-823
48.	Ishu' *bar Nun*	823-828
49.	Giwargis II	828-831?
50.	Sabrishu' II	831-835
51.	Abraham II *d'Margaa*	837-850
	INTERREGNUM	
52.	T'iyadusis (Solomon)	853-858
53.	Sargis *Subaya*	860-872
	INTERREGNUM	
54.	Israyil I *of Kashkar* [unconsecrated]	877
55.	Anush *d'Bit' Garmai*	877-884
56.	Yukhannan II *bar Akhiha*	884-891
57.	Yukhannan III *bar Narsai*	893-899

58.	Yukhannan IV *bar Agbara*	900-905
59.	Abraham III *Abraza*	905-936
60.	'Ummanu'il I	937-960
61.	Israyil II *Karkaya*	961
62.	'Abdishu' I	963-986
63.	Mari II *bar Tubi At'uraya*	987-999
64.	Yukhannan V *bar Ishu'*	1000-1011
65.	Yukhannan VI *Nazuk*	1012-1016
	INTERREGNUM	
66.	Ishu'yabh IV *bar Khazqi'il*	1020-1025
	INTERREGNUM	
67.	Iliya I	1028-1049
68.	Yukhannan VII *bar Targali*	1049-1057
	INTERREGNUM	
69.	Sabrishu' III *bar Zanbur*	1064-1072
	INTERREGNUM	
70.	'Abdishu' II *bar Arus Anraya*	1075-1090
71.	Makkikha I *bar Shlimun*	1092-1110
72.	Iliya II *bar Mulki*	1111-1132
73.	Bar Suma *d'Subi*	1134-1136
74.	'Abdishu' III *bar Mulki* [nephew of #72]	1139-1148
75.	Ishu'yabh V *Baladaya*	1149-1175
76.	Iliya III *Abu Khalim*	1176-1190
77.	Yabhalaha II *bar Qayyuma*	1190-1222
78.	Sabrishu' IV *bar Qayyuma*	1222-1224
79.	Sabrishu' V *bar Masikh*	1226-1256
80.	Makkikha II	1257-1265
81.	Dinkha I *Arbilaya*	1265-1281
82.	Yabhalaha III *bar Turkaya*	1283-1318
83.	Timat'ius II	1318-1332
84.	Dinkha II	1332-1364
85.	Shim'un II	1364-
86.	Shim'un III	1400?
87.	Iliya IV	-1437
88.	Shim'un IV *d'Bat' Sadi*	1437-1497
89.	Shim'un V	1497-1502?
90.	Iliya V	1502-1503
91.	Shim'un VI	1504-1538
92.	Ishu'yabh Shim'un VII *bar Mama* [brother of #91]	1538-1551
93.	Dinkha Shim'un VIII *bar Mama* [nephew of #92]	1551-1558
94.	Iliya VI *bar Mama*	1558-1576
97.	Shim'un Iliya VII *bar Mama*	1576-1591
99.	Iliya VIII *bar Mama*	1591-1617
100.	Shim'un Iliya IX *bar Mama*	1617-1660
101.	Yukhannan Iliya X *bar Mama*	1660-1700
104.	Marugin Iliya XI *bar Mama*	1700-1722

106. Dinkha Iliya XII *bar Mama*	1722-1778
108. Ishu'yabh Iliya XIII *bar Mama* [nephew of #106]	1778-1804
INTERREGNUM	
Yukhannan *Khurmiz* [locum tenens; cousin of #108]	1804-1830

PATRIARCHS OF THE CHALDEANS AT DJARBAKIR (SEERT)

95. Yukhannan Shim'un IX *Sulaqa (Sa'ud bar Dani'il)*	1551-1555
96. Marun 'Abdishu' IV	1555-1567
INTERREGNUM	
98. Shim'un Yabhalaha IV	1578-1580

PATRIARCHS OF BABYLON
OF THE CHALDEANS AT DJARBAKIR

102. Yusip II (I)	1681-1695
103. Ma'ruf Yusip III (II) *Sliba*	1696-1712
105. Timat'ius Yusip IV (III) *Mushi*	1713-1757
107. Lazar Yusip V (IV) *Khindi*	1757-1781
INTERREGNUM	
Agustinus Yusip (V) *Khindi* [nephew of #107; unconsecrated]	1804-1828

PATRIARCHS OF BABYLON OF THE CHALDEANS AT BAGHDAD

109. Yukhannan VIII *Khurmiz* [cousin of #108]	1830-1838
110. Niqula I Ishai Ya'qub *Zaya*	1838-1847
111. Yusip VI *Audu*	1848-1878
112. Pitrus Iliya XIV *Abulyunan*	1879-1894
113. Giwargis 'Abdishu' V *Khayyat'*	1895-1899
114. Yusip 'Ummanu'il II *T'uma*	1900-1947
115. Yusip VII *Ghanima*	1947-1958
116. Pulus II *Shaikhu*	1958-1989
117. Rapa'il *Bidawid*	1989-

XIX.

THE CHURCH OF BELARUS

The White Russians were strong opponents of the Bolsheviks during the Russian Civil War. Following the Soviet victory, the Bishop of Minsk, Melhisedek Paieuski, proclaimed the independence of the B(y)elorussian Church on 23 July 1922, and assumed the title of Metropolitan, not so much from nationalistic fervor, but to protect his flock from the reform movement then sweeping Russian Orthodoxy. In 1925 he renounced his title in Moscow, at the insistence of the *Locum Tenens*. Two years later, however, a group of influential communicants met in Minsk to reaffirm their Church's autocephaly, publishing a constitution which proclaimed a Belorussian Autocephalous Orthodox Church. In 1929 the Soviets moved against the nationalists, completely eradicating organized religion in the Republic.

When the Germans invaded in 1941, the movement revived, nominally under Metropolitan Panteleiman, although an actual Church structure was never achieved in the chaos of the Nazi administration. The 1944 German withdrawal forced the Church into exile in West Germany. Panteleiman later rejoined the Russian Patriarchate; other surviving prelates, under the leadership of Metropolitan Archbishop Syrhiey Okhotenko, organized the Byelorussian Autocephalic Orthodox Church on 5 June 1948 at Constanz, Switzerland; Syrhiey later settled at Adelaide, Australia. A second group of exiles formed the Byelorussian Orthodox Church, which later joined the Greek Orthodox Archdiocese of North and South America, under the Ecumenical Patriarch. Other prelates, led by Archbishops Benedykt and Filofey, joined the Russian Orthodox Church Outside of Russia, on 6 May 1946.

After Syrhiey's death on 2 October 1971, the Second Sabor of the Church met on 27-29 May 1972 at Highland Park, New Jersey, electing Andrey Kryt the new Metropolitan, with his residence at Cleveland, Ohio. He died in 1983, and was succeeded by his suffragan, Metropolitan Mikalay Mucukievich, who resides at Toronto, Canada. In the former Soviet Union, the Church of Russia granted the Belarussian Church autonomy under its own synod and Exarch on 30 January 1990.

The primate bears the title Metropolitan Archbishop of Minsk and Slutsk, Patriarchal Exarch of All Belarus; the later Metropolitans of the exiled Church also bear titles corresponding to their individual sees. The official language of the Church is Belorussian.

SOURCES: *Échos d'Orient*; *Orthodoxia*; personal communication; *Profiles in Belief* (Piepkorn); *Religion in the Soviet Union* (Kolarz).

METROPOLITANS OF BELARUS

1.	Melhisedek *Paieuski*	1922-1925
2.	Panteleiman *Rozhnovskiî*	1942-1946

RUSSIAN METROPOLITANS AND EXARCHS OF BELARUS

1.	Nikodim *Rotov*	1963
2.	Sergiî *Petrov*	1963-1965
3.	Antoniî *Melnikov*	1965-1978
4.	Filaret *Vakhromeev*	1978-

METROPOLITANS OF THE BELORUSSIAN CHURCH IN EXILE

1.	Syrhiey (or Siarhiey) *Okhotsenko*	1948-1971
2.	Andrey *Kryt*	1972-1983
3.	Mikalay *Mucukievich*	1984-

XX.

THE CHURCH OF BULGARIA

The rise of the autocephalous Church of Bulgaria closely coincides with the founding of an independent Bulgarian Empire. Tsar Boris I was converted to Christianity about 865, and asked the Patriarch of Constantinople for a prelate to organize a Bulgarian Church. Fifty years later, Archbishop Leontiî was the first Bulgarian Church leader to be called Patriarch. When the Byzantine Emperor conquered Bulgaria in 1018, the Church was reunited to Constantinople, its chief see being moved to Okhrid. Eastern Bulgaria regained independence in 1186, with the patriarchate being re-established at Turnovo, but it was again placed under Okhrid when Bulgaria fell in 1393. The Patriarchate of Okhrid was itself dismantled in 1767, and all of the South Slavic churches were transferred to the direct control of the Ecumenical Patriarch.

The rise of Bulgarian nationalism in the mid-1800s revived interest in a Bulgarian Church. In 1870 the Ottoman Empire recognized the Bulgarian Church as autocephalous; the Patriarchate of Constantinople declared the Church schismatic in 1872. That same year the first Exarch, Ilarion, was elected, but was replaced after a few days with Exarch Antim. On the death of Exarch Iosif, in 1915, the government of Tsar Ferdinand (and later Tsar Boris III) set up a synodal council patterned after the Russian model, and dispensed with the office of primate. Following the Soviet occupation, a new Exarch was elected in 1945. He immediately sought reconciliation with Constantinople, which finally recognized his Church's independence that same year.

Exarch Stefan soon had difficulties with the new government, however, and was forced to resign in 1948. The state issued a new constitution for the Church in 1950, which specified that its head would now be called Patriarch. Metropolitan Kiril was the first to receive the revived title, on 10 May 1953. He (and his title) were finally recognized by the Ecumenical Patriarch of Constantinople in 1961, thereby healing a major breach in Eastern Orthodoxy.

A major controversy arose in the aftermath of the fall of the Communist regime in the early 1990s. Khristofor Subev, a dissent priest who headed a reformist group of synodalists, mounted a campaign to depose Patriarch Maksim, on the grounds that he had been uncanonically appointed by the secular Communist government. Maksim was declared illegitimate by the Bulgarian Supreme Court, but was still able to maintain his position into the mid-1990s.

The primate bears the title Patriarch of Bulgaria, Metropolitan Archbishop of Sofia. The official Church language is Bulgarian. Roughly eight million communicants are located primarily in Bulgaria, with a strong overseas contingent in the United States.

SOURCES: *Deset Godini Bulgarska Patriarshiia*; *Dictionnaire de Théologie Catholique*; *Dictionnaire d'Histoire et de Géographie Ecclésiastique*; *Eastern Christianity and Politics in the Twentieth Century* (Ramet, ed.); *Échos d'Orient*; *Episkepsis*; *Gegenwartslage der Ostkirchen* (Spuler); *A History of Christianity in the Balkans* (Spinka); *History of the Church* (Jedin, ed.); *Istoricheski Pregled' na Bulgarskata TSurkva* (Drinov); *Jahrbuch der Orthodoxie* (Proc); *Orthodoxia*; *Profiles in Belief* (Piepkorn).

PATRIARCHS OF BULGARIA AT PRESLAV
(Archbishops at Pliska 870; Patriarchs at Preslav 919)

1.	Iosif I (or Stefan I)	870-878?
2.	Georgi I	878?-919?
3.	Leontiî	919-
4.	Dimitriî I	923?
5.	Sergiî I	925?
6.	Grigoriî I	-927
7.	Damian	927?-972?
8.	German I	972?-1000?
9.	Filip	1000?-1015?
10.	David	1015?-1018

ARCHBISHOPS OF OKHRID (OHRID)
(See also the Church of Macedonia and Ohrid)

11.	Ioan I	1018-1037?
12.	Luv I (León *ek Rómaión*)	1037?-1054?
13.	Teodul I (Theodoulos *apo Mókiou*)	1056?-1065
14.	Ioan II *Lakapin* (Ióannés *Lampénos*)	1065-1078?
15.	Ioan III *Ainos* (Ióannés *Aoinos*)	1079?-1084
16.	Teofilakt (Theophylaktos *ex Euripou*)	1085?-1108?
17.	Luv II *Mung* (León *Boungos*)	1108?-1120?
18.	Mikhail *Maksim* (Michaél *Maximos*)	1120?-
19.	Ioan IV *Komnin* (Ióannés *Komnénos*)	1143?-1157?
20.	Evstatiî (Eustathios)	1159?
21.	Konstantin I	1160?-1170?
22.	name unknown	1178?-1182?

PATRIARCHS OF BULGARIA AT TURNOVO

23.	Vasiliî I	1185-1233
24.	Ioakim I	1233?-1246
25.	Vasiliî II	1246-
26.	Ioakim II	-1272
27.	Ignatiî I	1272?-1277?
28.	Makariî I	-1291
29.	Ioakim III	1291-1300
30.	Visarion	1310?
31.	Doroteî I	1320?
32.	Roman	1330?
33.	Teodosiî I	1337?
34.	Ioanikiî II	1340?
35.	Simeon I	1346?
36.	Teodosiî II (or Teodosije)	1363?
37.	Ioanikiî III	1370?
38.	Evtimiî	1375-1393

ARCHBISHOPS (1818) AND PATRIARCHS (1558) OF OKHRID
(See also the Church of Macedonia and Ohrid)

39.	Ioan V *Kamatir* (Ióannés *Kamatéros*)	1183?-1215?
40.	Dimitriî II *Khomatian* (Démétrios *Chómatianos* [or *Chómaténos*])	1216?-1234?
41.	Ioanikiî I	1240?
42.	Sergiî II	1250?
43.	Konstantin II *Kavasila* (Kónstantinos *Kabasilas*)	1254?-1259?
44.	IAkov *Proarkhiî*	1265?
45.	Adrian	1275?
46.	Gen(n)adiî	1285?
47.	Makariî II	1295?-1299?
48.	Grigoriî II	1317?
49.	Antim I *Metokhit* (Anthimos *Metochités*)	1341?
50.	Nikolaî I	1347?
51.	Grigoriî III	1364?-1378?
52.	name unknown	1389?-1394
53.	Mateî	1408-1411?
54.	name unknown	1430?
55.	Nikodim	1452?
56.	Doroteî II	1466?
57.	Marko *Ksilokarav* (Markos *Xylokarabés*) [#163 of Constantinople]	1467?-
58.	Nikolaî II	1486-1502?
59.	Zakhariî	1515?

60.	Prokhor	1528?-1550
61.	Simeon II	1550
62.	Grigoriî IV	1551-
63.	Nikanor	-1557
64.	Païsiî I	1558-1566
65.	Parteniî I	1566-1567
66.	Sofroniî	1567-1572?
67.	Gavriil	1572-1587
68.	Teodul II	1588-1590
69.	Ioakim IV	1590-1593
70.	Atanasiî I	1593-1596
71.	Valaam	1596-1598
72.	Nektariî I	1598-1604
	Atanasiî I [2nd time]	1604-1614
73.	Mitrofan	1614-1616
74.	Georgi II	1616-1617
75.	Nektariî II	1617-1622?
76.	Porfiriî *Paleolog* (Porphyrios *Palaiologos*)	1624?
77.	Ioasaf I	1628?
78.	Avraamiî *Mesapsa* (Abraamios)	1629?-1634?
	INTERREGNUM	
79.	Meletiî I	1637-1643
80.	Khariton	1643-1647?
81.	Daniil	1647?-1650
	Khariton [2nd time]	1651-1652
82.	Dionisiî I	1652-1653
83.	Atanasiî II	1653-1660
84.	Pafnutiî	1660
85.	Ignatiî II	1660-1662
86.	Arseniî I	1662-1663?
87.	Zosima I	1663-1670
88.	Panaret I	1671
89.	Nektariî III	1673?
90.	Ignatiî III	1673-1675?
91.	Grigoriî V	1675-1676
92.	Teofan	1676
93.	Meletiî II	1676-1677
94.	Parteniî II	1677-1683
	Grigoriî V [2nd time]	1683-1688
95.	German II	1688-1690
96.	Grigoriî VI	1691-1693
97.	Ignatiî IV	1693-1695
98.	Zosima II	1695-1699
99.	Rafaïl	1699-1702
	German II [2nd time]	1702-1703
100.	Dionisiî II (Dionysios) *of Chios*	1703-1706

Zosima II [2nd time]	1707-1708
101. Metodiî I	1708
Zosima II [3rd time]	1708-1709
Dionisiî II [2nd time]	1709-1714
102. Filoteî	1714-1718
103. Ioasaf II	1719-1745
104. Iosif II	1746-1751
105. Dionisiî III	1751-1756
106. Metodiî II	1757-1758
107. Kiril I	1759-1762
108. Ieremiia	1762-1763
109. Ananiî	1763
110. Arseniî II	1763-1767

PATRIARCHS OF BULGARIA AT TSARIGRAD AND SOFIA
(Metropolitans 1767, Exarchs 1872, Patriarchs 1953)

111. Ilarion I	-1838
112. Panaret II	1838-1840?
113. Neofit	1840?-1850?
114. Païsiî II	1850?-1856?
Neofit [2nd time]	1856?-1857?
Païsiî II [2nd time]	1861-
115. Ilarion II	1872
116. Antim II	1872-1877
117. Iosif III	1877-1915
INTERREGNUM	
Stefan *Giorgiev* [locum tenens]	1922-1934
Neofit [locum tenens]	1934-1944
Stefan *Giorgiev* [2nd time]	1944-1945
118. Stefan II *Giorgiev*	1945-1948
INTERREGNUM	
Mikhail [locum tenens]	1948-1949
Païsiî [locum tenens]	1949-1951
Kiril *Markov* [locum tenens]	1951-1953
119. Kiril II *Markov*	1953-1971
120. Maksim *Minkov*	1971-

XXI.

THE ARMENIAN APOSTOLIC CHURCH OF CILICIA

The residence of the Armenian Catholicos was moved from Armenia Major (the capital city of Ani) to Cilicia (Lesser Armenia), first to Romkla (1149) and then to Sis (1293), where a thriving Armenian and Latin kingdom had recently been founded. As the kingdom grew and expanded, so the Church also thrived. By the middle of the fourteenth century, however, the Mamluk Arabs began to exert pressure on Lesser Armenia, eventually conquering it in 1375; the last king, Ghevon (Leo) VI, was driven into exile, and the Armenian cathedral was destroyed. Nonetheless, the Catholicos remained in Sis until the year 1441, when an Armenian National Church Council elected a Catholicos in Armenia Major, at Etchmiadzin, with Catholicos Grigor IX staying in Sis as the Catholicos of Cilicia. The line of succession continues unroken until today.

During the massacres of 1890-1915, the Church of Cilicia was severely affected; many Church members were forced to leave Turkey or be killed, and many of those who fled settled just over the border in Syria and Lebanon. The Catholicos was among those who moved south, finally settling at Antelias, a suburb of Beirut, in 1921. Through an agreement with the Armenian Patriarch of Jerusalem, certain of the latter's churches in Lebanon and Cyria were ceded to Cilicia. In 1956 Catholicos Vazgên I of Etchmiadzin attempted to interfere in the election of the new Catholicos for the Great House of Cilicia, and to subordinate Cilicia to the level of a patriarchate; the electors rejected his moves, and elected a pro-independence Archbishop, Zareh. In 1995 Catholicos Garegin II was elected Vazgên's successor, in the hope that the two churches could again be reunited.

The Armenian Apostolic Church, as it is now known, differs from the other Armenian churches in claiming complete autocephaly; it acknowledges the Patriarch at Etchmiadzin as first among equals in Armenian Christianity. The primate bears the title Catholicos of the Great House of Cilicia. The official Church language is Armenian. Roughly one million communicants are located in Lebanon, Syria, and Cyprus, with thriving overseas communities in Greece, Iran, Kuwait, the United Arab Emirates, and the Americas.

SOURCES: *Dictionnaire d'Histoire et de Géographie Ecclési-
astique*; *Eastern Christianity and Politics in the Twentieth Century*
(Ramet, ed.); *Europa World Yearbook*; *Gegenwartslage der Ostkirchen*
(Spuler); *History of the Church* (Jedin, ed.); *The Middle East and North
Africa*; *Orthodoxia*; *Patmutium Katoghikosats Kilikoy* (Giwleserean;
regarded as official by the Church); *Profiles in Belief* (Piepkorn).

ARMENIAN CATHOLICOSES OF CILICIA

1.	Grigor I *Musabêgiants'* [#97 of Armenia]	1441-1451
2.	Karapet	1446-1478
3.	Step'anos	1477?-1483
	INTERREGNUM	
4.	Hovhannês I	1488-1489
5.	Hovhannês II	1489-1525
6.	Hovhannês III	1525-1539
7.	Simêon I	1539-1545
8.	Ghazar	1545-1547
9.	T'oros I	1548-1550?
10.	Khach'atur I *Chorik*	1550?-1560
11.	Khach'atur II *"The Musician"*	1560-1584
12.	Azaria I	1584-1601
	Tiratur [anti-catholicos; #8 of Constantinople]	1586-1592
13.	Hovhannês IV	1602-1621
	Petros I [coadjutor]	1601-1608
14.	Minas	1621-1632
15.	Simêon II	1633-1648
16.	Nersês	1648-1654
17.	T'oros II	1654-1657
18.	Khach'atur III	1657-1674
	Dawit' [anti-catholicos]	1663-1679
19.	Sahak I *Mêykhachêchi*	1674-1686
29.	Azaria II	1683?-1686?
21.	Grigor II	1686-1693?
22.	Astuatsatur	1693-1694?
23.	Matt'êos	1694-1705
24.	Hovhannês V	1705-1721
	Petros (II) [anti-catholicos]	1708-1710
25.	Grigor III	1721?-1729
26.	Hovhannês VI	1729-1733
27.	Ghukas [brother of #28]	1733-1737
28.	Mik'ayêl I [brother of #27]	1737-1758
29.	Gabriêl [brother of #28]	1757-1770
30.	Ep'rem I [nephew of #30]	1771-1784
	Eghiazar *Adshapahian* [coadjutor]	1780?
31.	T'oros III *Adshapahian*	1784-1796

32.	Kirakos I *"The Great"*	1797-1822
33.	Ep'rem II	1823-1831
	Hovhannês [coadjutor]	1831-1833
34.	Mik'ayêl II	1832-1855
35.	Kirakos II	1855-1865
	INTERREGNUM	
	Kirakos [locum tenens]	1866-1871
36.	Mkrtich' *K'êfsizian Marach'ts'i*	1871-1894
	INTERREGNUM	
	Grigor *Aleadjian* [locum tenens]	1895
37.	Sahak II *Khapayan*	1902-1939
	Babkên *Giwlêserian* [coadjutor]	1931-1936
	INTERREGNUM	
38.	Petros II *Sarachian*	1939-1941
39.	Garegin I *Hovsêp'ian(ts)*	1943-1952
	INTERREGNUM	
	Khat *Adjapahian* [locum tenens]	1952-1955
	Khorên *Baroyan* [locum tenens]	1955-1956
40.	Zareh *Payaslian*	1956-1963
41.	Khorên *Baroyan*	1963-1983
42.	Garegin II *Sargisian* [coadjutor 1977; #141 of Armenia]	1983-1995
43.	Aram *K'êshishian*	1995-

XXII.

THE ARMENIAN CATHOLIC CHURCH OF CILICIA

The Armenian Church in Turkey had uniate factions as long ago as the fourteenth century. These were nurtured and developed by Roman Catholic missionaries sent to Asia Minor by the Popes. In 1740 the uniates elected a patriarch in succession to Armenian Cilician Patriarch Ghukas; he was confirmed by Pope Benedictus XIV in 1742. He established a tradition by appending "Petros" (Peter) to his name, in honor of the founder of the Roman Church; his successors have followed his pattern, and have numbered themselves consecutively from the first Patriarch.

In 1867 Pope Pius IX caused great controversy by issuing his bull, *Reversurus*, which outlined the powers and rights of the Armenian and Chaldean sees, established a new election law, and gave the Pope the right to appoint or veto new bishops. A number of the existing bishops blamed the new Patriarch, Anton Hassun, an outsider, for the regulations, and elected their own primate; the schism was not healed until the resignation of Hassun in 1879. Hassun had been Archbishop-Primate of Constantinople since 1846, and had been named by the Pope specifically to unite the two jurisdictions; after his resignation, he was made a cardinal in 1880, and died in Rome four years later. The residence of the Catholicos remained at Constantinople until 1928. Among recent patriarchs, Grigor Petros XV Aghajanian was widely known for his efforts to reunite Eastern Christianity.

The primate bears the title Patriarch of the Catholic Armenians and Catholicos of Cilicia. His chief see is located in a suburb of Beirut, Lebanon, with an estimated 143,000 adherents in Lebanon and Southeastern Turkey, as well as several congregations in the Americas. The official Church language is Armenian.

SOURCES: *The Catholic Eastern Churches* (Attwater); *Catholic Encyclopedia*; *The Christian Churches of the East* (Attwater); *Gegenwartslage der Ostkirchen* (Spuler); *The Middle East and North Africa*; *Die Morgenlandischen Kirchen* (Spuler); *New Catholic Encyclopedia*; "Pope Calls for Broad Mideast Peace" (Montalbano).

ARMENIAN CATHOLIC CATHOLICOS-PATRIARCHS OF CILICIA

1.	Abraham Petros I *Ardzivian*	1740-1749
2.	Hakob Petros II *Hovsêp'ian*	1749-1753
3.	Mik'ayêl Petros III *Gasparian*	1753-1780
4.	Barsegh Petros IV *Avkadian*	1780-1788
5.	Grigor Petros V *Kupelian*	1788-1812
	INTERREGNUM	
6.	Grigor Petros VI	1815-1841
7.	Hakob Petros VII *Holasian*	1842-1843
8.	Grigor Petros VIII *Astuatsaturian*	1844-1866
9.	Anton Petros IX *Hassun(ian)*	1866-1879
	Hakob Petros IX *Bak'darian* [anti-catholicos]	1870-1880?
10.	Step'anos Petros X *Azarian*	1881-1899
11.	Poghos Petros XI *Emmanuelian*	1899-1904
12.	Poghos Petros XII *Sabbaghian*	1904-1910
13.	Poghos Petros XIII *Terzian*	1910-1931
14.	Awetis Petros XIV *Arpiarian*	1931-1937
15.	Grigor Petros XV *Aghajanian*	1937-1962
16.	Ignatios Petros XVI *Batanian*	1962-1976
17.	Hemayag Petros XVII *Ghedighian*	1976-1982
18.	Hovhannês Petros XVIII *Gasparian*	1982-

XXIII.

THE ARMENIAN CHURCH OF CONSTANTINOPLE

When Ottoman Sultan Mehmet II conquered Constantinople in 1453, he summoned the new Ecumenical Patriarch, and made him responsible for the Greek populations in the empire, with corresponding judicial and administrative powers.   Similarly, the Armenian Bishop of Constantinople was given temporal powers over the Armenian subjects of the Ottoman Empire, with the new title of Patriarch, in 1461. Like the Ecumenical Patriarch, the Armenian primate was subjected to intense political pressures and behind-the-scenes machinations; the result was constant Turkish interference in the governance of the Armenian Patriarchate, with individual prelates being appointed or removed at the will of the Sultan or his viziers. At the same time, the size and influence of the Patriarchate expanded with the Ottoman Empire, rivalling at times that of the Catholicos at Echmiadzin.

When the Empire began to fail, however, the Church gradually saw its power diminish; the Armenian massacres of 1890-1915, with the subsequent exile of most of the survivors, reduced it to less than one-tenth of its former size, its territory shrinking to the state of Turkey proper. As with the Ecumenical Patriarchate, the Turkish government has followed a pattern of interference even in the twentieth century, preventing the Church from filling seats on its Council in the 1960s and '70s. However, the civilian government elected in Turkey during the late 1980s appeared to adopt a policy of reducing tensions, and allowed several new bishops and other church officials to be appointed.

The primate bears the title Patriarch of Constantinople. The official Church language is Armenian. The number of communicants is unknown.

SOURCES: *Dictionnaire d'Histoire et de Géographie Ecclési-astique*; *Gegenwartslage der Ostkirchen* (Spuler); *The History of the Armenian People* (Morgan); *Orthodoxia*; "Zhamanakagrowt'iwn T'oir-k'ioy Hayots' Patriark'nerow" (regarded by the Church as official).

ARMENIAN PATRIARCHS OF CONSTANTINOPLE

1.	Hovakim	1461-1478
2.	Nikoghayos	1478-1489
3.	Karapet I	1489-1509
4.	Martiros I	1509-1526
5.	Grigor I	1526-1537
6.	Astuatsatur I	1537-1550
7.	Step'anos I	1550-1561
8.	Tiratur	1561-1563
9.	Hakob I	1563-1573
10.	Hovhannês I	1573-1581
11.	T'ovmas I	1581-1587
12.	Sargis I	1587-1590
13.	Hovhannês II	1590-1591
14.	Azaria	1591-1592
15.	Sargis II	1592-1596
	Tiratur [2nd time]	1596-1599
16.	Melk'isedek I	1599-1600
17.	Hovhannês III	1600-1601
18.	Grigor II	1601-1608
	Hovhannês III [2nd time]	1609-1611
	Grigor II [2nd time]	1611-1621
	Hovhannês III [3rd time]	1621-1623
	Grigor II [3rd time]	1623-1626
19.	Zak'aria I	1626-1631
	Hovhannês III [4th time]	1631-1636
	Zak'aria I [2nd time]	1636-1640
20.	Dawit'	1640-1641
21.	Kirakos	1641-1642
22.	Khach'atur I	1642-1643
	Dawit' [2nd time]	1643-1644
23.	T'ovma II	1644
	Dawit' [3rd time]	1644-1649
	Dawit' [4th time]	1650-1651
24.	Eghiazar	1651-1652
25.	Hovhannês IV	1652-1655
	T'ovma II [2nd time]	1657-1659
26.	Martiros II	1659-1660
27.	Ghazar	1660-1663
28.	Hovhannês V	1663-1664
29.	Sargis III	1664-1665
	Hovhannês V [2nd time]	1665-1667
	Sargis III [2nd time]	1667-1670
30.	Step'anos II	1670-1674

31.	Hovhannês VI	1674-1675
32.	Andrêas	1675-1676
33.	Karapet II	1676-1679
34.	Sargis IV	1679-1680
	Karapet II [2nd time]	1680-1681
35.	T'oros	1681
	Karapet II [3rd time]	1681-1684
36.	Ep'rem	1684-1686
	Karapet II [4th time]	1686-1687
	T'oros [2nd time]	1687-1688
37.	Khach'atur II	1688
	Karapet II [5th time]	1688-1689
	INTERREGNUM	
38.	Matt'êos I [#61 of Jerusalem]	1692-1694
	Ep'rem [2nd time]	1694-1698
39.	Melk'isedek II	1698-1699
40.	Mkhit'ar	1699-1700
	Melk'isedek II [2nd time]	1700-1701
	Ep'rem [3rd time]	1701-1702
41.	Awetik' [#60 of Jerusalem]	1702-1703
42.	Galust *Vayzhavk*	1703-1704
43.	Nersês I	1704
	Awetik' [2nd time]	1704-1706
	Matt'êos I [2nd time]	1706
44.	Martiros III [#62 of Jerusalem]	1706
45.	Mik'ayêl [#63 of Jerusalem]	1706-1707
46.	Sahak [#64 of Jerusalem]	1707
47.	Hovhannês VII [#65 of Jerusalem]	1707-1708
	Sahak [2nd time]	1708-1714
48.	Hovhannês VIII [#66 of Jerusalem]	1714-1715
49.	Hovhannês IX *Kolot*	1715-1741
50.	Hakob II *Nalian Zmarats'i* [#68 of Jerusalem]	1741-1748
51.	Prokhoron	1749
52.	Minas	1749-1751
53.	Gêorg I	1751-1752
	Hakob II [2nd time]	1752-1764
54.	Grigor III *Pasmachian*	1764-1773
55.	Zak'aria II	1773-1781
56.	Hovhannês X	1781-1782
	Zak'aria II [2nd time]	1782-1799
57.	Daniêl	1799-1800
58.	Hovhannês XI *Zamach'erchian*	1800-1801
59.	Grigor IV *Khamsets'i*	1801-1802
	Hovhannês XI [2nd time]	1802-1813
60.	Abraham *Gholian*	1813-1815
61.	Poghos I *Grigorian*	1815-1823

62.	Karapet III *Palat'ts'i*	1823-1831
63.	Step'anos III *Zak'arian*	1831-1839
64.	Hakobos III *Serobian*	1839-1840
	Step'anos III [2nd time]	1840-1841
65.	Astuatsatur II	1841-1844
66.	Matt'êos II *Ch'ukhachian* [#132 of Armenia]	1844-1848
	Hakobus III [2nd time]	1848-1858
67.	Gêorg II *K'êrêst'êchian* [#133 of Armenia]	1858-1860
68.	Sargis V *Guyumchian*	1860-1861
	Stêp'an (IV) *Maghak'ian* [locum tenens]	1861-1863
69.	Poghos II *T'agt'agian*	1863-1869
70.	Ignatios *Gagmachian*	1869
71.	Mkrtich' *Khrimian* [#135 of Armenia]	1869-1873
72.	Nersês II *Vartsapetian*	1874-1884
73.	Harut'iwn *Vehapetian* [#80 of Jerusalem]	1885-1888
74.	Khorên *Ashegian*	1888-1894
75.	Matt'êos III *Izmirlian* [#136 of Armenia]	1894-1896
76.	Maghak'ia *Örmanian*	1896-1908
	Matt'êos III *Izmirlian* [2nd time]	1908-1909
77.	Eghishê *Durian* [#81 of Jerusalem]	1909-1911
78.	Hovhannês XII *Arsharuni*	1912-1913
79.	Zawên *Eghiayan*	1913-1915
	INTERREGNUM	
	Zawên *Eghiayan* [2nd time]	1919-1922
	INTERREGNUM	
	Gêorg *Arslanian* [locum tenens]	1922-1927
80.	Mesrop *Naroyan*	1927-1944
	INTERREGNUM	
	Gêorg *Arslanian* [locum tenens]	1944-1950
81.	Garegin I *Khach'aturian*	1951-1961
82.	Shnorhk' *Galustian*	1961-1990
	Sahan *Sivakian* [locum tenens]	1990
83.	Garegin II Petros *Kazanjian*	1990-

XXIV.

THE GREEK CHURCH OF CONSTANTINOPLE

The Ecumenical Patriarchate is first in honor among the original Orthodox churches, having been founded, according to tradition, by the
apostle Andrew, at the small town of Byzantium. Byzantium was trans-
formed by the Emperor Constantine I into the imperial capital, Constantinople, and made the center of a new Christian empire; simultaneously, the Church of Constantinople became the "New Rome," growing
rapidly in size and power as the Empire flourished. By the Council of
Chalcedon, in 451, Constantinople was recognized as having prece-
dence over Antioch and Alexandria, and by 590 the primate was calling
himself the "Ecumenical Patriarch." Gradually, a split developed between East and West, as Constantinople and Rome both strived to gain
absolute primacy over the Christian world. The strains were exacer-
bated by the intrusion of the temporal authorities and politics into both
religious worlds, including interference with the elections of the primates, and manipulation of the hierarchies.

The differences between East and West came into the open in
the years 857-878, with the struggle between Patriarchs Ignatios and
Phótios for the Patriarchal throne of Constantinople. The Pope supported Ignatios, while much of the Eastern hierarchy supported Phótios.
In the end, Phótios outlasted Ignatios; his outspoken opposition to Roman rule proved to be the example which all of the Eastern churches
would soon come to follow. The formal breach came during the reign
of Michaél I Kéroularios, when the two churches exchanged mutual
excommunications (1054). Two attempts at reconciliation both failed:
in 1274 Emperor Michael VIII ordered his prelates to reach a compro-
mise with Rome, which they did; it was never popular, however, and
was repudiated by Andronicus II in 1282. During the last few decades
of the Empire, while it was under severe pressure from the Turks, Emperors John VIII and Constantine XI sought aid from the West by again
forcing a reunion at the Council of Florence in 1439. The marriage of
churches was unsuccessful in gaining any significant military aid for the
beleaguered Greeks, and the city fell to the Turks on 29 May 1453.
The union was repudiated in 1472.

The invasion of the Turks benefited the Patriarchate in curious
ways: the new ruler, Sultan Mehmet II, appointed Gennadios II to the

empty patriarchal throne, and gave him temporal powers over the Orthodox faithful in the new Empire. Thereafter the Patriarchs served at the pleasure of the Sultans and their Viziers, being deposed or murdered virtually at will. In recompense, however, the Church gained domination over all the other Eastern churches, save only the non-Chalcedonian denominations and the Patriarchate of Russia, which Constantinople was forced to acknowledge as independent in 1589. In 1766-1767 the Patriarch managed to have the Sultan suppress the ancient Patriarchates of Pec (Serbia) and Ohrid (Macedonian), replacing the hierarchies there with Greek prelates. The Church had reached the apex of its power and influence.

In 1833 the Church of Greece set a precedent by demanding ecclesiastical independence from Constantinople, as the forces of nationalism began sweeping Eastern Europe. One by one, as each country achieved independence, the temporal and religious authorities of those states insisted on autocephaly for their own churches. By the end of World War I, the once-great Patriarchate was reduced in size to Turkey proper, and to overseas colonies of Orthodox immigrants in the Americas and elsewhere. The overthrow of the Ottoman Empire in 1922 did not end Turkish governmental interference in Orthodox affairs; on the contrary, Patriarch Meletios IV was forced into exile in 1923, as was Kónstantinos VI in 1925. Other direct or indirect pressures, including Turkish support of the independent Turkish Orthodox Church, have continued to this day; in the 1972 patriarchal election, for example, the Turks insisted on excluding several potential candidates from consideration, including the frontrunner, Metropolitan Melitón. As a result, the most junior member of that body, Démétrios, then a virtual unknown, was elected. At the latter's death in 1991, his assistant, Metropolitan Bartholomaios, was unanimously elected Patriarch without interference from the Turkish officials, the first such instance in modern history.

Noteworthy among recent primates of the Church was Patriarch Athénagoras I, former Archbishop of North and South America, and a friend of President Harry S. Truman, who became Patriarch in 1948. This extraordinary primate was the first Patriarch of Constantinople to meet with the Pope of Rome in 500 years; together, they lifted the excommunications imposed by each church on the other in 1054, and did much to lessen the atmosphere of antagonism that had overshadowed relations between East and West over many centuries. His two successors have continued his ecumenical work.

The primate bears the title Ecumenical Patriarch, Archbishop of Constantinople and New Rome. The official Church language is Greek. The Patriarch resides in a section of Istanbul (Constantinople) called the Phanar, a name which is sometimes applied to the Church itself, much as the Church of Rome is sometimes called the Vatican. Communicants number in the millions, most located in Turkey, the Americas, Western Europe, Australia, and other points overseas; the

Ecumenical Patriarch also has authority over the autonomous Churches of Crete and Finland, Mount Athos, and the Dodecanese islands of the Aegean Sea.

SOURCES: *Dictionnaire de Théologie Catholique*; *Dictionnaire d'Histoire et de Géographie Ecclésiastique*; *Eastern Christianity and Politics in the Twentieth Century* (Ramet, ed.); *Échos d'Orient*; *Eleutheroudaké Enkyklopaidikon Lexikon*; *Episkepsis*; *Gegenwartslage der Ostkirchen* (Spuler); *History of the Church* (Jedin, ed.); *Jahrbuch der Orthodoxie* (Proc); "Oikoumenikon (Patriarcheion)"; *Oriens Christianus* (Le Quien); *Orthodoxia*; *The Oxford Dictionary of Byzantium* (Kazhdan); *Patriarchikoi Pinakes* (Gedeón); *The Patriarchs of Constantinople* (Cobham); "Pinakes Patriarchón"; *Profiles in Belief* (Piepkorn). The list below is based primarily on Gedeón (regarded as official at the time of its publication) and Kazhdan.

ECUMENICAL PATRIARCHS OF CONSTANTINOPLE

1.	Andreas *Prótoklétos*	30?-38
2.	Stachys *Apostolos*	38-54
3.	Onésimos	54-68
	INTERREGNUM	
4.	Polykarpos I	71-89
5.	Ploutarchos	89-105
6.	Sedekión	105-114
7.	Diogenés	114-129
8.	Eleutherios	129-136
9.	Phélix (or Philix)	136-141
10.	Polykarpos II	141-144
11.	Athénodóros	144-148
12.	Euzóïos	148-154
13.	Laurentios	154-166
14.	Alypios	166-169
15.	Pertinax	169-187
16.	Olympianos	187-198
17.	Markos I	198-211
18.	Philadelphos	211-214
19.	Kyriakos I (or Kyrillianos)	214-230
20.	Kastinos	230-237
21.	Eugenios I	237-242
22.	Titos	242-272
23.	Dometios	272-303
24.	Rhouphinos	303
25.	Probos	303-315
26.	Métrophanés I	315-325
27.	Alexandros	325-337?
28.	Paulos I	337?-339

29.	Eusebios *Nikomédeias*	341-342?
	Paulos I [2nd time]	342-344
30.	Makedonios I	344-346
	Paulos I [3rd time]	346-351
	Makedonios I [2nd time]	350-360
31.	Eudoxios *Antiocheias* [#30 of Antioch]	360-369
32.	Démophilos	369-379
33.	Euagrios	379
	Démophilos [Arian anti-patriarch; 2nd time]	379-386
34.	Grégorios I *Nazianzénos Theologos*	380-381
35.	Maximos I *Kynikos*	381
36.	Nektarios [brother of #38]	381-397
	Marinos [Arian anti-patriarch]	386-
37.	Ióannés I *Chrysostomos*	398-404
38.	Arsakios [brother of #36]	404-405
39.	Attikos	406-425
	Dórotheos [Arian anti-patriarch]	-407
	Bardas [Arian anti-patriarch]	407-
40.	Sisinnios I	426-427
41.	Nestorios	428-431
42.	Maximianos	431-434
43.	Proklos	434-446
44.	Phlabianos (Flavianus)	446-449
45.	Anatolios	449-458
46.	Gennadios I	458-471
47.	Akakios	472-489
48.	Phrabitas (Fravitas)	489-490
49.	Euphémios	490-496
50.	Makedonios II	496-511
51.	Timotheos I *Kélón*	511-518
52.	Ióannés II *Kappadokés* (or *Kappadokos*)	518-520
53.	Epiphanios	520-535
54.	Anthimos I	536
55.	Ménas *Sampsón*	536-552
56.	Eutychios	552-565
57.	Ióannés III *Scholastikos* (or *Scholastikón*)	565-577
	Eutychios [2nd time]	577-582
58.	Ióannés IV *Nésteutés*	582-595
59.	Kyriakos II	595?-606
60.	Thómas I	607-610
61.	Sergios I	610-638
62.	Pyrrhos	638-641
63.	Paulos II	641-653
	Pyrrhos [2nd time]	654
64.	Petros	654-666
65.	Thómas II	667-669

66.	Ióannés V	669-675
67.	Kónstantinos I	675-677
68.	Theodóros I	677-679
69.	Geórgios I	679-686
	Theodóros I [2nd time]	686-687
70.	Paulos III	688-694
71.	Kallinikos I	694-706
72.	Kyros	706-712
73.	Ióannés VI	712-715
74.	Germanos I	715-730
75.	Anastasios	730-754
76.	Kónstantinos II	754-766
77.	Nikétas I	766-780
78.	Paulos IV	780-784
79.	Tarasios [uncle of #86]	784-806
80.	Niképhoros I	806-815
81.	Theodotos I *Kassitéras Melissénos*	815-821
82.	Antónios I *Kassimatas* (or *Kassimatés* or *Kasymatas*) *Byrsodepsés*	821-837?
83.	Ióannés VII *Grammatikos Pankratiou*	837?-843
84.	Methodios I	843-847
85.	Ignatios *Rhangabe*	847-858
86.	Phótios I [nephew of #79]	858-867
	Ignatios [2nd time]	867-877
	Phótios I [2nd time]	877-886
87.	Stephanos I	886-893
88.	Antónios II *Kauleas* (or *Kaulias*)	893-901
89.	Nikolaos I *Mystikos*	901-907
90.	Euthymios I	907-912
	Nikolaos I [2nd time]	912-925
91.	Stephanos II *apo Amaseias*	925-927
92.	Tryphón	927-931
93.	Theophylaktos *Lekapénos*	933-956
94.	Polyeuktos	956-970
95.	Basileios I *Skamandrénos*	970-974
96.	Antónios III *Stoudités Pachen*	974-979
97.	Nikolaos II *Chrysobergios* (or *Chrysobergés*)	979-991
	INTERREGNUM	
98.	Sisinnios II	996-998
	INTERREGNUM	
99.	Sergios II	1001-1019
100.	Eustathios *apo Palatiou*	1019-1025
101.	Alexios *Stoudités*	1025-1043
102.	Michaél I *Kéroul(l)arios* (or *Kéroularis*)	1043-1058
103.	Kónstantinos III *Leichoudés*	1059-1063
104.	Ióannés VIII *Xiphilinos*	1064-1075

105. Kosmas I *Hierosolymités*	1075-1081
106. Eustratios *Garidas*	1081-1084
107. Nikolaos III *Grammatikos Kyrdiniatés*	1084-1111
108. Ióannés IX *Agapétos Hieromnémón*	1111-1134
109. León *Styppés* (or *Styppeiótés*)	1134-1143
110. Michaél II *Kourkouas Oxeités*	1143-1146
111. Kosmas II *Attikos*	1146-1147
112. Nikolaos IV *Mouzalón* [#26 of Cyprus]	1147-1151
113. Theodotos II	1151?-1153?
114. Neophytos I *Enkleistos Klaustrarios*	1153?
115. Kónstantinos IV *Chliarénos*	1154-1157
116. Loukas *Chrysobergés*	1157-1169?
117. Michaél III *Anchialou*	1170-1178
118. Charitón *Eugeneiótés*	1178-1179
119. Theodosios I *Bo(r)rhadiótés*	1179-1183
120. Basileios II *Kamatéros Phylakopoulos*	1183-1186
121. Nikétas II *Mountanés*	1186-1189
122. Dositheos *Hierosolymités* [#93 of Jerusalem]	1189
123. Leontios *Theotokités*	1189
Dositheos *Hierosolymités* [2nd time]	1189-1191
124. Geórgios II *Xiphilinos*	1191-1198
125. Ióannés X *Kamatéros* (or *Kamateros*)	1198-1206
126. Michaél IV *Autóreianos* (or *Autoreianos*)	1208-1214
127. Theodóros II *Eirénikos Kópas*	1214-1216
128. Maximos II *apo Akoimétón*	1216
129. Manouél I *Saranténos Charitopoulos*	1216?-1222
130. Germanos II	1223-1240
131. Methodios II	1240?-1241?
132. Manouél II	1243?-1254
133. Arsenios *Autóreianos*	1254-1260
134. Niképhoros II *apo Ephesou*	1260-1261
Arsenios [2nd time]	1261-1265
135. Germanos III	1265-1266
136. Ióséph I	1266-1275
137. Ióannés XI *Bekkos*	1275-1282
Ióséph I [2nd time]	1282-1283
138. Grégorios II *Kyprios*	1283-1289
139. Athanasios I	1289-1293
140. Ióannés XII *Kosmas*	1294-1303
Athanasios I [2nd time]	1303-1309
141. Néphón I (or Niphón) *apo Kyzikou*	1310-1314
142. Ióannés XIII *Glykys*	1315-1319
143. Gerasimos I	1320-1321
144. Hésaïas	1323-1332
145. Ióannés XIV *Kalekas*	1334-1347
146. Isidóros I *Boucheiras apo Monembasias*	1347-1350

147. Kallistos I	1350-1353
148. Philotheos *Kokkinos apo Hérakleias*	1353-1354?
Kallistos I [2nd time]	1355-1363
Philotheos [2nd time]	1364-1376
149. Makarios	1376?-1379
150. Neilos *Kerameus* (or *Kerameós*)	1380-1388
151. Antónios IV	1389-1390
Makarios [2nd time]	1390-1391
Antónios IV [2nd time]	1391-1397
152. Kallistos II *Xanthopoulos*	1397
153. Matthaios I *apo Kyzikou*	1397-1402
Matthaios I *apo Kyzikou* [2nd time]	1403-1410
154. Euthymios II	1410-1416
155. Ióséph II *apo Ephesou*	1416-1439
156. Métrophanés II *apo Kyzikou*	1440-1443
157. Grégorios III *Mammas* (or *Mammés*)	1443-1451?
158. Athanasios II [locum tenens]	1451-1453

INTERREGNUM

159. Gennadios II *Scholarios Kourtesés*	1454-1456
160. Isidóros II *Xanthopoulos*	1456-1462
Gennadios II [2nd time]	1462-1463
161. Sóphronios I *Syropoulos*	1463-1464
Gennadios II [3rd time]	1464
162. Ióasaph I *Kokkas*	1464-1466?
163. Markos II *Xylokarabés Eugenikos* [#34 of Macedonia; #57 of Bulgaria]	1466
164. Symeón *Trapezountios*	1466?-1467
165. Dionysios I *Symeónés apo Philippoupoleós*	1467-1471
Symeón [2nd time]	1471-1475
166. Raphaél I *Serbos*	1475-1476
167. Maximos III *Manassés*	1476-1482
Symeón [3rd time]	1482-1486
168. Néphón II (or Nyphón) *apo Thessalonikés* [#8 of Romania]	1486-1488
Dionysios I [2nd time]	1488-1490
169. Maximos IV *apo Serrón*	1491-1497
Néphón II [2nd time]	1497-1498
170. Ióakeim I	1498-1502
Néphón II [3rd time]	1502
171. Pachómios I *apo Zichnón*	1503-1504
Ióakeim I [2nd time]	1504
Pachómios I [2nd time]	1504-1513
172. Theoléptos I *apo Ióanninón*	1513-1522
173. Hieremias I *apo Sophias*	1520-1522
174. Ióannikios I *apo Sózopoleós*	1522-1523
Hieremias I [2nd time]	1523-1537

175. Dionysios II	1537
Hieremias I [3rd time]	1537-1546
Dionysios II [2nd time]	1546-1555
176. Ióasaph II *Megaloprepés apo Adrianoupoleós*	1555-1565
177. Métrophanés III *apo Kaisareias*	1565-1572
178. Hieremias II *Tranos apo Larissés*	1572-1579
Métrophanés III [2nd time]	1579-1580
Hieremias II [2nd time]	1580-1584
179. Pachómios II *Patestos apo Kaisareias*	1584-1585
180. Theoléptos II *apo Philippoupoleós*	1585-1586?

INTERREGNUM

Niképhoros *Hierodiakonos* [locum tenens]	1586?
Dionysios [locum tenens]	1586?
Niképhoros *Hierodiakonos* [2nd time]	1586?-
Hieremias II [3rd time]	1589-1595
181. Matthaios II *apo Ióanninón*	1595
182. Gabriél I	1596
183. Theophanés I *Karykés* [#77 of Greece]	1596-1597
184. Meletios I *Pégas* [locum tenens; #85 of Alexandria]	1597-1598?
Matthaios II [2nd time]	1598?-1602?
185. Neophytos II *Karykés* [#78 of Greece]	1602-1603
Matthaios II [3rd time]	1603
186. Raphaél II *apo Methymnés*	1603-1607
Neophytos II [2nd time]	1607-1612
187. Kyrillos I *Loukaris* [locum tenens; #86 of Alexandria]	1612
188. Timotheos II *apo Palaión Patrón*	1612-1620
Kyrillos I [2nd time]	1620-1623
189. Grégorios IV *Straboamaseias*	1623
190. Anthimos II *apo Adrianoupoleós*	1623
Kyrillos I [3rd time]	1623-1630
191. Isaak	1630
Kyrillos I [4th time]	1630-1633
192. Kyrillos II *Kontarés apo Borrhoias*	1633
Kyrillos I [5th time]	1633-1634
193. Athanasios III *Patellarios apo Thessalonikés*	1634
Kyrillos I [6th time]	1634-1635
Kyrillos II [2nd time]	1635-1636
194. Neophytos III *apo Hérakleias*	1636-1637
Kyrillos I [7th time]	1637-1638
Kyrillos II [3rd time]	1638-1639
195. Parthenios I *Gerón apo Naupaktou*	1639-1644
196. Parthenios II *Oxys Keskinés*	1644-1646
197. Ióannikios II *Lindios apo Hérakleias*	1646-1648
Parthenios II [2nd time]	1648-1651
Ióannikios II [2nd time]	1651-1652

198.	Kyrillos III *Spanos apo Tornobou*	1652
	Athanasios III [2nd time]	1652
199.	Païsios I *apo Larissés*	1652-1653
	Ióannikios II [3rd time]	1653-1654
	Kyrillos III [2nd time]	1654
	Païsios I [2nd time]	1654-1655
	Ióannikios II [4th time]	1655-1656
200.	Parthenios III *Parthenakés apo Chiou*	1656-1657
201.	Gabriél II *apo Ganou kai Chóras*	1657
202.	Theophanés II *apo Melekinou*	1657
203.	Parthenios IV *Mogilalos Koukoumés*	1657-1662
204.	Dionysios III *Bardalis Spanos*	1662-1665
	Parthenios IV [2nd time]	1665-1667
205.	Klémés *apo Ikoniou*	1667
206.	Methodios III *Morónés apo Hérakleias*	1668-1671
	Parthenios IV [3rd time]	1671
207.	Dionysios IV *Mouselimés Komnénos*	1671-1673
208.	Gerasimos II *apo Tornobou*	1673-1674
	Parthenios IV [4th time]	1675-1676
	Dionysios IV [2nd time]	1676-1679
209.	Athanasios IV *apo Rhaidestou*	1679
210.	Iakóbos *apo Larissés*	1679-1682
	Dionysios IV [3rd time]	1682-1684
	Parthenios IV [5th time]	1684-1685
	Iakóbos [2nd time]	1685-1686
	Dionysios IV [4th time]	1686-1687
	Iakóbos [3rd time]	1687-1688
211.	Kallinikos II *Akarnan apo Prousés*	1688
212.	Neophytos IV *apo Adrianoupoleós*	1688-1689
	Kallinikos II [2nd time]	1689-1693
	Dionysios IV [5th time]	1693-1694
	Kallinikos II [3rd time]	1694-1702
213.	Gabriél III *Smyrnaios apo Chalkédonos*	1702-1707
214.	Neophytos V *apo Hérakleias* [unconsecrated]	1707
215.	Kyprianos *apo Kaisareias Kappadokias*	1707-1709
216.	Athanasios V *Krés apo Adrianoupoleós*	1709-1711
217.	Kyrillos IV *apo Kyzikou*	1711-1713
	Kyprianos [2nd time]	1713-1714
218.	Kosmas III *Chalkédonios* [#96 of Alexandria; #60 of Sinai]	1714-1716
219.	Hieremias III *apo Kaisareias Kappadokias*	1716-1726
	Kyrillos (V) *apo Prousés* [anti-patriarch]	1720
220.	Kallinikos III *apo Hérakleias* [one day]	1726
221.	Païsios II *Kiomourtzoglous apo Nikomédeias*	1726-1732
	Hieremias III [2nd time]	1732-1733
222.	Serapheim I *apo Nikomédeias*	1733-1734

223. Neophytos VI *apo Kaisareias Kappadokias*	1734-1740	
Païsios II [2nd time]	1740-1743	
Neophytos VI [2nd time]	1743-1744	
Païsios II [3rd time]	1744-1748	
224. Kyrillos V *Karakalos apo Nikomédeias*	1748-1751	
Païsios II [4th time]	1751-1752	
Kyrillos V [2nd time]	1752-1757	
225. Kallinikos IV *apo Proïlabou*	1757	
226. Serapheim II *apo Philippoupoleós*	1757-1761	
227. Ióannikios III *Karatzas apo Chalkédonos*	1761-1763	
228. Samouél *Chantzerés apo Derkón*	1763-1768	
229. Meletios II *apo Larissés*	1768-1769	
230. Theodosios II *Maridakés apo Thessalonikés*	1769-1773	
Samouél [2nd time]	1773-1774	
231. Sóphronios II [#125 of Jerusalem]	1774-1780	
232. Gabriél IV *apo Palaión Patrón*	1780-1785	
233. Prokopios *apo Smyrnés*	1785-1789	
234. Neophytos VII *apo Maróneias*	1789-1794	
235. Gerasimos III *apo Derkón*	1794-1797	
236. Grégorios V *Angelopoulos apo Smyrnés*	1797-1798	
Neophytos VII [2nd time]	1798-1801	
237. Kallinikos V *apo Nikaias*	1801-1806	
Parthenios [locum tenens]	1806	
Grégorios V [2nd time]	1806-1808	
Kallinikos V [2nd time]	1808-1809	
238. Hieremias IV *apo Mitylénés*	1809-1813	
239. Kyrillos VI *Serbetsoglous apo Adrianoupoleós*	1813-1818	
Grégorios V [3rd time]	1818-1821	
240. Eugenios II *apo Pissideias*	1821-1822	
241. Anthimos III *apo Chalkédonos*	1822-1824	
242. Chrysanthos *apo Serrón*	1824-1826	
243. Agathangelos *apo Chalkédonos* [#66 of Serbia]	1826-1830	
244. Kónstantios I [#68 of Sinai]	1830-1834	
245. Kónstantios II *apo Tornobou*	1834-1835	
246. Grégorios VI *Phourtouniados apo Serrón*	1835-1840	
247. Anthimos IV *Bambakés apo Nikomédeias*	1840-1841	
248. Anthimos V *apo Kyzikou*	1841-1842	
249. Germanos IV *apo Derkón*	1842-1845	
250. Meletios III *Pankalos apo Kyzikou*	1845	
251. Anthimos VI *Ióannidés apo Ephesou*	1845-1848	
Anthimos IV [2nd time]	1848-1852	
Germanos IV [2nd time]	1852-1853	
Anthimos VI [2nd time]	1853-1855	
252. Kyrillos VII *apo Amaseias*	1855-1860	
253. Ióakeim II *Kokkodés apo Kyzikou*	1860-1863	
254. Sóphronios III *apo Amaseias* [#109 of Alexandria]	1863-1866	

	Grégorios VI [2nd time]	1867-1871
	Anthimos VI [3rd time]	1871-1873
	Ióakeim II [2nd time]	1873-1878
255.	Ióakeim III *apo Thessalonikés*	1878-1884
256.	Ióakeim IV	1884-1886
257.	Dionysios V	1887-1891
258.	Neophytos VIII	1891-1894
259.	Anthimos VII	1895-1896
260.	Kónstantinos V	1897-1901
	Ióakeim III [2nd time]	1901-1912
261.	Germanos V	1913-1918
	INTERREGNUM	
	Dórotheos *apo Prousés* [locum tenens]	1918-1921
262.	Meletios IV *Metaxakés* [#114 of Greece; #111 of Alexandria]	1921-1923
263.	Grégorios VII *Serbydakés*	1923-1924
264.	Kónstantinos VI *Araboglou*	1924-1925
265.	Basileios III *Geórgiadés*	1925-1929
266.	Phótios II *Maniatés*	1929-1935
267.	Beniaminos *Christodoulos*	1936-1946
268.	Maximos V *Baportzés*	1946-1948
269.	Athénagoras *Spyrou* [#2 of America]	1948-1972
270.	Démétrios *Papadopoulos*	1972-1991
271.	Bartholomaios *Archondonés*	1991-

THE CHURCH OF TURKEY

The Turkish Orthodox Church was founded by an Orthodox priest, Paulos Euthymios Karachissaridés, who called himself Papa Eftim (the Turkish version of Euthymios). Desiring to establish a national church independent of Constantinople for Turkish-speaking Christians, particularly in Anatolia, Eftim began urging Turkish parishes of the Orthodox Church to rally around his standard. On 1 April 1922 he proclaimed the independence of the Turkish Orthodox Church, stating that Patriarch Meletios IV of Constantinople had occupied the throne uncanonically; this was followed by the first Church Congress on 21 September. The government of Turkey, eager to drive a wedge into the Greek communities, supported Eftim's claims, ultimately causing the flight of Meletios, and later the exile of his second successor, Kónstantinos VI. The Holy Synod of Constantinople responded by excommunicating Eftim in 1924. Undaunted, Eftim established his headquarters in Istanbul, issued a statement that two members of the Synod had lifted the anathema and had then consecrated him as bishop, and in 1926 proclaimed himself Archbishop of the Independent Turkish Orthodox Church of Istanbul, and Exarch of All Turkish Orthodox. To provide for the succession, he ordained his son and nephew to the priesthood, and raised a second son to the deaconate. Eftim resigned his leadership in 1962, dying six years later; he was succeeded by his second son, Turgut Erenerol, as Papa Eftim II. In December 1965 the two Turkish churches renounced their mutual excommunications. The Turkish Orthodox Church was at one time favored by the Turkish government, which supported its efforts to take over parishes and churches formerly controlled by Constantinople; but it has diminished in size over the decades, now numbering no more than a thousand communicants. **Sources:** "An Autocephalous Turkish Orthodox Church" (Jacob); *Eastern Christianity and Politics in the Twentieth Century* (Ramet, ed.); *Gegenwartslage der Ostkirchen* (Spuler).

ARCHBISHOPS OF THE TURKISH ORTHODOX CHURCH

1.	Papa Eftim I (Euthymios) *Karachissaridés*	1926-1962
2.	Papa Eftim II *Erenerol*	1962-

XXV.

THE LATIN CHURCH OF CONSTANTINOPLE

The Latin Patriarchate of Constantinople was established in the year 1204, as a direct result of the fourth crusade, which stopped short of the Holy Land and instead conquered the capital of the Byzantine Empire. When the Greek patriarch fled the city, Thomas Morosini was named his successor. This church was one of four such creations made during the period of the crusades to correspond to the patriarchates of the ancient world, and to provide rival jurisdictions to the Greek churches and prelates. The Latin Church of Constantinople survived until the reconquest of that city by the Greeks in 1261, after which time it became a purely titular honor, with the patriarchs being based in Rome. During the renaissance the rank of "patriarch" in the Latin church became a kind of intermediate level between archbishop and cardinal, many patriarchs relinquishing their titles when promoted to the College of Cardinals. The title was abolished by Pope Pius XII about 1953.

SOURCES: *The Catholic Encyclopedia*; *Dictionnaire d'Histoire et de Géographie Ecclésiastiques*; *The New Catholic Encyclopedia*; *Oriens Christianus* (Le Quien).

LATIN PATRIARCHS OF CONSTANTINOPLE

1.	Thomas I *Morosini*	1204-1211
	INTERREGNUM	
2.	Gervasius (or Everardus)	1215-1219
3.	Matthæus (or Matthias)	1221-1226
	Ioannes I *Halegrin* [unconsecrated]	1226
4.	Simon	1227-1232
5.	Nicolaus I *de Castro Arquato*	1234-1251
6.	Pantaleon *Giustiniani*	1253-1286
7.	Petrus I *Correr*	1286-1302
8.	Leonardus *Faliero*	1302-1305?
	INTERREGNUM	
9.	Nicolaus II	1308-1331?
10.	Petrus II *de Bolonesio*	1331?-
11.	Cardinalis (?)	1332-1335
12.	Gotius (or Goctius) *Battaglia*	1335-1339

13.	Rolandus *de Ast*	1339
14.	Stephanus I	1339-1345
15.	Stephanus II	1346
16.	Guillelmus I *de Castello*	1346-1361
	INTERREGNUM	
17.	Petrus III *Thomas*	1364-1366
18.	Paulus I *Guillelmus*	1366-1370
19.	Hugolinus *de Malabranca*	1371-1375?
20.	Iacobus I *d'Itri*	1376-1378
21.	Guillelmus II	1379
22.	Thomas II *Palaiologos Tagaris* [rival]	1379?-1384?
23.	Paulus II	1379?-
24.	Ludovicus I	1405
25.	Angelus *Correr*	1405
26.	Antonius I *Correr* [nephew of #25]	1405-1408
27.	Alphonsus	1408-
28.	Franciscus I *Landus*	1409
29.	Ioannes II *Contarini*	1409-
30.	Ioannes III *de la Rochetaillée*	1412-1423
	Ioannes II *Contarini* [2nd time]	1424-
31.	Franciscus II *de Conzié*	1430-
32.	Franciscus III *Condulmer*	1438-
33.	Gregorius (Grégorios) *Mammas* [#157 of Greek Church of Constantinople]	1454?-1459
34.	Isidorus (Isidor) *of Kiev*	1459-1463
35.	Bessarion	1463-1472
36.	Petrus IV *Riario*	1472-1474
37.	Hieronymus *Lando*	1474-1497
38.	Ioannes IV *Michele*	1497-1503
39.	Ioannes V *Borgia*	1503
40.	Franciscus IV *de Lorris*	1503-1506
41.	Marcus *Cornaro*	1506-1507
42.	Thomas III *Bakócz de Erdoed*	1507-1521
	Marcus *Cornaro* [2nd time]	1522-1524
43.	Gillus *Caninio*	1524-1530
44.	Franciscus V *Pesaro*	1530-1544
45.	Marinus *Grimani*	1545-1546
46.	Ranucius *Farnese*	1546-1549
47.	Fabius I *Colonna*	1550-1554
	Ranucius *Farnese* [2nd time]	1554-1565
48.	Scipio *Rebiba*	1565-1573
49.	Prosperus *Rebiba* [nephew of #49]	1573-1594
50.	Silvius *Savelli*	1594-1596
51.	Hercules *Tassoni*	1596-1597
52.	Bonifacius *Bevilacqua*	1598-1599
53.	Bonaventurus Secusius *de Caltagirone*	1599-1618?

54.	Ascanius *Gesualdi*	1618-1640
55.	Franciscus VI Maria *Machiavelli*	1640-1641
56.	Ioannes VI Iacobus *Panciroli*	1641-1643
57.	Ioannes VII Baptistus *Spada*	1643-1658
58.	Volunnius *Bandinelli*	1658-1667
59.	Stephanus III *Ugolini*	1667-1670
60.	Fredericus *Borromée* [#25 of Alexandria]	1670-1673
	INTERREGNUM	
61.	Odoardus *Cybò*	1689-1700
	INTERREGNUM	
62.	Ludovicus II *Pic de la Mirandole*	1706-1712
	INTERREGNUM	
63.	Andreas *Riggio*	1716-1717
64.	Camillus *Cybò*	1718-1729
65.	Mondillus *Orsini*	1729-
66.	Ferdinandus Maria *de Rossi*	1751-1759
67.	Philippus Ioshua *Caucci*	1760-1771
68.	Ioannes VIII *de la Puebla*	1771-1779
69.	Franciscus VII Antonius *Marcucci*	1781-1799
	INTERREGNUM	
70.	Benedictus *Fenoja*	1805-1812
	INTERREGNUM	
71.	Iosephus I *della Porta Rodiani*	1823-1835
72.	Ioannes IX *Soglia-Ceroni*	1835-1839
73.	Antonius II Maria *Traversi*	1839-1842
74.	Iacobus II *Sinibaldi*	1843-1844?
75.	Fabius II Maria *Asquini*	1844-1845
76.	Ioannes X Ludovicus *Canali*	1845-1851
77.	Dominicus *Lucciardi*	1851
	INTERREGNUM	
78.	Iosephus II Melchiades *Ferlisi* [#53 of Antioch]	1860-1865
79.	Rogerus Ludovicus Æmilius *Antici-Mattei*	1866-1875
	INTERREGNUM	
80.	Iacobus III Gregorius *Gallo*	1878-1881
	INTERREGNUM	
81.	Iulius *Lenti*	1887-1894
82.	Ioannes XI Baptistus *Casali del Drago*	1895-1899
83.	Alexander *Sanminiatelli-Zabarella*	1899-1901
84.	Carolus Antonius *Nocella* [#60 of Antioch]	1901-1903
85.	Iosephus III *Capetelli*	1903-1921?
85.	Michael *Zezza di Zapponeta*	1923-1927
86.	Antonius III Anastasius *Rossi*	1927-1948
	THE PATRIARCHATE DISCONTINUED	

XXVI.

THE CHURCH OF CRETE

The autonomous Church of Crete was founded in the year 65 A.D., according to tradition, by the Apostle Paul, the first known bishop being his disciple, Titos (a name which has remained popular among the island's clergy). Although Crete is a province of the Republic of Greece, the Church resisted being placed under the Archbishop of Athens after the Greek Revolution of the 1820s, and instead maintained itself as an appendage of the Ecumenical Patriarchate. In 1878 the Church was granted self-governance, and in 1961 autonomy by Constantinople, now managing all of its own affairs except for the consecration of each new primate.

The primate bears the title Archbishop of Crete and Metropolitan of Herakleion. The official language of the Church is Greek. The number of communicants is probably equal to the population of the island, about a half million.

SOURCES: *Dictionnaire d'Histoire et de Géographie Ecclésiastiques*; *Échos d'Orient*; *Episkepsis*; *History of the Church* (Jedin, ed.); *Jahrbuch der Orthodoxie* (Proc); "Kréte—Ekklés." (Benerés; regarded as official by the Church); *Oriens Christianus* (Le Quien); *Orthodoxia*.

METROPOLITAN ARCHBISHOPS OF CRETE

1.	Paulos I	64?
2.	Titos I *Apostolos*	64?
3.	Philippos	
4.	Dioskoros	
5.	Myrón *Thaumatourgos*	249?
6.	Kriskés	256?
7.	Kyrillos I	393?
8.	Petros I *Eikonios*	431?
9.	Martyrios	451?
10.	Theodóros	553?
11.	Ióannés I	597?
12.	Paulos II	667?
13.	Eumenios I *Thaumatourgos*	668?

14.	Basileios I	680?-692?
15.	Andreas	710-720
16.	Petros II *Kolybités*	761?
17.	Élias I	787?
18.	Kyrillos II	824?
19.	Basileios II	879?
20.	Ióannés II	
21.	Stephanos	1027?-1030?
22.	Nikétas I	
23.	Nikétas II	
24.	Basileios III	
25.	Élias II	1081-1092
26.	Nikétas III	1086?
27.	Ióannés III	1106?
28.	León	
29.	Michaél	
30.	Kónstantinos I	
31.	Basileios IV	
32.	Kónstantinos II	
33.	Nikolaos I	
34.	Ióannés IV	1166-1177
35.	Manouél I	
36.	Manouél II	
37.	Nikolaos II	1195?-1221?
38.	Niképhoros I	1296?
39.	Antónios *Homologétés*	1306?
40.	Niképhoros II	1312?-1318?
41.	Élias III	
42.	Makarios	1357?
43.	Anthimos I *Homologétés* [#58 of Greece]	1365-1370

INTERREGNUM

44.	Neophytos *Patelaros*	1645?-1679
45.	Niképhoros III *Skótakés*	1679-1681?
46.	Kallinikos I	1683-1687
47.	Arsenios I	1687-1688
48.	Athanasios *Kalliopolités*	1688-1697
49.	Kallinikos II	1697-1699?
50.	Arsenios II	1699-1701
51.	Ióasaph	1701?-1710

INTERREGNUM

52.	Kónstantios *Chalkiopoulos*	1716-1722?
53.	Daniél *apo Pethymnés*	1722-1725
54.	Gerasimos I *Letitzés Gerontas*	1725-1755?
55.	Anthimos II	1756
56.	Gerasimos II *apo Chiou*	1756-1769
57.	Zacharias *Maridakés*	1769-1786

58.	Maximos *Progiannakopoulos*	1786-1800
59.	Gerasimos III *Pardalés*	1800-1821
60.	Methodios *apo Karpathou*	1823
61.	Kallinikos III *ex Ankialou*	1823-1831
62.	Meletios I *Nikoletakés*	1831-1839
63.	Porphyrios *Phótiadés*	1839
51.	Kallinikos IV *Gargalados*	1839-1842
52.	Kallinikos V *Chougias*	1842-1843
53.	Chrysanthos *Lesbos*	1843-1850
54.	Sóphronios I *apo Ainou*	1850
55.	Dionysios I *Byzantios*	1850-1856
56.	Ióannikios *Zagorésios*	1856-1858
57.	Dionysios II *Charitóniadés*	1858-1868
58.	Meletios II *Kalymnios*	1868-1873?
59.	Sóphronios II *apo Dioumoteichou*	1874?-1877
	Meletios II [2nd time]	1877-1882
60.	Timotheos I *Kastrinogiannakés*	1882-1897
61.	Eumenios II *Xéroudakés*	1897-1920
62.	Titos II *Zógraphidés*	1922-1933
63.	Timotheos II *Benerés*	1933-1941
64.	Basileios V	1941-1950
65.	Eugenios *Psallidakés*	1950-1978
66.	Timotheos III *Papoutsakés*	1978-

XXVII.

THE CHURCH OF CYPRUS

Tradition states that the Church of Cyprus was founded by St. Barnabas, an early disciple of the apostles. It was recognized as autocephalous in 431, under an independent Archbishop. When the island was captured by the Crusaders in 1191, the Orthodox bishops were put under the authority of the Latin Archbishop of Nikosia, and were systematically suppressed. Finally, when Archbishop Germanos died, about 1275, no elections were allowed for a new primate, although the principal Greek sees continued to have Greek bishops. Three centuries later, the Ottomans took possession of Cyprus, in 1571, and the native population began lobbying for a new primate, whom they received a year later in the person of Timotheos. In 1821 the Turks murdered Archbishop Kyprianos and his three bishops for sending aid to the Greek rebels on the mainland.

In the twentieth century both Church and state have been plagued with continual struggles between the Greek and Turkish populations, and between the British administration and those seeking either independence or union with Greece. The Archbishop's throne remained vacant for nine years between 1900-1909, as various factions sought to control the election. The abortive revolution of 1931 resulted in chaos; when Kyrillos III died in 1933, the British administration delayed new elections for fourteen years. Finally, the Locum Tenens, Metropolitan Leontios, was allowed to assume the throne (1947), but died a month after his election.

Archbishop Makarios III was a major figure in the Cypriot struggle for independence; following his election in 1950 at the early age of 37, he led the forces seeking to free Cyprus from British rule. He was subsequently exiled, but returned as first President of Cyprus in 1959. His later years were troubled with a series of unsettling events. First, three of his Metropolitans attempted to unseat him in 1973, claiming that canon law prevented a church official from also holding a secular political office, and demanding Makarios resign his Presidency; when he refused, they named Gennadios of Paphos as new Archbishop. Makarios convened an extraordinary Synod, presided over by the three Greek Patriarchs of Alexandria, Jerusalem, and Antioch; the Synod condemned the insurrection, and revalidated Makarios's authority. A year later Makarios was again forced into exile, following a political revolution, but returned in 1975, after the Turkish Army had invaded the island and established a separate Turkish state of North Cyprus. This extraordinary churchman died in 1977, at the age of sixty-three, and was succeeded by Archbishop Chrysostomos.

The primate bears the title Archbishop of Nova Justiniana and All Cyprus, but resides at Nikosia. The official Church language is Greek. The approximately 442,000 members of this island church are all located on Cyprus.

SOURCES: *Dictionnaire d'Histoire et de Géographie Ecclési-astique*; *Échos d'Orient*; *Hé Ekklésia tés Kyprou* (Mitsidés; regarded by the Church as official); *Episkepsis*; *Europa World Yearbook*; *Gegen-wartslage der Ostkirchen* (Spuler); *Hémerlogion Ekklésias Kyprou 1992* (regarded as official by the Church); *History of the Church* (Jedin, ed.); *History of the Orthodox Church of Cyprus* (Hackett); *Jahrbuch der Or-thodoxie* (Proc); *The Middle East and North Africa*; *Orthodoxia*.

ARCHBISHOPS OF CYPRUS

1.	Barnabas I *Apostolos*	45?
	Aristión [not officially recognized]	70?
	Hérakleidés [not officially recognized]	90?
2.	Gelasios	325?
3.	Epiphanios I	368-403
4.	Sabinos I	403-
5.	Tróïlos	-431
	Theodóros [not officially recognized]	431?
6.	Rhéginos	431-
7.	Olympios I	449?-451?
8.	Sabinos II	457?-458?
9.	Anthemios	478?
10.	Olympios II	490?
11.	Philoxenos	510?
12.	Damianos	530?
13.	Sóphronios I	550?
14.	Grégorios (I)	570?
15.	Arkadios I	600?
16.	Ploutarchos	620?-625?
17.	Arkadios II	630?-641?
18.	Sergios	643?
19.	Epiphanios II	681?-685?
20.	Ióannés I	691?
21.	Geórgios I	753?
22.	Kónstantinos	783?-787?
23.	Epiphanios III	870?
24.	Eustathios	890?

25.	Basileios	1080?
26.	Nikolaos *Mouzalón* [#112 of Constantinople]	1110?
27.	Ióannés II *Krétikos*	1151?-1174
28.	Barnabas II	1175-
29.	Sóphronios II	1191?
30.	Hésaïas	1209?-1218?
	Symeón (or Hilarión) [anti-archbishop]	1218?-1220
31.	Neophytos I	1222?-1251
32.	Geórgios II (or Grégorios II)	1254?
33.	Germanos I *Pésimandros*	1260?-1275?

INTERREGNUM

THE GREEK CHURCH RESTORED

34.	Timotheos	1572-1588?
35.	Laurentios	1588?
36.	Neophytos II	-1592
37.	Athanasios I	1592-1600
38.	Beniamin	1600-1605
39.	Christodoulos I	1606-1638?
	Timotheos (II) [anti-archbishop]	1622-
	Ignatios [anti-archbishop]	1634-
	Christodoulos (II) [anti-archbishop]	1637-1638
40.	Niképhoros	1640?-1674
41.	Hilarión (II) *Tzigalas* (or *Kigalas*)	1674-1682
42.	Christodoulos II	1682-1685?

INTERREGNUM

43.	Iakóbos I	1691?-1692?

INTERREGNUM

44.	Germanos II	1695?-1705
45.	Athanasios II *al-Dabbas* [#145 of Antioch]	1705-1708
46.	Iakóbos II	1709-1718
	Ephraim [anti-archbishop]	1715
47.	Silbestros	1718-1733
48.	Philotheos	1734-1745
	Neophytos (III) [anti-archbishop]	1745
	Philotheos [2nd time]	1745-1759
49.	Païsios	1759-1761
	Kyprianos [anti-archbishop; #99 of Alexandria]	1761
	Païsios [2nd time]	1761-1767
50.	Chrysanthos	1767-1783
	Ióannikios [anti-archbishop]	1783
	Chrysanthos [2nd time]	1783-1810
51.	Kyprianos	1810-1821
52.	Ióakeim	1821-1824
53.	Damaskénos	1824-1827

THE CHURCH OF CYPRUS

54.	Panaretos	1827-1840
55.	Ióannikios	1840-1849
56.	Kyrillos I [cousin of #52]	1849-1854
57.	Makarios I	1854-1865
58.	Sóphronios III	1865-1900
	INTERREGNUM	
	Kyrillos *Papadopoulos* [locum tenens]	1900-1909
59.	Kyrillos II *Papadopoulos*	1909-1916
60.	Kyrillos III *Basileiou*	1916-1933
	INTERREGNUM	
	Leontios *Leontiou* [locum tenens]	1933-1947
61.	Leontios *Leontiou*	1947
62.	Makarios II *Myriantheus*	1947-1950
63.	Makarios III *Mouskos*	1950-1973
	Gennadios [anti-archbishop]	1973
	Makarios III [2nd time]	1973-1977
64.	Chrysostomos *Kykkotés*	1977-

LATIN ARCHBISHOPS OF CYPRUS

1.	Alanus	1196-
2.	Terrius	1206-1211
3.	Albertus	1211-
4.	Durandus [unconsecrated]	1212-1213
	INTERREGNUM	
5.	Eustorgius *de Montaigu* (or *d'Auvergne*)	1217?-1239
6.	Elias I	1240-1251
7.	Hugo I *de Pise* (or *de Fagiano*)	1251-1260
	INTERREGNUM	
8.	Raphael	1264-
9.	Ranulphus (or Arnulphus)	1275?-1280
	INTERREGNUM	
10.	Ioannes I *d'Ancone*	1288-1295
11.	Gerardus *de Langres*	1295-1312?
12.	Ioannes II *de Polo* (or *del Conte*)	1312-1332
13.	Helias II *des Nabinaux*	1332-1342
14.	Philippus I *de Chambarlhac*	1344-1360
	INTERREGNUM	
15.	Raymundus *de la Pradèle*	1366-
16.	Paloungerus	1370?
17.	Michael	1375?
18.	Andreas I	1380?
19.	Conradus I	1396-
20.	Ioannes III	1400?
21.	Conradus II *Caraccioli*	1402-1405
22.	Stephanus *de Carrare*	1406-1412

23.	Ugo II *de Lusignan*	1413-1442
	Iacobus I *Benoît* [locum tenens]	1442
24.	Galesius *de Montolif*	1445-1447
25.	Andreas II	1447-
26.	Iacobus II *de Lusignan*	1459
27.	Elias III	1460-1463?
28.	Isidorus	1463?-
29.	Antonius *Tuneto*	1464?
30.	Ioannes IV Franciscus *Brusato*	1464?
31.	Fabricius	1464-
32.	Guillelmus *Gonème*	1467-
33.	Ludovicus *Perez Fabrice*	1471-1483
34.	Victor *Marcello*	1477-
35.	Benedictus *Soranzo*	1484-
36.	Sebastianus *Priuli*	1496-1498?

INTERREGNUM

37.	Aldobrandinus *des Ursins*	1502-1517?
38.	Livius *Podocator*	1524-
39.	Guido *Brunelli*	1530?
40.	Cæsar *Podocator*	1553-
41.	Philippus II *Mocenigo*	1560-1571?
42.	Iulianus	1571-1577

THE LATIN ARCHBISHOPRIC DISCONTINUED

XXVIII.

THE CHURCH OF CZECHOSLOVAKIA

Czechoslovakia, like Poland, is predominately a Catholic nation. The proclamation of Czech independence following World War I led to a resurgence of nationalism in this small Slavic country, including demands by Orthodox believers in Slovakia (the eastern half of the country) for their own independent church. Some of these petitioned the Serbian patriarch for their own bishop; he organized the Church on 8 August 1921, and consecrated Matthias Pavlík on 24 September under the religious name of Gorazd. Little more than a year later, on 8 February 1923, the Ecumenical Patriarch consecrated a rival Archbishop in the person of Sabbazd (or Savatij); his Church was declared autocephalous a month later, on 8 March. Most of the Czech church remained under nominal Serbian control until the second World War, when Gorazd was murdered by the Nazis (1942) for harboring refugees on church property; his rival Bishop Sabbazd was imprisoned at Dachau for five years. Gorazd was later canonized in the 1980s by the Czech Church.

In 1946, following the Soviet occupation of Czechoslovakia, the Church was put under the authority of the Moscow Patriarchate, and a new (Russian) Exarch was appointed; the Soviets then forcibly attempted (1950) to merge the Byzantine-Rite Catholics in Slovakia into the Orthodox body. On 23 November (or December) 1951 Patriarch Aleksiî I of Russia granted the Czechs their autocephaly, and on 8 December Exarch Jelevferij was elected Metropolitan. Gradually the Russian prelates were displaced by Czech bishops, until an all-native hierarchy was constituted. The Czech Church's autocephaly was recognized a second time by the Ecumenical Patriarch in 1960.

The impending division of Czechoslovakia on 1 January 1993 into the Czech Republic and Slovakia prompted much discussion on the future of the Czech church. Ultimately, at a synod held on 12 December 1992, church leaders decided to separate Slovakia into an autonomous metropolitanate under the Archbishop of Presov, with the unity of the overall church still being maintained. The future remains uncertain, however, since neither of the autonomous halves of this small church has sufficient followers to maintain a stable hierarchical structure.

The primate bears the title Archbishop of Prague and Metropolitan of the Czech Lands and Slovakia (since 1992), having formerly
been called Metropolitan of Prague and All Czechoslovakia. The official language is Czech. Of the 55,000 communicants, 20,000 are located in the Czech Republic and 35,000 in Slovakia.

SOURCES: *Czechoslovakia* (Busek and Spulber); *Eastern
Christianity and Politics in the Twentieth Century* (Ramet, ed.); *Échos
d'Orient*; *Episkepsis*; *Europa World Yearbook*; *Gegenwartslage der
Ostkirchen* (Spuler); *History of the Church* (Jedin, ed.); *Jahrbuch der
Orthodoxie* (Proc); *Orthodoxia*; personal communication; *Profiles in
Belief* (Piepkorn).

METROPOLITAN ARCHBISHOPS OF CZECHOSLOVAKIA
(Bishops 1921, Exarchs 1946, Metropolitans 1951)

1.	Gorazd *Pavlík* [rival metropolitan]	1921-1942
1.	Sabbazd (Savatij) *Vrabec* [rival metropolitan]	1923-1945
	INTERREGNUM	
2.	Jelevferij *Voronzov*	1946-1955
3.	Jan *Kuchtin*	1956-1964
4.	Dorotej *Filipp*	1964-

METROPOLITAN ARCHBISHOPS OF SLOVAKIA

1.	Nikolaj *Kocvar*	1993-

THE SLAVONIC ORTHODOX CHURCH

The Russian takeover of the Czech Church in 1946 prompted a group of
communicants and prelates to form an underground church. One of the
leaders of this movement, Archbishop Filotej, fled the country in 1968,
settling in the United States, where he founded the Slavonic Orthodox
Church. A year later, Andrei Prazsky was consecrated Coadjutor
Archbishop, succeeding Filotej on his death in 1970. Andrei established communion with the Ukrainian Orthodox Church in the U.S.A.
(q.v.), and was provisionally reconsecrated by Archbishops Hryhoriî
and Hennadiî in the early 1970s. Further talks led to a joint sobor of
bishops from both churches on 11 May 1980; Andrei voluntarily va-
cated his position in favor of Hryhoriî. On 9 June 1982 Andrei was
elected Metropolitan Archbishop of Prague and All Czechoslovakia; he
died in 1990. The Church is located in the Bronx, where it ministers to
roughly 5,000 Slovaks, Ukrainians, and other Slavic nationalities in
America. SOURCES: Bishop Andrew Prazsky; news reports.

METROPOLITAN ARCHBISHOPS OF THE
SLAVONIC ORTHODOX CHURCH

1.	Filotej	1968-1970
2.	Andrej *Prazsky* [coadjutor 1969]	1970-1980
3.	Hryhorij *Ohiîchuk* (or *Osijchuk*)	1980-1982
	Andrej *Prazsky* [2nd time]	1982-1990
4.	Alexis Nizza	1991-
	Efthimious Kontargiris [coadjutor]	1991-

XXIX.

THE CHURCH OF ESTONIA

Estonia existed as an independent state between the two World Wars. Like its two neighbors on the Baltic Sea, Latvia and Lithuania, Estonia's population was largely Roman Catholic, with perhaps one-fifth of believers there professing orthodoxy. Following the declaration of Estonian independence, on 12 April 1917, the Estonian Apostolic Orthodox Church was organized, and a bishop elected, in the person of Paul Kulbusch (Bishop Platon); he was consecrated on 31 December 1917, and murdered by the Bolsheviks on 14 January 1919. On 20 May 1920, the Estonian Church was granted autonomy by Russian Patriarch Tikhon. The Estonian Church unilaterally seceded from Russian jurisdiction on 23 September 1922, and on 7 July 1923, the Church's autonomy (or autocephaly, according to current members of the Church) was recognized by Ecumenical Patriarch Meletios III of Constantinople. Many Russians living in Estonia refused to accept the Church's jurisdiction, however, preferring to have a Russian prelate; the dispute was settled by placing the Estonian parishes under the independent Metropolitan of the Estonian Apostolic Orthodox Church, and the Russian churches under the Archbishop of Narva and Izhborsk.

The Russian invasion of 1940 forced Metropolitan Aleksander to renounce his status in March 1941, but he re-established the Church a few months later, when the Nazis occupied the country. The withdrawal of the German armies in 1944 was the beginning of the end; those members of the Church who did not go into exile were forced to submit a second time on 5 March 1945. Metropolitan Aleksander settled at Stockholm, Sweden, where he organized the Estonian Orthodox Church in Exile, under the overall jurisdiction of the Patriarchate of Constantinople; other émigrés established Church branches in the United States and Canada. Aleksander died in 1954, and was succeeded by Archbishop Athénagoras I of Thyateira and Great Britain as *Locum Tenens*. The exiled Estonian priest Jüri was consecrated Bishop in 1956; when he died in 1961, Athénagoras again assumed administration of the Church. On 1 September 1968, an assembly of exiled Estonians in Stockholm, Sweden, elected Archpriest Sergi Samon to be their bishop, and again pressed for his appointment in 1973, but consecration was refused by the Ecumenical Patriarchate.

THE CHURCH OF ESTONIA

In September 1991 Estonia once again achieved independence from the Soviet Union; the Estonian Apostolic Orthodox Church was granted autonomy by the Russian Church on 28 April 1993. Most of the native Estonians who had professed the Orthodox faith died, left, or were exiled during the Soviet occupation. The remaining believers consist largely of minority Russians still living in Estonia, under the jurisdiction of the Patriarch of Russia.

The primate bears the title Bishop of Tallinn and All Estonia. The official language of the Church is Estonian. There were roughly 212,000 communicants of the Church in 1935, one-third of them Russian; the number today is unknown.

SOURCES: *Échos d'Orient*; *Eesti Apostlik Ortodoksne Kirik Eksilis, 1944-1960*; *Episkepsis*; *Europa World Yearbook*; *The Latvian Orthodox Church* (Cherney); *Profiles in Belief* (Piepkorn); *Religion in the Soviet Union* (Kolarz).

METROPOLITAN ARCHBISHOPS OF ESTONIA

1.	Platon *Kulbusch*	1917-1919
2.	Aleksander *Paulus*	1920-1953

PRIMATES OF THE ESTONIAN ORTHODOX CHURCH IN EXILE

	Athénagoras I *Kabbadas* [locum tenens]	1954-1956
3.	Jüri *Välbe*	1956-1961
	Athénagoras I *Kabbadas* [2nd time]	1961-1962
	Athénagoras II *Kokkinakés* [locum tenens]	1964-1973
4.	Sergi(us) *Samon* [unconsecrated]	1973-1974
	Paul *Menebisoglou* [locum tenens]	1974-

RUSSIAN BISHOPS OF ESTONIA

1.	Aleksius (Aleksiî) *Ridiger* [#15 of Russia]	1961-1987
	INTERREGNUM	
2.	Kornelius (Korneliî) *Jakobs*	1990-

XXX.

THE CHURCH OF ETHIOPIA

Traditionally, the Ethiopian Church was founded by a Coptic monk of the Church of Alexandria, St. Frumentios, who took the name Salama when he became the first Abuna (Father) in 245. However, the early history of the Ethiopian Church is obscure, and the early list of Abunas cannot be confirmed. It is known that the Ethiopians were from the first dependent on the Coptic Church of Alexandria for their primates, and that all of their bishops until recent times were Coptic monks who had to make the arduous journey from Alexandria to take up their duties. During the medieval period several attempts were made by Catholic missionaries to convert the population, but they were ultimately suppressed. Emperor Haile Selassie demanded the independence of the Church when the old Abuna died in 1926. Coptic Pope Yuannis XIX ended three years of negotiations in 1929 by appointed a Copt as Abuna, and by simultaneously consecrating four native bishops to help provide a future Ethiopian hierarchy.

During the Italian occupation, the government deposed the Coptic primate, unilaterally declared the Church autocephalous, and appointed a blind Bishop, Abraha, as first Patriarch; he was followed by Mika'el. When the allies freed Ethiopia, Abuna Qerlos was restored— he died in 1950. Basilyos was elected the first Ethiopian Metropolitan in 1951, and was consecrated as the first Catholicos-Patriarch of Ethiopia on 28 June 1959. His successor, Tewoflos, was deposed in 1976 by the Marxist government, who replaced him with a junior bishop, Takla Haymanot, who died in 1988.

When the Communist president was overthrown in 1991, Patriarch Merkorewos, who had been appointed by the Dergue (the government council), was deposed later that same year. A reformer, Paulos Gebre-Yohannes, was elected as his successor on 7 July 1992. Two months later, on 22 September 1992, the head of the American branch of the Church, Archbishop Yes(e)haq, a supporter of Merkorewos, refused to accept the election, declaring that the previous patriarch had been illegally deposed, and proclaiming his Archdiocese independent of the mother Church. The matter remains unresolved in 1995. In Sept. 1993, following the declaration of Eritrea's independence after a long civil war with Ethiopia, the Ethiopian Church recognized the Eritrean Church as an autonomous ecclesiastical jurisdiction.

The Patriarch's official residence is Axum, but he actually resides in the capital, Addis Ababa. His title is Catholicos Patriarch of Addis Ababa and All Ethiopia. The official Church language is Amharic. The official list of abunas differs so widely from the historical record (so far as it can be determined) that both lists have reproduced here separately. Roughly twenty million communicants are located primarily in Ethiopia, with approximately 80,000 members located in the U.S.

SOURCES: *Church and State in Ethiopia: 1270-1527* (Tamrat); *The Church of Abyssinia* (Hyatt); *Dictionnaire d'Histoire et de Géographie Ecclésiastique*; *Eastern Christianity and Politics in the Twentieth Century* (Ramet, ed.); *Episkepsis*; *The Ethiopian Church* (O'Leary); *The Ethiopian Orthodox Church* (Molnar); *Ethiopiens Ortodokse Kirke* (Andersen); *Europa World Yearbook*; *Gegenwartslage der Ostkirchen* (Spuler); *History of the Church* (Jedin, ed.); "Le Liste dei Metropoliti d'Abissinia" (Guidi); *Die Morgenlandischen Kirchen* (Spuler); *Orthodoxia*; *Profiles in Belief* (Piepkorn).

ABUNAS AND CATHOLICOS-PATRIARCHS OF ETHIOPIA
OFFICIAL LIST

1. Salama I *Fremenatos*   245?
2. Salama II (or Minas I)
3. Petros I
4. Matewos I
5. Marqos I
6. Yohannes I
7. Gabr'el I
8. Yohannes II
9. Gabr'el II
10. Minas II
11. Mika'el I
12. Yes'aq I (or Ishaq)
13. Sem'on I
14. Petros II
15. Mika'el II
16. Gabr'el III
17. Yohannes III
18. Matewos II
19. Mika'el III
20. Sem'on II
21. Yohannes IV
22. Marqos II
23. Abreham I

24. Gerlos I (or Gerillos)
25. Takla Haymanot I
26. Yohannes V
27. Mika'el IV
28. Sem'on III
29. Petros III
30. Matewos III
31. Ya'eqob (or Ewostatewos)
32. Fiqtor I (or Salama III)
33. Qerlos II (or Qerillos)
34. Qozmos I
35. Yostos I
36. Mika'el V
37. Gabr'el IV
38. Mika'el VI
39. Matewos IV
40. Yosab I
41. Yosef
42. Qozmos II
43. Filatawos I
44. Petros IV
45. Yohannes VI
46. Fiqtor II
47. Yostos II
48. Barmeya (or Barmeyu)
49. Mika'el VII
50. Gabr'el V
51. Minas III
52. Yohannes VII
53. Yohannes VIII
54. Abreham II
55. Marqos III
56. Maqares
57. Mika'el VIII
58. Matewos V
59. Marqos IV
60. Mika'el IX
61. Gabr'el VI
62. Yohannes IX
63. Qerlos III
64. Minas IV
65. Matewos VI
66. Mika'el X
67. Gabr'el VII
68. Marqos V
69. Gabr'el VIII

70.	Matewos VII	
71.	Yohannes X	
72.	Minas V	
73.	Marqos VI	
74.	Krestodolo I	
75.	Zakaryas	
76.	Filatawos II	
77.	Suntyos (or Sentyos)	
78.	Gabr'el IX	
79.	Yohannes XI	1437?
80.	Mika'el XI	1438-1458?
81.	Gabr'el X	1438-1458?
82.	Bartalomewos	
83.	Matewos VIII	
84.	Yohannes XII	
85.	Yeshaq II	1481-1510?
86.	Marqos VII	1481-1530?
87.	Kaladyanu	
88.	Petros V	
89.	Matewos IX	
90.	Sem'on IV	
91.	Yosab II	1539?-1559?
92.	Mika'el XII	
93.	Matewos X	
94.	Marqos VIII	1576?-1588?
95.	Petros VI	1600?-1607
96.	Sem'on V	1600?-1617
	Se'la Krestos [anti-abuna]	1617?-1633?
97.	Marqos IX	1634?-1648?
98.	Mika'el XIII	1648?
99.	Yohannes XIII	1648?-
100.	Krestodolo II	1663?-1671
101.	Sinoda	1671?-1693?
102.	Marqos X	1693?-1716
	INTERREGNUM	
103.	Krestodolo III	1720-1735
	INTERREGNUM	
104.	Yohannes XIV	1743-1761
	INTERREGNUM	
105.	Yosab III	1770-1803
106.	Makaryos	1804-1808?
	INTERREGNUM	
107.	Qerlos IV	1815?-1828?
	INTERREGNUM	
108.	Salama IV Andreyas	1841-1867
109.	Atnatewos	1869-1876

	INTERREGNUM	
110. Petros VII		1881-1889
111. Matewos XI		1889-1926
	INTERREGNUM	
112. Qerlos V		1929-1936
Abraha (III) [anti-abuna]		1937-1939
Yohannes XV [anti-abuna]		1939-1941
Qerlos V [2nd time]		1941-1950
113. Basilyos		1951-1970
114. Tewoflos *Melaktu*		1971-1976
Yohannes [locum tenens]		1976
115. Takla Haymanot II *Wolde Mika'el*		1976-1988
116. Merkorewos *Fenta*		1988-1991
Zena Marqos *Bogosew* [locum tenens]		1991-1992
117. Paulos *Gebre Yohannes*		1992-

ABUNAS AND CATHOLICOS-PATRIARCHS OF ETHIOPIA
HISTORICAL LIST

1.	Salama I *Fremenatos*	245?
2.	Minas I	270?
3.	Qerlos I	623?
4.	Yohannes I	820?-840?
5.	Ya'eqob I	848?
6.	Salama II	870?
7.	Petros I	923?
8.	Minas II	923?
9.	Bartalomewos I	950?
10.	Dengel (or Dan'el)	969?
11.	Fiqtor	1050?-1077
12.	Qerlos II *Abdon*	1077-
13.	Sawiros [nephew of #11]	1078?
14.	Giyorgis I	1102?
15.	Mika'el I *Habib al-Atfihi*	1105?-1153
	[alternate dates for reign]:	1130?-1199?
	Qerlos III [anti-abuna]	1144?
16.	Mika'el II *Kilus ibn al-Mulabbas*	1205-1210?
17.	Yes'aq I (or Yeshaq)	1210?-
18.	Ezra	1215?
19.	Yerda' Mika'el III	1220?
20.	Samu'el	1223?
21.	Giyorgis II	1225
22.	Tomas	1237
23.	Ya'eqob II	1250?
24.	Qerlos IV	1260?-1273
25.	Takla Haymanot I	1280

26.	Salama III	1285?
27.	Yohannes II	1310?
28.	Honoriwos	1315?
29.	Maqares	1320?
30.	Ya'eqob III *Madhinana Egzie*	1337-1344
31.	Gabra Krestos	1344?-1348?
32.	Salama IV	1348-1388
33.	Bartalomewos II	1398?-1436
34.	Yohannes III	1437?
35.	Mika'el IV	1438-1455?
36.	Gabr'el	1438-1458?
	INTERREGNUM	
37.	Yeshaq II	1481-1505?
38.	Marqos I	1481-1530?
39.	Yohannes IV	1530?
40.	Marqos II	1538-1546?
41.	Yusab I (or Yosab)	1547?-1559?
42.	Petros II	1559?-1570?
43.	Marqos III	1576?-1588?
44.	Krestodolo I	1588?-
45.	Petros III	1600?-1607
46.	Sem'on	1607?-1617
47.	Se'la Krestos (or Rezq Allah)	1617?-1633
48.	Marqos IV	1634-1648?
49.	Mika'el V	1649?
50.	Yohannes V	1649?-
	INTERREGNUM	
51.	Krestodolo II	1663?-1671?
52.	Marqos V	1671?
53.	Sinoda	1671?-1693?
54.	Marqos VI	1693?-1716
	INTERREGNUM	
55.	Krestodolo III	1720-1735
	INTERREGNUM	
56.	Yohannes VI	1743-1761
57.	Salama V	1762-1770?
58.	Yusab II	1770-1803
59.	Makaryos	1804-1808?
	INTERREGNUM	
60.	Qerlos V	1815?-1828?
	INTERREGNUM	
61.	Andreyas (or Indriyas)	1841
62.	Salama VI (same as Andreyas?)	1841-1867
63.	Atnatewos	1869-1876
	INTERREGNUM	
64.	Petros IV	1881-1889

65.	Matewos	1889-1926
	INTERREGNUM	
66.	Qerlos VI	1929-1936
	Abraha [anti-abuna]	1937-1939
	Yohannes VII [anti-abuna]	1939-1941
	Qerlos VI [2nd time]	1941-1950
67.	Basilyos	1951-1970
68.	Tewoflos *Melaktu*	1971-1976
	Yohannes [locum tenens]	1976
69.	Takla Haymanot II *Wolde Mika'el*	1976-1988
70.	Merkorewos *Fenta*	1988-1991
	Zena Marqos *Bogosew* [locum tenens]	1991-1992
71.	Paulos *Gebre Yohannes*	1992-

THE CHURCH OF ERITREA

Following the declaration of Eritrean independence from Ethiopia on 24 May 1993, after a long civil war, the Church of Eritrea also separated from its mother church in September 1993, becoming an autonomous ecclesiastical body. The primate bears the title Archbishop of Asmara and All Eritrea. The principal language is Amharic. The size of the church is unknown.

SOURCES: *Europa World Yearbook*; news reports; *Orthodoxia*.

ARCHBISHOPS OF ERITREA

1.	Mika'el *Wolde Mika'el*	-1980?
2.	Gabr'el *Iyasu*	1980-1985
3.	Tadewos *Biwonegin*	1985-1988
4.	Nikodimos *Abebe*	1988-1991
5.	Filippos *Berhan*	1991-

XXXI.

THE CHURCH OF FINLAND

The autonomous Church of Finland was originally an adjunct of the Patriarchate of Russia during the years when Finland was a province of the Russian Empire. With the outbreak of the Russian Revolution in 1917, the Finns secured their independence from the Soviets, and reinforced that claim in the Second World War, in a series of battles which ultimately resulted in the ceding of much of Karelia to the Soviet Union. The vast majority of Finns belong to the Lutheran Church. The small Finnish Orthodox Church was granted autonomy by the Russians in 1921, and then sent a petition to Constantinople in 1923, requesting autocephaly. The Ecumenical Patriarch stated that the Church was too small to support autocephalous status, but granted autonomy under the aegis of Constantinople on 9 July 1923 (Moscow did not recognize the split until 1957). The Archbishop was granted the status of Metropolitan on 1 February 1972, but continues to use the former title. The Finnish Church is now self-governing in every respect, except that the consecration of a new Archbishop must include a representative of the Ecumenical Patriarch (and thus his approval).

The primate bears the title Archbishop of Karelia and all Finland. The official language of the Church is Finnish. Approximately 57,000 adherents are centered primarily in eastern Finland (Karelia), around Helsinki, the national capital, and near Kuopia.

SOURCES: *Eastern Christianity and Politics in the Twentieth Century* (Ramet, ed.); *Échos d'Orient*; *Episkepsis*; *Europa World Yearbook*; *Gegenwartslage der Ostkirchen* (Spuler); *History of the Church* (Jedin, ed.); *Jahrbuch der Orthodoxie* (Proc); *The Latvian Orthodox Church* (Cherney); *Orthodoxia*; *Profiles in Belief* (Piepkorn).

ARCHBISHOPS OF FINLAND

1.	Nikolaî	1898-1905
2.	Sergi *Stragorodskiî* [#12 of Russia]	1906-1917
3.	Seraphim *Lukianov*	1918-1924
4.	Herman *Aav(a)*	1925-1960
5.	Paavali *Olmari*	1960-1987
6.	Johannes *Rinne*	1987-

XXXII.

THE CHURCH OF GEORGIA

The ancient Kingdom of Georgia, located in the Caucasus Mountains between the Black and Caspian Seas, was an autonomous kingdom as early as the first century B.C., but did not convert to Christianity until the 4th century A.D. Its physical isolation from the West promoted the independence of its bishops and archbishops, who gradually became recognized as autonomous and finally autocephalous, in the year 1089 (however, the Church itself dates its autocephaly from the appointment by Constantinople of the first Catholicos-Archbishop, Petre I, in 467). King Giorgi XII willed his country to Russia on his death in late 1800; the Russian army promptly occupied Georgia in 1801. The last Georgian Patriarch, Anton II, who had been in secular life Prince Theimuraz, younger brother of the King, was deposed from his position in 1811, the Georgian Church being put under the authority of the Synod of the Russian Orthodox Church at Moscow. Russian exarchs governed the Georgian Orthodox Church from 1811 until the Russian Revolution of 1917, when the breakdown in governmental and ecclesiastical authority allowed the Georgian Church to re-establish its autocephaly (12 March 1917), and elect a new Patriarch, Kirion III, in September 1917; he died a year later under mysterious circumstances.

Georgia joined the Transcaucasian Republic in 1917, but proclaimed its independence as a socialist republic a year later. Soviet forces occupied Georgia in February 1921; the Georgian Soviet Socialist Republic became a constituent republic of the U.S.S.R. in 1936. With the arrival of the Soviets, persecution to limit the Church's influence on the political and social life of the Georgian people was harsh and immediate: Patriarch Ambrosi was arrested in February 1923, together with most of the Church hierarchy, and sent to prison. Following his death in March of 1927, his newly elected successor, K'ristep'ore III, moved toward support of the Soviet state, although official pressure on the Church was maintained, with parishioners being harassed and churches being closed on a continuing basis. The autocephaly of the Georgian Orthodox Apostolic Church was finally acknowledged by Moscow (and the Russian Patriarchate) on 31 October 1943. The Church gradually managed to promote its independence from government control during the post-World War II period, with many setbacks, including one rumor that Catholicos Davit' V was actually chosen for his post by the KGB.

His successor, Ilia II, was just forty-four at his election on 23 December 1977, and has revitalized the Church considerably in recent years, appointing many new bishops, reopening churches, initiating new journals and other publications, and generally exciting the interest of the Georgian youth. Under his firm tutelage, the Church of Georgia seems to have a bright future, as the country of Georgia again moves toward full independence. The Church was officially recognized as autocephalous (and the patriarchal title confirmed) by the Ecumenical Patriarch of Constantinople in early 1990. Georgia regained its independence on 25 August 1991; civil war broke out within the year, threatening the fragile unity of the new country, and conflict has continued in Abkhazia and other regions.

The official language of the church is Georgian. The primate bears the title Catholicos-Patriarch of All Georgia, Archbishop of Mtshet and Tbilisi, his chief see being the latter city. The roughly five million communicants are mostly located within the confines of the Georgian Republic.

SOURCES: *Dictionnaire de Théologie Catholique*; *Dictionnaire d'Histoire et de Géographie Ecclésiastique*; *Eastern Christianity and Politics in the Twentieth Century* (Ramet, ed.); *Échos d'Orient*; *Episkepsis*; *Europa World Yearbook*; *History of the Church* (Jedin, ed.); *Jahrbuch der Orthodoxie* (Proc); *Gegenwartslage der Ostkirchen* (Spuler); Catholicos Ilia II; *Orthodoxia*; *Profiles in Belief* (Piepkorn); *Religion in the Soviet Union* (Kolarz).

CATHOLICOS-PATRIARCHS OF GEORGIA
(Bishops 335, Catholicos-Archbishops 467, Catholicos-Patriarchs 1012)

1.	Ioane I	335-363
2.	Iakobi	363-375
3.	Iobi	375-390
4.	Elia I	390-400
5.	Svimeon I	400-410
6.	Mose	410-425
7.	Iona	425-429
8.	Ieremia	429-433
9.	Grigol I	433-434
10.	Basil I	434-436
11.	Mobidani	436-448
12.	Iovel I	448-452
13.	Mik'el I	452-467
14.	Petre I	467-474
15.	Samoel I	474-502

16.	Gabriel I	502-510
17.	T'avp'ech'agh I	510-516
18.	Ch'irmagi	516-523
19.	Saba I	523-533
20.	Evlavi	533-544
21.	Samoel II	544-553
22.	Makari	553-569
23.	Svimon II	569-575
24.	Samoel III	575-582
25.	Samoel IV	582-591
26.	Bart'lome	591-595
27.	Kirion I (or Svimon Petre)	595-610
28.	Ioan II	610-619
29.	Babila	619-629
30.	T'abori	629-634
31.	Samoel V	634-640
32.	Evnoni	640-649
33.	T'avp'ech'agh II	649-664
34.	Evlale	664-668
35.	Ioveli II	668-670
36.	Samoel VI	670-677
37.	Giorgi I	677-678
38.	Kirion II	678-683
39.	Izid-Bozidi	683-685
40.	T'eodore I	685-689
41.	Petre II	689-720
42.	T'alale	720-731
43.	Mamai	731-744
44.	Ioane III	744-760
45.	Grigol II	760-767
46.	Sarmeane	767-774
47.	Mik'el II	774-780
48.	Samoel VII	780-790
49.	Kirile I	791-802
50.	Grigol III	802-814
51.	Samoel VIII	814-826
52.	Giorgi II	826-838
53.	Gabriel II	838-860
54.	Arsen I	860-887
55.	Evsuk'i	887-908
56.	Klimentos	908-914
57.	Basil II	914-930
58.	Mik'el III	930-944
59.	Davit' I	944-955
60.	Arsen II	955-980
61.	Ok'ropir I	980-1001

62.	Svimon III	1001-1012
63.	Melk'isedek I	1012-1045
64.	Ok'ropir II	1045-1049
65.	Ek'vt'ime I	1049-1055
66.	Giorgi III	1055-1065
67.	Gabriel III	1065-1080
68.	Dimitri	1080-1090
69.	Basil III	1090-1100
70.	Ioane IV	1100-1142
71.	Svimeon IV	1142-1146
72.	Saba II	1146-1150
73.	Nikoloz I	1150-1178
74.	Mik'el IV	1178-1186
75.	T'eodore II	1186-1206
76.	Basili IV	1206-1208
77.	Ioane V	1208-1210
78.	Epip'ane	1210-1220
79.	Ek'vt'ime II	1220-1222
80.	Arsen III	1222-1225
81.	Giorgi IV	1225-1230
82.	Arsen IV	1230-1240
83.	Nikoloz II	1240-1280
84.	Abram I	1280-1310
85.	Ek'vt'ime III	1310-1325
86.	Mik'el V	1325-1330
87.	Basil V	1330-1350
88.	Dorot'eoz I	1350-1356
89.	Shio I	1356-1364
90.	Nikoloz III	1364-1380
91.	Giorgi V	1380-1397
92.	Eliozi	1399-1411
93.	Mik'el VI	1411-1426
94.	Davit' II	1426-1430
95.	T'eodore III	1430-1435
96.	Davit' III	1435-1439
97.	Shio II	1440-1443
	Davit' III [2nd time]	1443-1459
98.	Markozi	1460-1466
99.	Davit' IV	1466-1479
100.	Evagre	1480-1492
101.	Abram II	1492-1497
102.	Ep'rem I	1497-1500
	Evagre [2nd time]	1500-1503
103.	Dorot'eos II	1503-1510
104.	Dionise	1510-1511
	Dorot'eos II [2nd time]	1511-1516

105.	Basil VI	1517-1528
106.	Malak'ia	1528-1538
107.	Melk'isedek II	1538-1541
108.	Germane	1541-1547
109.	Svimon V	1547-1550
110.	Zebede I	1550-1557
	INTERREGNUM	
111.	Nikoloz IV	1562-1584
112.	Nikoloz V	1584-1591
113.	Dorot'eoz III	1592-1599
114.	Domenti I	1599-1603
115.	Zebede II	1603-1610
116.	Ioane VI	1610-1613
	INTERREGNUM	
117.	K'ristep'ore I	1616-1622
118.	Zak'aria	1623-1630
119.	Evdemoz I	1630-1637
120.	K'ristep'ore II	1638-1660
121.	Domenti II	1660-1676
122.	Nikoloz VI	1678-1688
123.	Ioane VII	1688-1691
	Nikoloz VI [2nd time]	1691-1696
	Ioane VII [2nd time]	1696-1700
124.	Evdemoz II	1701-1705
125.	Domenti III	1705-1725
126.	Besarioni	1725-1737
127.	Kirile II	1737-1739
	Domenti III [2nd time]	1739-1741
128.	Nikoloz VII	1741-1744
129.	Anton I	1744-1755
130.	Iosebi	1755-1764
	Anton I [2nd time]	1764-1788
131.	Anton II (Teymuraz) *Bagrationi*	1788-1811
	INTERREGNUM	

RUSSIAN EXARCHS OF GEORGIA

1.	Varlaam *Eristavi*	1811-1817
2.	Feofilakt *Rusanov*	1817-1821
3.	Iona *Vasil'evskiî*	1821-1832
4.	Moiseî *Bogdanov-Platonov*	1832-1834
5.	Evgeniî *Baenov*	1834-1844
6.	Isidor *Nikolskiî*	1844-1858
7.	Evsebiî *Ilinskiî*	1858-1877
8.	Ioannikiî *Rudnev* [#32 of Russia]	1877-1882
9.	Pavel *Lebedev*	1882-1887

THE CHURCH OF GEORGIA

10.	Palladiî *Raev*	1887-1892
11.	Vladimir *Bogoiavlens'kyî* [#79 of Ukraine]	1892-1898
12.	Flavian *Gorodetskiî*	1898-1903
13.	Aleksandr *Opotskiî*	1903-1905
14.	Nikolaî	1905-1906
15.	Nikon *Sofiîskiî*	1906-1908
16.	Innokentiî	1910-1913
17.	Aleksiî	1913-1917

CATHOLICOS-PATRIARCHS OF GEORGIA

	Leonide *Okropiridze* [locum tenens]	1917
132.	Kirion(i) III *Sadzaglishvili* (or *Sagzagelidze*)	1917-1918
133.	Leonide *Okropiridze* (or *Okroperidze*)	1918-1921
134.	Ambrosi *K'elava* (or *K'elaia* or *Kelaya*)	1921-1927
	INTERREGNUM	
	Kalistrate *Tsintsadze* [locum tenens]	1924-1927
135.	K'ristep'ore III *Tsitskishvili*	1927-1932
136.	Kalistrate *Tsintsadze*	1932-1952
137.	Melk'isedek III *Pk'aladze*	1952-1960
138.	Ep'rem II *Sidamonidze* [cousin of #133]	1960-1972
139.	Davit' V *Devdariani*	1972-1977
140.	Ilia II *Shiolashvili*	1977-

THE GEORGIAN CHURCH OF ABKHAZIA

The independent Church of Abkhazia developed in the kingdom of the same name, and was extinguished with the Russian occupation in the late eighteenth and early nineteenth centuries. Records of the primates of this church are fragmentary. Both lists are adapted from the official records of the Patriarchate of Georgia at Tbilisi.

CATHOLICOS-PATRIARCHS OF ABKHAZIA

1.	Nikoloz	1290?
2.	Danieli	1375?
3.	Arseni	1390
4.	Ioane	1455-1474
5.	Step'ane	1470-1516
	INTERREGNUM	
6.	Malak'ia I	1529-1532
	INTERREGNUM	
7.	Evdemoz I	1557-1578
8.	Ek'vt'ime I	1578-1605
	INTERREGNUM	
9.	Grigol I	1612-1616?

145

10.	Malak'ia II	1616-1639
11.	Mak'sime I	1639-1657
12.	Zak'aria	1657-1660
13.	Svimon	1660-1666
14.	Evdemoz II	1666-1669
15.	Ek'vt'ime II	1669-1673
16.	Davit'i	1673-1696
17.	Grigoli II	1696-1742
18.	Germane	1742-1750?

INTERREGNUM

19.	Besarioni	1755-1769
20.	Iosebi	1769-1776
21.	Mak'sime II	1776-1795

THE CATHOLICOSATE DISCONTINUED

XXXIII.

THE CHURCH OF GREECE

The history of the Orthodox Church of Greece is closely tied to the Greek War of Independence in the early nineteenth century. Many of the clergy had supported the revolutionaries, so it was natural that they should demand ecclesiastical reforms once independence had been won. At two national assemblies, in 1821 and 1829, they pressed the issue, and on 15 July 1833 King Othón promulgated a charter of autocephaly. The Patriarch of Constantinople refused to acknowledge the break until 1850. When subsequent events added territory to the kingdom, these areas were absorbed into the Church as well, making it among the largest national Orthodox churches in the world today in population. Beginning in 1917, the government followed a consistent pattern of interference in Church affairs, often deposing or appointing Archbishops virtually at will.   Thus, following the military *coup d'état* of 1967, Chrysostomos II was forced to resign, and Hierónymos took his place; the latter then resigned when the generals were overthrown in 1973, and Archbishop Serapheim took his place. The democratic government which assumed power in 1974 has left the Church in relative peace, and Serapheim has enjoyed a stable reign, the longest of any Greek primate in the twentieth century.

The primate bears the title Archbishop of Athens and All Greece. The official Church language is Greek. Roughly nine million members are located primarily within the confines of the Greek Republic.

SOURCES: *Dictionnaire d'Histoire et de Géographie Ecclésiastiques*; *Eastern Christianity and Politics in the Twentieth Century* (Ramet); *Échos d'Orient*; *Episkepsis*; *Episkopikoi Katalogoi Hellados* (Basileios); *Europa World Yearbook*; *Gegenwartslage der Ostkirchen* (Spuler); *Historia tés Ekklésias Hellados* (Papadopoulos); *History of the Church* (Jedin, ed.); *Jahrbuch der Orthodoxie* (Proc); *The Orthodox Church and Independent Greece, 1821-1852* (Frazee); *Orthodoxia*.

ARCHBISHOPS OF GREECE

1.	Dionysios I *Areopagités*	93?
2.	Narkissos	117-138

147

3.	Pouplios (Publius)	161-180
4.	Kodratos (Quadratus)	200?
5.	Leónidés	250?
6.	Olympios	300?
7.	Pistos	325?
8.	Klématios	400?
9.	Modestos	431?
10.	Athanasios I	451-458
11.	Anatolios	459?
12.	Ióannés I	550?
13.	Grégorios I	600?
14.	Ióannés II	680?
15.	Andreas	692-693?
16.	Theocharistos	694-702
17.	Marinos	702-704
18.	Ióannés III	704-714
19.	Grégorios II	780?
20.	Theodosios I	800?
21.	Adamantios	810?
22.	Ióannés IV	810-819
23.	Theodosios II	820?
24.	Hypatios	827?
25.	Démétrios I	835?
26.	Germanos I	-841
	INTERREGNUM	
27.	Démétrios II	846-857
28.	Gabriél I	858-860
29.	Grégorios III	860-867
30.	Kosmas I	867
31.	Nikétas I	867-877
32.	Sabbas I	877-880
33.	Anastasios	880-889
34.	Sabbas II	889-914
35.	Geórgios I	914-922
36.	Nikétas II	922-927
37.	Kónstantinos	965?
38.	Philippos	981?
39.	Theodégios	985-1007
40.	Michaél I	1007-1030
41.	León I *Synkellos*	1054?-1061?
42.	León II *Synkellos*	1061?-1069?
43.	Ióannés V *Blachernités*	1069-1087
44.	Nikétas III *Kourtés*	1086-1103
45.	Niképhoros	1103-1121
46.	Gerasimos	1127?
47.	Michaél II	1133?

48.	Theophylaktos	1140?
49.	Geórgios II	1145-1160
	INTERREGNUM	
50.	Nikétas IV (or Nikolaos) *Hagiotheodórités*	1166-1175
51.	Geórgios III *Xéros*	1175-1179
52.	Geórgios IV *Bourtzés*	1180
53.	Ióannés VI	1180-1181
54.	Michaél III *Akominatos Chóniatés*	1182-1222
	INTERREGNUM	
55.	Meletios I	1275-1289
56.	Lazaros *apo Sina*	1300?
57.	Kosmas II	1339
58.	Anthimos I *Homologétés* [#43 of Crete]	1339-1366
59.	Neophytos I	1366
60.	Nikodémos	1371?
61.	name unknown	1380?
62.	Dórotheos I	1387-1393?
63.	Makarios I	1394-1404
64.	Gerbasios I	1432?
65.	Theodóros	1438-1453?
66.	Isidóros	1456?
67.	Theophanés I	1458?
68.	Gerbasios II	1462?
68.	name unknown	1465?-1466?
70.	Dórotheos II	-1472
71.	Anthimos II	1489?
72.	Neophytos II	1492-1498
	INTERREGNUM	
73.	Laurentios	1528-1550
74.	Kallistos	1550-1564
75.	Sóphronios I	1565-1570
76.	Nikanór	1570-1592
77.	Theophanés II *Karykés* [#183 of Constantinople]	1592-1597
78.	Neophytos III *Karykés* [#185 of Constantinople]	1597-1602
79.	Samouél *Primpetos*	1602
80.	Nathanaél *Emporos*	1602-1604
81.	Anthimos III *apo Naupliou kai Argous*	1604-1610
82.	Kyrillos I	-1611
83.	Métrophanés	-1619
84.	Theophanés III	1620-1633
85.	Sóphronios II	1633-1636
86.	Daniél *apo Talantiou*	1636-1655
87.	Anthimos IV *apo Talantiou*	1655-1676
88.	Iakóbos I *apo Mytilénés*	1676-1686
89.	Athanasios II	1686-1689
90.	Makarios II *Pelekanos*	1689-1693

149

91.	Anthimos V	1693-1699
92.	Kyrillos II	1699-1703
93.	Meletios II *Métrou apo Naupaktou kai Artés*	1703-1713
94.	Iakóbos II	1713-1734
95.	Zacharias	1734-1741
96.	Anthimos VI	1741-1756
97.	Athanasios III	1756-1760
	Anthimos VI [2nd time]	1760-1764
98.	Bartholomaios *apo Drystras*	1764-1780
99.	Neophytos IV	1774-1776
100.	Gabriél II	1781
101.	Benediktos *apo Pisidias*	1781-1785
102.	Athanasios IV *Taklikartés* (or *T[s]alikarés*)	1785-1787
	Benediktos [2nd time]	1787-1796
	Athanasios IV [2nd time]	1796-1799
103.	Grégorios IV	1799-1820
104.	Dionysios II	1820-1823
105.	Grégorios V *Argyrokastrités apo Euripou*	1827-1828
106.	Anthimos VII *apo Artés*	1828-1830

INTERREGNUM

107.	Neophytos V *Metaxas apo Talantiou*	1833-1861
108.	Misaél *Apostolidés*	1862
109.	Theophilos *Blachopapadopoulos*	1862-1873
110.	Prokopios I *Geórgiadés*	1874-1889
111.	Germanos II *Kalligas*	1889-1896
112.	Prokopios II *Oikonomidés*	1896-1901
113.	Theoklétos I *Ménopoulos*	1902-1917
114.	Meletios III *Metaxakés* [#111 of Alexandria; #262 of Constantinople]	1918-1920
	Theoklétos I *Ménopoulos* [2nd time]	1920-1922
115.	Chrysostomos I *Papadopoulos*	1923-1938
116.	Damaskénos *Papandreou*	1938
117.	Chrysanthos *Philippidés*	1938-1941
	Damaskénos *Papandreou* [2nd time]	1941-1949
118.	Spyridón *Blachos*	1949-1956
119.	Dórotheos III *Kottaras*	1956-1957
120.	Theoklétos II *Panagiótopoulos*	1957-1962
121.	Iakóbos III *Babanatsos*	1962
122.	Chrysostomos II *Chatzéstaurou*	1962-1967
123.	Hierónymos *Kotsónés*	1967-1973
124.	Serapheim *Tikas*	1974-

XXXV.

THE CHURCHES OF INDIA

The St. Thomas Christians are located primarily in Kerala, along the southwest coast of India. According to legend, some of the natives were converted by St. Thomas the Apostle in the decades following the death of Christ; real historical evidence is scarce, however, until the coming of European missionaries in the sixteenth century, when a flourishing Eastern Church was found. The existing communities were governed by bishops appointed by the Catholicos-Patriarch of Assyria (East Syria); when Roman Catholic missionaries began making inroads into the established churches, some of the local parishes, feeling strong local leadership was needed to resist this threat, revolted against their Patriarch, and on 22 May 1643 consecrated one of their archdeacons as Metropolitan, under the title Mar Thoma I. Thus begins the independent existence of the Syrian churches of Malabar.

From the first the churches were plagued by schisms and disputes, a trend which continues to this day. Succession was often hereditary, from brother to brother or uncle to nephew; thus, Mar Thoma I was followed by his brother, Mar Thoma II, also a member of the Pakalomarram family. Since the original Mar Thoma was consecrated only by a laying-on of hands, and not by two other bishops, his successors have striven through the centuries to obtain recognition either from Rome or from the West Syrian Patriarch of Antioch. Mar Thoma VI approached both Churches, offering to join either if new bishops were sent to India; the Jacobite Patriarch was the first to respond, sending three prelates in the late 1760s; Mar Thoma was reconsecrated in 1772, taking the new name of Dionysios I. Consecrated with him was Mar Koorilose, whom Dionysios feared as a potential rival. He promptly exiled Koorilose to Thozhiyoor (Toliyur), where the latter founded the first of the splinter churches, which has continued to this day; it remains the smallest of the Malabar Orthodox groups. Curiously, the Church of Toliyur eventually developed during the nineteenth century a kind of symbiotic relationship with the Mar Thoma family, each line providing properly-consecrated bishops for the other when their respective sees fell vacant.

By the mid-nineteenth century, dissidents in the Mar Thoma Church had begun pressing for reforms in the liturgy and clergy. They placed their hopes on Mathews Mar Athanasios, who was consecrated bishop by the West Syrian patriarch in 1843. After a period of struggle, Mar Dionysios IV was forced to retire, and Mar Athanasios was recognized as sole Metropolitan of the Malabar Church. But a dissident priest, Joseph, was consecrated as Mar Dionysios V in 1865, causing a new split, each Metropolitan claiming to be the rightful heir to the church properties. Ultimately, the secular courts of Travancore State ruled in favor of Athanasios. This did not end the controversy, however, for Dionysios then appealed to the Syrian patriarch, Ighnatiyus Butrus IV, to adjudicate the argument in person; this he did in 1875, excommunicating Athanasios and proclaiming Dionysios the only true leader of the Malabar Church. The result of these difficulties was an increasing polarization of the Malankara communities, a further split in the churches, and the establishment of an unfortunate precedent whereby ecclesiastical disputes would now be settled by the temporal authorities.

The price of Dionysios's recognition as head of the Syrian Church in Malabar was his acknowledgement of the supremacy of the West Syrian patriarch, whose aid he had sought. When Dionysios V died in 1909, the Syrian Patriarch consecrated Geevarghese Dionysios VI in his place. Later that year the new Syrian Patriarch (Ighnatiyus 'Abd Allah II), came to India, where he became embroiled in a jurisdictional dispute with his supposed agent. 'Abd Allah excommunicated Dionysios in 1911, and appointed Mar Koorilose the new Metropolitan. Dionysios refused to accept the Patriarch's actions, and each side again went to court. The matter was further complicated by the arrival in 1912 of ex-Syrian Patriarch Ighnatiyus 'Abd al-Masih II, who immediately consecrated Paulose Mar Ivanios as Catholicos of Malankara, thus in effect creating (with the best of intentions) a third church. When Dionysios died in 1934, the Catholicos was named his successor, thereby reducing the churches to two factions, one supporting the Syrian patriarch, one claiming ecclesiastical independence.

The split was finally healed in 1958, and reinforced with the installation of Baselios Mar Augen I as Catholicos in 1964; Syrian Patriarch Ighnatiyus Afram I travelled to India to participate in the ceremony. Ten years later, the dispute flared anew, with Augen claiming equality with his Syrian counterpart. Augen was suspended by Afram from his ecclesiastical functions, an action Augen angrily refused to recognize. Augen died at an advanced age a few months later, in 1975. At his death, the Syrian Patriarch appointed Paulose Mar Philoksenos the new Catholicos, even though Mathews Mar Athanasios had already been named Augen's designated successor. Once more the churches went to court.

The autocephalous Malankara Orthodox Syrian Church is located at Kottayam, Kerala; its primate uses the title Catholicos of Malankara. Approximately 1.6 million communicants are located primarily in southwestern India, with a few members overseas (mostly in the United States). The autonomous Malankara Jacobite Syrian Church is located at Moovattupuzha, Kerala; its primate bears the title Catholicos Metropolitan of Malabar, and acknowledges the supremacy of the Syrian Patriarch of Antioch, to which it contributes about half (1.5 million) of that church's three million communicants.

SOURCES: *Catholicate Sapthathi Souvenir*; *Eastern Christianity in India* (Tisserant); *Eastern Churches Review*; *Gegenwartslage der Ostkirchen* (Spuler); *History of the Church* (Jedin, ed.); *The Indian Christians of St Thomas* (Brown); *The Malabar Church and Other Orthodox Churches* (Daniel); *The Orthodox Church of India* (Daniel); *Orthodoxia*; *Profiles in Belief* (Piepkorn); *The St. Thomas Christian Encyclopedia of India* (Menachery); *The Syrian Christians of Kerala* (Pothan); *The Syrian Church of Malabar* (Daniel); *Die Syrischen Kirchen in Indien* (Verghese); *The Thomas Christians* (Podipara); Bishop Thomas Mar Makarios (personal communication).

METRANS OF THE MALANKARA SYRIAN CHURCH
(Bishops 1665 and 1772, Metrans 1876)

1.	Mar Thoma I *Pakalomarram*	1652-1670
	Mar Gregorios (I)	1665-1672
2.	Mar Thoma II [nephew of #1]	1670-1686
	Mar Thoma	1674
	Mar Baselios (I)	1685
	Mar Yuhanna	1685-1693
3.	Mar Thoma III	1686-1688
4.	Mar Thoma IV	1688-1728
5.	Mar Thoma V	1728-1765
	Mar Baselios (II)	1751-1763
	Mar Gregorios (II)	1751-1772
	Mar Ivanios	1751-1794
6.	Mar Thoma VI [suffragan 1761; nephew of #5]	1765-1772
	[under the title Mar Dionysios I]:	1772-1808
7.	Mathew Mar Thoma VII [suffragan 1796; nephew of #6]	1808-1809
8.	Mar Thoma VIII [suffragan 1806]	1809-1816
9.	Pulikkottil Mar Dionysios II	1815-1816
10.	Mar Thoma IX [uncle of #8]	1816
11.	Geevarghese Mar Phileksinose [#4 of Thozhiyoor]	1816-1817
12.	Punnathra Mar Dionysios III *Ittoop*	1817-1825
	Geevarghese Mar Phileksinose [2nd time]	1825-1829
13.	Cheepat Mar Dionysios IV *Kattanar*	1829-1852
14.	Yoyakin Mar Koorilose (or Yoakim) [rival]	1846-1852
15.	Mathews Mar Athanasios *Palakunnath* [suffragan 1842; #1 of Mar Thoma]	1852-1875

16.	Joseph Mar Dionysios V *Putikkottil*	1865-1909
17.	Geevarghese Mar Dionysios VI *Vattasseril* [suffragan 1908]	1909-1934

MERGED WITH THE MALANKARA ORTHODOX SYRIAN CHURCH

CATHOLICOSES OF THE EAST AND MALANKARA METROPOLITANS (MALANKARA ORTHODOX SYRIAN CHURCH)

1.	Thomas I	35-72
2.	Addai	72-120
3.	Aggai	120-152
4.	Mari	152-185
5.	Abrosios	185-201
6.	Abraham I	201-213
7.	Yakoub	213-231
8.	Ahod Abuci	231-246
9.	Shahluppa	246-266
10.	Pappa	267-336
11.	Simun I *Bar Sheba*	337-350
12.	Shahoudoth	350-352
13.	Bar Bosomin	352-360
14.	Thomuso	360-368
15.	Quoyumo	370-375
16.	Ishaq	375-386
17.	Oah	386-393
18.	Yahb Allaho	393-398
19.	Magina	398-400
20.	Merbukhat	401-420
21.	Daudesh	421-456
22.	Babuyah	457-484
23.	Acasios	485-498
24.	Babi	499-502
25.	Shilo	502-504
26.	Elisho	504-536
27.	Paulose I	537-539
28.	Aabo	540-552
29.	Joseph I	552-556
	INTERREGNUM	
30.	Ahoudemme	559-577
31.	Qoum Yesu	578-579
	INTERREGNUM	
32.	Samuel	614-624
	INTERREGNUM	
33.	Morooso	628-649
34.	Denha I	650-659

INTERREGNUM

35.	Bar Yesu	669-684
36.	Abraham II	686-687
37.	David	687
38.	Youhanon I *Soubo*	687-688
39.	Denha II	688-728
40.	Paulose II	728-757
41.	Youhanon II *Keeyunoyo*	758-788
42.	Joseph II	789-793
43.	Sharbeel	794-810
44.	Simun II	812-828
45.	Baselios I *Bar Baldoyo*	828-838
46.	Daniel	838-847
47.	Thoma II *of Tigris*	848-856
48.	Lo Asar	856-869

INTERREGNUM

49.	Sargis	872-883

INTERREGNUM

50.	Athanasios I	887-904

INTERREGNUM

51.	Thoma III *Asthunoro*	912-913
52.	Denha III	915-935

INTERREGNUM

53.	Baselios II	938-962
54.	Kooriakose	964-982

INTERREGNUM

55.	Youhanan III *Damascus*	991-997
56.	Ignatios I *Barkiki*	997-1022

INTERREGNUM

57.	Athanasios II *of Edessa*	1027-1041

INTERREGNUM

58.	Baselios III *of Tigris*	1046-1069

INTERREGNUM

59.	Youhanan IV *Sleeba*	1075-1106

INTERREGNUM

60.	Dionysios I *Moosa*	1112-1142
61.	Ignatios II *Lo Asar*	1143-1164
62.	Youhanan V *Srugayo*	1165-1188
63.	Dionysios II *Bar Msah*	1188-1204
64.	Gregorios I *Yakoub*	1204-1215
65.	Ignatios III *David*	1215-1222
66.	Dionysios III *Sleeba*	1222-1231
67.	Youhanan VI *Bar Madan*	1232-1253
68.	Ignatios IV *Sleeba of Edessa*	1253-1258

INTERREGNUM

69.	Gregorios II *Bar Hebraeus*	1266-1286

	INTERREGNUM	
70.	Gregorios III *Bar Sauma*	1289-1308
	INTERREGNUM	
71.	Gregorios IV *Mathai*	1317-1360
	INTERREGNUM	
72.	Athanasios Mar Abraham III	1365-1379
	INTERREGNUM	
73.	Baselios Mar Bahnam I	1404-1412
	INTERREGNUM	
74.	Dioscoros Mar Bahnam II	1415-1417
	INTERREGNUM	
75.	Baselios Mar Barsauma	1422-1455
	INTERREGNUM	
76.	Baselios Mar Asiz	1471-1487
	INTERREGNUM	
77.	Ignatios Mar Nuh *of Homs* [#115 of Syrian Orthodox Church of Antioch]	1490-1494
78.	Baselios Mar Abraham IV	1494-1496
	INTERREGNUM	
79.	Baselios IV	1560-1589
	INTERREGNUM	
80.	Baselios Mar Yalda	1634-1685
	INTERREGNUM	
81.	Baselios Mar Shakrulla	1751-1764
	INTERREGNUM	
82.	Baselios Mar Elias	1838-1840
	INTERREGNUM	
83.	Baselios Mar Bahnam III	1850-1860
	INTERREGNUM	
84.	Baselios Mar Paulose I (or III) *Kathanar*	1912-1914
	INTERREGNUM	
	Geevarghese Mar Dionysios VI [administrator]	1914-1925
85.	Baselios Mar Geevarghese I *Karnchira*	1925-1928
	Geevarghese Mar Dionysios VI [2nd time]	1928-1929
86.	Baselios Mar Geevarghese II *Kallacheril*	1929-1964
87.	Baselios Mar Augen (or Ougen) *Turuthi* [suffragan 1962]	1964-1975
88.	Baselios Mar Thoma Mathews I *Vattakunnel* [suffragan 1970]	1975-1991
89.	Baselios Mar Thoma Mathews II [suffragan 1980] Thomas Mar Timotheos [suffragan 1992]	1991-

CATHOLICOS-METROPOLITANS OF THE
MALANKARA JACOBITE SYRIAN CHURCH
(Under the Syrian "Jacobite" Church of Antioch)

84.	Paulose Mar Koorilose	1911-1917
	INTERREGNUM	
	Paulose Mar Athanasios [locum tenens]	1917-1935
85.	Paulose Mar Athanasios	1935-1953
	INTERREGNUM	
86.	Abraham Mar Climis	1957-1958
87.	Baselios Mar Geevarghese *Kallacheril*	1958-1964
88.	Baselios Mar Augen (or Ougen) *Turuthi*	1964-1975
89.	Baselios Mar Paulose II	1975-

THE MALANKARA MAR THOMA SYRIAN CHURCH

On the death of Mathews Mar Athanasios, Metran of the Malankara Syrian Church, in 1877, he was succeeded by Thomas Mar Athanasios, who lost control over most of his parishes and church buildings in a series of lawsuits filed during his sixteen-year reign by rival Metran Dionysios V. Subsequently, his movement was renamed the Malankara Mar Thoma Syrian Church, and gradually absorbed elements of both Anglicanism and evangelism, as new parishes were established and reforms effected. It remains today the most Protestant of all the Malabar Syrian churches. At the death or resignation of the primate, the most senior bishop automatically succeeds. The official language of the Church (and of its brother churches) is Malayalam. The primate, who since Titos I has always taken the additional surname Mar Thoma, bears the title Metropolitan (Metran), and resides at Tiruvalla, Kerala. Roughly 700,000 communicants are located mostly in southwestern India.

SOURCES: *Eastern Christianity in India* (Tisserant); *Europa World Yearbook*; *History of the Church* (Jedin, ed.); *The Indian Christians of St Thomas* (Brown); *The Malabar Church and Other Orthodox Churches* (Daniel); *The Malabar Independent Syrian Church* (Fenwick); *The Orthodox Church of India* (Daniel); *The St. Thomas Christian Encyclopedia of India*; *The Syrian Church of Malabar* (Daniel).

METRANS OF THE MAR THOMA SYRIAN CHURCH

1.	Mathews Mar Athanasios *Palakunnath* [#16 of Malankara]	1843-1877
2.	Thomas Mar Athanasios [suffragan 1868; cousin of #1]	1877-1893
3.	Titos I *Mar Thoma*	1894-1910

4.	Titos II *Mar Thoma* [suffragan 1899]	1910-1944
5.	Abraham *Mar Thoma* [suffragan 1917]	1944-1947
6.	Juhanon *Mar Thoma* [suffragan 1937]	1947-1976
7.	Aleksander *Mar Thoma* [suffragan 1954]	1976-
	Philipose Mar Chrysostom [suffragan]	
	Thomas Mar Athanasios [suffragan 1982]	

THE CHALDEAN SYRIAN (MELLUSIAN) CHURCH
(Under the Jurisdiction of The Church of the East)

The Chaldean Syrian Church, which patterns some of its liturgy after the Assyrian (East Syrian) Church, originally acknowledged the supremacy of the Catholic Chaldean Patriarchate of Babylon. The church switched allegiance to the Church of the East in the 1890s, when Mar Abdisho made himself an autonomous Metropolitan. Mar Thoma Darmo, who had for years opposed the principle of heredity succession used by the Assyrian Church, was elected Patriarch of an anti-Shim'un faction in 1968; his successor in India, Mar Aprem, continues to acknowledge Darmo's church as paramount. The church's headquarters are located at Trichur, Kerala, where most of the church's 15,000 communicants reside.

SOURCES: *Eastern Christianity in India* (Tisserant); *History of the Church* (Jedin, ed.); *The Indian Christians of St Thomas* (Brown); *The Malabar Church and Other Orthodox Churches* (Daniel); *The Orthodox Church of India* (Daniel); *The St. Thomas Christian Encyclopedia of India*; *The Syrian Church of Malabar* (Daniel).

METROPOLITANS OF THE CHALDEAN SYRIAN CHURCH

1.	Yusip I *of Edessa*	345?
2.	T'uma I	795?-824?
3.	Sabrishu'	880?
4.	Piruz	880?
5.	Yukhannan I	1000?
6.	T'uma II	1056?
7.	Yukhannan II	1110?
8.	Yukhannan III	1122?-1129?
9.	Yusip II	1231
10.	Da'ud	1285?
11.	Pulus	1295?
12.	Ya'qub I	1328?
13.	Yabhalaha I	1407?
14.	T'uma III	1490?
15.	Yukhannan IV	1490?
16.	Yabhalaha II	1503?
17.	Dinkha	1503?

18.	Ya'qub II	1503-1549?
19.	Yusip III	1556-1569
20.	Abraham	1568-1597
	INTERREGNUM	
21.	Mar Thoma (IV) *Rocos*	1861-1862
22.	Mar Abdisho *Thondanatta*	1864-1874
23.	Mar Yohannon (V) Elia *Mellus*	1874-1882
	Mar Abdisho *Thondanatta* [2nd time]	1882-1900
24.	Mar Michael *Augustine*	1900-1911
25.	Mar Abimaleck *Timotheus*	1908-1945
	INTERREGNUM	
	Poulos *Konikara* [locum tenens]	1945-1952
26.	Mar Thoma (V) *Darmo* [#1 of Church of the East]	1952-1968
27.	Mar Aprem	1968-

THE MALABAR INDEPENDENT SYRIAN CHURCH OF THOZHIYOOR (TOLIYUR)

The small Independent Syrian Church of Thozhiyoor was founded in 1772 by Mar Koorilose, who fled from Mar Dionysios I, and has maintained itself as a small independent church body ever since. Since the Church usually supports only one or two bishops at a time, when the Metropolitan dies or resigns with an appointed heir, the new primate is elected by representatives of each of the congregations from a list of eligible priests, and the candidate is then consecrated by the Metran of the Malankara Mar Thoma Syrian Church. As is often the case with the other Keralan churches, a successor may be chosen before the death of the previous occupant of the Metropolitan office, and consecrated by both the old Metropolitan and the Metran; two of these suffragans did not live long enough to become undisputed Metropolitan. In 1977 Paulose Mar Phileksinose III joined the Catholic Church, taking some of his communicants with him, and resigned without leaving a successor. The chief see is located in Thozhiyoor, where most of the roughly 10,000 communicants live. The language of the Church is Malayalam. The primate bears the title Metropolitan of Thozhiyoor.

SOURCES: *Eastern Christianity in India* (Tisserant); *History of the Church* (Jedin, ed.); *The Indian Christians of St Thomas* (Brown); *The Malabar Church and Other Orthodox Churches* (Daniel); *The Malabar Independent Syrian Church* (Fenwick; regarded as official by the Church); *The Orthodox Church of India* (Daniel); *The St. Thomas Christian Encyclopedia of India*; *The Syrian Church of Malabar* (Daniel).

METROPOLITANS OF THE MALABAR INDEPENDENT SYRIAN CHURCH OF THOZHIYOOR

1. Abraham Mar Koorilose I *Kattumangat*   1771-1802
2. Geevarghese Mar Koorilose II [brother of #1;
   suffragan 1794]   1802-1808
   Joseph Mar Ivanios *Kasseesa* [suffragan]   1807
3. Skaria Mar Phileksinose I *Kasseesa* [suffragan 1807] 1808-1811
4. Geevarghese Mar Phileksinose II [#11 of Malankara
   Syrian Church]   1811-1829
5. Geevarghese Mar Koorilose III *Koothoor*   1829-1856
6. Joseph Mar Koorilose IV *Kasseesa*   1856-1888
7. Joseph Mar Athanasios I [suffragan 1883]   1888-1898
8. Geevarghese Mar Koorilose V *Pulikottil* [suffragan
   1892]   1898-1935
   Paulose Mar Athanasios II *Panakal* [suffragan]   1917-1927
9. Kooriakose Mar Koorilose VI   1936-1947
10. Geevarghese Mar Koorilose VII *Kasseesa*   1948-1967
11. Paulose Mar Phileksinose III [suffragan 1967]   1967-1977
12. Mathews Mar Koorilose VIII   1978-1986
13. Joseph Mar Koorilose IX *Panakal* [suffragan 1981]   1986-

XXXV.

THE CHURCH OF JAPAN

The autonomous Church of Japan was an adjunct for many years of the Patriarchate of Moscow and All Russia; following World War II, the Church split into two factions, one supported by Moscow, the other by the former Russian Archdiocese of North America. Both churches were given independence from Moscow on the same day in 1970, and merged into one small Church; the Russian-consecrated bishop returned to the Soviet Union. Although the autonomous Japanese Church remains too small to consecrate its own primates, native-born Archbishop Theodosius assumed authority over the Church on 19 March 1972.

The primate bears the title Archbishop of Tokyo, Primate and Metropolitan of All Japan. The official language of the Holy Orthodox Church of Japan is Japanese. Roughly 25,000 communicants are spread throughout Japan, concentrated in the major cities.

SOURCES: *Europa World Yearbook*; *Gegenwartslage der Ostkirchen* (Spuler); *History of the Church* (Jedin, ed.); "Holy Orthodox Church" (Onami); *Jahrbuch der Orthodoxie* (Proc); *Orthodoxia*.

METROPOLITAN ARCHBISHOPS OF JAPAN

1.	Nikolaî I *Kassatkin*	1880-1912
2.	Sergiî *Tykhomirov*	1912-1940
	Arsen *Tsakawa* [locum tenens]	1940-1941
3.	Nikolaî II *Ono*	1941-1967?
4.	Nikolaî III *Sayama*	1967-1970
	MERGED WITH THE AUTONOMOUS CHURCH	

AMERICAN JURISDICTION

4.	Veniamin *Babalich* (or *Bassalyga*)	1946-1953
5.	Ireney *Bekish* [#15 of America]	1953-1960
6.	Nikon *de Greve*	1960-1962
7.	Amvrosiî	1962
8.	Vladimir *Nagoskiî*	1962-1972
9.	Theodosius *Nagashima*	1972-

XXXVI.

THE ARMENIAN CHURCH OF JERUSALEM

The Armenian Church of Jerusalem has traditionally claimed the title of Patriarch since the year 638, as the keeper of the sacred sites of Palestine. It does not appear to have been recognized elsewhere, however, until 1311, when the Patriarch Sargis obtained permission from the Mamluk Sultan to assume the title. It was then regranted by the Armenian Patriarch of Constantinople about 1720. The Church acknowledges the supremacy of Echmiadzin, which ordains new bishops and prepares new chrism. Its territory includes Israel and Jordan, and a small overseas contingent in California. On 20 March 1957 Tiran Nersoyan (who later was chosen primate of the American branch of the Church) was elected Patriarch of Jerusalem, but the Jordanian government, which controlled eastern Jerusalem at the time, did not recognize the new primate, and forcibly deported him on 30 August 1958.

The primate bears the title Patriarch of Jerusalem. The official Church language is Armenian. The Patriarch of this small group of roughly 900 celebrants resides at the monastery of St. James on Mount Zion, in Jerusalem, and is elected by the General Clerical Assembly there.

SOURCES: *Dictionnaire d'Histoire et de Géographie Ecclésiastique*; *Gegenwartslage der Ostkirchen* (Spuler); *Hay Erowsagheme Darerow Mejen* (Keok'chian); *The History of the Armenian People* (Morgan); *Jerusalem and the Armenians* (Antreassian); *Orthodoxia*.

ARMENIAN PATRIARCHS OF JERUSALEM

1.	Abraham I	638-669
2.	Grigor I *Ezekielian*	669-696
3.	Georg	696-708
4.	Mkrtich' I	708-730
5.	Hovhannês I	730-758
6.	Step'anos	758-774
7.	Eghia	774-797
	INTERREGNUM	
8.	Abraham II	885-909
	INTERREGNUM	

9.	Grigor II	981-1006
10.	Arsen	1006-1038
	Mesrop I [coadjutor]	1008
	INTERREGNUM	
11.	Simêon I	1090-1109
12.	Movsês	1109-1133
13.	Esayi I	1133-1152
14.	Sahak I	1152-1180
15.	Abraham III *of Jerusalem*	1180-1191
16.	Minas I	1191-1205
17.	Abraham IV	1205-1218
18.	Arakel	1218-1230
19.	Hovhannês II *of Garin*	1230-1238
20.	Karapet I *of Jerusalem*	1238-1254
21.	Hakobus I	1254-1281
22.	Sargis I	1281-1313
23.	Astuatsatur I	1313-1316
24.	Dawit' I	1316-1321
25.	Poghos I	1321-1323
26.	Vrt'anês I	1323-1332
27.	Hovhannês III *Joslin*	1332-1341
28.	Barsegh	1341-1356
	Karapet II [locum tenens]	1356
29.	Grigor III	1356-1363
	Kirakos I [locum tenens]	1363
30.	Mkrtich' II	1363-1378
31.	Hovhannês IV	1378-1386
32.	Grigor IV *of Egypt*	1386-1391
33.	Esayi II	1391-1394
34.	Sargis II	1394-1415
	Martiros I [coadjutor]	1399
	Mesrop II [coadjutor]	1402
35.	Poghos II *of Karni*	1415-1419
36.	Martiros II *of Egypt*	1419-1430
	Minas II [coadjutor]	1426
37.	Esayi III	1430-1431
38.	Hovhannês V	1431-1441
	Muron [coadjutor]	1436-1437
39.	Abraham V *of Egypt*	1441-1454
40.	Mesrop III	1454-1461
41.	Petros I	1461-1476
42.	Mkrtich' III	1476-1479
43.	Abraham VI *of Aleppo*	1479-1485
44.	Hovhannês VI *of Egypt*	1485-1491
45.	Martiros III *of Broussa*	1491-1501
46.	Petros II	1501-1507

LORDS TEMPORAL AND LORDS SPIRITUAL

47.	Sargis III	1507-1517
48.	Hovhannês VII	1517-1522
49.	Astuatsatur II *of Melitene*	1522-1542
50.	P'ilippos	1542-1550
	Astuatsatur II [2nd time]	1550-1551
51.	Andrêas *of Melitene*	1551-1583
52.	Dawit' II *of Melitene*	1583-1613
53.	Grigor V *Baron-Ter*	1613-1645
54.	Astuatsatur III *of Daron*	1645-1664
55.	Eghiazar *of Hromkla*	1664-1665
	Astuatsatur III [2nd time]	1665-1666
	Eghiazar [2nd time]	1666-1668
	Astuatsatur III [3rd time]	1668-1670
	Eghiazar [3rd time]	1670-1677
56.	Martiros IV	1677-1680
57.	Hovhannês VIII *of Amasia*	1680-1681
	Martiros IV [2nd time]	1681-1683
58.	Hovhannês IX *of Constantinople*	1684-1697
	Simêon II [coadjutor]	1688-1691
59.	Minas III	1697-1704
	Galust [coadjutor]	1697-1704
	Grigor VI [coadjutor]	1697-1704
60.	Awetik' [#41 of Constantinople]	1704-1706
61.	Matt'êos [#38 of Constantinople]	1706
62.	Martiros V [#44 of Constantinople]	1706
63.	Mik'ayêl [#45 of Constantinople]	1706-1707
64.	Sahak II [#46 of Constantinople]	1707
65.	Hovhannês X [#47 of Constantinople]	1707-1708
	Sahak II [2nd time]	1708-1714
66.	Hovhannês XI [#48 of Constantinople]	1714-1715
67.	Grigor VII *"The Chain-Bearer"*	1715-1749
68.	Hakob II *Nalian Zmarats'i* [#50 of Constantinople]	1749-1752
69.	T'êodoros I *of Khorên*	1752-1761
70.	Karapet III *of Kantsag*	1761-1768
71.	Poghos III *of Van*	1768-1775
72.	Hovakim *of Kanaker*	1775-1793
73.	Petros III	1794-1800
74.	T'êodoros II *of Van*	1800-1818
75.	Gabriêl	1818-1840
	Poghos (IV) [vicar general]	1824-1847
76.	Zak'aria *Ter-Grigorian of Gop*	1841-1846
77.	Kirakos II *Mnatsakanian of Jerusalem*	1847-1850
78.	Hovhannês XII *Movsêsian of Zmurnia*	1850-1860
	INTERREGNUM	
	Vrt'anês (II) [locum tenens]	1860-1864
79.	Esayi IV *Karapetian*	1864-1885

	INTERREGNUM	
	Eremia *Sahagian* [locum tenens]	1885-1889
80.	Harut'iwn *Vehapetian* [#73 of Constantinople]	1889-1910
	INTERREGNUM	
81.	Eghishê I *Durian* [#77 of Constantinople]	1921-1930
	Mesrop *Nishanian* [locum tenens]	1930-1931
82.	T'orgom I *Gushakian*	1931-1939
83.	Mesrop IV *Nishanian*	1939-1944
84.	Kuregh *Israelian*	1944-1949
	INTERREGNUM	
	Eghishê II *Derderian* [locum tenens]	1949-1957
85.	Tiran *Nersoyan*	1957-1958
	Eghishê II *Derderian* [locum tenens]	1958-1960
86.	Eghishê II *Derderian*	1960-1990
87.	T'orgom II *Manugian*	1990-

XXXVII.

THE GREEK CHURCH OF JERUSALEM

Of the ancient Orthodox patriarchates, Jerusalem ranks fourth in honor. Having been founded, according to tradition, by the apostle James, it has always been a small church, being confined in territory to the current states of Israel and Jordan; it was recognized as a Patriarchate in 451, as keeper of the holy places in Palestine. During the Ottoman period, the Church became heavily dependent on the Ecumenical Patriarch, who consecrated (and often chose) the new patriarchs. In 1872, for example, Patriarch Kyrillos II was deposed for refusing to condemn the secession of the Bulgarian Church. In 1908, the revolution of the Young Turks prompted the Palestinian Orthodox faithful, who comprised a majority of believers in the Church, to demand concessions from the hierarchy, which had been completely comprised of Greeks, many of them foreigners, for at least 400 years.

When Patriarch Damianos died in 1931, the struggle went public, causing a four-year delay in the patriarchal election. The new Patriarch, Timotheos, was another Greek, but he promised reforms, giving a voice in Church matters to the native Christians—these reforms were duly enacted in 1938. Further changes were made by his successor, Benediktos, who in 1958 provided for the election of two Arab bishops. The Patriarch of Jerusalem also consecrates the Abbot-Archbishop of the Sinai (q.v.).

The primate bears the title Patriarch of the Holy City of Jerusalem and of All Palestine. The official Church language is Greek. The roughly 260,000 communicants are located primarily in Israel, Jordan, and the Sinai peninsula.

SOURCES: *Échos d'Orient*; *Episkepsis*; *Europa World Yearbook*; *Gegenwartslage der Ostkirchen* (Spuler); *Historia tés Ekklésias Hierosolymón* (Papadopoulos; regarded as official by the Church); *History of the Church* (Jedin, ed.); *Jahrbuch der Orthodoxie* (Proc); *The Middle East and North Africa*; *Oriens Christianus* (Le Quien); *Orthodoxia*; "Pinakes Patriarchón"; *La Question de Palestine et Le Patriarcat de Jerusalem* (Moschopoulos).

GREEK PATRIARCHS OF JERUSALEM

1.	Iakóbos I *Adelphotheos*	50?-62
2.	Symeón I *Kleópa*	62?-107?
3.	Ioustos I (or Ioudas) I	107?-111
4.	Zakchaios	111?-
5.	Tóbias	
6.	Beniamin *Philippos*	
7.	Ióannés I	
8.	Matthias	
9.	Philippos	
10.	Senekas	
11.	Ioustos II	
12.	Leuis	
13.	Ephraim I	
14.	Ióséph I	
15.	Ioudas II	-134?
16.	Markos I	134?-
17.	Kassianos	
18.	Pouplios	
19.	Maximos I	
20.	Ioulianos I	
21.	Gaïos I (or Gaïanos)	
22.	Gaïos II	
23.	Symmachos	
24.	Ioulianos II (or Oualés I)	
25.	Kapión	
26.	Maximos II	
27.	Antónios	
28.	Oualés II	
29.	Dolichianos	-185?
30.	Narkissos	185-211
31.	Dios (or Ailios)	213
32.	Germanión	213
33.	Gordios	213
34.	Alexandros	213-251
35.	Mazabanés	251-260
36.	Hymenaios	260-298
37.	Zambdas	298-300
38.	Hermón	300-314
39.	Makarios I	314-333
40.	Maximos III	333-348
41.	Kyrillos I	348?-357
	Kyrillos I [2nd time]	358-360
	Kyrillos I [3rd time]	362-367

		INTERREGNUM	
	Kyrillos I [4th time]		378-386?
42.	Ióannés II		386-417
43.	Praulios		417-422
44.	Ioubenalios		422-458
45.	Anastasios I		458-478
46.	Martyrios		478-486
47.	Salloustios		486-494
48.	Élias I		494-516
49.	Ióannés III		516-524
50.	Petros		524-552
51.	Makarios II		552
52.	Eustochios		552-564
	Makarios II [2nd time]		564-575
53.	Ióannés IV		575-594
54.	Amós		594-601
55.	Isaakios		601-609
56.	Zacharias		609-632
57.	Modestos		632-634
58.	Sóphronios I		634-638
		INTERREGNUM	
59.	Anastasios II		-706
60.	Ióannés V		706-735
61.	Theodóros		735-770
62.	Élias II		770-797
63.	Geórgios		797-807
64.	Thómas I		807-820
65.	Basileios		820-838
66.	Ióannés VI		838-842
67.	Sergios I		842-844
		INTERREGNUM	
68.	Solomón		855-860
69.	Theodosios		862-878
70.	Élias III		878-907
71.	Sergios II		908-911
72.	Leontios I		912-929
73.	Athanasios I		929-937
74.	Christodoulos I		937-
75.	Agathón		950-964
76.	Ióannés VII		964-966
77.	Christodoulos II		966-969
78.	Thómas II		969-977
		INTERREGNUM	
79.	Ióséph II		980-983
80.	Orestés (or Hieremias)		983-1005
		INTERREGNUM	

81.	Theophilos I	1012-1020
82.	Niképhoros I	1020
83.	Ióannikios	1020-1040
84.	Sóphronios II	1040-1059
85.	Euthymios I	-1084
86.	Symeón II	1084-1098
87.	Sab(b)as	1098
88.	Ióannés VIII *Chrysostomités Merkouropólos*	1098?-1107?
	INTERREGNUM	
89.	Nikolaos	1156
90.	Ióannés IX	1156-1166
91.	Niképhoros II	1166-1170
92.	Leontios II	1170-1190
93.	Dositheos I [#122 of Constantinople]	1191
94.	Markos II	1191
95.	Euthymios II	-1223
96.	Anastasios II	1224-1236
97.	Sóphronios III	1236
	INTERREGNUM	
98.	Grégorios I	-1298
99.	Thaddaios	1298
	INTERREGNUM	
100.	Athanasios III	1313?-1334
101.	Grégorios II	1332
102.	Lazaros	1334?-1368
	Gerasimos [anti-patriarch]	1334?-1349
103.	Arsenios	1344
	INTERREGNUM	
104.	Dórotheos I	1376-1417
105.	Theophilos II	1417-1424
106.	Theophanés I	1424-1431
107.	Ióakeim	1431-1450
108.	Theophanés II	1450-1452
109.	Athanasios IV	1452-1460
110.	Iakóbos II	1460-
111.	Abraam	1468
112.	Grégorios III	1468-1493
	INTERREGNUM	
113.	Markos III	1503
	INTERREGNUM	
114.	Dórotheos II	1506-1537
115.	Germanos *Peloponnesios*	1537-1579
116.	Sóphronios IV	1579-1608
117.	Theophanés III	1608-1644
118.	Païsios	1645-1660
119.	Nektarios [#58 of Sinai]	1660-1669

120. Dositheos II	1669-1707
121. Chrysanthos *Notaras*	1707-1731
122. Meletios *apo Kaisareias*	1731-1737
123. Parthenios	1737-1766
124. Ephraim II	1766-1771
125. Sóphronios V [#231 of Constantinople]	1771-1775
126. Abramios	1775-1787
127. Prokopios I	1787-1788
128. Anthimos	1788-1808
129. Polykarpos	1808-1827
130. Athanasios V	1827-1845
131. Kyrillos II	1845-1872
132. Prokopios II	1873-1875
133. Hierotheos	1875-1882
134. Nikodémos	1883-1890
135. Gerasimos *Propapas* [#154 of Antioch]	1891-1896
136. Damianos *Kassiótés*	1897-1931
INTERREGNUM	
Keladión [locum tenens]	1931-1935
137. Timotheos *Themelés*	1935-1955
138. Benediktos *Papadopoulos*	1957-1980
Germanos *Mamaladés* [locum tenens]	1980-1981
139. Diodóros *Karibalés*	1981-

XXXVIII.

THE LATIN CHURCH OF JERUSALEM

The Latin Patriarchate of Jerusalem was established in the year 1099, as a direct result of the first crusade, which conquered the Holy Land and erected a Latin kingdom centered at Jerusalem. This church was one of four such creations made during the period of the crusades to correspond to the patriarchates of the ancient world, and to provide rival jurisdictions to the Greek churches and prelates. The Church of Jerusalem survived in actuality until the conquest of Acre by the Muslims in 1291, after which time it became a purely titular honor, with the patriarchs being based in Rome. The title was suspended between 1374-1830. When the honor was restored, the patriarch eventually came actually to reside (1847) in his primatial see of Jerusalem, unlike the three Latin patriarchs of Constantinople, Alexandria, and Antioch, who continued to function as titular leaders residing in Rome. Thus, when the ancient Latin titles were abolished by Pope Pius XII in 1953 to promote ecumenism, that of Jerusalem was retained. The first native-born Palestinian leader, Michael Sabbah, was elected in 1987 on the resignation of his predecessor. The primate bears the title Patriarch of Jerusalem of the Latins. Some 63,000 communicants are located primarily in Israel and Jordan.

SOURCES: *The Catholic Encyclopedia*; *Dictionnaire d'Histoire et de Géographie Ecclésiastiques*; *The New Catholic Encyclopedia*; *Oriens Christianus* (Le Quien); "Pope Calls for Broad Mideast Peace."

LATIN PATRIARCHS OF JERUSALEM

1.	Arnulphus	1099-1100
2.	Dai(m)bertus (or Dagobertus) *of Pisa*	1100-1107
	Ehremarus [anti-patriarch]	1105?
3.	Gibelinus *of Arles*	1107-1111
	Arnulphus [2nd time]	1111-1118
4.	Gormundus	1118-1128
5.	Stephanus	1128-1130
6.	Willelmus (or Guillelmus) I	1130-1145
7.	Fulcherus	1146-1157
8.	Amalricus	1157-1180

9.	Eraclius (or Eracleus)	1180-1191
10.	Sulpitius	1191-
11.	Michael I	1194
12.	Monachus	1194-
13.	Soffredus	1203-
14.	Albertus I	1204-1214
15.	Gualterus (or Lotharius)	1214?-
16.	Radulphus I	-1225
17.	Giroldus (or Geraldus)	1225-1239
18.	Robertus	1240-1254
19.	Iacobus I *Pantaléon* [#180 of Rome]	1255-1261
20.	Bartholomæus *de Braganza*	1261-
21.	Humbertus *de Romanis*	1262?
22.	Guillelmus II	1263-1270
23.	Thomas *Angi de Lentino*	1272-1277
24.	Aiglerius (or Angelus)	1275?
25.	Ioannes *de Vercellis*	1278-
26.	Elias I	1279-1287
27.	Nicolaus *de Hanapis*	1288-1294
28.	Radulphus II	1294-1304
29.	Antonius *Beccus*	1305-1310

INTERREGNUM

30.	Petrus I *de Plana-Cassano*	1314-1322
31.	Petrus II *Nicosiensis*	1322-1324
32.	Raymundus *Bequin*	1324-1328
33.	Petrus III *de Palude*	1329-1342
34.	Elias II *de Nabinallis*	1342-
35.	Guillelmus III	1351-
36.	Philippus I *de Cabassole*	1361-1368
37.	Guillelmus IV	1369-1374

INTERREGNUM

38.	Augustus *Foscolo*	1830-1847
39.	Iosephus *Valerga*	1847-1872
40.	Vincentius *Bracco*	1873-1889
41.	Aloysius I *Piavi*	1889-1905
42.	Philippus II *Camassei*	1906-1919
43.	Aloysius II *Barlassina* [auxiliary 1918]	1920-1947
44.	Albertus II *Gori*	1949-1970
45.	Iacobus II Iosephus *Beltritti* [coadjutor 1965]	1970-1987
46.	Michael II *Sabbah*	1987-

XXXIX.

THE CHURCH OF LATVIA

Latvia, which existed as an independent Republic between the world wars, is largely Roman Catholic, with just 9% of the faithful being Orthodox. Nonetheless, the same nationalistic forces that ultimately led to separate Orthodox Churches in Poland and Czechoslovakia also prompted demands by the clergy and populace for their own church. Autonomy (or autocephaly, according to some current Church members) was declared on 26 February 1920, and confirmed by Patriarch Tikhon of Russia on 19 July 1921. The Latvian Church transferred its autonomous jurisdiction to the Ecumenical Patriarch of Constantinople on 4 February 1936, when the new Archbishop, Augustins Petersons, was created a Metropolitan. Petersons was forced to renounce independence on 17 June 1940, during the Soviet occupation of the Baltic republics, and the Church was returned to the direct jurisdiction of the Russian Church on 4 January 1941.

No independent, organized Latvian Church structure survived the Russian suppression, either in Latvia or in the West, although scattered Latvian parishes exist in the United States and in Europe. They continued to acknowledge Metropolitan Augustins until his death in 1955. Thereafter, the Ecumenical Patriarch placed the Latvian Church under the guardianship of the Metropolitans of Thyateira and Great Britain. Between 1941-90 Russian primates were appointed by the Patriarch to govern the mostly Russian communicants remaining in Latvia. Latvia seceded from the Soviet Union in March 1990. On 4 January 1993 the Latvian Church declared that it would return to an autonomous status under the overall jurisdiction of the Constantinople, based on the ruling of the Ecumenical Patriarch in 1936. Patriarch Aleksiî II of Russia confirmed the Latvian Church's independence two days later. The primate bears the title Bishop of Riga and All Latvia. The official language of the Church is Latvian. Roughly 240,000 communicants belonged to the Church in 1936; current membership is unknown.

SOURCES: *Échos d'Orient*; *Episkepsis*; *The Latvian Orthodox Church* (Cherney); *Orthodoxia*; *Profiles in Belief* (Piepkorn); *Religion in the Soviet Union* (Kolarz).

METROPOLITANS OF LATVIA
(Archbishops 1920, Metropolitans 1936,
Russian Bishops 1941 and 1993)

1.	Janis *Pommers*	1920-1934
2.	Augustins *Petersons*	1936-1955
	Athénagoras I *Kabbadas* [locum tenens]	1955-1962
	Athénagoras II *Kokkinakés* [locum tenens]	1964-1979
	Methodios *Fougas* [locum tenens]	1979-1988
	Grégorios *Hadgitophés* [locum tenens]	1988-1993

RUSSIAN BISHOPS OF LATVIA

3.	Nikon *Fomichev*	1963-1966
4.	Aleksiî *Konoplev*	1966
5.	Leonid *Poliakov*	1966-1989
6.	Aleksandrs *Kudrjasovs*	1989-

XL.

THE CHURCH OF MACEDONIA (OHRID)

The Orthodox Church of Macedonia is unique among the old Slavic churches in not being tied directly to one of the great Slavic states that arose in the early middle ages. The first Archbishop of Ohrid, Filip, was head of the Bulgarian Church; and for almost two hundred years, the two jurisdictions were synonymous. When the second Bulgarian patriarchate was established in 1186, Ohrid managed to maintain its independence, its primate eventually assuming the title of Patriarch. The territory comprising the Patriarchate of Ohrid varied over the centuries, but generally included present-day Macedonia, and parts of what are now northern Albania, western Bulgaria, and northwestern Greece. Ohrid itself is located in the former Yugoslavia, on Lake Ohrid, near its current border with Albania. At the behest of the Ecumenical Patriarch, Ottoman Sultan Mustafa III issued a decree in 1766 subordinating Ohrid and Pec under the jurisdiction of Constantinople; when Serbia attained its independence, the Ohrid Metropolitanate was transferred to Pec, the modern Patriarchate of Serbia.

After World War II, the new Soviet state of Yugoslavia divided the country into six constituent republics, one of which was Macedonia. The large Orthodox population there began petitioning the state for re-establishment of a church separate from the Patriarchate of Serbia. When Serbian Patriarch Vikentije died on 5 July 1958, the leading churchmen in Macedonia called for a general assembly of clergy and lay people. These met at Ohrid on 5 October 1958. The assembly declared the ancient Church of Ohrid restored, and elected Vicar-Bishop Dositej unilaterally as the new Metropolitan Archbishop of the restored see. These actions were immediately attacked by the Serbian patriarch, who asked the government to deny the new Church recognition. President Tito, however, fully supported the move, and the new Serbian Patriarch, German, finally recognized the Macedonian Church's autonomy on 18 July 1959.

German later assisted Metropolitan Dositej in consecrating a second Macedonian bishop, Kliment. This enabled Dositej canonically to create a new Macedonian Synod which would be self-perpetuating. The new church continued to press for complete independence, and when the Serbians refused to agree, an assembly of the Macedonian

Church and people declared the Church autocephalous on 19 July 1967. Thus far, few of the other Orthodox churches have recognized the Macedonian Church's claim to autocephaly (as few nations have recognized the Macedonian state's independence), but, given the history of Eastern Orthodoxy since 1800, such recognition seems likely over the long term. On 15 December 1992, in the midst of the Yugoslavian civil war, the Serbian Church declared the hierarchy of the Macedonian Church to be illegal, and appointed an administrator of the Macedonian Metropolitanate; the new Republic of Macedonia refused to grant the Serbian administrator, Jovan Mladenovic, a visa, and he was transferred to the United States a year later; he was replaced by Pahomije Gachic.

Archbishop Gavril resigned his office for reasons of ill health on 9 June 1993, and was replaced by Archbishop Mihail on 5 December 1993. On 22 June 1994 the Church of Serbia threatened to excommunicate the entire hierarchy of the Macedonian Church.

The primate bears the title Metropolitan Archbishop of Ohrid and Macedonia; he resides at Skopje, the capital of Macedonia. The official Church language is Macedonian. There are eight bishops (including the ruling Archbishop and four metropolitans), with roughly one million communicants in the Republic of Macedonia, and another 400,000 in the Americas, Western Europe, and Australia.

SOURCES: *Church and State in Yugoslavia Since 1945* (Alexander); *Eastern Christianity and Politics in the Twentieth Century* (Ramet, ed.); *Europa World Yearbook*; *Gegenwartslage der Ostkirchen* (Spuler); *History of the Church* (Jedin, ed.); *Jahrbuch der Orthodoxie* (Proc); "The Orthodox Church in Yugoslavia: The Problem of the Macedonian Church" (Pavlowitch); *Orthodoxia*; *Profiles in Belief* (Piepkorn).

PATRIARCHS OF OHRID
(Archbishops 1018, Patriarchs 1000, 1558)
(See also the CHURCH OF BULGARIA)

1.	Filip	1000?-1015
2.	David	1015-1018
3.	Jovan I	1018-1027
4.	Lev I (León *ek Rómaión*)	1027-1056
5.	Teodul I (Theodoulos *apo Mókiou*)	1056-1065
6.	Jovan II *Lampin* (Ióannés *Lampénos*)	1065-1078
7.	Jovan III (Ióannés *Aoinos*) *"The Sober"*	1079-1081?
8.	Teofilakt (Theophylaktos *ex Euripou*)	1081-1112?
9.	Lev II (León *Boungos*)	-1120
10.	Mihail I *Maksim* (Michaél *Maximos*)	1120-
11.	Jevstatij (Eustathios)	1134?
12.	Jovan IV *Komnen* (Ióannés *Komnénos*)	1143-1157
13.	Konstantin I	1157-1166

INTERREGNUM

14.	name unknown	1180-1183
15.	Jovan V *Kamatir* (Ióannés *Kamatéros*)	1183-1215
16.	Dimitrij *Homatian* (Démétrios *Chómatianos* [or *Chómaténos*])	1216-1235
17.	Joanikij	1238?
18.	Sergej	1241?
19.	Konstantin II (Kónstantinos *Kabasilas*)	1250-1261
20.	Hefajst (Hephaistos)	1265?
21.	Jakov *Proarhij*	1275?
22.	Adrian	1285?
23.	Genadij	1289?
24.	Makarij	1294-1299
25.	Grigorij I	1316?
26.	Antim *Metohit* (Anthimos *Metochités*)	1328?
27.	Nikolaj I	1345-1348?
28.	Grigorij II	1348-1378
29.	name unknown	1383-1394

INTERREGNUM

30.	Matej	1408-1410

INTERREGNUM

31.	Nikodim	1452?
32.	Dorotej	1456-1466
33.	Dositej I	1466
34.	Mark *Ksilocarf* (Markos *Xylokarabés*) [#163 of Constantinople]	1466-1467
35.	Dionisij I	1467-
36.	Maksim	1477-1481
37.	Nikolaj II	1481?-1487?
38.	Zaharij (Zacharias)	1487?-
39.	Prohor	1523-1550
40.	Simeon I	1550
41.	Neofit	1551
42.	Grigorij III	1553?
43.	Nikanor	1555?-1557
44.	Akakij	1557?-1564?
45.	Pajsij	1565-1566
46.	Partenij I	1566?-1567?
47.	Sofronij	1567-1572
48.	Gavril I	1572?-1588
49.	Teodul II	1588
50.	Joahim	1588?-1593
	Gavril I [2nd time]	1593
51.	Atanasij I	1593-1596
52.	Valaam	1597-1598
53.	Nektarij I	1598-

	Atanasij I [2nd time]	1606-
54.	Mitrofan	1610?-1614
	Atanasij I [3rd time]	1614-1615
55.	Nektarij II	1616-1623?
56.	Porfirij *Paleolog* (Porphyrios *Palaiologos*)	1623-1624
57.	Georgij	1627?
58.	Joasav I	1628?
59.	Avram	1629-1634
60.	Simeon II	1634-
61.	Meletij I	1637-1641
62.	Hariton	1641-1646

INTERREGNUM

63.	Danil	1650?
64.	Dionsij II	1651-1656
65.	Arsenij I	1656-1657
66.	Atanasij II	1657
	Arsenij I [2nd time]	1658-1659?
67.	Ignatij I	1659
	Arsenij I [3rd time]	1659
	Ignatij I [2nd time]	1659-1662
68.	Zosim I	1662-1669
69.	Grigorij IV	1669-1670
70.	Panaret	1671
71.	Nektarij III	1671-1673
72.	Ignatij II	1673?
73.	Teofan	1675?-1676
74.	Meletij II	1677-1679
75.	Partenij II	1679-1683
76.	Grigorij V	1683-1687
77.	German I *of Voden*	1688-1691
	Grigorij V [2nd time]	1691-1693
78.	Ignatij III	1693-1695
79.	Zosim II	1695-1699
80.	Rafaïl	1699-1702
	German I [2nd time]	1702-1703
	Ignatij III [2nd time]	1703?-
81.	Dionisij III (Dionysios *apo Chiou*)	1706-1707
	Zosim II [2nd time]	1707?-1708?
82.	Metodij I	1708
	Zosim II [3rd time]	1708-1709
83.	Ermenus	1709-1710?
	Dionisij III [2nd time]	1710-1714
84.	Tilotej	1714-1718
85.	Joasav II	1719-1745
86.	Josif	1746-1752
87.	Dionisij IV	1752-1757

THE CHURCH OF MACEDONIA

88.	Metodij II	1757-1758
89.	German II	1758-1759
90.	Kiril	1759-1762
91.	Eremij	1761-1763
92.	Ananij	1763
93.	Arsenij II	1764-1767

THE ARCHBISHOPRIC DISCONTINUED

METROPOLITAN ARCHBISHOPS OF OHRID AND MACEDONIA

94.	Dositej II *Stojkovic*	1958-1981
95.	Angelarij *Krstevski*	1981-1986
96.	Gavril II *Miloshevski*	1986-1993
97.	Mihail II *Gogov*	1993-

SERBIAN ADMINISTRATORS OF MACEDONIA

1.	Jovan *Mladenovic*	1993-1994
2.	Pahomije *Gachic*	1994-

XLI.

THE CHURCH OF MOLDOVA

Prior to World War II, Moldova was part of Bessarabia in Romania, but this narrow strip of land was annexed by the Soviet Union in June 1940, merged with other territory, and was renamed the Moldavian Soviet Socialist Republic. Following the breakup of the Soviet Union in 1991, Moldavia declared its independence, changing its name to Moldova. Although there was speculation that Moldova might reunite with Romania, since much of the population speaks Romanian, the government has resisted efforts to be merged with any other state.

The Church of Moldova was originally part of the Church of Romania, and then of Russia after 1940. On 24 December 1992 Russian Patriarch Aleksiî II declared the Eparchy of Molodova autonomous under its own self-governing synod; the Eparch received a new title, Metropolitan. In 1993 a number of priests broke away from the church and received recognition from Patriarch Teoctist of Romania as the Metropolitanate of Bessarabia (its original name), but the Moldovan government blocked the move, and Patriarch Aleksiî II reaffirmed the Russian Church's paramountcy. The government favors the eventual creation of an autocephalous religious body independent of both the Russian and Romanian churches. The head of the Church bears the title Metropolitan of Kishinev (or Chisinau) and All Moldova. The Church uses both Russian and Romanian as languages. The current number of communicants is unknown, but the official Moldovan Church claims 839 active parishes under its jurisdiction.

SOURCES: current news reports; *Orthodoxia*.

METROPOLITANS OF MOLDOVA

1.	Varfolomeî *Gondarovskiî*	1969-1972
2.	Ionafan *Kopolovich*	1972-1986
3.	Serapion *Fadeev*	1986-1989
4.	Vladimir *Cantarian*	1989-

METROPOLITANS OF BESSARABIA (ROMANIA)

Petru *Peduraru* [locum tenens]	1992-

XLII.

THE CHURCH OF POLAND

Poland has historically been an anomaly among the Eastern European states, the Polish kings having been converted at an early date to Roman Catholicism; most of the population remains Catholic to this day. However, an Orthodox Church diocese was established as early as the year 1087 in Przemysl, in eastern Poland, under the direct control of the Patriarchate of Russia. During the seventeenth century, Polish Orthodoxy was subject to persecution at the hands of the state, many believers being forced to acknowledge Catholic Eastern Rite bishops. Following the partitions of the late 1700s, Russia occupied the eastern half of Poland, and encouraged the re-establishment of the Orthodox hierarchy, against much resistance from the populace.

The Russian Revolution of 1917 resulted in the eventual independence of the Polish state, with administration of the Orthodox Church of Poland being transferred to the Ecumenical Patriarch at Constantinople. Following the lead of the other Slavic churches, the Polish Orthodox Church promptly sought autocephaly, a general synod unilaterally declaring the church's independence in 1922. The Patriarch of Russia refused recognition, and the controversy lead to the assassination of Archbishop Jerzy by a Russian monk a year later. Autocephaly was recognized by the Ecumenical Patriarch of Constantinople on 13 November 1924. When the Soviets occupied the country during World War II, they immediately reestablished control over the Church, finally deposing Metropolitan Dionizus in 1948, and replacing him with a Russian administrator. Autocephaly was then regranted by the Moscow Patriarchate on 15 June 1951, with a new Metropolitan being elected a month later.

The primate bears the title Metropolitan Archbishop of Warsaw and All Poland. The official Church language is Polish. The Polish Orthodox Church remains small in comparison with the powerful Polish Catholic Church, having just 870,000 communicants; most Orthodox believers live in the eastern sections of Poland, near the Russian border.

SOURCES: *Eastern Christianity and Politics in the Twentieth Century* (Ramet, ed.); *Échos d'Orient*; *Episkepsis*; *Europa World Yearbook*; *Gegenwartslage der Ostkirchen* (Spuler); *History of the Church*

(Jedin, ed.); *Jahrbuch der Orthodoxie* (Proc); *Orthodoxia*; *Profiles in Belief* (Piepkorn).

METROPOLITAN ARCHBISHOPS OF POLAND
(Archbishops 1922, Metropolitans 1924)

1.	Jerzy *Jaroszewski*	1921-1923
2.	Dionizus *Waledynski*	1923-1948
	INTERREGNUM	
	Tymoteusz *Szretter* [locum tenens]	1948-1951
3.	Makariusz *Oksijuk*	1951-1961
	Tymoteusz *Szretter* [locum tenens]	1959-1961
4.	Tymoteusz *Szretter*	1961-1962
	INTERREGNUM	
	Jerzy *Korenistow* [locum tenens]	1962-1964
5.	Stefan *Rudyk*	1965-1969
6.	Bazyli *Doroszkiewicz*	1970-

XLIII.

THE CHURCH OF ROMANIA

The Orthodox Church of Romania developed in tandem with the secular Romanian state. The princes of Moldavia and Wallachia sought ecclesiastical autonomy as a means of furthering the growth of their realms. Thus, the Voievode of Wallachia petitioned the Patriarch of Constantinople for the establishment of a separate Metropolitanate at Curtea de Arges, a request which was granted in 1359. Similarly, Moldavia secured its own Metropolitan in 1401, in the person of Iosif Musat. The union of the two states in 1861, and the international recognition of its independence in 1878, led to demands for an autocephalous church. These were granted by Constantinople on 13 April 1885, with the Metropolitan of Ungro-Vlachia (Wallachia) being acknowledged as Metropolitan Primate of Romania. The patriarchate was established on 4 February 1925, and recognized by Constantinople on 30 July 1925.

The Soviet occupation in 1944, and the subsequent establishment of a communist government, imposed many hardships on the Church; it became, as in Russia, the semi-official religion for believers. The harshness of the Ceausescu regime resulted in further setbacks for an already besieged church. The civil chaos which resulted from the latter's fall at the end of 1989 resulted in the resignation of Patriarch Teoctist in January 1990, but he was restored to his position three months later. However, many of the Romanian Church's hierarchs continue to be criticized for having cooperated with the Communist regime. The church of the neighboring newly-independent state of Moldova, a territory which had been a part of Romania prior to World War II (when it was annexed to the Soviet Union), was declared autonomous by the Patriarch of Russia on 24 December 1992. In 1993 Patriarch Teoctist attempted to reassert the authority of the Romanian Church over Moldova, but the government of Moldova adamantly opposed what it regarded as interference by a foreign power, as did Patriarch Aleksiî II of Russia.

The primate bears the title Patriarch of All Romania, Locum Tenens of Caesarea in Cappadocia, Metropolitan of Ungro-Vlachia (*i.e.*, Wallachia), Archbishop of Bucuresti. The official language is Romanian. Roughly eighteen million communicants reside in Romania and the United States.

SOURCES: *Eastern Christianity and Politics in the Twentieth Century* (Ramet, ed.); *Échos d'Orient*; *Episkepsis*; *Europa World Yearbook*; *Gegenwartslage der Ostkirchen* (Spuler); *History of the Church* (Jedin, ed.); *Istoria Bisericii Ortodoxe Române* (Pacurariu; regarded as official by the Church); *Jahrbuch der Orthodoxie* (Proc); *Orthodoxia*; *Profiles in Belief* (Piepkorn); *The Romanian Orthodox Church, Yesterday and Today*.

PATRIARCHS OF ROMANIA
(Metropolitans of Ungro-Vlachia 1359, Metropolitan Primates 1865, Patriarchs 1925)

1.	Iachint	1359-1372
2.	Hariton	1372-1380?
3.	Antim I *Critopol*	1380?-1401
4.	Teodor I	15th cent.
5.	Iosif I	1464-1477?
6.	Macarie I	1477-1487?
7.	Ilarion I	1487?-1502?
8.	Nifon I [#168 of Constantinople]	1503?-1505
9.	Maxim *Brancovici*	1505-1508
	INTERREGNUM	
10.	Macarie II	1512-1521?
11.	Teodor II	1521?-1523
12.	Ilarion II	1523-1526?
13.	Mitrofan I	1526?-1534?
14.	Varlaam I	1534?-1544
15.	Anania	1544-1558
16.	Efrem	1558?-1566?
17.	Daniil I	1566?-1568
18.	Eftimie I	1568-1576
19.	Serafim	1576-1585
20.	Mihail I	1585?-1589
21.	Nichifor	1589-1592
22.	Mihail II	1592-1594
23.	Eftimie II	1594-1602
24.	Luca	1602-1629
25.	Grigorie I	1629-1636
26.	Teofil	1636-1648
27.	Stefan I	1648-1653
28.	Ignatie I	1653-1655
	Stefan I [2nd time]	1655-1668
29.	Teodosie	1668-1672
30.	Dionisie I	1672
31.	Varlaam II	1672-1679
	Teodosie [2nd time]	1679-1708

32.	Antim II *Ivireanul*	1708-1716
33.	Mitrofan II	1716-1719
34.	Daniil II	1719-1731
35.	Stefan II	1732-1738
36.	Neofit I *Cretanul*	1738-1753
37.	Filaret I *Mihalitzis*	1753-1760
38.	Grigorie II	1760-1787
39.	Grigorie III *Socoteanu* [locum tenens]	1770-1771
40.	Cosma *Popescu*	1787-1792
41.	Filaret II	1792-1793
42.	Dositei *Filitti*	1793-1810
43.	Gavriil *Banulescu* [exarch]	1808-1812
44.	Ignatie II	1810-1812
	Iosif *al Argesului* [locum tenens]	1812
45.	Nectarie	1812-1819
46.	Dionisie II *Lupu*	1819-1821
	Dionisie [locum tenens]	1821-1822
	Benedict *Troadas* [locum tenens]	1822
	Gherasim *al Buzaului* [locum tenens]	1822
	Benedict *Troadas* [locum tenens]	1822
47.	Grigorie IV *Dascalul*	1823-1829

INTERREGNUM

	Neofit [locum tenens]	1829-1833
	Grigorie IV *Dascalul* [2nd time]	1833-1834

INTERREGNUM

	Neofit [locum tenens]	1833-1840
	Chesarie [locum tenens]	1833-1840
	Ilarion [locum tenens]	1833-1840
48.	Neofit II	1840-1849
	Nifon [locum tenens]	1849-1850
49.	Nifon II	1850-1875
50.	Calinic *Miclescu*	1875-1886
	Inochentie *Moisiu* [locum tenens]	1886
51.	Iosif II *Gheorghian*	1886-1893
	Gherasim *Timus* [locum tenens]	1893
52.	Ghenadie *Petrescu*	1893-1896
	Iosif *Naniescu* [locum tenens]	1896
	Gherasim *Timus* [locum tenens]	1896
	Partenie *Clinceni* [locum tenens]	1896
	Iosif II *Gheorghian* [2nd time]	1896-1909
53.	Athanasie *Mironescu*	1909-1911
	Teodosie *Atanasiu* [locum tenens]	1911-1912
54.	Conon *Aramescu-Donici*	1912-1919
	Platon *Ciosu* [locum tenens]	1919
55.	Miron *Cristea*	1919-1939
	Nicodim *Munteanu* [locum tenens]	1939

56.	Nicodim *Munteanu*	1939-1948
	Justinian *Marina* [locum tenens]	1948
57.	Justinian *Marina*	1948-1977
	Iustin *Moïsescu* [locum tenens]	1977
58.	Iustin *Moïsescu* [#43 of Austria—Sibiu]	1977-1986
59.	Teoctist *Arapas(u)*	1986-

XLIV.

THE CHURCH OF ROME

The Roman Catholic Church is the largest of the ancient Christian patriarchates, the Pope of Rome having been regarded as either first among equals or first in primacy during the early centuries of Christianity. The traditions, language, and history of the Catholic church gradually moved it away from its Eastern brethren, particularly during the decline of the Roman Empire, to which it was so closely tied. As the temporal center of the Empire shifted to Byzantium (Constantinople), the Byzantine emperors sought to make their church pre-eminent among the five original patriarchates. The collapse of the Western Empire, ironically, forced the Popes to become more self-sufficient, and injected them directly into local and international politics.

In 754 the Vatican acquired the first pieces of land in what would eventually become the "Papal States," the temporal domains of the pontiffs in central Italy. After a succession of weak Popes in the ninth and tenth centuries, the continuing political struggle between East and West came to a head in 1054, when the Pope and the Patriarch of Constantinople exchanged excommunications. The other major patriarchates gradually followed Constantinople's lead, although Rome continues to have supporters in the East to the present day. These loyalists have often split away from their Orthodox counterparts to form rival patriarchates which acknowledge the supremacy of the Pope.

The Church went through a period of reform and reorganization during the early Middle Ages. By the year 1200 the Pope had more feudal vassals than any other ruler in Europe, and could impose his will upon the most intransigent of monarchs. In the fourteenth century political turmoil at Rome forced the Pope to move his seat of power to Avignon, in France, under the protection of the French king. In 1378 the newly-elected Pontiff, Urbanus VI, was persuaded to return to Rome, thereby precipating the Great Schism. Disgruntled French cardinals immediately elected their own Pope at Avignon, and all of Europe began dividing itself into two equal camps. Neither side would renounce its claims, and as Pope succeeded Pope, men of good will began to despair that the breach would ever be healed. Finally, a great Council was called at Pisa in 1409 to resolve the issue; it deposed both claimants, and elected its own Pope. Neither of the other pontiffs recognized the actions of the Council, so there were now three papal courts.

In 1415, two of the Popes were persuaded to resign, and a new leader was elected in 1417, whereupon the third line of pontiffs, although it continued until 1430, rapidly lost its legitimacy and supporters. A second great schism occurred with the Protestant Revolution of the sixteenth century; this was met with the reforming Council of Trent in 1545. The Church's temporal powers were directly affected by the rise of nationalism in Europe in the mid-nineteenth century; in 1870 the last remnants of the Papal States were occupied by revolutionary forces, and the Pope withdrew to the Vatican, vowing never to venture forth until his lands were restored. This dispute was settled in 1929 by the Lateran Treaty, through which Italy ceded to the Pope 300 acres of land surrounding the Vatican in Rome. The Pope remains the only patriarch to possess temporal authority, as Head of Vatican City State; this status gives him an international authority and voice shared by no other religious leader in the world.

The Roman Catholic Church remains the most successful of all Christian denominations, with the greatest number of followers worldwide, the largest number of parishes, the largest and most pervasive infrastructure, the greatest financial resources. The primate bears the title Pope, Bishop of Rome, Vicar of Jesus Christ, Successor of the Prince of the Apostles, Supreme Pontiff of the Universal Church, Patriarch of the West, Primate of Italy, Sovereign of Vatican City State. The official language of the Church is Latin, which is used for all official publications; however, Italian is spoken in Vatican City State.

SOURCES: *Annuario Pontificio per l'Annò...* (regarded as official by the Church); *Échos d'Orient*; *Manuel d'Histoire, de Généalogie et de Chronologie* (Stokvis); *The Oxford Dictionary of Popes* (Kelly).

POPES OF ROME

1.	Petrus	40?-67?
2.	Linus	67?-76?
3.	Anacletus (I) (or Cletus)	76?-88?
4.	Clemens I	88?-97?
5.	Evaristus	97?-105?
6.	Alexander I	105?-115?
7.	Sixtus I	115?-125?
8.	Telesphorus	125?-136?
9.	Hyginus	136?-140?
10.	Pius I	140?-155?
11.	Anicetus	155?-166?
12.	Soter	166?-175?
13.	Eleutherius	175?-189
14.	Victor I	189-199

15.	Zephyrinus	199-217
16.	Calixtus I	217-222
	Hippolytus [anti-pope]	217-235
17.	Urbanus I	222-230
18.	Pontianus	230-235
19.	Anterus	235-236
20.	Fabianus	236-250
21.	Cornelius	251-253
	Novatianus [anti-pope]	251
22.	Lucius I	253-254
23.	Stephanus I	254-257
24.	Sixtus II	257-258
25.	Dionysius	259-268
26.	Felix I	269-274
27.	Eutychianus	275-283
28.	Gaius	283-296
29.	Marcellinus	296-304

INTERREGNUM

30.	Marcellus I	308-309
31.	Eusebius	309
32.	Miltiades (or Melchiades)	311-314
33.	Sylvester I	314-335
34.	Marcus	336
35.	Iulius I	337-352
36.	Liberius	352-366
	Felix II [anti-pope]	355-365
37.	Damasus I	366-384
	Ursinus [anti-pope]	366-367
38.	Siricius	384-399
39.	Anastasius I	399-401
40.	Innocentius I	401-417
41.	Zosimus	417-418
42.	Bonifacius I	418-422
	Eulalius [anti-pope]	418-419
43.	Coelestinus I	422-432
44.	Sixtus III	432-440
45.	Leo I *Magnus* "The Great"	440-461
46.	Hilarius	461-468
47.	Simplicius	468-483
48.	Felix III	483-492
49.	Gelasius I	492-496
50.	Anastasius II	496-498
51.	Symmachus	498-514
	Laurentius [anti-pope]	498
	Laurentius [anti-pope; 2nd time]	501-505
52.	Hormisdas	514-523

53.	Ioannes I	523-526
54.	Felix IV	526-530
55.	Bonifacius II	530-532
	Dioscorus [anti-pope]	530
56.	Ioannes II (Mercurius)	533-535
57.	Agapetus I	535-536
58.	Silverius	536-537
59.	Vigilius	537-555
60.	Pelagius I	556-561
61.	Ioannes III	561-574
62.	Benedictus I	575-579
63.	Pelagius II	579-590
64.	Gregorius I *Magnus "The Great"*	590-604
65.	Sabinianus	604-606
66.	Bonifacius III	607
67.	Bonifacius IV	608-615
68.	Deusdedit (or Adeodatus I)	615-618
69.	Bonifacius V	619-625
70.	Honorius I	625-638
71.	Severinus	640
72.	Ioannes IV	640-642
73.	Theodorus I	642-649
74.	Martinus I	649-655
75.	Eugenius I	654-657
76.	Vitalianus	657-672
77.	Adeodatus II	672-676
78.	Donus	676-678
79.	Agatho	678-681
80.	Leo II	682-683
81.	Benedictus II	684-685
82.	Ioannes V	685-686
83.	Conon	686-687
	Theodorus II [anti-pope]	687
	Paschalis I [anti-pope]	687
84.	Sergius I	687-701
85.	Ioannes VI	701-705
86.	Ioannes VII	705-707
87.	Sisinnius	708
88.	Constantinus (I)	708-715
89.	Gregorius II	715-731
90.	Gregorius III	731-741
91.	Zacharias	741-752
	Stephanus (II) [unconsecrated]	752
92.	Stephanus II (III)	752-757
93.	Paulus I	757-767
	Constantinus II [anti-pope]	767-769

	Philippus [anti-pope]	768
94.	Stephanus III (IV)	768-772
95.	Adrianus I	772-795
96.	Leo III	795-816
97.	Stephanus IV (V)	816-817
98.	Paschalis I	817-824
99.	Eugenius II	824-827
100.	Valentinus	827
101.	Gregorius IV	827-844
	Ioannes VIII [anti-pope]	844
102.	Sergius II	844-847
103.	Leo IV	847-855
104.	Benedictus III	855-858
	Anastasius III [anti-pope]	855
105.	Nicolaus I *Magnus "The Great"*	858-867
106.	Adrianus II	867-872
107.	Ioannes VIII	872-882
108.	Marinus I	882-884
109.	Adrianus III	884-885
110.	Stephanus V (VI)	885-891
111.	Formosus	891-896
112.	Bonifacius VI	896
113.	Stephanus VI (VII)	896-897
114.	Romanus	897
115.	Theodorus II	897
116.	Ioannes IX	898-900
117.	Benedictus IV	900-903
118.	Leo V	903
	Christophorus [anti-pope]	903-904
119.	Sergius III	904-911
120.	Anastasius III	911-913
121.	Lando (or Landus)	913-914
122.	Ioannes X	914-928
123.	Leo VI	928
124.	Stephanus VII (VIII)	928-931
125.	Ioannes XI	931-935
126.	Leo VII	936-939
127.	Stephanus VIII (IX)	939-942
128.	Marinus II	942-946
129.	Agapetus II	946-955
130.	Ioannes XII (Octavianus)	955-964
131.	Leo VIII	963-965
132.	Benedictus V	964-966
133.	Ioannes XIII	965-972
134.	Benedictus VI	973-974
	Bonifacius VII (Franco) [anti-pope]	974

135. Benedictus VII	974-983
136. Ioannes XIV *Canepanova*	983-984
Bonifacius VII [2nd time]	984-985
137. Ioannes XV	985-996
138. Gregorius V (Bruno)	996-999
Ioannes XVI *Philagathos* [anti-pope]	997-998
139. Sylvester II (Gerbert)	999-1003
140. Ioannes XVII *Sicco*	1003
141. Ioannes XVIII *Fasanus*	1004-1009
142. Sergius IV (Petrus)	1009-1012
143. Benedictus VIII (Theophylactus)	1012-1024
Gregorius VI [anti-pope]	1012
144. Ioannes XIX (Romanus)	1024-1032
145. Benedictus IX (Theophylactus)	1032-1044
146. Sylvester III (Ioannes) *of Sabina*	1045
Benedictus IX [2nd time]	1045
147. Gregorius VI *Gratianus*	1045-1046
148. Clemens II (Suidger)	1046-1047
Benedictus IX [3rd time]	1047-1048
149. Damasus II (Poppo)	1048
150. Leo IX *von Egisheim*	1049-1054
151. Victor II *von Dollnstein-Hirschberg*	1055-1057
152. Stephanus IX (X) (Frederick)	1057-1058
Benedictus X *Mincius* [anti-pope]	1058-1059
153. Nicolaus II (Gérard)	1059-1061
154. Alexander II *da Baggio*	1061-1073
Honorius II *Cadalus* [anti-pope]	1061-1072
155. Gregorius VII (Hildebrand)	1073-1085
Clemens III (Guibert) [anti-pope]	1080
Clemens III (Guibert) [anti-pope; 2nd time]	1084-1100
156. Victor III (Desiderius)	1086-1087
157. Urbanus II (Odo)	1088-1099
158. Paschalis II (Rainerius)	1099-1118
Theodoricus [anti-pope]	1100
Albertus [anti-pope]	1102
Sylvester IV (Maginulf) [anti-pope]	1105-1111
159. Gelasius II *Caetani*	1118-1119
Gregorius VIII *Burdinus* [anti-pope]	1118-1121
160. Calixtus II *di Borgogna*	1119-1124
161. Honorius II (Lamberto)	1124-1130
Coelestinus II *Buccapecus* [anti-pope]	1124
162. Innocentius II *Papareschi*	1130-1143
Anacletus II *Leonis* [anti-pope]	1130-1138
Victor IV *Conti* [anti-pope]	1138
163. Coelestinus II (Guido)	1143-1144
164. Lucius II *Caccianemici*	1144-1145

165. Eugenius III *Pignatelli* (or *Paganelli*)	1145-1153
166. Anastasius IV (Corrado)	1153-1154
167. Adrianus IV *Breakspear*	1154-1159
168. Alexander III *Bandinelli*	1159-1181
Victor IV *de Monticelli* [anti-pope]	1159-1164
Paschalis III *da Crema* [anti-pope]	1164-1168
Calixtus III (Giovanni) [anti-pope]	1168-1178
Innocentius III (Lando) [anti-pope]	1179-1180
169. Lucius III *Allucingoli*	1181-1185
170. Urbanus III *Crivelli*	1185-1187
171. Gregorius VIII *de Morra*	1187
172. Clemens III *Scolari*	1187-1191
173. Coelestinus III *Bobone*	1191-1198
174. Innocentius III *di Segni*	1198-1216
175. Honorius III *Savelli*	1216-1227
176. Gregorius IX *di Segni* [nephew of #174]	1227-1241
177. Coelestinus IV *da Castiglione*	1241
178. Innocentius IV *Fieschi*	1243-1254
179. Alexander IV *Segni* [nephew of #176]	1254-1261
180. Urbanus IV *Pantaléon* [#19 of Jerusalem]	1261-1264
181. Clemens IV *Foulques*	1265-1268
INTERREGNUM	
182. Gregorius X *Visconti*	1271-1276
183. Innocentius V *de Tarentaise*	1276
184. Adrianus V *Fieschi* [nephew of #178]	1276
185. Ioannes XXI *Juliao*	1276-1277
186. Nicolaus III *Orsini*	1277-1280
187. Martinus IV *de Brie*	1281-1285
188. Honorius IV *Savelli* [great-nephew of #175]	1285-1287
189. Nicolaus IV *Masci*	1288-1292
190. Coelestinus V *del Morrone*	1294
191. Bonifacius VIII *Caetani*	1294-1303
192. Benedictus XI *Boccasini*	1303-1304
193. Clemens V *de Got*	1305-1314
194. Ioannes XXII *Duèse*	1316-1334
Nicolaus V *Rainalducci* [anti-pope]	1328-1330
195. Benedictus XII *Fournier*	1334-1342
196. Clemens VI *Roger*	1342-1352
197. Innocentius VI *Aubert*	1352-1362
198. Urbanus V *de Grimoard*	1362-1370
199. Gregorius XI *de Beaufort*	1370-1378
200. Urbanus VI *Prignano*	1378-1389
Clemens VII *de Boulogne* [anti-pope]	1378-1394
201. Bonifacius IX *Tomacelli*	1389-1404
Benedictus XIII *de Luna* [anti-pope]	1394-1423
202. Innocentius VII *de' Migliorati*	1404-1406

203. Gregorius XII *Correr*	1406-1415
Alexander V *Philarghi* (or *Filargo*) [anti-pope]	1409-1410
Ioannes XXIII *Cossa* [anti-pope]	1410-1415
204. Martinus V *Colonna*	1417-1431
Clemens VIII *Sánchez Muñoz* [anti-pope]	1423-1429
Benedictus XIV *Garnier* [anti-pope]	1425-1430
205. Eugenius IV *Condulmaro*	1431-1447
Felix V *di Savoia* [anti-pope]	1439-1449
206. Nicolaus V *Parentucelli*	1447-1455
207. Calixtus III *de Borja* [uncle of #212]	1455-1458
208. Pius II *Piccolomini* [uncle of #213]	1458-1464
209. Paulus II *Barbo*	1464-1471
210. Sixtus IV *della Rovere*	1471-1484
211. Innocentius VIII *Cibò*	1484-1492
212. Alexander VI *de Borja* [nephew of #207]	1492-1503
213. Pius III *Todeschini-Piccolomini* [nephew of #208]	1503
214. Iulius II *della Rovere* [nephew of #210]	1503-1513
215. Leo X *de' Medici*	1513-1521
216. Adrianus VI *Florensz*	1522-1523
217. Clemens VII *de' Medici* [cousin of #215]	1523-1534
218. Paulus III *Farnese*	1534-1549
219. Iulius III *Ciocchi del Monte*	1550-1555
220. Marcellus II *Cervini*	1555
221. Paulus IV *Carafa*	1555-1559
222. Pius IV *de' Medici*	1559-1565
223. Pius V *Ghislieri*	1566-1572
224. Gregorius XIII *Boncompagni*	1572-1585
225. Sixtus V *Peretti*	1585-1590
226. Urbanus VII *Castagna*	1590
227. Gregorius XIV *Sfondrati*	1590-1591
228. Innocentius IX *Facchinetti*	1591
229. Clemens VIII *Aldobrandini*	1592-1605
230. Leo XI *de' Medici* [nephew of #215]	1605
231. Paulus V *Borghese*	1605-1621
232. Gregorius XV *Ludovisi*	1621-1623
233. Urbanus VIII *Barberini*	1623-1644
234. Innocentius X *Pamfili* (or *Pamphilj*) [#34 of Antioch]	1644-1655
235. Alexander VII *Chigi*	1655-1667
236. Clemens IX *Rospigliosi*	1667-1669
237. Clemens X *Altieri*	1670-1676
238. Innocentius XI *Odescalchi*	1676-1689
239. Alexander VIII *Ottoboni*	1689-1691
240. Innocentius XII *Pignatelli*	1691-1700
241. Clemens XI *Albani*	1700-1721
242. Innocentius XIII *dei Conti*	1721-1724
243. Benedictus XIII *Orsini*	1724-1730

THE CHURCH OF ROME

244. Clemens XII *Corsini*	1730-1740
245. Benedictus XIV *Lambertini*	1740-1758
246. Clemens XIII *della Torre Rezzonico*	1758-1769
247. Clemens XIV *Ganganelli*	1769-1774
248. Pius VI *Braschi*	1775-1799
249. Pius VII *Chiaramonti*	1800-1823
250. Leo XII *della Genga*	1823-1829
251. Pius VIII *Castiglione*	1829-1830
252. Gregorius XVI *Cappellari*	1831-1846
253. Pius IX *Mastai-Ferretti*	1846-1878
254. Leo XIII *Pecci*	1878-1903
255. Pius X *Sarto*	1903-1914
256. Benedictus XV *della Chiesa*	1914-1922
257. Pius XI *Ratti*	1922-1939
258. Pius XII *Pacelli*	1939-1958
259. Ioannes XXIII *Roncalli*	1958-1963
260. Paulus VI *Montini*	1963-1978
261. Ioannes Paulus I *Luciani*	1978
262. Ioannes Paulus II *Wojtyla*	1978-

THE RENOVATED CHURCH OF JESUS CHRIST

The Renovated Church was founded by Michel Collin, who claimed to have had a vision in which Christ told him that he would succeed Pope John XXIII in 1963. Accordingly, on 31 May 1963 he claimed the title of Pope Clement XV at Lourdes, France, and was crowned on 9 June, at the "Little Vatican," in Clemery, France. The Renovated Church rejects Vatican Council II and has amended many of the teachings of the Roman Catholic Church; among others, it permits women priests. Gaston Tremblay, a native of French Quebec, reported a similar vision in 1947, and subsequently founded the Apostles and Disciples of the Infinite Love, Order of the Mother of God, at Saint-Jovite, Québec, in 1958, later bringing it in communion with Clement's church. Tremblay took the religious name Jean de la Trinité. In 1967 Clement expelled Jean and many of his followers; a year later Jean issued a statement that God had now raised up a new pope (himself) to carry on the work of Clement, and that he would be known as Gregory XVII. Clement died during a hundred-days' fast on 24 June 1974. SOURCES: *The Encyclopedia of American Religions* (Melton); *Directory of Autocephalous Bishops* (Prüter); *The Old Catholic Sourcebook* (Prüter & Melton); *Profiles in Belief* (Piepkorn).

POPES OF THE RENOVATED CHURCH OF JESUS CHRIST

260. Clemens XV *Collin*	1963-1974
261. Gregorius XVII *Tremblay*	1968-

XLV.

THE CHURCH OF RUSSIA

The establishment of an independent Russian Church coincided with the decline of the Byzantine Empire, and the simultaneous rise of the Russian Empire. When Emperor Ivan III married the niece of the last Emperor of Constantinople, the claim of succession passed to the Russian state, the princes of which began calling themselves "tsars" (*i.e.*, "caesars"). It was natural that they would seek the independence of their church to bolster their temporal claims. Although the Russian Church claimed autocephaly from 1448, the recognition of Constantinople and the other ancient patriarchates was not secured until 1589, when Patriarch Hieremias II invested Metropolitan Iov as the first Russian primate. The Civil War which ensued sixteen years later, at the death of Tsar Boris Godunov, increased the patriarchs' political influence; this reached its height under Patriarch Filaret Romanov, whose son Mikhail became the first Tsar of the Romanov Dynasty. When Patriarch Adrian died in 1700, Peter the Great refused to allow the election of a new Patriarch, leaving Stefan IAvorskiî (Yavorsky) as *Locum Tenens* for 21 years. In 1721 Peter promulgated a new constitution for the Church, which abolished the office of Patriarch, and placed its governance under a Holy Synod administered by a lay official appointed by the Tsar.

Thus was established the precedent of direct governmental interference in, and control of, the Russian Orthodox Church, a practice which was later continued by the Soviet state; the new constitution made the Tsar the head of the Church, and provided for a procurator, a minister of the crown, to administer its day-to-day affairs. When Tsar Nikolaî II was overthrown in March of 1917, the Russian Orthodox Church convened a national sobor to elect a new Patriarch; Metropolitan Tikhon assumed office in November of that year, almost simultaneously with the outbreak of the Bolshevik Revolution.

The Soviets placed severe restrictions on the revitalized Church, finally imprisoning Tikhon in 1922, and refusing to allow an election for his successor when he died in 1925. Metropolitan Petr became *Locum Tenens*, but was almost immediately arrested; the Metropolitan of Nizhni-Novgorod, Sergiî (previously Metropolitan of Finland), succeeded him later that year. Sergiî issued a declaration in July 1927 in which he altered the Church's official stance toward the

Moscow government from one of hostility to outright praise and cooperation. Outside observers have called this statement either the great betrayal or the great salvation of the Russian Church. With the invasion of the German armies in 1941, the political climate in Moscow changed, as every segment of society unified behind the Russian war effort.

Sergiĭ himself gathered funds, issued calls to arms, organized rallies, and did everything possible to hasten the Nazi defeat. His many contributions gained him the favorable attention of Iosif Stalin, who granted his request for new patriarchal elections. Sergiĭ assumed office in late 1943, and died within six months. During the next forty years the government permitted subsequent elections within a year of each vacancy, and made the Church one of the few officially-recognized Christian organizations in the Soviet Union, thereby setting a precedent for the other Eastern block countries to follow. All other potential "national" Orthodox churches within the USSR, with the exception of the ancient, well-established patriarchates of Armenia and Georgia, were merged into the Moscow Patriarchate, as were some Eastern-rite Catholics (particularly the Ukrainians), and many other Christian denominations and sects. The Church became increasingly active in international Orthodox and ecumenical affairs in the 1970s-1980s, and has been particularly vocal before the World Council of Churches and elsewhere in encouraging anti-nuclear and anti-war movements throughout the world.

During the "glasnost" period of the late 1980s and early '90s, governmental restrictions on the practice of religion in the Soviet Union were gradually lifted, permitting the reopening of old churches, monasteries, cathedrals, and seminaries. At the death of Patriarch Pimen, in 1990, the Russian Orthodox Church was able to conduct relatively free, immediate elections for the first time since 1917, resulting in the selection of a young, vigorous patriarch, Aleksiĭ II. The relaxation of controls has also, however, seen demands from outlying Soviet republics for the reinstitution of national churches as each of these states has declared its independence, and seems certain to result in the same kind of proliferation of religious groups and sects as has already occurred in the West. In the 1990s the Russian Church has been forced to agree to the autonomy of several jurisdictions in the newly independent ex-Soviet republics.

The primate bears the title Patriarch of Moscow and All Russia. The official language of the Church is Russian. The number of believers in Russia is unknown, but certainly numbers in the millions.

SOURCES: *Eastern Christianity and Politics in the Twentieth Century* (Ramet, ed.); *Échos d'Orient*; *Episkepsis*; *Gegenwartslage der Ostkirchen* (Spuler); *History of the Church* (Jedin, ed.); *Jahrbuch der Orthodoxie* (Proc); "Patriarkh" (Buganov); *Orthodoxia*; "50-Letie

Vosstanovleniia Patariarshestva"; *Profiles in Belief* (Piepkorn); *Religion in the Soviet Union* (Kolarz); *The Russian Orthodox Church* (Ellis).

METROPOLITANS OF MOSCOW

1.	Petr	1305-1325
	INTERREGNUM	
2.	Feognost	1328-1352
3.	Aleksiî	1354-1378
4.	Kiprian	1378-1410
5.	Fotiî	1410-1436
6.	Isidor	1436-1448
7.	Iona	1448-1462
8.	Feodor	1462-1467
9.	Filipp I	1467-1472
10.	Gerontiî	1472-1491
11.	Zosima	1491-1496
12.	Simeon	1496-1511
13.	Varlaam	1511-1521
14.	Porfiriî	1521-1522
15.	Daniil	1522-1539
	INTERREGNUM	
16.	Makariî (I)	1542-1563
17.	German	1563-1565
	INTERREGNUM	
18.	Filipp II	1568-1572
19.	Antoniî	1572-1582
20.	Dionisiî	1582-1587
21.	Iov	1587-1589

PATRIARCHS OF RUSSIA
(The Tsarist Patriarchate)

1.	Iov	1589-1605
	Ignatiî [anti-patriarch]	1605-1606
2.	Germogen	1606-1612
	INTERREGNUM	
3.	Filaret *Romanov*	1619-1633
4.	Ioasaf I	1634-1641
5.	Iosif	1642-1652
6.	Nikon	1652-1658
	INTERREGNUM	
7.	Ioasaf II	1667-1672
8.	Pitirim	1672-1673
9.	Ioakim *Savelov*	1674-1690
10.	Adrian	1690-1700

Stefan *IAvorskiî* [locum tenens]	1700-1721

THE PATRIARCHATE DISCONTINUED

ARCHBISHOPS AND METROPOLITANS OF MOSCOW

22.	Iosif (II) *Volchanskiî*	1742-1745
23.	Platon I *Malinovskiî*	1748-1754
	INTERREGNUM	
24.	Timofeî *Sacherbatskiî*	1764-1767
25.	Amvrosiî *Zertis-Kamenskiî*	1768-1771
	INTERREGNUM	
26.	Platon II *Levshin*	1775-1812
	INTERREGNUM	
27.	Avgustin *Vinogradskiî*	1818-1819
28.	Serafim *Glagolevskiî*	1819-1821
29.	Filaret *Drozdov*	1821-1867
30.	Innokentiî *Veniaminov* [#2 of America]	1868-1879
31.	Makariî (II) *Bulgakov*	1879-1882
32.	Ioannikiî *Rudnev* [#8 of Georgia]	1882-1891
33.	Leontiî *Lebedinskiî*	1891-1893
34.	Sergiî *Liapidevksiî*	1893-1898
	INTERREGNUM	
35.	Makariî (III) *Nevskiî*	1912-1917

PATRIARCHS OF RUSSIA

11.	Tikhon *Belavin* [#9 of America]	1917-1925
	INTERREGNUM	
	Petr *Polianskiî* [locum tenens]	1925
	Sergiî *Stragorodskiî* [deputy locum tenens]	1925-1937
	Sergiî *Stragorodskiî* [locum tenens]	1937-1943
12.	Sergiî *Stragorodskiî* [#2 of Finland]	1943-1944
	Aleksiî *Simanskiî* [locum tenens]	1944-1945
13.	Aleksiî I *Simanskiî*	1945-1970
	Pimen *Izvekov* [locum tenens]	1970-1971
14.	Pimen *Izvekov*	1971-1990
15.	Aleksiî II *Ridiger* [#1 of Estonia]	1990-

THE RUSSIAN ORTHODOX CHURCH OUTSIDE RUSSIA

Patriarch Tikhon issued a statement in 1917 urging the faithful to act independently to preserve the Russian Church; subsequently, a group of exiled, pro-tsarist church members and prelates organized a sobor at Sremski Karlovci, Yugoslavia, on 21 November-2 December, 1921, under the presidency of Metropolitan Antoniî of Kiev. The result of this meeting was the organization of the Russian Orthodox Church Outside Russia, sometimes called the Synodal Church. The Church disapproves of the cooperation between the Patriarchal Church and the Russian government, as embodied in the letters issued by Metropolitan (later Patriarch) Sergiî Stragodorskiî in 1926 and 1927. Antoniî became the first head of the Church, with his see at Geneva, Switzerland. He was succeeded in 1936 by Metropolitan Anastasiî (who died in 1965), who was followed on his retirement by Metropolitan Filaret in 1964. The chief see of the Metropolitan was moved during the Second World War to Munich, Germany, and in 1952 to New York. Since then the Church has attracted dissident factions from other exiled churches, particularly those with origins in Eastern Europe. The membership of the Church (roughly 150,000 communicants) is centered primarily in the United States, Western Europe, and Australia, although three dioceses have been established within the former Soviet Union since 1990.

SOURCES: *Eastern Christianity and Politics in the Twentieth Century* (Ramet, ed.); *Episkepsis*; "The First Council of the Russian Church Abroad in Sremski Karlovtsi (21 November-2 December 1921)" (Zernov); *History of the Church* (Jedin, ed.); *Jahrbuch der Orthodoxie* (Proc); *Orthodoxia*; *The Russian Orthodox Church Outside Russia* (Young); *Profiles in Belief* (Piepkorn).

METROPOLITANS OF THE RUSSIAN ORTHODOX CHURCH OUTSIDE RUSSIA

1.	Antoniî *Khrapovitskiî* [#80 of Ukraine]	1921-1936
2.	Anastasiî *Gribanovskiî*	1936-1964
3.	Filaret *Voznesenskiî*	1964-1985
	Vitaliî *Ustinov* [locum tenens]	1985-1986
4.	Vitaliî *Ustinov*	1986-

XLVI.

THE CHURCH OF SERBIA (PEC)

As in the other Slavic countries of Eastern Europe, the fate of the Serbian Orthodox Church has been closely tied to the rise and fall of the secular state. The first King of Serbia, Stefan II, made his brother, Sava, the first Metropolitan of the Church, in 1219; Sava organized the Church, crowned his brother, and established his see at Pec (also called Pech or Ipek). In 1346 a synod proclaimed the Church autocephalous, awarding the primate the title of Patriarch. Except for a brief period from about 1463 to 1557, during which the Church was ruled by Ohrid, it remained independent until the suppression of the South Slav patriarchates in 1766-67, when, at the behest of the Ecumenical Patriarch, Ottoman Sultan Mustafa III placed Pec and Ohrid under Constantinople.

The Serbs revolted against their Turkish overlords beginning in 1806, finally attaining autonomy in 1829, and independence in 1878. Correspondingly, the Serbian Church was given autonomy by Constantinople in 1832, and autocephaly in 1879, the primates using the title Metropolitan Archbishops of Serbia. After World War I, when Serbia became the nucleus of the new state of Yugoslavia, the five autonomous South Slav churches agreed in mid-1919 to the unification of the Serbian Churches, and in August 1920 unified their administrations under a common Patriarch.

Serbian Metropolitan Dimitrije was elected first head of the revived Church on 12 November 1920. Constantinople did not recognized the autocephaly of the new Serbian Church until 1922. The Nazi invasion of 1941 severely disrupted the Church administration, forcing the Patriarch into exile. In addition, the newly-organized Nazi puppet state of Croatia insisted that all subjects in its territory become Roman Catholics; those members of the Orthodox churches who refused to submit were systematically arrested, beaten, and/or murdered.

The primate bears the title Archbishop of Pec, Metropolitan of Belgrade and Karlovci, and Patriarch of Serbia. The official Church language is Serbian. The chief see is located at Belgrade (Beograd). Roughly eleven million communicants are located primarily in Serbia and Montenegro, plus parts of Bosnic-Hercegovina and Croatia, with a strong overseas contingent in the United States.

SOURCES: *Biographisches Lexikon zur Geschichte Südosteuropas* (Bernath & Nehring); *The Bosnian Church* (Fine); *Church and State in Yugoslavia Since 1945* (Alexander); *Eastern Christianity and Politics in the Twentieth Century* (Ramet, ed.); *Échos d'Orient*; *Episkepis*; *Europa World Yearbook*; *Gegenwartslage der Ostkirchen* (Spuler); *The Hapsburg Empire, 1790-1918* (Macartney); *A History of Christianity in the Balkans* (Spinka); *A History of Modern Serbia, 1804-1918* (Petrovich); *History of the Church* (Jedin, ed.); *Jahrbuch der Orthodoxie* (Proc); *Orthodoxia*; "Pecska Patrijarsija" (Grujic); *Profiles in Belief* (Piepkorn); *Srpska Pravoslavna Crkva, 1219-1969* (Lavrentije).

[For information on the former autocephalous Serbian Church of Karlovci, see the chapter on The Churches of Austria-Hungary.]

PATRIARCHS OF PEC
(Metropolitan Archbishops, 1219 and 1506;
Patriarchs, 1346 and 1557)
[Greek primates are listed with both their Serbian and Greek names]

1.	Sava I *Nemanjic*	1219-1233
2.	Arsenije I *Sremac*	1233-1263
3.	Sava II *Nemanjic* [nephew of #1]	1263-1271
4.	Danilo I	1271-1272
5.	Joanikije I	1272-1276
6.	Jevstatije I	1279-1286
7.	Jakov	1286-1292
8.	Jevstatije II	1292-1309
9.	Sava III	1309-1316
10.	Nikodim I	1317-1324
11.	Danilo II (or Daniil)	1324-1337
12.	Joanikije II	1338-1354
13.	Sava IV	1354-1375
14.	Jefrem	1375-1379
15.	Spiridon	1379-1382
	Jefrem [2nd time]	1382-1387
16.	Danilo III	1389
17.	Sava V	1389-1404
18.	Danilo IV	1406
19.	Kirilo I (or Cirilo)	1407-1419
20.	Nikon	1420-1435
	INTERREGNUM	
21.	Teofan I	1446
22.	Nikodim II	1446-1452
	INTERREGNUM	
23.	Arsenije II	1457-1463
24.	Joanikije III	1506?

25.	Jovan I	1508?-1509?
26.	Teodosije I	1520?
27.	Marko	1524?
28.	Simeon	1528-1532?
29.	Pavle I	1530?-1541?
30.	Teofan II	1544?
31.	Josif	1544?
	INTERREGNUM	
32.	Makarije *Sokolovic*	1557-1574
33.	Antonije *Sokolovic*	1572-1575
34.	Gerasim (or Gherasim) *Sokolovic*	1575-1586
35.	Savatije *Sokolovic*	1587
36.	Nikanor	1589?
37.	Jerotej	1589-1591
38.	Filip	1591-1592
39.	Jovan II *Kantul*	1592-1614
40.	Pajsije I *Janjevac*	1614-1647
41.	Gavrilo I *Rajic*	1648-1655
42.	Maksim *Skopljanac*	1655-1674
43.	Arsenije III *Crnojevic* [#1 of Karlovci]	1674-1690
44.	Kalinik I *Skopljanac*	1691-1710
45.	Atanasije I *Ljubojevic*	1711-1712
46.	Mojsije *Rajovic*	1712-1725?
47.	Arsenije IV *Jovanovic Shakabenda* [#8 of Karlovci]	1725?-1737
48.	Joanikije IV (Ióannikios) *Karadza*	1737-1746
49.	Atanasije II *Gavrilovic*	1746-1752
50.	Gavrilo II *Mihailovic Sarajevac*	1752
51.	Gavrilo III (Gabriél)	1752-
52.	Vikentije I (or Vicentije) *Stefanovic*	1756?
53.	Pajsije II (Païsios)	1757?
54.	Gavrilo IV (Gabriél)	1757?-1758
55.	Kiril II	1758-1763
56.	Vasilije *Jovanovic Brkic* (died 1772)	1763-1765
57.	Kalinik II (Kallinikos)	1765-1766
	THE PATRIARCHATE DISCONTINUED	

PATRIARCHS OF SERBIA
(Metropolitans of Beograd 1766, Metropolitan Archbishops 1831, Patriarchs 1920)

58.	Antim I (Anthimos)	
59.	Danilo V (Daniél)	
60.	Jeremije (Hieremias)	-1786
61.	Dionisije I (Dionysios)	1786-1793
62.	Metodije (Methodios)	1793-1801
63.	Leontije (Leontios) *Lambrovic*	1801-1809

64.	Melentije I *Stefanovic* [unconsecrated]	1809-1811
	Leontije [2nd time]	1811-1813
65.	Dionisije II (Dionysios)	1813-1815
66.	Agatangel (Agathangelos) [#243 of Constantinople]	1815-1825
67.	Kirilo III (Kyrillos)	1826-1827
68.	Antim II (Anthimos)	1827-1831
69.	Melentije II *Pavlovic*	1831-1833
70.	Petar *Jovanovic*	1833-1858
71.	Mihaïlo *Jovanovic*	1859-1881
72.	Teodosije II *Mraovic*	1883-1889
	Mihaïlo [2nd time]	1889-1898
73.	Inokentije *Pavlovic*	1898-1905
74.	Dimitrije *Pavlovic*	1905-1930
75.	Varnava *Rosic*	1930-1937
76.	Gavrilo V *Dozhic* [#26 of Montenegro]	1937-1950
	Josif *Zvijanovic* [locum tenens]	1941-1946
77.	Vikentije II *Prodanov*	1950-1958
78.	German *Djoric*	1958-1990
	Jovan *Pavlovic* [locum tenens]	1989-1990
79.	Pavle II *Stojchevic*	1990-

THE CHURCH OF MONTENEGRO

The autonomous Church of Montenegro (Crna Gora) was independent from at least 1491, when Vladika Vavyla assumed temporal as well as spiritual authority after the abdication of the previous ruler. Vladika Danilo I, who succeeded in 1697, restricted future candidates for the office to members of his own family, erecting an hereditary succession similar to that of the Catholicos-Patriarchs of Assyria (q.v.). For the next one hundred and fifty years, each Vladika was followed at his death or deposition by his nephew or cousin. Ironically, it was the second Danilo, in 1852, who broke the string, renouncing his religious authority, and assuming the temporal title of "Prince," while simultaneously announcing his intention to marry. Thereafter, until the end of the Montenegrin state in the aftermath of World War I, the Vladikas maintained religious authority only. In 1920, following the unification of the South Serbs into the new state of Yugoslavia, Metropolitan Gavrilo helped lead the integration of the five autocephalous/autonomous Serbian churches (Serbia, Montenegro, Sremski Karlovci, Bukovina Dalmatia, and the remaining provinces of southeastern Yugoslavia then under the direct control of the Ecumenical Patriarch) into one body. On 12 November 1920, Metropolitan Dimitrij of Serbia was elected Patriarch of the unified Church; Gavrilo himself was elected Patriarch of Serbia in 1937.

Earlier primates bore the title Vladika or Metropolitan of Cetinje and All Montenegro; current church leaders use the title Metropolitan of Montenegro and Primorje (or The Littoral). The Church had roughly 220,000 communicants in 1906. Following the disintegration of Yugoslavia in the early 1990s, there has much local agitation for the re-establishment of an autocephalous church. On 31 October 1993 the "Committee of the Restoration of the Autocephaly of the Montenegrin Orthodox Church" demonstrated in Cetinje during a Serbian Church synod, and chose an exiled bishop, Antonije Abramovic, as the first "Patriarch of Montenegro." He has not been recognized by Serbia or the other orthodox churches.

SOURCES: *Biographisches Lexikon zur Geschichte Südosteuropas* (Bernath & Nehring); *Eastern Europe and the Commonwealth States*; *Échos d'Orient*; *The Falcon & the Eagle* (Treadway); *Manuel d'Histoire, de Généalogie et de Chronologie* (Stokvis); *Rodoslovne Tablice i Grbovi.*

VLADIKAS AND METROPOLITANS OF MONTENEGRO
(Hereditary Prince-Bishops "Vladikas"
of the House of Petrovic-Njegosh, 1697-1852;
Metropolitans of Cetinje, 1852-1920)

1.	Vavyla	1491-1520
2.	German	1520-
3.	Pavel	
4.	Vasilije I	
5.	Nikodim	-1551
6.	Romul	1551-1568
7.	Paonije *Komanin*	1568-1582
8.	Venijamin	1582-1631
9.	Rufim I *Njegosh*	1631-1659
10.	Makarije *Korneciani*	1659-1675
11.	Rufim II *Boljevic*	1675-
12.	Vasilije II *Veljekraïski*	-1689
13.	Visarion I *Baïca*	1689-1695
14.	Sava I *Kalugericic*	1695-1697
15.	Danilo I *Petrovic-Njegosh*	1697-1735
16.	Sava II [coadjutor 1719; cousin of #15]	1735-1750
17.	Vasilije III [coadjutor 1744; nephew of #15]	1750-1766
	Sava II [2nd time]	1766-1767
	Arsenije I *Plamenac* [anti-vladika]	1767-1773
	Sava II [3rd time]	1773-1781
18.	Arsenije I *Plamenac* [2nd time]	1781-1784
19.	Petar I [cousin of #17]	1784-1830
20.	Petar II [nephew of #19]	1830-1851
21.	Danilo II [unconsecrated; nephew of #20]	1851-1852
	INTERREGNUM	
22.	Nikanor *Ivanovic-Njegush*	1855-1860

INTERREGNUM

23.	Ilari(j)on *Roganovic*	1863-1882
24.	Visarion II *Ljubisha*	1882-1884
25.	Mitrofan *Ban*	1885-1920
26.	Gavrilo *Dozhic* [#76 of Serbia]	1920

SERBIAN METROPOLITANS OF MONTENEGRO

	Gavrilo *Dozhic* [as local metropolitan]	1920-1938
27.	Joanikije *Lipovac*	1940-1945
28.	Arsenije II *Bradvarevic*	1947-1960
29.	Danilo III *Dajkovic*	1961-1990
30.	Amfilohije *Radovic*	1990-

PATRIARCHS OF MONTENEGRO

27.	Antonije *Abramovic*	1993-

XLVII.

THE CHURCH OF THE SINAI

The smallest of the universally-recognized autocephalous Orthodox churches is the Church of the Sinai, consisting of the monastery of St. Catherine in the Southern Sinai Desert, and the small neighboring dioceses of Pharan and Raithu. One of the oldest continually-occupied monasteries in the world, having been founded by Emperor Justinian I in 530, St. Catherine's Monastery was autonomous from an early date, as both the Greek Patriarchates of Alexandria and Jerusalem tried to bring it under their jurisdiction; autocephaly was finally granted by Constantinople in 1575, and recognized by the other Orthodox churches in 1782. In the last hundred years the monastery has become known to the outside world for its enormous treasure of original manuscripts dating from early Christian times. The abbot is elected by a council (*synaxis*) of senior monks, and is consecrated by the Greek Orthodox Patriarch of Jerusalem. A church office is also maintained in Cairo, Egypt.

The primate bears the title Archbishop of Sinai, Pharan, and Raithu. The official Church language is Greek. Approximately one hundred communicants worship at the several parishes controlled by the Church of the Sinai, plus the central community of twenty to fifty monks.

SOURCES: "Les Archevêques du Sinai" (Cheikho); "Die Autokephale Kirche des Berges Sinai" (Lubeck); *Échos d'Orient*; *Episkepis*; *History of the Church* (Jedin, ed.); *A History of the Sinai* (Eckenstein); *Jahrbuch der Orthodoxie* (Proc); *Hé Moné tou Horous Sina* (Papamichalopoulos); *Oriens Christianus* (Le Quien); *Orthodoxia*; *Syntomos Historia tés Hieras Monés tou Sina* (Amantos).

ABBOTS AND ARCHBISHOPS OF THE SINAI
(Bishops of Pharan 530, Bishops of Sinai 869, Archbishops 1203?)

1.	Geórgios I	
2.	Netras (or Natéras)	
3.	Móüsés	
4.	Martyrios	400?
5.	Makarios I	454?

6.	Phótios	544?-546?
7.	Theodóros	649?-680?
8.	Kónstantinos	-869?
9.	Markos I	869-
10.	Élias	900?
11.	Makarios II	967?
12.	Petros	985?
13.	Symeón I	1003-1035
14.	Iórios	1035-
15.	Ióannés I *Athénaios*	1081-1091
16.	Markos II	1100?
17.	Zacharias	1103-1114
	INTERREGNUM	
18.	Geórgios II	1130-1149
	INTERREGNUM	
19.	Gabriél I	1154-1160
20.	Ióannés II	1164?
21.	Germanos I	1177?
22.	Markos III	1181?
23.	Symeón II	1203-1223
24.	Euthymios	1223-1224
25.	Makarios III	1224-
26.	Germanos II	1228?
27.	Theodosios	1239?
28.	Symeón III	1258?
29.	Ióannés III	1265-1290
30.	Arsenios I	1290-1299?
31.	Ióannés IV	1299?-
32.	Symeón IV	1306-1324
33.	Dórotheos I	1324-1333
34.	Germanos III	1333-
35.	Arsenios II	1338?
36.	Markos IV	1375?
37.	Iób	1395?
38.	Athanasios I	1410?
39.	Sabbas	1429?
40.	Abraamios (or Abramios)	1435?
41.	Gabriél II	1445?
42.	Michaél	1455?
43.	Silouanos	1465?
44.	Kyrillos I	1470?
45.	Solomón	1480?
46.	Makarios IV	1486?
47.	Lazaros	1491?
48.	Markos V	1496?
49.	Daniél	1507?

50.	Klémés	1514?
51.	Sóphronios	1540?-1545
52.	Makarios V *Kyprios*	1547-
53.	Neilos *Kouerinos*	1555?
54.	Eugenios	1567-1583
55.	Anastasios	1583-1592
56.	Laurentios	1592-1617
57.	Ióasaph *apo Rhodou*	1617-1660
58.	Nektarios [#119 of Jerusalem]	1660-1661
59.	Ananias	1661-1671
60.	Ióannikios I *Laskaris*	1671-1702
61.	Kosmas *Byzantios* [#218 of Constantinople; #96 of Alexandria]	1703-1706
62.	Athanasios II *apo Naousés tés Makedonias*	1708-1720
63.	Ióannikios II *Lesbios*	1721-1728
64.	Niképhoros *Marthalés Glykys*	1728-1747
65.	Kónstantios I	1748-1759
66.	Kyrillos II *Krés*	1759-1790
	INTERREGNUM	
67.	Dórotheos II *Byzantios*	1794-1797
	INTERREGNUM	
68.	Kónstantios II [#244 of Constantinople]	1804-1859
69.	Kyrillos III *Byzantios*	1859-1867
70.	Kallistratos	1867-1884
71.	Porphyrios I *apo Zakynthou*	1885-1904
72.	Porphyrios II *Logothetés*	1904-1926
73.	Porphyrios III *Paulinos*	1926-1968
74.	Grégorios	1969-1973
75.	Damianos *Samartsés*	1973-

XLVIII.

THE CHURCHES OF UKRAINE

The Russian Revolution of 1917 revitalized the long-dormant movement for Ukrainian independence, and simultaneously led to demands for a separate Ukrainian Orthodox Church. A series of sobors during the height of the Russian Civil War resulted in a split in the Church, with the hierarchy unanimously supporting the Moscow patriarchate, and many laymen and lesser clergy calling for autocephaly. The Ukrainian government issued the "Law on the Supreme Authority of the Ukrainian Church" on 1 January 1919, establishing an autonomous Ukrainian Church, but was unable to implement it, due to the ensuing Soviet invasion of Ukraine.

The reform movement organized the All-Ukrainian Orthodox Church Council in 1919-20, taking over a number of parishes previously controlled by Moscow. The Russian bishop of Kiev then suspended the priestly functions of any clergy supporting the movement; the Council responded by declaring unilateral autocephaly on 5 May 1920. Having no bishops, the movement elected Archpriest Vasyl' Lypkivskiî Metropolitan of Kiev and All Ukraine on 23 October 1921, making him bishop through a laying-on of hands by the members of the sobor. He in turn ordained other bishops.

Many of the other Orthodox churches refused to recognize the validity of Lypkivskiî's election or consecration, or the validity of the consecrations made unilaterally by him, in violation of usual Orthodox practice; and he also faced increasingly harsh repression from the Soviets, finally being deposed by them in October 1927. The sobor then elected Mykolaî Boretskiî as his successor. The government forcibly convened an extraordinary sobor in January 1930, for the sole purpose of dissolving the Church; its leaders were then imprisoned or exiled.

The German occupation of Ukraine led to a revitalization of Orthodox religious life there, and the establishment of two churches: the Autonomous Orthodox Church in Ukraine was founded in August 1941, under the leadership of Metropolitan Aleksiî Hromadskiî; it acknowledged the supremacy of the Moscow Patriarchate, but refused its authority while the Soviets controlled Russia; the Ukrainian Autocephalous Orthodox Church was founded in 1942 by Metropolitan Dionizus of Poland, who consecrated Polykarp Sikorskiî Metropolitan.

Attempts to unite the two churches failed in 1942. Metropolitan Aleksiî was assassinated by partisans in 1943. When the Germans withdrew from Ukraine in 1943-44, most of the clergy followed them into exile; those who remained were arrested or deposed, their parishes being reincorporated against their will into the Patriarchate of Russia, which established its own metropolitanate at Kiev.

Metropolitan Polykarp and his followers settled in western Europe. At a sobor in 1947 the Church split into two factions, the larger following Polykarp, the smaller Archbishop Hryhoriî (for which see below). Polykarp died in Paris in 1953, when he was succeeded by Nikanor Abramovych, whose seat was located at Karlsruhe, West Germany. Nikanor established communion with the Canadian Ukrainian Church and the UOC-USA in 1957; at his death in 1969, he was succeeded by Mstyslav Skrypnyk, who became head of the UOC-USA in 1971. The administrative offices of the Church were then transferred to South Bound Brook, New Jersey, although the two churches remain legally and canonically independent.

Following the election of Russian Patriarch Aleksiî II in 1990, the Synod of the Russian Church announced that it had granted the metropolitanate Ukrainian Orthodox Church (hereafter known as the Ukrainian Orthodox Church—Moscow) complete autonomy, and that the latter body would henceforth be allowed to be self-governing, with its own Synod. However, nonagenarian Metropolitan Mstyslav Skrypnyk of the Ukrainian Autocephalous Orthodox Church, head of one of the largest independent jurisdictions outside the former Soviet Union, and himself one of the last survivors of the remnants of the original Ukrainian hierarchy, returned to Kiev and was proclaimed Patriarch Mstyslav I on 18 November 1990.

Russian-appointed Metropolitan Filaret Denisenko at first opposed Mstyslav, but when scandals in the former's personal life resulted in him being stripped of all authority by Russian Patriarch Aleksiî II in May 1992, he abruptly recognized Mstyslav and tried to subsume his Church, proclaiming the deposition of the elderly primate on 16 December 1992. Meanwhile, the Holy Synod of the Church of Russia elected on 27 May 1992 a new Metropolitan (soon elevated to the title of Exarch), Volodymyr Slobodan, leaving three distinct factions in Kiev, neither of them recognizing the others' jurisdictions, and all fighting over legal and actual possession of church parishes and properties. Patriarch Mstyslav died on 11 June 1993. One faction (the Ukrainian Orthodox Church—Kiev) elected Volodymyr Romaniuk the new Patriarch, with Metropolitan Filaret as Deputy Head; the other (the Ukrainian Autocephalous Orthodox Church) named Dmytro IArema as Patriarch. The two rival patriarchs were consecrated within ten days of each other in October 1993. The Ukrainian government has variously supported the factions of Denisenko, Romaniuk, and Slobodan, depending on the political winds.

The primate bears the title Exarch or Patriarch of Kiev and All Ukraine. Romaniuk's church claims 15 million communicants and 3,000 parishes under its control; IArema's church claims 1,500 parishes; Slobodan's church claims 5,000 parishes; all of these figures are likely exaggerated. The official language of these churches is Ukrainian.

SOURCES: *Échos d'Orient*; *The Encyclopedia of American Religions* (Melton); *Episkepsis*; *Gegenwartslage der Ostkirchen* (Spuler); *History of the Church* (Jedin, ed.); *Jahrbuch der Orthodoxie* (Proc); *The Old Catholic Sourcebook* (Prüter & Melton); *Narys Istorii Ukraïns'koi Pravoslavnoi Tserkby (An Outline of the History of the Ukrainian Orthodox Church)* (Vlasovs'kyî); *Die Orthodoxe Kirche in der Ukraine von 1917 bis 1945* (Heyer); *Orthodoxia*; *Profiles in Belief* (Piepkorn); *Religion in the Soviet Union* (Kolarz); *Ukraine: A Concise Encyclopaedia* (Nubijovyc).

METROPOLITAN ARCHBISHOPS OF UKRAINE
(Metropolitans of Kiev 988, Metropolitans of Kiev and All Rus' 1243, Metropolitans of Kiev and Halych 1507)

1.	Mykhaïl I	988-991
2.	Leontiî	991-1004
3.	Ioann I	1004-1038
4.	Feopempt	1039-
5.	Ilarion	1051-1054
6.	IEfrem I	1055-
7.	Hryhoriî I	1072-1073
8.	Kyryl I	1073-1077
9.	Ioann II	1077-1089
10.	Ioann III	1089-1090
11.	IEfrem II	1090-1096
12.	Mykolaî I	1097-1101
13.	Nikyfor I	1103-1121
14.	Nykyta	1122-1126
	INTERREGNUM	
15.	Mykhaïl II	1130-1145
16.	Klyment	1147-1154
17.	Konstantyn I	1154-1158
18.	Feodor	1160-1163
19.	Ioann IV	1164-1165
20.	Konstantyn II	1167-1183?
21.	Nikyfor II	1183-1197
	INTERREGNUM	
22.	Matfeî	1210-1220
	INTERREGNUM	
23.	Kyryl II	1224-1233

	INTERREGNUM	
24.	Iosyf I	1237-1240?
	INTERREGNUM	
25.	Kyryl III	1243-1281
26.	Maksym *Hrek "The Greek"* (Maximos)	1283-1305
	INTERREGNUM	
27.	Petr I (or Petro)	1308-1326
28.	Feognost	1328-1353
29.	Aleksiî	1354-1378
30.	Mykhaïl-Mitay	1378?-1380?
31.	Pimen	
32.	Dionysiî I	
33.	Kyprian	1389-1406
34.	Fotiî	1408-1431
35.	Herasym	1431-1435
36.	Isydor I	1437
	INTERREGNUM	
38.	Iona I	1448-1458
39.	Hryhoriî II *Bolharyn*	1458-1475
40.	Mysaïl	1475-1480
41.	Symeon	1480-1488
	INTERREGNUM	
42.	Iona II *Hlezna*	1492-1494
43.	Makariî I	1495-1497
44.	Iosyf II *Bolharynovych*	1498-1501
45.	Iona III	1502-1507
46.	Iosyf III *Soltan*	1507-1522
47.	Iosyf IV	1522-1534
48.	Makariî II	1534-1556
49.	Syl'vestr I *Belkuvych*	1556-1567
50.	Iona IV *Protasevych-Ostrovskiî*	1568-1577
51.	Iliia *Kucha*	1577-1579
52.	Onysyfor *Petrovych-Divochka*	1579-1589
53.	Mykhaïl III *Rohoza*	1589-1596
	INTERREGNUM	

RUSSIAN METROPOLITANS OF UKRAINE

54.	Ipatiî *Potsifi*	1599-1613
	INTERREGNUM	
55.	Iov *Borets'kiî*	1620-1631
56.	Isaiia *Kopynskiî*	1631-1632
57.	Isaak *Boryshevych*	1633
58.	Petr II *Mohyla*	1633-1647
59.	Syl'vestr II *Kosiv*	1647-1653
60.	Dionysiî II *Balaban*	1657-1663

61.	Iosyf V *Neliubovych-Tukals'kyî*	1663-1675
62.	Antoniî I *Vynkyî*	1675-1679

INTERREGNUM

63.	Hedeon *Sviatopolk-Chetveryns'kyî*	1685-1690
64.	Varlaam I *IAsyns'kyî*	1690-1707
65.	Iosyf VI *Krokovs'kyî*	1708-1718

INTERREGNUM

66.	Varlaam II *Vonatovych*	1722-1730
67.	Rafaïl *Zaborovs'kyî*	1731-1747
68.	Tymofiî *Shcherbants'kiî*	1748-1757
69.	Arseniî I *Mohylians'kyî*	1757-1770
70.	Havryïl I *Kremianets'kyî*	1770-1783
71.	Samuïl *Myslavs'kyî*	1783-1796
72.	IErofei *Malits'kyî*	1796-1799
73.	Havryïl II *Banulesko-Bodoni*	1799-1803
74.	Serapion *Aleksandrovych*	1803-1822
75.	IEvgeniî *Bolkhovytynov*	1822-1837
76.	Filaret I *Amfiteatrov*	1837-1857
77.	Isydor II *Nikol's'kyî*	1858-1860
78.	Arseniî II *Moskvin*	1860-

[METROPOLITANS UNKNOWN]

79.	Volodymyr I *Bogoiavlens'skyî* [#11 of Georgia]	1915-1918
80.	Anton II *Khrapovits'kyî* [#1 of Russia—Synodal]	1918-1920
81.	Mykhaïl IV	1921-1929
82.	Konstantyn III *Dzhakov*	1929-1937

INTERREGNUM

83.	Mykolaî II *IArushevych*	1940-1944
84.	Ioann V *Sokolov*	1944-1964
85.	Ioasaf *Leluchyn*	1964-1966
86.	Filaret II *Denisenko*	1966-1992
87.	Volodymyr II *Slobodan*	1992-

PATRIARCHS OF THE UKRAINIAN AUTOCEPHALOUS ORTHODOX CHURCH
(Metropolitans 1921, Patriarchs 1990)

81.	Vasyl'(iî) *Lypkivs'kyî*	1921-1927
82.	Mykolaî II *Borets'kyî*	1927-1930

INTERREGNUM

83.	Polykarp *Sikors'kyî*	1942-1953
84.	Nikanor *Burshak-Abramovych*	1953-1969
85.	Mstyslav *Skrypnyk* [#3 of Canada; #2 of USA]	1969-1993
	Mykolaî Hrokh [locum tenens]	1990-1991
	Antoniî Masendych [locum tenens]	1991-1993
86.	Dymytrii *IArema*	1993-

PATRIARCHS OF THE UKRAINIAN ORTHODOX CHURCH—KIEVAN PATRIARCHATE

86.	Volodymyr II *Romaniuk*	1993-

METROPOLITANS OF THE UKRAINIAN AUTONOMOUS CHURCH

1.	Aleksiî *Hromads'kyî*	1942-1943

METROPOLITANS OF THE UKRAINIAN CHURCH OF HALYCH

1.	Aleksiî	1140?
2.	Kuz'ma	1156?
3.	Nifont	1303-1305
4.	Havryïl	1331?
5.	Feodor	1337-1347
6.	Antoniî	1371-1391

MERGED WITH THE METROPOLITANATE OF KIEV

UKRAINIAN ORTHODOX CHURCHES IN EXILE

THE UKRAINIAN GREEK ORTHODOX CHURCH OF CANADA

The Ukrainian Greek Orthodox Church in Canada was organized in 1918 as an autocephalous church, under a Syrian bishop, Germanos. In 1924 Ioan Teodorovich came to America, and became head of both the Canadian and American churches. Ilarion Ohiîenko was consecrated as the first Metropolitan Archbishop of the Canadian Church in 1951. Communion was established in 1957 with the UOC-USA and with the church in Europe. After the election of Ukrainian Patriarch Mstyslav I in 1990, Metropolitan Vasyl' severed the connections with the American church, and joined the Greek Orthodox Archdiocese of North and South America, acknowledging the supremacy of the Ecumenical Patriarch, and giving up any claims of autocephaly. The chief see of the Church is located at Winnipeg, Manitoba. The primate uses the title Metropolitan of Winnipeg and of All Canada. The roughly 150,000 communicants are located mostly in the large cities of central Canada.

SOURCES: *Eastern Christianity and Politics in the Twentieth Century* (Ramet, ed.); *The Encyclopedia of American Religions* (Melton); *History of the Church* (Jedin, ed.); *Jahrbuch der Orthodoxie* (Proc); *The Old Catholic Sourcebook* (Prüter & Melton); *Profiles in Belief* (Piepkorn).

METROPOLITAN ARCHBISHOPS OF THE
UKRAINIAN GREEK ORTHODOX CHURCH OF CANADA
(Bishops 1918, Metropolitans 1951)

1.	Herman (Germanos)	1918-1924
2.	Ioann *Teodorovych* [#1 of USA]	1924-1947
3.	Mstyslav *Skrypnyk* [#85 of Autocephalous]	1947-1950
4.	Ilarion *Ohiîenko*	1951-1972
5.	Mykhaïl *Horoshyî*	1972-1975
6.	Andreî *Metiiuk*	1975-1985
7.	Vasyl' *Fedak*	1985-

THE UKRAINIAN ORTHODOX CHURCH
OF THE UNITED STATES

The Ukrainian Orthodox Church of the United States of America
(Autocephalous) was organized in 1919 by Ukrainian immigrants, re-
ceiving its first Metropolitan, Ioan Teodorovych, in 1924. Since questions were raised concerning the validity of his consecration, he was
provisionally reconsecrated by two Ukrainian bishops in 1949. At his
death on 3 March 1971, he was succeeded by Metropolitan Archbishop
Mstyslav Skrypnyk, head of the Ukrainian Autocephalous Orthodox
Church (of Europe), who made himself Patriarch of the newly independent Church in Ukraine in 1990. When he died in 1993, the mother
church split, and the American branch declined to support either of the
new patriarchs, maintaining its independence by electing its own
metropolitan, Konstantyn. Following the lead of its Canadian counterpart, the Church joined the Greek Orthodox Archdiocese of North and
South America early in 1995, acknowledging the supremacy of the Ecumenical Patriarch, and giving up its claim to autocephaly. The chief
see of the church is located in South Holland, Illinois. The church has
branches in Great Britain, Franch, and South America, with about
87,000 communicants. The primate now uses the title Metropolitan of
Chicago and of the Ukrainian Orthodox Church in the Diaspora.
SOURCES: *The Encyclopedia of American Religions* (Melton); *History
of the Church* (Jedin, ed.); *Jahrbuch der Orthodoxie* (Proc); *The Old
Catholic Sourcebook* (Prüter & Melton); *Profiles in Belief* (Piepkorn).

METROPOLITAN ARCHBISHOPS OF THE UKRAINIAN
ORTHODOX CHURCH OF THE USA

1.	Ioann *Teodorovych* [#2 of Canada]	1924-1971
2.	Mstyslav *Skrypnyk* [#3 of Canada; #85 of Ukraine]	1971-1993
3.	Konstantyn Buggan	1993-

THE UKRAINIAN ORTHODOX CHURCH OF AMERICA

Other exiles organized the Ukrainian Autocephalic Orthodox Church in Exile in 1954 at Brooklyn, under the leadership of Archbishops Palladiî Vydybida-Rudenko and Ihor Huba. After Palladiî's death, on 1 September 1971, the Church broke into factions, the largest of which merged with the Ukrainian Orthodox Church of America and Canada. The latter had been founded in 1931 under the leadership of Iosyf Zuk and the aegis of the Greek Orthodox Archdiocese of North and South America of the Ecumenical Patriarchate. Bishop Andreî Kushchak succeeded Bohdan Shpylka in 1967, and was named Metropolitan in 1983 by the Ecumenical Patriarch; his successor dropped the Canadian affiliation when the Ukrainian Greek Orthodox Church of Canada joined with Constantinople in 1990. This church is said to have about 25,000 members in North America. SOURCES: *The Encyclopedia of American Religions* (Melton); *History of the Church* (Jedin, ed.); *Jahrbuch der Orthodoxie* (Proc); *The Old Catholic Sourcebook* (Prüter & Melton); *Profiles in Belief* (Piepkorn).

ARCHBISHOP OF THE UKRAINIAN AUTOCEPHALOUS ORTHODOX CHURCH IN EXILE

1. Palladiî *Vydybida-Rudenko*   1954-1971
    MERGED WITH THE UKRAINIAN ORTHODOX CHURCH OF AMERICA.

METROPOLITANS OF THE UKRAINIAN ORTHODOX CHURCH OF AMERICA AND CANADA

1.	Iosyf *Zuk*	1928-1934
2.	Bohdan *Shpylka*	1937-1965
3.	Andreî *Kushchak*	1966-1986
4.	Vsevolod *Maîdanskiî*	1987-

THE UKRAINIAN AUTOCEPHALOUS CHURCH IN THE USA

The Ukrainian Autocephalous Orthodox Church in the United States of America, sometimes called the Synodical or Sobornopravnaia Church, was founded in Germany in 1947 by Metropolitan Hryhoriî Ohiîchuk, who was consecrated at Kiev in 1942 by Metropolitan Polykarp, and fled the Ukraine in 1944. He withdrew from Polykarp's group in 1947, and organized his own church in Chicago in 1950. The UAOC-USA regards itself the successor in spirit to the church of Lypkivskyî. On 11 May 1980 a joint sobor with bishops of the Slavonic Orthodox Church (see Czechoslovakia) led to a declaration of communion. Two years

217

later, on 3 July 1982, Metropolitan Andreî Prazsky of the Slavonic Church was elected Metropolitan Archbishop Coadjutor with the right of succession. He automatically succeeded Hryhoriî when the latter died on 16 February 1985. The administrative offices of the Ukrainian Church were then transferred to Bronx, New York, and merged with those of the Slavonic Church; however, the two churches remained canonically and legally independent. On Prazsky's death on 16 December 1990, the churches again separated. The Church is said to have roughly 5,000 members located chiefly in the northeastern United States. SOURCES: *The Encyclopedia of American Religions* (Melton); *History of the Church* (Jedin, ed.); *Jahrbuch der Orthodoxie* (Proc); *The Old Catholic Sourcebook* (Prüter & Melton); *Profiles in Belief* (Piepkorn); Bishop Andrew Prazsky.

METROPOLITAN ARCHBISHOPS OF THE UKRAINIAN AUTOCEPHALOUS ORTHODOX CHURCH IN THE USA

1.	Hryhoriî *Ohiîchuk*	1947-1985
2.	Andreî *Prazsky*	1985-1990

THE AUTOCEPHALOUS GREEK ORTHODOX CHURCH OF AUSTRALIA

Affiliated with the UAOC-USA is the Autocephalous Greek Orthodox Church of Australia, whose Metropolitan Archbishop, Spyridon, was consecrated in 1969 by Metropolitan Hryhoriî and Archbishop Hennadiî to serve Greek-speaking communities. His seat is located at Sydney, Australia. Sources: *Profiles in Belief* (Piepkorn).

METROPOLITAN ARCHBISHOPS OF THE AUTOCEPHALOUS GREEK ORTHODOX CHURCH OF AUSTRALIA

1.	Spyridón	1969-

SELECTED BIBLIOGRAPHY

This bibliography makes no attempt to provide a comprehensive listing of resources on the Eastern churches; rather, it reflects the materials which I personally found useful in compiling this book. I have also listed complete runs of those journals which were consulted for their news and obituary sections over a long span of years.

Alexander, Stella. *Church and State in Yugoslavia Since 1945.* Cambridge: Cambridge University Press, 1979.

Almanach of the Melkite-Greek Catholic Church 1986. Journieh, Lebanon: Le Lien, 1986.

Amantos, Kónstantinos. *Syntomos Historia tés Hieras Monés tou Sina.* Thessaloniké: [s.n.], 1953.

Andersen, Knud Tage. *Ethiopiens Ortodokse Kirke.* København: Udg. af Dansk Ethioper Mission, 1971.

Annuario Pontificio per l'Annò 1982- . Città del Vaticano: Libreria Editrice Vaticana, 1982- .

Antreassian, Assadour. *Jerusalem and the Armenians.* Jerusalem: St. James Press, 1968.

Arbanités, Athanasios K. *Historia tés Assyriachés Nestorianikés Ekklésias.* Athénai: Athénais Philekpaideutikés Etaireias, 1968.

Assemani, Giuseppi Luigi [*i.e.*, Yusuf al-Sim'ani]. *De Catholicis Seu Patriarchis Chaldaeorum et Nestorianorum.* Romae: Monaldini, 1775. Reprinted: Farnborough, England: Gregg International Publishers, 1969.

Assemani, Giuseppi Simone [i.e., Yusuf Sim'an al-Sim'ani]. *Series Chronologica Patriarcharum Antiochiae.* Romae: Ex Typographia Polyglotta, 1881. Reprinted: Farnborough, England: Gregg International Publishers, 1969.

Atiya, Aziz Suryal, ed. *The Coptic Encyclopedia.* New York: Macmillan Publishing Co., 1991, 8 vols.

Atiya, Aziz Suryal. *History of Eastern Christianity.* Notre Dame, IN: University of Notre Dame Press, 1968.

Atiya, Aziz Suryal. *History of the Patriarchs of the Egyptian Church.* Cairo: [s.n.], 1943-59, 3 vols.

Attwater, Donald. *The Catholic Eastern Churches.* Milwaukee, WI: Bruce Publishing Co., 1935. Revised and expanded as: *The Christian Churches of the East.* Milwaukee, WI: Bruce Publishing Co., 1961, 2 vols.

Babken Giwleserean, Catholicos of Armenian Cilicia. *Patmutiun Katoghikosats Kilikoy: 1441-en Minchev Mer Orere.* Antelias, Lebanon: Tparan Tbrevanuts Katoghikosutean Kilikoy, 1939.

Barrett, David B. *World Christian Encyclopedia.* Oxford: Oxford University Press, 1982.

Basileios, Bishop of Lémnos. *Episkopikoi Katalogoi Hellados.* Athénai: [s.n.], 1972.

Batalden, Stephen K., ed. *Seeking God: The Recovery of Religious Identity in Orthodox Russia, Ukraine, and Georgia.* DeKalb, IL: Northern Illinois University Press, 1993.

Bernath, Mathias, and Karl Nehring, eds. *Biographisches Lexikon zur Geschichte Südosteuropas.* München: R. Oldenbourg Verlag, 1974-81, 4 vols.

Binder, Leonard, ed. *Politics in Lebanon.* New York: John Wiley & Sons, 1966.

Brown, Leslie. *The Indian Christians of St Thomas: An Account of the Ancient Syrian Church of Malabar.* Cambridge: Cambridge University Press, 1982.

Buganov, V. I. "Patriarkh," in *Bol'shaia Sovetskaia Entsiklopediia,* Vol. 19, p. 281. Moskva: Bol'shaia Sovetskaia Entsiklopediia, 197- .

Burgess, Michael. *Eastern Churches Review: An Index to Volumes I-X, 1966-1978.* San Bernardino, CA: St. Willibrord's Press, forthcoming.

Busek, Vratislav, and Nicolas Spulber, eds. *Czechoslovakia.* New York: Published for the Mid-European Studies Center of the Free Europe Committee by Frederick A. Praeger, 1957.

The Catholic Encyclopedia. New York: Encyclopedia Press, 1908, 15 vols.

Catholicate Sapthathi Souvenir. Kottayam, India: Malankara Orthodox Syrian Church, 1982.

Chabot, J. B. "Les Listes Patriarcales de L'Église Maronite: Étude Critique et Historique," in *Mémoires de L'Academie des Inscriptions et Belles-Lettres* 43 (1951): 21-43.

Cheikho, Louis. "Les Archevêques du Sinai," in *Mélanges de la Faculté Orientale de St. Joseph* 2 (1907): 408.

Cherney, Alexander. *The Latvian Orthodox Church.* Welshpool, Powys, Wales: Stylite Publishing Ltd., 1985.

Chrysostomos Papadopoulos, Archbishop of Greece. *Historia tés Ekklésias Alexandreias (62-1934).* Alexandreia: Patriarchikon Typographeion, 1935.

Chrysostomos Papadopoulos, Archbishop of Greece. *Historia tés Ekklésias Antiocheias.* Alexandreia: [Patriarchikon Typographeion], 1951.

Chrysostomos Papadopoulos, Archbishop of Greece. *Historia tés Ekklésias Hellados.* Athénai: P. A. Petrakos, 1920.

Chrysostomos Papadopoulos, Archbishop of Greece. *Historia tés Ekklésias Hierosolymón*. Alexandreia: Patriarchikon Typographeion, 1910.

Cobham, Claude Delaval. *The Patriarchs of Constantinople*. London: Ares Publishers, 1911.

Cramer, Maria. *Das Christlich-Koptische Agypten Einst und Heute*. Weisbaden: Otto Harrassowitz, 1959.

Daniel, David. *The Orthodox Church of India: History*. New Delhi: Rachel Daniel, 1972. 2nd ed., 1986.

Daniel, I. *The Malabar Church and Other Orthodox Churches*. Haripad, India: Suvarna Bharathi Press, 1950.

Daniel, I. *The Syrian Church of Malabar*. Madras: Diocesan Press, 1945.

Deset Godini Bulgarska Patriarshiia. Sofia: Sinodalno Izd-vo., 1963.

Dib, Pierre. *L'Église Maronite*. Beyrouth: Édition de la Sagesse, 1962-1973, 3 vols.

Dictionnaire d'Archéologie Chrétienne et de Liturgie. Paris: Letouzey, 1907-1953, 15 vols.

Dictionnaire de Théologie Catholique. Paris: Letouzey, 1909-1950, 15 vols.

Dictionnaire d'Histoire et de Géographie Ecclésiastique. Paris: Letouzey, 1912-1995+ (in progress), 24+ vols.

Dowsett, C. J. F. "The Albanian Chronicle of Mxit'ar Gos," in *Bulletin of the School of Oriental and African Studies* 21: 472-490.

Dowsett, C. J. F. "A Neglected Passage in the History of the Caucasian Albanians," in *Bulletin of the School of Oriental and African Studies* 19: 456-468.

Drinov, Marin. *Isturicheski Pregled' na Bulgarska-ta Tsurkva ot' Samo-to i Hachalo i do Dnes'*. Vienzh: L. Sommepovzh, 1869.

Eastern Churches News Letter. London: Anglican and Eastern Churches Association, n.s. Nos. 9- , 1979- . News sections.

Eastern Churches Review. London: Oxford University Press (and others), 1966-1978, 10 vols. News and Comments, Appointments, and Obituaries sections.

Eastern Europe and the Commonwealth States. London: Europa Publications, 1993- . 2nd ed., 1994.

Échos d'Orient. Paris: Échoes d'Orient, Vols. 1-40, 1897-1942. News sections.

Eckenstein, Lina. *A History of the Sinai*. New York: Macmillan, 1921.

Eesti Apostlik Ortodoksne Kirik Eksiilis, 1944-1960. Stockholm: Eesti Apostliku Ortodoksne Kiriku Kultuurfond, 1961.

Ellis, Jane. *The Russian Orthodox Church: A Contemporary History*. Bloomington & Indianapolis: Indiana University Press, 1986.

Episkepsis. Chambésy, Switzerland: Le Centre Orthodoxe du Patriarcat Oecuménique, 1982- . News and obituaries.

The Europa World Year Book. London: Europa Publications, 1947- .

Fenwick, John R. K. *The Malabar Independent Syrian Church*. Nottingham, England: Grove Books, 1992.

Fine, John V. A., Jr. *The Bosnian Church: A New Interpretation: A Study of the Bosnian Church of Its Place in State and Society from the 13th to the 15th Centuries*. Boulder, CO: East European Quarterly, 1975.

Fortescue, Adrian. *The Lesser Eastern Churches*. New York: AMS Press, 1972. First published 1913.

Frazee, Charles A. *The Orthodox Church and Independent Greece, 1821-1852*. Cambridge: Cambridge University Press, 1969.

Gedeón, Manouél I. *Patriarchikoi Pinakes*. Kónstantinopoleós: Lorenz & Keil, 1890.

Gennadios, Metropolitan of Hélioupoleós and Thierón, ed. *Historia tou Oikoumenikou Patriarcheiou*. Athénai: Kon. Theolokikés Scholés, 1953.

Ghabra'il, Mikha'il Abd Allah. *Histoire de L'Église Syriaque Maronite d'Antioche*. 1900.

Grbic, Manojlo. *Karlovacko Vladicanstvo: Prilog k Istoriji Srpske Pravoslavne Crkve*. Karlovac: Stamparija Karla Hauptfelda, 1891, 3 vols.

Grujic, R. "Pecska Patrijarsija," in *Narodna Enciklopedija Srpsko-Hrvatsko-Slovenacka*, Vol. III, p. 389-399. Zagreb: 1928.

Guidi, I. "Le Liste dei Metropoliti d'Abissinia," in *Bessarione* 4 (Luglio-Agosto, 1899): 1-16.

Hackett, John. *A History of the Orthodox Church of Cyprus from the Coming of the Apostles Paul and Barnabas to the Commencement of the British Occupation (A.D. 45-A.D.1878)*. London: Methuen, 1901.

Haddad, Robert M. *Syrian Christians in Muslim Society*. Princeton, NJ: Princeton University Press, 1970.

Hagiotaphitikon Hémerlologion. Hierosolyma: Ekdosis Hierou Koinou tou Panagiou Taphou, 1975?- .

Harik, Iliya F. *Politics and Change in a Traditional Society: Lebanon, 1711-1845*. Princeton, NJ: Princeton University Press, 1968.

Heyer, Friedrich. *Die Orthodoxe Kirche in der Ukraine von 1917 bis 1945*. Koln-Braunsfeld: Rudolf Muller, 1953.

Hussey, J. M. *The Orthodox Church in the Byzantine Empire*. Oxford: Clarendon Press, 1986.

Hyatt, Harry Middleton. *The Church of Abyssinia*. London: Luzac & Co., 1928.

Jacob, Xavier. "An Autocephalous Turkish Orthodox Church," in *Eastern Chur-ches Review* 3 (Spring, 1970): 59-71.

Jedin, Hubert. *History of the Church*. New York: Crossroad, 1980-81, 10 vols.

Kamil, Jill. *Coptic Egypt: History and Guide*. Cairo: American University in Cairo Press, 1987.

Kazhdan, Alexander P., ed. *The Oxford Dictionary of Byzantium*. New York, Oxford: Oxford University Press, 1991, 3 vols.

Keok'chian, Vahram. *Hay Erowsagheme Darerow Mejen*. Erowsaghem: Tp. Srbots' Yakoreants', 1965.

Kidd, B. J. *The Churches of Eastern Christendom*. London: Faith Press, 1927.

King, Archdale A. *The Rites of Eastern Christendom*. Rome: Catholic Book Agency, 1947, 2 vols.

King, Rev. Demetrius J. *A History of the American Orthodox Catholic Church*. Unpublished manuscript used by permission of the author.

Kolarz, Walter. *Religion in the Soviet Union*. London: Macmillan & Co., 1962.

Lavrentije, Bishop, *et al.*, eds. *Srpska Pravoslavna Crkva, 1219-1969: Spomenica o 750-Godishnjici Autokefalnosti*. Beograd: Izdanje Cvetog Arhijerejskog Cinoda, Crpske Pravoslavne Crkve, 1969.

Le Quien, Michel. *Oriens Christianus*. Graz: Akademische Druck u. Verlagsanstalt, 1958, 3 vols. First published 1740.

Lubeck, Konrad. "Die Autokephale Kirche des Berges Sinai," in *Wissenschaft Liche Beilage zur Germania* no. 16 (1911): .

Macartney, C. A. *The Hapsburg Empire, 1790-1918*. New York: Macmillan Co., 1969.

MacLean, Arthur John. *A Dictionary of the Dialects of Vernacular Syriac*. Oxford: Clarendon Press, 1901.

Maghak'ia Örmanian, Armenian Patriarch of Constantinople. *The Church of Armenia: Her History, Doctrine, Rule, Discipline, Liturgy, Literature, and Existing Condition*, translated by G. Marcar Gregory, edited by Terenig Poladian. 2nd ed. London: A. R. Mowbray, 1955.

Marshall, Richard H. Jr., editor. *Aspects of Religion in the Soviet Union, 1917-1967*. Chicago and London: University of Chicago Press, 1971.

Maximos, Metropolitan of Sardés. *The Oecumenical Patriarchate in the Orthodox Church: A Study in the History and Canons of the Church*. Thessaloniki, Greece: Patriarchal Institute for Patristic Studies, 1976.

McCullough, W. Stewart. *A Short History of Syriac Christianity to the Rise of Islam*. Chico, CA: Scholars Press, 1982.

Meinardus, Otto F. A. *Christian Egypt Ancient and Modern*. Cairo: American University at Cairo Press, 1977.

Meinardus, Otto F. A. *Monks and Monasteries of the Egyptian Desert*. Cairo: American University at Cairo Press, 1961. Expanded 2nd ed., 1989.

Melton, J. Gordon. *The Encyclopedia of American Religions.* Wilmington, NC: McGrath Publishing Co., 1978, 2 vols. 2nd ed. Detroit: Gale Research Co., 1987. Plus 1987 Supplement.

Menachery, Thomas, ed. *The St. Thomas Christian Encyclopedia of India.* Trichur, India: St. Thomas Christian Encyclopedia of India, 1970, 3 vols.

Michael I, Syrian Orthodox Patriarch of Antioch. *Chronique de Michel Le Syrien,* edited by J. B. Chabot. Paris: Culture et Civilisation, 1963, 4 vols. Originally published 1899.

The Middle East and North Africa. London: Unesco Publications, 195_-. Annual.

Mishaqā, Mikhayil, translated by W. M. Thackston Jr. *Murder, Mayhem, Pillage, and Plunder: The History of Lebanon in the 18th and 19th Centuries.* Albany, NY: State University of New York Press, 1988.

al-Misri, Iris Habib. *Qissat al-Khanisah al-Qibtiyah.* Cairo: 196- , 4 vols.

Mitsidés, Andreas N. *Hé Ekklésia tés Kyprou.* Leukósia: Anagennésé, 1980.

Mnatsakanian, A. Sh. *O Literature Kavkazskoi Albanii.* Erevan: Izdatel'stvo Akademii Nauk Armianskoi SSR, 1969.

Molnar, Enricot S. *The Ethiopian Orthodox Church.* Pasadena, CA: Bloy House Theological School, 1969.

Montalbano, William D. "Pope Calls for Broad Mideast Peace," in *Los Angeles Times* (March 5, 1991): A16.

Moosa, Matti. *The Maronites in History.* Syracuse, NY: Syracuse University Press, 1986.

Morgan, Jacques de. *The History of the Armenian People.* Boston: Hairenik Press, 1956. Originally published in 1916 in French.

Movsês Daskhuranci. *The History of the Caucasian Albanians,* translated by C. J. F. Dowsett. London: Oxford University Press, 1961.

Munier, H. *Précis de L'Histoire d'Égypte.* Caire: Institut Français d'Archéologie Orientale du Caire, 1932-35.

Nasrallah, Joseph. *Chronologie des Patriarches Melchites d'Antioche de 1250 à 1500.* Jerusalem: 1968.

Nasrallah, Joseph. *Notes et Documents pour Servir à l'Histoire du Patriarchat Melchite d'Antioche.* Jerusalem: 1965.

Nasrallah, Joseph. *Sa Béatitude Maximos IV et la Succession Apostolique du Siège d'Antioche.* Paris: 1963.

Nasrallah, Joseph. *Vie de la Chrétiente Melkite sous la Domination Turque.* Paris: Geuthner, 1949.

Neal, J. *A History of the Holy Eastern Church.* London: 1850.

The New Catholic Encyclopedia. New York: McGraw-Hill, 1967-79, 17 vols, plus annual yearbooks and several multi-volume supplements.

Nicol, Donald M. *The Last Centuries of Byzantium, 1261-1453.* 2nd ed. Cambridge: Cambridge University Press, 1993.

Nubijovyc, Volodymyr. *Ukraine: A Concise Encyclopaedia.* 1971.

Official Catholic Directory. Chicago: P. J. Kenedy & Sons, 1910-DATE.

"Oikoumenikon (Patriarcheion)," in *Megalé Helleniké Enkyklopaideia,* Vol. 18, p. 766-775. Athénai: Pyrsos, 1932.

O'Leary, De Lacy. *The Ethiopian Church.* London: SPCK, 1936.

Onami, Yuji. "Holy Orthodox Church," in *Kodansha Encyclopedia of Japan,* Vol. 3. Tokyo: Kodansha, 1983.

Orthodox News. London: St. George Orthodox Information Service, Vol. 2- , 1984- . News and obituaries.

Orthodoxia, ed. by Dr. Nikolaus Wyrwoll. Regensburg, Germany: Ortkirchliches Institut, 1982- . 8th ed., 1995.

The Oxford Dictionary of Byzantium. New York, Oxford: Oxford University Press, 1991, 3 vols.

Pacurariu, Mircea. *Istoria Bisericii Ortodoxe Române.* Bucuresti: Editura Institutului Biblic si de Misiune al Bisericii Ortodoxe Române, 1980-81, 3 vols.

Papamichalopoulos, Kónstantinos. *Hé Moné tou Horous Sina.* Athénai: E. D. Papas, 1932.

Pavlowitch, Stevan K. "The Orthodox Church in Yugoslavia: The Problem of the Macedonian Church," in *Eastern Churches Review* 1 (Winter 1967/68): 374-388.

Petrovich, Michael Boro. *A History of Modern Serbia, 1804-1918.* New York: Harcourt Brace Jovanovich, 1976, 2 vols.

"50-Letie Vosstanovleniia Patriarshestva," in *Zhurnal Moskovskoi Patriarkhii* (1971): .

Piepkorn, Arthur Carl. *Profiles in Belief: The Religious Bodies of the United States and Canada.* New York: Harper & Row, 1977, 2 vols.

"Pinakes Patriarchón," in *Eleutheroudaké Enkyklopaidikon Lexikon,* Vol. 10, p. 521-523, plus four-page insert between p. 520-521, and p. 487 of the Supplement. Athénai: Ekdotikos Oikos "Eleutheroudakes," 1930.

Podipara, Placid J. *The Thomas Christians.* London: Darton, Longman & Todd; Bombay: St. Paul Publications, 1970.

Pothan, S. G. *The Syrian Christians of Kerala.* New York: Asia Publishing House, 1963.

Proc, Alex. *Jahrbuch der Orthodoxie: Schematismus 1976/77.* West Germany: Athos-Verlag, 1976? Only one year was published.

Prüter, Karl, Bishop. *Bishops Extraordinary.* Highlandville, MO: St. Willibrord Press, 1985.

Prüter, Karl, Bishop. *A Directory of Autocephalous Bishops of the Apostolic Succession.* 7th ed. San Bernardino, CA: St. Willibrord's Press, 1995. New editions published every eighteen months.

Prüter, Karl, Bishop. *The Strange Partnership of George Alexander McGuire and Marcus Garvey*. Highlandville, MO: St. Willibrord Press, 1986.

Prüter, Karl, Bishop, and J. Gordon Melton. *The Old Catholic Sourcebook*. New York: Garland Publishing, 1983.

Ramet, Pedro, ed. *Eastern Christianity and Politics in the Twentieth Century*. CHRISTIANITY UNDER STRESS, Volume I. Durham & London: Duke University Press, 1988.

Rodoslovhe Tablice i Grbovi: Srpskih Dinastijai Vlastele. Beograd: Nova Knjiga, 1987.

The Romanian Orthodox Church, Yesterday and Today, translated by Andrei Bantas. Bucharest: Publishing House of the Bible and Mission Institute of the Romanian Orthodox Church, 1979.

Roncaglia, Martiniano. *Histoire de L'Église Copte*. Beirut: Dar al-Kalima, 1966.

Runciman, Steven. *The Orthodox Churches and the Secular State*. The Sir Douglas Robb Lectures, 1970. Auckland: Auckland University Press, 1971.

Sergeî Voskresenskiî, Metropolitan. "The Orthodox Church Under German Occupation: An Unpublished Memorandum by the Exarch of the Baltic Area, Metropolitan Sergei," in *Eastern Churches Review* 6 (Autumn 1971): 131-161.

Smith, J. Payne (and R. Payne). *A Compendious Syriac Dictionary, Founded upon the Thesaurus Syriacus of R. Payne Smith*. Oxford: Clarendon Press, 1979. Originally published in 1903.

Sobornost. London: Fellowship of St. Alban & St. Sergius, Series 7, 1975-1978; N.S. no. 1, 1979- . News sections.

Spinka, Matthew. *A History of Christianity in the Balkans*. Archon Books, 1968. Originally published 1933.

Spuler, Bertold. *Gegenwartslage der Ostkirchen in Ihrer Volkishen und Staatlichen Umwelt*. Wiesbaden: Metopin Verlag, 1948.

Spuler, Bertold. *Die Morgenlandischen Kirchen*. Leiden: E. J. Brill, 1964.

Stokvis, A. M. H. J. *Manuel d'Histoire, de Généalogie et de Chronologie de Touts les États du Globe*. Leiden: E. J. Brill, 1888-93, 3 vols. Reprinted: Leiden: B. M. Israël, 1966, 3 vols. in 4.

Tamrat, Taddesse. *Church and State in Ethiopia: 1270-1527*. Oxford: Clarendon Press, 1972.

Tarasar, Constance J. *Orthodox America: 1794-1976: Development of the Orthodox Church in America*. Syosset, NY: Orthodox Church in America, Dept. of History and Archives, 1975.

Tarrazi, Philippe de. *Al-Salasil al-Tarikhiyah fi Asaqifat al Abrashiyat al-Suryaniyah*. Bayrut: 1910.

Timotheos Benerés, Archbishop of Crete. "Krété—Ekklés.," in *Megalé Helléniké Enkyklopaideia*, Vol. 15. Athénai: Ekdotikos Organismos, 1950?

Tisserant, Eugene, Cardinal. *Eastern Christianity in India*. Westminster, MD: Newman Press, 1957.

Treadway, John D. *The Falcon & the Eagle: Montenegro and Austria-Hungary, 1908-1914*. West Lafayette, IN: Purdue University Press, 1983.

Tseng, Sally C., with David C. Tseng and Linda C. Tseng. *LC Romanization Tables and Cataloging Policies*. Metuchen, NJ: Scarecrow Press, 1990.

al-Unaysi, Tubiyya. *Silsilah Tarikhiyah lil-Batarikah al-Antakiyin al-Mawarinah*. Rome: 1927.

Ursal, George R. "From Political Freedom to Religious Independence: The Romanian Orthodox Church, 1877-1925," in *Romania Between East and West: Historical Essays in Memory of Constantin C. Giurescu*, edited by Stephen Fischer-Galati, Radu R. Florescu, and George R. Ursal. Boulder, CO: East European Monographs, 1982.

Verghese, Paul. *Die Syrischen Kirchen in Indien*. Stuttgart: Evangelisches Verlagswerk, 1974.

Vlasovs'kyi, Ivan. *An Outline of the History of the Ukrainian Orthodox Church = Naris Istorii Ukrainskoi Pravoslavnoi TSerkvi*. New York: Ukrainian Orthodox Church of U.S.A., 1957, 3 vols. 2nd ed. 1974.

Wakin, Edward. *A Lonely Minority: The Modern Story of Egypt's Copts*. New York: William Morrow, 1963.

Walker, Christopher J. *Armenia: The Survival of a Nation*. New York: St. Martin's Press, 1980. Rev. ed. 1990.

Watha'iq-Tarikhiyah lil-Kursi al-Malaki al-Antaki. Bayrut: 1932.

Who's Who in Lebanon. Beyrouth: Éditions Publictec, 1963- .

Year Book and Church Directory of the Russian Orthodox Greek Catholic Church of America [later the ...*Orthodox Church in America*]. 1968- .

Young, Rev. Father Alexey. *The Russian Orthodox Church Outside Russia: A History and Chronology*. San Bernardino, CA: St. Willibrord's Press, 1993.

Zernov, Nicolas. "The First Council of the Russian Church Abroad in Sremski Karlovtsi (21 November-2 December 1921): The Notes of One of the Participants," in *Eastern Churches Review* 7 (1975): 164-185.

"Zhamanakagrowt'iwn T'oirk'ioy Hayots' Patriark'nerow," in *Shoghakat'* (Autumn, 1961): 59-73.

STATISTICAL TABLES

HIGHEST POST-NOMINAL NUMBER—(tied): Ishai Shim'un XXIII (Assyria), Ioannes XXIII (Rome). Two of the Shim'uns are disputed, as are two of the Johns, so both should actually be numbered as XXI.

HIGHEST POST-NOMINAL NUMBER CURRENTLY BEING USED—Hovhannês Petros XVIII (Armenian Catholic Church of Cilicia); since every Patriarch uses the name Petros, the number increases with each reign.

LONGEST CURRENTLY REIGNING PRIMATE—31+ years: Dorotej (Czechoslovakia); or 37+ years: Iakóbos (America; not an autocephalous church).

SHORTEST REIGN—One day (1726): Kallinikos III (Ecumenical Patriarchate of Constantinople). It should be noted that all of the very short reigns of this and the other churches are disputed by scholars.

THE LONGEST VERIFIABLE REIGN

Verifiable reigns exceeding 45 years are rare. Step'anos IV (Caucasian Albania) is listed with 61 years, Shim'un IV (Babylon) with 60 years in one source, and Dinkha Iliya XII (Babylon) with 56 years, but none of these can be validated. The longest reign that can be regarded as proven is 55 years for Kónstantios II (Sinai). The longest reigns by major church are listed below:

ALBANIA—17 years: Païsi (1949-1966)
ALEXANDRIA (COPTIC)—53 years: Kirillus V (1874-1927)
ALEXANDRIA (COPTIC CATHOLIC)—45 years: Athanasiyus I (328-373)
ALEXANDRIA (GREEK)—45 years: Athanasios I (328-373)
AMERICA—37+ years: Iakóbos (1958-1995+)
ANTIOCH (GREEK)—42 years: Silfistrus (Silbestros) (1724-1766)
ANTIOCH (GREEK MELKITE)—39 years: Kirillus V (1672, 1682-1720)
ANTIOCH (MARONITE)—43 years: Musi (1524-1567)
ANTIOCH (SYRIAN CATHOLIC)—43 years: Ighnatiyus Bihnam I (1412-1455)
ANTIOCH (SYRIAN ORTHODOX)—42 years: Ighnatiyus Bihnam I (1412-1454)
ARMENIA—53 years: Grigor III (1113-1166)

ASSYRIA—45 years: Ishai Shim'un XXIII (1920-1975); Iliya Shim'un XII is listed with a reign of 53 years (1600-1653), but this is unverifiable, although certainly possible, given the hereditary nature of this catholicosate

AUSTRIA-HUNGARY (KARLOVCI)—46 years: Stevan II (1790-1836)

BABYLON—47 years: Yusip 'Ummanu'il II (1900-1947); Dinkha Iliya XII is listed with 56 years (1722-1778), Shim'un IV with 60 years (1437-1497), but none of these are verifiable, although certainly possible, given the hereditary nature of this catholicosate

BULGARIA—48 years: Vasiliî I (1185-1233)

CILICIA (ARMENIAN APOSTOLIC)—37 years: Sahak II (1902-1939)

CILICIA (ARMENIAN CATHOLIC)—27 years: Mik'ayêl Petros III (1753-1780)

CONSTANTINOPLE (ARMENIAN)—29 years: Shnorhk' (1961-1990)

CONSTANTINOPLE (GREEK)—31 years: Dometios (272-303)

CRETE—34 years: Neophytos (1645?-1679)

CYPRUS—43 years: Chrysanthos (1767-1810)

CZECHOSLOVAKIA—31+ years: Dorotej (1964-1995+)

ETHIOPIA—37 years: Matewos (1889-1926); Marqos I is listed with 49 years (1481-1530?) and Salama IV with 40 years (1348-1388), but none of these are verifiable

FINLAND—35 years: Herman (1925-1960)

GEORGIA—42 years: Ioane IV (1100-1142)

GREECE—40 years: Michaél III (1182-1222)

INDIA—44 years: Joseph Mar Dionysios V (1865-1909)

JAPAN—32 years: Nikolaî I (1880-1912)

JERUSALEM (ARMENIAN)—34 years: Grigor VII (1715-1749)

JERUSALEM (GREEK)—42 years: Germanos (1537-1579)

JERUSALEM (LATIN)—27 years: Aloysius II (1920-1947)

MACEDONIA—32 years: Jovan V (1183-1215)

POLAND—25+ years: Bazyli (1970-1995+)

ROMANIA—29 years: Justinian (1948-1977)

ROME—32 years: Pius IX (1846-1878)

RUSSIA—25 years: Aleksiî I (1945-1970)

SERBIA—33 years: Pajsije I (1614-1647)

SINAI—55 years: Kónstantios II (1804-1859)

UKRAINE—34 years: Ioann I (1004-1038)

COMPARATIVE NAME TABLES

The names listed below are given in their best-known English-language or Latin-language versions first, with other variants following in alphabetical order.

AARON—Aharon (Arabic, Armenian)
ABILIUS—Abilios (Greek), Abiliyus (Arabic)
ABRAHAM—Abraam(ios) (Greek), Abraha (Amharic), Abraham (Armenian), Abram (Arabic, Georgian), Abramios (Greek), Abreham (Amharic), Avraamiî (Bulgarian), Avram (Macedonian), Avramiî (Bulgarian), Ibrahim (Arabic)
ACACIUS—Akakios (Greek), Akakij (Macedonian), Akakiyus (Arabic), Aqaq (Arabic, Syriac)
ADAM—Atom (Armenian)
ADRIAN—Adrian (Bulgarian), Adrianus (Latin), Hadrianus (Latin)
AGAPIUS—Agapios (Greek), Aghabiyus (Arabic)
AGATHO—Agathón (Greek), Aghathun (Arabic)
AGRIPPINUS—Agrippinos (Greek), Aghribbinus (Arabic)
ALAN—Alanus (Latin)
ALBERT—Albertus (Latin)
ALEXANDER—Aghek'sandr (Armenian), Aleksandr (Russian), Aleksandrs (Latvian), Alexander (Latin), Alexandros (Greek), Aliksandarus (Arabic), Iskandar (Arabic)
ALEXIUS—Aleksiî (Russian, Ukrainian), Alexios (Greek)
ALPHONSE—Alphonsus (Latin)
AMBROSE—Ambrosi (Georgian), Amvrosiî (Russian)
AMOS—Amós (Greek)
AMPHILOCHIUS—Amfilohie (Romanian), Amfilohije (Serbian)
ANANIAS—Anania (Armenian, Romanian), Ananiî (Bulgarian), Ananij (Macedonian)
ANASTASIUS—Anastas (Albanian, Armenian), Anastasie (Romanian), Anastasiî (Russian), Anastasios (Greek), Anastasius (Latin), Anastasiyus (Arabic)
ANATOLIUS—Anatolios (Greek)
ANDREW—Andrawus (Arabic), Andreas (Greek, Latin), Andrêas (Armenian), Andreî (Czech, Romanian, Ukrainian), Andrey (Belorussian), Andreyas (Amharic), Indriyas (Amharic)
ANDRONICUS—Andruniqus (Arabic)
ANGEL—Angelus (Latin)

ANGELARIUS—Angelarij (Macedonian)

ANIANUS—Anianos (Greek), Aniyanus (Arabic)

ANTHEMIUS—Anthemios (Greek), Antimiyus (Arabic)

ANTHIMUS—Anthimos (Greek), Antim (Bulgarian, Macedonian, Romanian)

ANTHONY—Anton (Armenian, Georgian, Ukrainian), Antonie (Romanian), Antoniî (Russian, Ukrainian), Antonije (Montenegrin, Serbian), Antonios (Greek), Antonius (Latin), Antun (Arabic)

APOLLINARIUS—Apollinarios (Greek)

ARCADIUS—Arcadie (Romanian), Arkadios (Greek)

ARISTARCES—Aristakês (Armenian)

ARNOLD—Arnaldus (Latin)

ARSENIUS—Arsaniyus (Arabic), Arsen (Armenian, Georgian), Arseni (Georgian), Arseniî (Bulgarian, Ukrainian), Arsenij (Macedonian), Arsenije (Montenegrin, Serbian), Arsenios (Greek)

ARTEMUS—Artemios (Greek)

ASCLEPIADES—Asklépiadés (Greek), Asqlibiyad(h)(is) (Arabic)

ATHANASIUS—Atanasie (Romanian), Atanasiî (Bulgarian), Atanasij (Macedonian), Atanasije (Serbian), At'anasios (Armenian), Athanasie (Romanian), Athanasios (Greek), Athanasius (Latin), Athanasius (Latin), Athanasiyus (Arabic), Atnatewos (Amharic)

ATHENAGORAS—Athénagoras (Greek)

ATHENODORUS—Athénodóros (Greek)

ATTICUS—Attikos (Greek)

AUGUSTINE—Augustins (Latvian), Avgustin (Russian)

AUGUST—Augustus (Latin)

AYMERIC—Aymericus (Latin)

AZARIAH—Azaria (Armenian)

BABYLAS—Babila (Georgian), Babilas (Arabic), Babylas (Greek), Vavyla (Montenegrin)

BALTHAZAR—Baghdasar (Armenian)

BARLAAM—Valaam (Bulgarian, Macedonian), Varlaam (Romanian, Russian, Ukrainian)

BARNABAS—Barnabas (Greek), Varnava (Serbian)

BARTHOLOMEW—Bartalomewos (Amharic), Bartholomæus (Latin), Bartholomaios (Greek), Bart'lome (Georgian), Bart'oghimêos (Armenian), Bar T'ulmai (Syriac), Varfolomeî (Russian)

BASIL—Barsegh (Armenian), Baselios (Malayalam), Basileios (Greek), Basili (Georgian), Basiliyus (Arabic), Basilyos (Amharic), Bazyli (Polish), Vasile (Romanian), Vasiliî (Bulgarian, Russian), Vasilije (Montenegrin, Serbian), Vasyl'(iî) (Ukrainian)

BENEDICT—Benedict (Romanian), Benedictus (Latin), Benediktos (Greek)

BENJAMIN—Banyamin (Arabic), Beniamin(os) (Greek), Venijamin (Montenegrin)

BERNARD—Bernardus (Latin)

231

BERNARDINE—Bernardinus (Latin)

BESSARION—Besarioni (Georgian), Visarion (Bulgarian, Montenegrin, Romanian), Vissarion (Albanian)

BONAVENTURE—Bonaventurus (Latin)

BONIFACE—Bonifacius (Latin)

CAESAR—Cæsar (Latin), Chesarie (Romanian)

CALLANDION—Kaladyanu (Amharic), Kalandhiyun (Arabic), Kallandión (Greek), Qalandiyun (Arabic), Qalandun (Arabic)

CALLINICUS—Calinic (Romanian), Kalinik (Serbian), Kallinikos (Greek)

CALLISTRATUS—Calistru (Romanian), Kallistrate (Georgian), Kallistratos (Greek)

CALLISTUS—Kallistos (Greek)

CASSIAN—Kassianos (Greek)

CELADION—Keladión (Greek)

CERDON—Kerdón (Greek)

CHARITON—Charitón (Greek), Hariton (Macedonian, Romanian), Khariton (Bulgaria)

CHARLES—Carolus (Latin)

CHRISTIAN—Christianus (Latin)

CHRISTODOULUS—Akhristudulus (Arabic), Christodoulos (Greek), Krestodolo (Amharic)

CHRISTOPHER—Christophoros (Greek), Christophorus (Latin), Hristofor (Romanian), Kristufurus (Arabic), K'ristap'or (Armenian), K'ristep'ore (Georgian), Kristofor (Albanian)

CHRYSANTHUS—Chrysanthos (Greek)

CHRYSOSTOM—Chrysostomos (Greek)

CLEMATIUS—Klématios (Greek)

CLEMENT—Aklimandus (Arabic), Clemens (Latin), Klémés (Greek), Klimentos (Georgian), Klyment (Ukrainian)

CONON—Conon (Latin, Romanian), Konón (Greek)

CONSTANT—Kónstantios (Greek)

CONSTANTINE—Constantinus (Latin), Konstantin (Bulgarian, Macedonian), Kónstantinos (Greek), Konstantyn (Ukrainian), Kostandin (Armenian), Qustantinus (Arabic)

CORNELIUS—Kornélios (Greek), Kurniliyus (Arabic), Qurnil(iyus) (Arabic)

COSMAS—Cosma (Romanian), Kosmas (Greek), Kuz'ma (Ukrainian), Qosmos (Amharic), Qusma(n) (Arabic)

CYPRIAN—Kiprian (Russian), Kyprian (Ukrainian), Kyprianos (Greek)

CYRIACUS—Kirakos (Armenian), Kyriakos (Greek), Quriyaqus (Arabic)

CYRIL—Gerlos (Amharic), Kiril (Bulgarian, Macedonian, Serbian), Kirile (Georgian), Kirillus (Arabic), Kirilo (Serbian), Kuregh (Armenian), Kurilos (Malayalam), Kyrillos (Greek), Kyryl (Ukrainian), Qer(i)los (Amharic), Qurillus (Arabic)

CYRUS—Kurush (Arabic), Kyros (Greek)

DAMASCENUS—Damaskénos (Greek)

DAMIAN—Damian (Albanian, Bulgarian), Damianos (Greek), Damiyanus (Arabic)

DANIEL—Dan'el (Amharic), Daniêl (Armenian), Danieli (Georgian), Daniil (Bulgarian, Romanian, Russian), Danil (Arabic, Macedonian), Danilo (Montenegrin, Serbian), Daniyal (Arabic), Dengel (Amharic)

DAVID—David (Bulgarian), Davit'(i) (Georgian), Dawit' (Armenian), Dawud (Arabic)

DEMETRIAN—Démétrianos (Greek), Dimitriyanus (Arabic)

DEMETRIUS—Démétrios (Greek), Dimitri (Georgian), Dimitrie (Romanian), Dimitriî (Bulgarian), Dimitrij (Macedonian), Dimitrije (Serbian), Dimitriyanus (Arabic), Dimitriyus (Arabic), Dymytrii (Ukrainian)

DEMOPHILUS—Démophilos (Greek)

DENNIS—Dengel (Amharic), Dhiyunisiyus (Arabic), Dionise (Georgian), Dionisie (Romanian), Dionisiî (Bulgarian, Russian), Dionisij (Macedonian), Dionizus (Polish), Dionysiî (Ukrainian), Dionysios (Greek), Dionysius (Latin), Diyunisiyus (Arabic)

DIODORUS—Diodóros (Greek)

DIOSCORUS—Dioskoros (Armenian, Greek), Disqurus (Arabic)

DOMETIUS—Domenti (Georgian), Dometios (Greek), Dumitiyus (Arabic)

DOMINIC—Domenicus (Latin)

DOMNUS—Domnos (Greek), Dumnus (Arabic)

DOROTHEUS—Dorot'eos/z (Georgian), Doroteî (Bulgarian), Dorotej (Macedonian), Dórotheos (Greek), Duruthiyus (Arabic)

DOSITHEUS—Dositei (Romanian), Dositej (Macedonian), Dositheos (Greek), Dosoftei (Romanian)

ELEUTHERIUS/LUTHER—Eleutherios (Greek), Jelevferij (Czech)

ELIAZAR—Eghiazar (Armenian)

ELIJAH/ELIAS—Eghia (Armenian), Elia (Georgian), Elias (Latin), Élias (Greek), Eliozi (Georgian), Helias (Latin), Ilia (Georgian), Ilie (Romanian), Iliia (Ukrainian), Iliya (Syriac), Ilyas (Arabic)

ELISHA—Eghishê (Armenian), Ilisha' (Syriac)

EMILIAN—Aimilianos (Greek), Amiliyanus (Arabic), Emilian (Romanian)

EMMANUEL—Manouél (Greek), 'Ummanu'il (Syriac)

ENOCH—Hinukh (Arabic)

ENOS—Anush (Syriac)

EPHREM/EPHRAIM—Afram (Arabic), Aprem (Syriac), Efrem (Romanian), Ep'rem (Armenian, Georgian), Ephraim (Greek), IEfrem (Ukrainian), Jefrem (Serbian)

EPIPHANY—Apifaniyus (Greek), Epip'ane (Georgian), Epiphanios (Greek)

Eros—Awrus (Arabic), Ayrus (Arabic), Erós (Greek), Irus (Arabic)

Eudocimus—Evdokim (Russian)

Eudoxius—Afduksiyus (Arabic), Awduksiyus (Arabic), Eudoxios (Greek)

Eugene—Augen (Malayalam), Eugenie (Romanian), Eugenios (Greek), Eugenius (Latin), Evgeniî (Russian), Evghenie (Romanian), IEvgeniî (Ukrainian), Ougen (Malayalam)

Eulalius—Aflaliyus (Arabic), Awlaliyus (Arabic), Eulalios (Greek), Evlale (Georgian)

Eulogius—Eulogios (Greek), Evloghie (Romanian)

Eumenius—Awminiyus (Arabic), Eumenés/Eumenios (Greek)

Euphemius—Euphemios (Greek)

Euphrasius—Afrasiyus (Arabic)

Euphronius—Afrun(iyus) (Arabic), Awfruniyus (Arabic), Euphronios (Greek)

Eusebius—Awsabiyus (Arabic), Eusebios (Greek), Evsebiî (Russian)

Eustace—Astatiyus (Arabic), Awstathiyus (Arabic), Eustathios (Greek), Evstatiî (Bulgarian), Ewostatewos (Amharic), Jevstatij (Macedonian), Jevstatije (Serbian)

Eustochius—Eustochios (Greek)

Eustratius—Afstratiyus (Arabic), Eustratios (Greek)

Euthymius—Aftimios (American), Aftimiyus (Arabic), Eftim (Turkish), Eftimie (Romanian), Ek'vt'ime (Georgian), Euthymios (Greek), Evtimiî (Bulgarian)

Eutychius—Eutychios (Greek)

Euzoius—Afzuyus (Arabic), Euzóïos (Greek)

Evagrius—Awghris (Arabic), Awighriyus (Arabic), Euagrios (Greek), Evagre (Georgian)

Evodius—Afudiyus (Arabic), Awdiyus (Arabic), Euodios (Greek)

Ezekiel—Iezekiél (Greek), Kazqi'il (Syriac)

Ezra—Ezr (Armenian)

Fabian—Fabianus (Latin)

Fabius—Fabiyus (Arabic), Phabios (Greek)

Felix—Phélix/Philix (Greek)

Ferdinand—Ferdinandus (Latin)

Flacillus—Filaqas (Arabic), Phlakilos (Greek)

Flavian—Flabiyanus (Arabic), Flafiyanus (Arabic), Flavian (Russian), Phlabianos (Greek)

Francis—Franciscus (Latin)

Fravitas—Phrabitas (Greek)

Frederick—Fredericus (Latin)

Gabriel—Gabr'el (Amharic), Gabriêl (Armenian), Gavriil (Bulgarian, Romanian), Gavril (Macedonian), Gavrilo (Montenegrin, Serbian), Ghubriyal (Arabic), Havryïl (Ukrainian), Jibra'il (Arabic)

Gaianus—Gaïanos (Greek), Kayanus (Arabic)

Gaius/Caius—Gaïos (Greek)

GEDEON—Ghedeon (Romanian), Hedeon (Ukrainian)

GELASIUS—Gelasios (Greek), Ghelasie (Romanian)

GENNADIUS—Gen(n)adiî (Bulgarian), Genadij (Macedonian), Gennadios (Greek), Ghenadie (Romanian)

GEORGE—Geevarghese (Malayalam), Gêorg (Armenian), Georgi (Bulgarian), Georgij (Macedonian), Georgije (Serbian), Geórgios (Greek), Georgius (Latin), Gheorghe (Romanian), Giorgi (Georgian), Giwargis (Syriac), Giyorgis (Amharic), Jawrji(yus) (Arabic), Jerzy (Polish), Jirjis (Arabic), Jüri (Estonian)

GERALD—Geraldus (Latin)

GERARD—Gerardus (Latin)

GERASIMUS—Gherasim (Romanian, Serbian), Gerasimos (Greek), Herasym (Ukrainian), Jirasimus (Arabic)

GERMAN/HERMAN—German (Bulgarian, Montenegrin, Russian, Serbian), Germane (Georgian), Germanos (Greek), Gherman (Serbian), Herman (Ukrainian)

GERMANION—Germanión (Greek)

GERONTIUS—Gerontiî (Russian)

GERVASE—Gerbasios (Greek), Gervasius (Latin)

GILBERT—Gilbertus (Latin)

GILES—Gillus (Latin)

GORDIUS—Gordios (Greek)

GREGORY—Ghrighuriyus (Arabic), Grégorios (Greek), Gregorius (Latin), Grigol(i) (Georgian), Grigor (Armenian), Grigorie (Romanian), Grigoriî (Bulgarian), Grigorij (Macedonian), Grigoris (Armenian), Grigur (Syriac), Hryhoriî (Ukrainian)

HENRY—Henricus (Latin)

HEPHÆSTUS—Hefajst (Macedonian), Hephaistos (Greek)

HERACLAS—Héraklas (Greek), Yaraklas (Arabic)

HERMOGENES—Germogen (Russian)

HERO—Irun (Arabic), Hérón (Greek)

HIEROTHEUS—Ayruthiyus (Arabic), Hierotheos (Greek), IErofei (Ukrainian), Jerotej (Serbian)

HILARY—Hilarión (Greek), Hilarius (Latin), Ilarion (Bulgarian, Romanian, Ukrainian), Ilarijon (Montenegrin)

HIPPOLYTE—Hippolytus (Latin)

HONOR—Honorius (Latin)

HUMBERT—Humbertus (Latin)

HYACINTH—Iachint (Romanian)

HYMENÆUS—Hymenaios (Greek)

HYPATIUS—Hypatios (Greek), Ipatiî (Ukrainian)

IGNATIUS—Ighnatiyus (Arabic), Ignatie (Romanian), Ignatiî (Bulgarian, Russian), Ignatij (Macedonian), Ignatios (Armenian, Greek)

INNOCENT—Inochentie (Romanian), Innocentius (Latin), Innokentiî (Russian), Inokentije (Serbian)

IRENÆUS—Ireneî/Ireney (Russian)

ISAAC—Husik (Armenian), Isaak (Ukrainian), Isaak(ios) (Greek), Ishaq (Arabic), Iskhaq (Syriac), Sahak (Armenian), Yes'aq (Amharic), Yeshaq (Amharic)

ISAIAH—Esayi (Armenian), Hésaïas (Greek), Isaia (Romanian), Isaiia (Ukrainian), Isaija (Serbian)

ISHMAEL—Isma'il/Ismil (Arabic)

ISIDOR—Isidor (Russian), Isidóros (Greek), Isidorus (Latin), Isydor (Ukrainian)

ISRAEL—Israyêl (Armenian), Israyil (Syriac)

JACOB/JAMES—Hakob(us) (Armenian), Iacob (Romanian), Iacobus (Latin), Iakobi (Georgian), Iakobos (Greek), IAkov (Bulgarian), Jakov (Macedonian, Serbian), Ya'eqob (Amharic), Ya'qub (Arabic)

JEREMY/JEREMIAH—Aramiya (Arabic), Eremia (Armenian), Eremij (Macedonian), Hieremias (Greek), Ieremia (Georgian), Ieremiia (Bulgarian)

JEROME—Hierónymos (Greek), Hieronymus (Latin)

JESUS/JOSHUA—Ishu' (Arabic, Syriac)

JOAB—Hovab (Armenian)

JOACHIM—Hovakim (Armenian), Ióakeim (Greek), Ioakim (Bulgarian, Russian), Ioaquim (Latin), Joahim (Macedonian), Yuwakim (Arabic)

JOANNICIUS—Ioanichie (Romanian), Ioanikiî (Bulgarian), Ioannikiî (Russian), Ióannikios (Greek), Joanikij (Macedonian), Joanikije (Montenegrin, Serbian)

JOASAPH—Ioasaf (Bulgarian, Romanian, Russian, Ukrainian), Ióasaph (Greek), Joasav (Macedonian), Yosab (Amharic), Yusab (Arabic)

JOB—Ayyub (Arabic), Iób (Greek), Iobi (Georgian), Iov (Romanian, Russian, Ukrainian)

JOHN—Hovhan(nes) (Armenian), Ioan (Bulgarian, Romanian), Ioane (Georgian), Ioann (Latvian, Russian, Ukrainian), Ioannes (Latin), Ióannes (Greek), Iyunnis (Arabic), Jan (Czech), Janis (Latvian), Jovan (Macedonian, Serbian), Juhanon (Malayalam), Yohannes (Amharic), Yohannon (Malayalam), Yuhanna (Arabic), Yuhannis (Arabic), Yukhannan (Syriac)

JONAH—Iona (Georgian, Russian, Ukrainian), Iónas (Greek), Yunan (Arabic, Syriac)

JONATHAN—Ionafan (Russian)

JORDAN—Iordanus (Latin)

JORY—Iórios (Greek)

JOSEPH—Hovsêp' (Armenian), Iosebi (Georgian), Ioseph (Greek), Iosephus (Latin), Iosif (Bulgarian, Romanian, Russian), Iosyf (Ukrainian), Josif (Macedonian, Serbian), Yosef (Amharic), Yusip (Syriac), Yusuf (Arabic)

JOSHUA—SEE: Jesus

JUDE—Ioudas (Greek)

JULIAN—Ioulianos (Greek), Iulianus (Latin), Yuliyanus (Arabic), Yulyan (Arabic)

JULIUS—Iulius (Latin)

JUSTIN—Ioustinos (Greek), Iustin (Romanian)

JUSTINIAN—Ioustinianos (Greek), Justinian (Romanian)

JUSTUS—Ioustos (Greek), Yostos (Amharic), Yustus (Arabic)

JUVENAL—Ioubenalios (Greek)

LAWRENCE—Laurentios (Greek), Laurentius (Latin), Lavrentie (Romanian)

LAZARUS—Ghazar (Armenian), Lazaros (Greek)

LEO(N)—Ghevond (Armenian), León (Greek), Lev (Macedonian), Luv (Bulgarian)

LEONARD—Leonardus (Latin)

LEONIDAS—Leonide (Georgian), Leónidés (Greek)

LEONTIUS—Ghevondius (Armenian), Leontiî (Bulgarian, Russian, Ukrainian), Leontios (Greek)

LEVI—Leuis (Greek)

LEWIS—Ludovicus (Latin)

LIVY—Livius (Latin)

LUCIAN—Loukianos (Greek), Lukijan (Serbian)

LUKE/LUCAS—Ghukas (Armenian), Loukas (Greek), Luca (Romanian), Lucas (Latin), Lucius (Latin), Luqa (Arabic)

MACARIUS—Macarie (Romanian), Makar (Armenian), Makari (Georgian), Makariî (Bulgarian, Russian, Ukrainian), Makarij (Macedonian), Makarije (Montenegrin, Serbian), Makarios (Greek), Makariusz (Polish), Makariyus (Arabic), Makaryos (Amharic), Maqares (Amharic)

MACEDONIUS—Makedonios (Greek), Maqiduniyus (Arabic)

MALACHI—Maghak'ia (Armenian), Malak'ia (Georgian)

MARCIAN—Markianos (Greek), Markiyanus (Arabic)

MARINUS—Marinos (Greek)

MARK—Marcu (Romanian), Marcus (Latin), Marko (Bulgarian, Serbian), Markos (Armenian, Greek), Markozi (Georgian), Marqos (Amharic), Murqus (Arabic)

MARTIN—Martinos (Greek), Martinus (Latin)

MARTYR(IUS)—Mardarie (Romanian), Martiriyus (Arabic), Martiros (Armenian), Martur(iyus) (Arabic), Martyrios (Greek)

MARY/MARION—Maria (Greek, Latin)

MATTHEW/MATTHIAS—Mateî (Bulgarian), Matej (Macedonian), Matewos (Amharic), Matfeî (Ukrainian), Mathews (Malayalam), Matiyus (Arabic), Matta(wus) (Arabic), Matt'e(os) (Armenian), Matthæus (Latin), Matthaios (Greek)

MAXIM—Maksim (Bulgarian, Macedonian, Serbian), Mak'sime (Georgian), Maksimus (Arabic), Maksym (Ukrainian), Maxim (Romanian), Maximos (Greek)

MAXIMIAN—Maksimiyanus (Arabic), Maximianos (Greek)

MAXIMIN—Maksiminus (Arabic), Maximinos (Greek)
MELCHIZEDEK—Melhisedek (Belorussian), Melkhisedek (Bulgarian), Melk'isedek (Armenian, Georgian)
MELETIUS—Malatiyus (Arabic), Melentije (Serbian), Meletie (Romanian), Meletiî (Bulgarian), Meletij (Macedonian), Meletios (Greek), Melitê (Armenian)
MENAS—Ménas (Greek), Mina (Arabic), Minas (Amharic, Armenian)
MERCURY—Mercurius (Latin), Merkorewos (Amharic)
METHODIUS—Methodios (Greek), Metodiî (Bulgarian), Metodij (Macedonian), Mithudiyus (Arabic)
METROPHANES—Métrophanés (Greek), Mitrofan (Bulgarian, Macedonian, Montenegrin, Romanian, Serbian)
MICHAEL—Khaél (Coptic), Kha'il (Arabic), Michael (Latin), Michaél (Greek), Mihail (Macedonian, Romanian), Mihaïlo (Serbian), Mika'el (Amharic), Mik'ayêl (Armenian), Mik'el (Georgian), Mikhail (Bulgarian, Ukrainian), Mikha'il (Arabic), Mykhaïl (Ukrainian)
MISAEL—Misaél (Greek), Misail (Romanian), Mysaïl (Ukrainian)
MODESTUS—Modestos (Greek)
MOSES—Móésés (Greek), Moïseî (Russian), Mojsej(e)/Mojsije (Serbian), Mose (Georgian), Móusés (Greek), Movsês (Armenian), Mowshe (Armenian), Musi/Musa (Arabic)
MYRON—Miron (Romanian, Serbian), Muron (Armenian), Myrón (Greek)
NARCISSUS—Narsai (Syriac), Narkissos (Greek), Nersês (Armenian)
NATHANIEL—Nathanaél (Greek)
NECTAR—Nectarie (Romanian), Nektariî (Bulgarian), Nektarij (Macedonian), Nektarios (Greek)
NEIL—Neilos (Greek), Nilus (Arabic)
NEOPHYTUS—Neofit (Bulgarian, Macedonian, Romanian), Neophytos (Greek), Niyufutus (Arabic)
NESTOR(IUS)—Nestorios (Greek), Nestor (Russian)
NICANOR—Nikanor (Bulgarian, Montenegrin, Serbian, Ukrainian), Nikanór (Greek)
NICEPHORUS—Nichifor (Romanian), Niképhoros (Greek), Nikyfor (Ukrainian), Niqifurus (Arabic)
NICETAS—Nikétas (Greek), Nykyta (Ukrainian)
NICHOLAS—Mikalay (Belorussian), Mykolaî (Ukrainian), Nicolae (Romanian), Nicolaus (Latin), Nikoghayos (Armenian), Nikolaî (Bulgarian, Russian), Nikolaj (Macedonian, Slovak), Nikolaos (Greek), Nikoloz (Georgian), Niqula (Syriac), Niqulawus (Arabic)
NICODEMUS—Nicodim (Romanian), Nikodémos (Greek), Nikodim (Bulgarian, Montenegrin), Nikodimos (Amharic)
NICON—Nikon (Russian), Nikón (Greek), Niqun (Arabic)
NIMROD—Nimrud (Arabic)
NIPHON—Néphón (Greek), Nifon (Romanian), Nifont (Ukrainian), Niphón (Greek)

NOAH—Nuh (Arabic)
OLYMPIUS—Olympios (Greek)
ONESIPHORUS—Onysyfor (Ukrainian)
ORESTES—Iorest (Romanian), Orestés (Greek)
PACHOMIUS—Bakhumiyus (Arabic), Pachomios (Greek), Pahomie (Romanian), Pahomije (Serbian)
PAISIUS—Païsi (Albanian), Païsiî (Bulgarian), Païsios (Greek), Pajsij (Macedonian), Pajsije (Serbian)
PALLADIUS—Baladhiyus (Arabic), Baladiyun (Arabic), Baladiyus (Arabic), Baladus (Arabic), Palladiî (Russian, Ukrainian)
PANARETUS—Panaret (Bulgarian, Macedonian), Panaretos (Greek)
PANTELEIMON—Pantaleon (Latin), Panteleémón (Greek), Panteleiman (Belorussian)
PAONIUS—Paonije (Montenegrin)
PAPHNYTIUS—Pafnutiî (Bulgarian), Paphnytios (Greek)
PARTHENIUS—Partenie (Romanian), Parteniî (Bulgarian), Partenij (Macedonian), Parthenios (Greek)
PASCHAL—Paschalis (Latin)
PAUL—Bulus (Arabic), Paulos (Greek), Paulose (Malayalam), Paulus (Latin), Pavel (Montenegrin, Russian), Pavle (Serbian), Poghos (Armenian), Pulus (Syriac)
PAULIN(US)—Baflinus (Arabic), Bulinus (Arabic), Fulin (Arabic), Paulinos (Greek)
PETER—Butrus (Arabic), Petar (Montenegrin, Serbian), Petr (Russian, Ukrainian), Petre (Georgian), Petro (Ukrainian), Petros (Amharic, Armenian, Greek), Petru (Romanian), Petrus (Latin)
PHILARET—Filaret (Romanian, Russian, Ukrainian)
PHILEMON—Filimun (Arabic), Philémón (Greek)
PHILETUS—Filitus (Arabic), Philétos (Greek)
PHILIP—Filibbus (Arabic), Filip (Bulgarian, Macedonian, Serbian), Filipp (Russian), Filippos (Amharic), Philippos (Greek), Philippus (Latin), P'ilippos (Armenian)
PHILOGON—Bilujin (Arabic), Filughunus (Arabic), Filujuniyus (Arabic), Philogon(i)os (Greek)
PHILOTHEUS—Filatawos (Amharic), Filoteî (Bulgarian), Filuthawus (Arabic), Filotej (Czech), Philotheos (Greek), Tilotej (Macedonian)
PHILOXENUS—Filuksinus (Arabic), Phileksinose (Malayalam), Philoxenos (Greek)
PHOTIUS—Fotiî (Russian, Ukrainian), Phótios (Greek)
PILATE—Bilatus (Arabic), Pilatos (Greek)
PISTUS—Pistos (Greek)
PLACID—Placidus (Latin)
PLATO—Platon (Estonian, Romanian, Russian), Platón (Greek)
PLUTARCH—Ploutarchos (Greek)
POIMEN—Pimen (Russian, Ukrainian), Poimén (Greek)
POLITIAN—Politianos (Greek)

POLYCARP—Polykarp (Ukrainian), Polykarpos (Greek)

PORPHYRIUS—Burfirus (Arabic), Burfuriyus (Arabic), Porfiriî (Bulgarian, Russian), Porfirij (Macedonian), Porphyrios (Greek)

PRIMUS—Abrimus (Arabic), Primos (Greek)

PROBUS—Probos (Greek)

PROCHORUS—Prohor (Macedonian), Prokhor (Bulgarian), Prokhoron (Armenian)

PROCLUS—Proklos (Greek)

PROCOPIUS—Procopie (Romanian), Prokopije (Serbian), Prokopios (Greek)

PROSPER—Prosperus (Latin)

PROTERIUS—Proterios (Greek)

PUBLIUS—Pouplios (Greek)

PYRRHUS—Pyrrhos (Greek)

QUADRATUS—Kodratos (Greek)

RAPHAEL—Rafaïl (Bulgarian, Macedonian, Ukrainian), Rapa'il (Syriac), Raphael (Latin), Raphaél (Greek)

RAYMOND—Raymundus (Latin)

REUBEN—Rupil (Syriac)

ROBERT—Robertus (Latin)

ROGER—Rogerus (Latin)

ROLAND—Rolandus (Latin)

ROMAN—Roman (Bulgarian), Rómanos (Greek), Romanus (Latin)

RUFINUS—Rhouphinos (Greek), Rufim (Montenegrin)

ROMULUS—Romul (Montenegrin)

SABBAS—Saba (Georgian), Sabbas (Arabic), Sava (Montenegrin, Romanian, Serbian)

SABBATIUS—Sabbazd (Czech), Savatije (Serbian)

SABINE—Sabinos (Greek)

SALLUST—Salloustios (Greek)

SAMPSON—Sampsón (Greek)

SAMUEL—Samoel (Georgian), Samouél (Greek), Samuel (Armenian), Samu'el (Amharic), Samuïl (Ukrainian), Samuïlo (Serbian)

SEBASTIAN—Sebastian (Romanian), Sebastianos (Greek), Sebastianus (Latin), Sibastiyanus (Arabic)

SENOUTHIUS—Sanutiyus (Arabic), Shanudah/Shinudah (Arabic), Sinoda (Amharic), Suntyos (Amharic)

SENECA—Senekas (Greek)

SERAPHIM—Serafim (Romanian, Russian), Serapheim (Greek), Seraphinus (Latin), Sirafim (Arabic)

SERAPION—Serapion (Russian, Ukrainian), Serapión (Greek), Sirabiyun (Arabic)

SERGIUS—Sargis (Armenian, Syriac), Sergej (Macedonian), Sergi (Estonian), Sergiî (Bulgarian, Russian), Sergios (Greek), Sergius (Latin), Sirjiyus (Arabic), Sirkis (Arabic), Syrhiey (Belorussian)

SEVERIN—Severinus (Latin)

SEVERUS—Sawira (Arabic), Sawiriyus (Arabic), Sawiros (Amharic), Sebéros (Greek), Subrus (Arabic)

SILVAN—Silouanos (Greek)

SIMON/SIMEON—Sem'on (Amharic), Shim'un (Arabic, Syriac), Sim'an (Arabic), Simawun (Arabic), Simeon (Bulgarian, Macedonian), Simêon (Armenian), Simion (Romanian), Simon (Latin), Svim(e)on (Georgian), Symeon (Ukrainian), Symeón (Greek)

SISINNIUS—Sisinnios (Greek)

SOLOMON—Soghomon (Armenian), Solomón (Greek)

SOPHRONIUS—Sofron (Albanian), Sofronie (Romanian), Sofroniî (Bulgarian), Sofronij (Macedonian), Sofronije (Serbian), Sóphronios (Greek), Sufruniyus (Arabic)

SPYRIDON—Asbiridun (Arabic), Spiridon (Serbian), Spyridón (Greek)

STEPHEN—Istifan(us) (Arabic), Stefan (Bulgarian, Polish, Romanian), Step'ane (Georgian), Step'an(os) (Armenian), Stephanos (Greek), Stephanus (Latin), Stevan (Serbian)

SYLVESTER—Silbestros (Greek), Silfistrus (Arabic), Silvestru (Romanian), Syl'vestr (Ukrainian)

SYMMACHUS—Symmachos (Greek)

TARASIUS—Tarasios (Greek)

THADDEUS—Addai (Syriac), T'addai (Syriac), T'adêos (Armenian), Tadewos (Amharic), Thaddaios (Greek)

THEOCHARISTUS—Theocharistos (Greek), Thiyukharistus (Arabic)

THEOCLETUS—Theoklétos (Greek)

THEOCTISTUS—Teoctist (Romanian)

THEODEGIUS—Theodégios (Greek)

THEODORE—Feodor (Russian, Ukrainian), Teodor (Romanian), T'eodore (Georgian), T'êodoros (Armenian), Thawdurus (Arabic), Theodoros (Greek), Theodorus (Latin), Thiyudhurus (Arabic), Thiyudur(us) (Arabic), Thiyuduritus (Arabic), T'iyadurus (Syriac)

THEODORIC—Theodoricus (Latin)

THEODOSIUS—Feodosiî (Russian), Teodosie (Romanian), Teodosiî (Bulgarian), Teodosije (Serbian), Thawdusiyus (Arabic), Theodosios (Greek), Thiyudusiyus (Arabic), T'iyadusis (Syriac)

THEODOTUS—Thawdutus (Arabic), Theodotos (Greek), Thiyudut(us) (Arabic)

THEODULUS—Teodul (Bulgarian, Macedonian)

THEOGNOSTUS—Feognost (Ukrainian)

THEOLEPTUS—Theoleptos (Greek)

THEONAS—Thawna (Arabic), Theónas (Greek)

THEOPEMPTUS—Feopempt (Ukrainian)

THEOPHANES—Teofan (Bulgarian, Macedonian, Romanian, Serbian), Thawfaniyus (Arabic), Theophanés (Greek), Thiyufanis (Arabic)

THEOPHILUS—Feofil (Russian), Teofil (Romanian), Tewoflos (Amharic), Thawfilus (Arabic), Theophilos (Greek), Thiyufilus (Arabic)

THEOPHYLACTUS—Feofilakt (Bulgarian, Russian), Theophylaktos (Greek), Thiyufilaktus (Arabic), Tufilaqtus (Arabic)

THOMAS—Thoma(s) (Malayalam), Thomas (Latin), Thómas (Greek), Tomas (Amharic), T'ovma(s) (Armenian), Tuma (Arabic), T'uma (Syriac)

TIMÆUS—Timaios (Greek), Timayus (Arabic), Timiyus (Arabic)

TIMOTHY—Timat'ius (Syriac), Timithiyus (Arabic), Timofeî (Russian), Timotheos (Greek), Timuthawus (Arabic), Tymofiî (Ukrainian), Tymoteusz (Polish)

TIRIDATES—Trdat (Armenian)

TITUS—Tit (Romanian), Titos (Greek)

TOBIAS—Tóbias (Greek), Tubiyya (Arabic)

TYCHON—Tikhon (Russian), Tychón (Greek)

TYRRANUS—Turanus (Arabic), Tyrannos (Greek)

URBAN—Urbanus (Latin)

VALENS—Oualés (Greek)

VALENTINE—Valentinus (Latin)

VICTOR—Fiqtor (Amharic), Victor (Latin)

VINCENT—Vicentije/Vikentije (Serbian), Vincentus (Latin)

VITALIAN—Vitalianus (Latin)

VITALIS—Bitalis (Arabic, Greek), Fitalis (Arabic), Fitaliyus (Arabic), Vitaliî (Russian)

VLADIMIR—Vladimir (Romanian, Russian), Volodymyr (Ukrainian)

WALTER—Gualterus (Latin)

WILLIAM—Guillelmus (Latin), Willelmus (Latin)

ZACHARY—Zacharias (Greek, Latin), Zaharij (Macedonian), Zak'aria (Armenian, Georgian), Zakaryas (Amharic), Zakhariî (Bulgarian), Zakhariya(s) (Arabic), Zakka (Arabic)

ZEBEDEE—Zebede (Georgian)

ZION—Sion (Armenian)

ZOILUS—Zóïlos (Greek)

ZOSIMUS—Zosim (Macedonian), Zosima (Bulgarian, Russian)

INDEX OF PRIMATES

NOTE: This index is arranged alphabetically by the first name of the primate, then alphabetically by church (primary see and denomination), then by dates of reign. A typical entry includes: name, other given name(s) or nickname(s), surname(s) (in italics), years of reign, church name. If the same individual is recorded on two or more separate lists, he is listed completely separately under each church unless reign styles and dates are exactly identical, even when it is obvious that the same prelate is involved.

Aabo : 540-552 (India—Malankara Orthodox)
Aba I *Raba* : 540-552 (Babylon)
Aba II : 741-751 (Babylon)
Abad *M'shikha* : 191-203 (Assyria)
Abas : 552-596 (Aghunie)
'Abd al-Ghani, Ighnatiyus : 1597-1598 (Antioch—Syrian Catholic)
'Abd Allah, Ighnatiyus : 1520-1557 (Antioch—Syrian Catholic)
'Abd Allah I, Ighnatiyus : 1520-1556 (Antioch—Syrian Orthodox)
'Abd Allah II *al-Saddi*, Ighnatiyus : 1906-1915 (Antioch—Syrian Orthodox)
'Abd al-Masih I *al-Rawhi*, Ighnatiyus : 1662-1686 (Antioch—Syrian Orthodox)
'Abd al-Masih II, Ighnatiyus : 1895-1905 (Antioch—Syrian Orthodox)
Abdisho *Thondanatta*, Mar : 1864-1874, 1882-1900 (India—Chaldean)
'Abdishu' I *Garmaqaya* : 963-986 (Assyria)
'Abdishu' II *bar Arus Anraya* : 1072-1090 (Assyria)
'Abdishu' III *bar Mulki* : 1138-1147 (Assyria)
'Abdishu' I : 963-986 (Babylon)
'Abdishu' II *bar Arus Anraya* : 1075-1090 (Babylon)
'Abdishu' III *bar Mulki* : 1139-1148 (Babylon)
'Abdishu' IV, Marun : 1555-1567 (Babylon)
'Abdishu' V *Khayyat'*, Giwargis : 1894-1899 (Babylon)
Abilios : 83-95 (Alexandria—Greek)
Abiliyus : 83-95 (Alexandria—Coptic Catholic)
Abimaleck *Timotheus*, Mar : 1908-1945 (India—Chaldean)
Abraam : 1468 (Jerusalem—Greek)
Abraha—SEE ALSO: Abreham
Abraha : 1937-1939 [anti-abuna] (Ethiopia—Historical)
Abraha III : 1937-1939 [anti-abuna] (Ethiopia—Official)
Abraham I : 607-615 (Armenia)
Abraham II : 1730-1734 (Armenia)
Abraham III : 1734-1737 (Armenia)
Abraham I : 130-152 (Assyria)
Abraham II *d'Margaa* : 837-850 (Assyria)
Abraham III *Abraza* : 906-937 (Assyria)
Abraham I : 2nd cent. (Babylon)

Abraham II *d'Margaa* : 837-850 (Babylon)
Abraham III *Abraza* : 905-936 (Babylon)
Abraham *Gholian* : 1813-1815 (Constantinople—Armenian)
Abraham : 1568-1597 (India—Chaldean)
Abraham I : 201-213 (India—Malankara Orthodox)
Abraham II : 686-687 (India—Malankara Orthodox)
Abraham III, Athanasios Mar : 1365-1379 (India—Malankara Orthodox)
Abraham IV, Baselios Mar : 1494-1496 (India—Malankara Orthodox)
Abraham I : 638-669 (Jerusalem—Armenian)
Abraham II : 885-909 (Jerusalem—Armenian)
Abraham III *of Jerusalem* : 1180-1191 (Jerusalem—Armenian)
Abraham IV : 1205-1218 (Jerusalem—Armenian)
Abraham V *of Egypt* : 1441-1454 (Jerusalem—Armenian)
Abraham VI *of Aleppo* : 1479-1485 (Jerusalem—Armenian)
Abraham Mar Climis : 1957-1958 (India—Malankara Jacobite)
Abraham Mar Koorilose I *Kattumangat* : 1771-1802 (India—Thozhiyoor)
Abraham *Mar Thoma* : 1917-1944 [suffragan], 1944-1947 (India—Mar Thoma
    Syrian)
Abraham Petros I *Ardzivian* : 1740-1749 (Cilicia—Armenian Catholic)
Abraham Shim'un XIX : 1820?-1860 (Assyria)
Abram : 975-978 (Alexandria—Coptic)
Abram I : 1280-1310 (Georgia)
Abram II : 1492-1497 (Georgia)
Abramios : 1775-1787 (Jerusalem—Greek)
Abramios : 1435? (Sinai)
Abreham—SEE ALSO: Abraha
Abreham I : unknown (Ethiopia—Official)
Abreham II : unknown (Ethiopia—Official)
Abrimus : 106-118 (Alexandria—Coptic)
Abrimus : 106-118 (Alexandria—Coptic Catholic)
Abris : 90-107 (Assyria)
Abris : 2nd cent. (Babylon)
Abrosios : 185-201 (India—Malankara Orthodox)
Acasios : 485-498 (India—Malankara Orthodox)
Achillas : 312-313 (Alexandria—Greek)
Adamantios : 810? (Greece)
Addai I *Shlikha* : 33-45 (Assyria)
Addai II *Giwargis* : 1972- (Assyria—Old Apostolic Church of the East)
Addai *Shlikha* : 33- (Babylon)
Addai : 72-120 (India—Malankara Orthodox)
Adeodatus I : 615-618 (Rome)
Adeodatus II : 672-676 (Rome)
Adrian : 1275? (Bulgaria)
Adrian : 1285? (Macedonia)
Adrian : 1690-1700 (Russia)
Adrianus I : 772-795 (Rome)
Adrianus II : 867-872 (Rome)
Adrianus III : 884-885 (Rome)
Adrianus IV *Breakspear* : 1154-1159 (Rome)
Adrianus V *Fieschi* : 1276 [unconsecrated] (Rome)
Adrianus VI *Florensz* : 1522-1523 (Rome)
Ægidius *de Ferrare* : 1295-1310 (Alexandria—Latin)
Afdhuksiyus : 358-359 (Antioch—Greek and Antioch—Greek Melkite)
Aflaliyus : 332 (Antioch—Greek)

Aflaliyus : 331-333 (Antioch—Greek Melkite)
Afram—SEE ALSO: Abram
Afram *of Amida* : 527-545 (Antioch—Greek)
Afram *of Amida* : 526-545 (Antioch—Greek Melkite)
Afram *Barsum*, Ighnatiyus : 1933-1957 (Antioch—Syrian Orthodox)
Afram I *of Amida* : 528-546 (Antioch—Syrian Catholic)
Afram II *Rahmani*, Ighnatiyus : 1898-1929 (Antioch—Syrian Catholic)
Afrasiyus *ibn Malaha* : 521-526 (Antioch—Greek)
Afrasiyus *ibn Malaha* : 521-526 (Antioch—Greek Melkite)
Afrasiyus *ibn Malaha* : 521-528 (Antioch—Syrian Catholic)
Afrun : 338-342 (Antioch—Syrian Catholic)
Afruniyus : 332-333 (Antioch—Greek)
Afruniyus : 333-334 (Antioch—Greek Melkite)
Afstatiyus : 325-330 (Antioch—Greek)
Afstatiyus : 325-331 (Antioch—Greek Melkite)
Afstratiyus : 939-960 (Antioch—Greek)
Aftimios : 1927-1933 (America—American Orthodox Catholic Church)
Aftimiyus I : 1159-1164 (Antioch—Greek)
Aftimiyus II : 1260-1269 (Antioch—Greek)
Aftimiyus III *al-Karmah* : 1635-1636 (Antioch—Greek)
Aftimiyus IV *apo Chiou* : 1636-1648 (Antioch—Greek)
Aftimiyus I : 1258?-1273? (Antioch—Greek Melkite)
Aftimiyus II *al-Karmah* : 1634 (Antioch—Greek Melkite)
Aftimiyus III *apo Chiou* : 1634-1647 (Antioch—Greek Melkite)
Afudiyus : 53-68 (Antioch—Greek)
Afudiyus : 43-70? (Antioch—Greek Melkite)
Afudiyus : 50-68 (Antioch—Syrian Orthodox)
Afzuyus : 361-376 (Antioch—Greek)
Afzuyus : 360-370 [anti-patriarch] (Antioch—Greek Melkite)
Agai : 45-48 (Assyria)
Agai : 1st cent. (Babylon)
Agapetus I : 535-536 (Rome)
Agapetus II : 946-955 (Rome)
Agatangel *apo Chalkédonos* : 1815-1825 (Serbia)
Agathangelos *apo Chalkédonos* : 1826-1830 (Constantinople—Greek)
Agatho : 678-681 (Rome)
Agathón : 950-964 (Jerusalem—Greek)
Aggai : 120-152 (India—Malankara Orthodox)
Aghabiyus *Bishai* : 1866-1887 (Alexandria—Coptic Catholic)
Aghabiyus : 977-995 (Antioch—Greek)
Aghabiyus I : 978-996 (Antioch—Greek Melkite)
Aghabiyus II *Matar* : 1796-1812 (Antioch—Greek Melkite)
Aghathu(n) : 662-680 (Alexandria—Coptic)
Aghek'sandr I : 1706-1714 (Armenia)
Aghek'sandr II *Karakashian* : 1753-1755 (Armenia)
Aghribbinus : 166-178 (Alexandria—Coptic and Alexandria—Coptic Catholic])
Agrippinos : 166-178 (Alexandria—Greek)
Agustinus Yusip (V) *Khindi* : 1804-1828 [unconsecrated] (Babylon)
Aharon : 779-781 (Aghunie)
Ahod Abuci : 231-246 (India—Malankara Orthodox)
Ahoudemme : 559-577 (India—Malankara Orthodox)
Aiglerius : 1275? (Jerusalem—Latin)
Ailios : 213 (Jerusalem—Greek)
Akakij : 1557?-1564? (Macedonia)

Akakios : 472-489 (Constantinople—Greek)
Akakiyus : 458-459 (Antioch—Greek and Antioch—Greek Melkite)
Akha *d'Abuhi* : 205-220 (Assyria)
Akha *d'Abuhi* : 3rd cent. (Babylon)
Akhkhi : 411-415 (Assyria)
Akhkhi : 411-414 (Babylon)
Akhristudulus : 1047-1077 (Alexandria—Coptic)
Aklimandus *Bahuth* : 1856-1864 (Antioch—Greek Melkite)
Alanus : 1196- (Cyprus—Latin)
Albertus I *de Robertis* : 1226-1246 (Antioch—Latin)
Albertus II *Barbolani* : 1856-1857 (Antioch—Latin)
Albertus : 1211- (Cyprus—Latin)
Albertus I : 1204-1214 (Jerusalem—Latin)
Albertus II *Gori* : 1949-1970 (Jerusalem—Latin)
Albertus : 1102 [anti-pope] (Rome)
Aldobrandinus *des Ursins* : 1500-1517? (Cyprus—Latin)
Aleksander *Mar Thoma* : 1954-1976 [suffragan], 1976-   (India—Mar Thoma
   Syrian)
Aleksander *Paulus* : 1920-1953 (Estonia)
Aleksandr *Nemolovskiĭ* : 1919-1922 (America—Orthodox Church)
Aleksandr *Opotskiĭ* : 1903-1905 [exarch] (Georgia)
Aleksandrs *Kudrjasovs* : 1993- (Latvia)
Aleksiĭ : 1913-1917 [exarch] (Georgia)
Aleksiĭ *Konoplev* : 1966 (Latvia)
Aleksiĭ I *Simanskiĭ* : 1944-1945 [locum tenens], 1945-1970 (Russia)
Aleksiĭ II *Ridiger* : 1990- (Russia)
Aleksiĭ : 1354-1378 (Russia—Moscow)
Aleksiĭ : 1354-1378 (Ukraine)
Aleksiĭ : 1140? (Ukraine—Halych)
Aleksiĭ *Hromads'kyĭ* : 1942-1943 (Ukraine—Autonomous Church)
Aleksius *Ridiger* : 1961-1987 (Estonia)
Alexander I *Riario* : 1570? (Alexandria—Latin)
Alexander II *Crescenzi* : 1675? (Alexandria—Latin)
Alexander *Crescenzi* : 1675?-1688 (Antioch—Latin)
Alexander *Sanminiatelli-Zabarella* : 1899-1901 (Constantinople—Latin)
Alexander I : 105?-115? (Rome)
Alexander II *da Baggio* : 1061-1073 (Rome)
Alexander III *Bandinelli* : 1159-1181 (Rome)
Alexander IV *Segni* : 1254-1261 (Rome)
Alexander V *Philarghi* : 1409-1410 [anti-pope] (Rome)
Alexander VI *de Borja* : 1492-1503 (Rome)
Alexander VII *Chigi* : 1655-1667 (Rome)
Alexander VIII *Ottoboni* : 1689-1691 (Rome)
Alexandros I : 313-328 (Alexandria—Greek)
Alexandros II : 1059-1062 (Alexandria—Greek)
Alexandros : 1922-1930? (America—Greek)
Alexandros : 325-337? (Constantinople—Greek)
Alexandros : 213-251 (Jerusalem—Greek)
Alexios *Stoudités* : 1025-1043 (Constantinople—Greek)
Aliksandarus I : 312-326 (Alexandria—Coptic)
Aliksandarus II : 705-730 (Alexandria—Coptic)
Aliksandarus : 312-328 (Alexandria—Coptic Catholic)
Aliksandarus I : 414-424 (Antioch—Greek)
Aliksandarus II : 695-702 (Antioch—Greek)

Aliksandarus III *Tahhan* : 1931-1958 (Antioch—Greek)
Aliksandarus : 416-417 (Antioch—Greek Melkite)
Aliksandarus : 413-417? (Antioch—Syrian Orthodox)
Aloysius I *Piavi* : 1889-1905 (Jerusalem—Latin)
Aloysius II *Barlassina* : 1918-1920 [auxiliary patriarch], 1920-1947 (Jerusalem—Latin)
Alphonsus *de Fonseca* : 1506? (Alexandria—Latin)
Alphonsus I *Carafa* : 1504- (Antioch—Latin)
Alphonsus II : -1529 (Antioch—Latin)
Alphonsus : 1408- (Constantinople—Latin)
Aluntiyus : 351-357 (Antioch—Syrian Catholic)
Alypios : 166-169 (Constantinople—Greek)
Amalricus : 1157-1180 (Jerusalem—Latin)
Ambrosi *K'elava* : 1921-1927 (Georgia)
Amfilohie : 1595-1598 (Austria—Cernovci)
Amfilohije *Radovic* : 1990- (Serbia—Montenegro)
Amiliyanus : 1062-1075 (Antioch—Greek)
Amiliyanus : 1074?-1090? (Antioch—Greek Melkite)
Amós : 594-601 (Jerusalem—Greek)
Amvrosiî : 1962 (Japan)
Amvrosiî *Zertis-Kamenskiî* : 1768-1771 (Russia—Moscow)
Anacletus (I) : 76?-88? (Rome)
Anacletus II *Leonis* : 1130-1138 [anti-pope] (Rome)
Anania (I) : 946-968 (Armenia)
Anania (II) : 1204-1208? [anti-catholicos] (Armenia)
Anania : 1544-1558 (Romania)
Ananias : 1661-1671 (Sinai)
Ananiî : 1763 (Bulgaria)
Ananij : 1763 (Macedonia)
Anastas : 741-745 (Aghunie)
Anastas *Xhanulatos* : 1990- (Albania)
Anastas : 661-667 (Armenia)
Anastasie I *Crimca* : 1600 (Austria—Cernovci)
Anastasie II : 1613-1616? (Austria—Cernovci)
Anastasie III : 1639?-1644? (Austria—Cernovci)
Anastasiî *Gribanovskiî* : 1936-1964 (Russia—Synodal Church)
Anastasios : 730-754 (Constantinople—Greek)
Anastasios : 880-889 (Greece)
Anastasios I : 458-478 (Jerusalem—Greek)
Anastasios II : -706 (Jerusalem—Greek)
Anastasios : 1583-1592 (Sinai)
Anastasius I : 399-401 (Rome)
Anastasius II : 496-498 (Rome)
Anastasius III : 855 [anti-pope] (Rome)
Anastasius III : 911-913 (Rome)
Anastasius IV : 1153-1154 (Rome)
Anastasiyus : 605-616 (Alexandria—Coptic)
Anastasiyus I *al-Sinaïtah* : 559-570, 593-598 (Antioch—Greek)
Anastasiyus II *al-Sinaïtah* : 599-609 (Antioch—Greek)
Anastasiyus III : 620-628 (Antioch—Greek)
Anastasiyus I *al-Sinaïtah* : 559-570, 593-598 (Antioch—Greek Melkite)
Anastasiyus II *al-Sinaïtah* : 599-609 (Antioch—Greek Melkite)
Anatolios : 449-458 (Constantinople—Greek)
Anatolios : 459? (Greece)

Andrawus *Akhijan Murabbi*, Ighnatiyus : 1662-1677 (Antioch—Syrian Catholic)
Andrêas : 1675-1676 (Constantinople—Armenian)
Andreas *Prótoklétos* : 30?-38 (Constantinople—Greek)
Andreas *Riggio* : 1716-1717 (Constantinople—Latin)
Andreas : 710-720 (Crete)
Andreas I : 1380? (Cyprus—Latin)
Andreas II : 1447- (Cyprus—Latin)
Andreas : 692-693? (Greece)
Andrêas *of Melitene* : 1551-1583 (Jerusalem—Armenian)
Andreî *Saguna* : 1846-1847 [locum tenens], 1847-1873 (Austria—Sibiu)
Andreî *Prazsky* : 1985-1990 (Ukraine—Autocephalous Church in USA)
Andreî *Metiiuk* : 1975-1985 (Ukraine—Canada)
Andreî *Kushchak* : 1967-1986 (Ukraine—America and Canada)
Andrej *Prazsky* : 1969-1970 [coadjutor], 1970-1980, 1982-1990 (Czechoslovakia—Slavonic)
Andrey *Kryt* : 1972-1983 (Belarus)
Andreyas : 1841 (Ethiopia—Historical)
Andruniqus : 616-622 (Alexandria—Coptic)
Angelarij *Krstevski* : 1981-1986 (Macedonia)
Angelus *Correr* : 1405 (Constantinople—Latin)
Anianos : 61-82 (Alexandria—Greek)
Anicetus : 155?-166? (Rome)
Aniyanus : 68-85 (Alexandria—Coptic)
Aniyanus : 68-83 (Alexandria—Coptic Catholic)
Aniyanus : 359 (Antioch—Greek)
Aniyanus : 360-362 (Antioch—Syrian Catholic)
Aniyus : 357-360 [anti-patriarch] (Antioch—Greek Melkite)
Aniyanus : 359 (Antioch—Syrian Orthodox)
Anterus : 235-236 (Rome)
Anthemios : 478? (Cyprus)
Anthimos I : 536 (Constantinople—Greek)
Anthimos II *apo Andrianoupoleós* : 1623 (Constantinople—Greek)
Anthimos III *apo Chalkédonos* : 1822-1824 (Constantinople—Greek)
Anthimos IV *Bambakés apo Nikomédeias* : 1840-1841, 1848-1852 (Constantinople—Greek)
Anthimos V *apo Kyzikou* : 1841-1842 (Constantinople—Greek)
Anthimos VI *Ióannidés apo Ephesou* : 1845-1848, 1853-1855, 1871-1873 (Constantinople—Greek)
Anthimos VII : 1895-1896 (Constantinople—Greek)
Anthimos I *Homologétés* : 1365-1370 (Crete)
Anthimos II : 1756 (Crete)
Anthimos I *Homologétés* : 1339-1366 (Greece)
Anthimos II : 1489? (Greece)
Anthimos III *apo Naupliou kai Argous* : 1604-1610 (Greece)
Anthimos IV *apo Talantiou* : 1655-1676 (Greece)
Anthimos V : 1693-1699 (Greece)
Anthimos VI : 1741-1756, 1760-1764 (Greece)
Anthimos VII *apo Artés* : 1828-1830 (Greece)
Anthimos : 1788-1808 (Jerusalem—Greek)
Antim I *Metokhit* : 1341? (Bulgaria)
Antim II : 1872-1877 (Bulgaria)
Antim *Metohit* : 1328? (Macedonia)
Antim I *Critopol* : 1380?-1401 (Romania)

Antim II *Ivireanul* : 1708-1716 (Romania)
Antim I : 18th cent. (Serbia)
Antim II : 1827-1831 (Serbia)
Antimiyus *of Helenopolis* : 1792-1813 (Antioch—Greek)
Anton—SEE ALSO: Antoniĭ
Anton I : 1744-1755, 1764-1788 (Georgia)
Anton II *Bagrationi* : 1788-1811 (Georgia)
Anton II *Khrapovits'kyĭ* : 1918-1920 (Ukraine)
Anton Petros IX *Hassun* : 1866-1879 (Cilicia—Armenian Catholic)
Antonie : 1728-1729 (Austria—Cernovci)
Antonie *Plamadeala* : 1982- (Austria—Sibiu)
Antoniĭ—SEE ALSO: Anton
Antoniĭ *Melnikov* : 1965-1978 (Belarus)
Antoniĭ : 1572-1582 (Russia—Moscow)
Antoniĭ *Khrapovitskiĭ* : 1921-1936 (Russia—Synodal Church)
Antoniĭ I *Vynkyĭ* : 1675-1679 (Ukraine)
Antoniĭ *Masendych* : 1991-1993 [locum tenens] (Ukraine—Autocephalous)
Antoniĭ : 1371-1391 (Ukraine—Halych)
Antonije *Abramovic* : 1993- (Montenegro)
Antonije *Sokolovic* : 1572-1575 (Serbia)
Antónios I *Kassimatas Byrsodepsés* : 821-837? (Constantinople—Greek)
Antónios II *Kauleas* : 893-901 (Constantinople—Greek)
Antónios III *Stoudités Pachen* : 974-979 (Constantinople—Greek)
Antónios IV : 1389-1390, 1391-1397 (Constantinople—Greek)
Antónios *Homologétés* : 1306? (Crete)
Antónios : 2nd cent. (Jerusalem—Greek)
Antonius I Maria *Pallavicino* : 1743-1749 (Antioch—Latin)
Antonius II *Despuig y Dameto* : 1799-1810 (Antioch—Latin)
Antonius III *Piatti* : 1837-1841 (Antioch—Latin)
Antonius I *Correr* : 1405-1408 (Constantinople—Latin)
Antonius II Maria *Traversi* : 1839-1842 (Constantinople—Latin)
Antonius III Anastasius *Rossi* : 1927-1948 (Constantinople—Latin)
Antonius *Tuneto* : 1464? (Cyprus—Latin)
Antonius *Beccus* : 1305-1310 (Jerusalem—Latin)
Antun I Butrus *'Aridah* : 1932-1955 (Antioch—Maronite)
Antun II Butrus *Khuraish* : 1975-1986 (Antioch—Maronite)
Antun I *Samhiri*, Ighnatiyus : 1853-1864 (Antioch—Syrian Catholic)
Antun II *Huwayyik*, Ighnatiyus : 1968- (Antioch—Syrian Catholic)
Anush *d'Bit' Garmai* : 873-884 (Assyria)
Anush *d'Bit' Garmai* : 877-884 (Babylon)
Apifaniyus : 1935- [anti-patriarch] (Antioch—Greek)
Apollinarios : 551-569 (Alexandria—Greek)
Aprem, Mar : 1968- (India—Chaldean)
Aqaq : 458-460 (Antioch—Syrian Catholic)
Aqaq : 458-459 (Antioch—Syrian Orthodox)
Aqaq : 484-496 (Assyria)
Aqaq : 485-496? (Babylon)
Arakel : 1495-1511 (Aghunie)
Arakel : 1577- [coadjutor] (Armenia)
Arakel : 1218-1230 (Jerusalem—Armenian)
Aram *K'êshishian* : 1995- (Cilicia—Armenian Apostolic)
Aramiya I : unknown (Antioch—Maronite)
Aramiya II *al-Amshiti* : 1209?-1230 (Antioch—Maronite)
Aramiya III *al-Dimlisawi* : 1272-1297 (Antioch—Maronite)

Arcadie *Ciupercovic* : 1896-1902 (Austria—Cernovci)
Aristakês I : -1478 (Aghunie)
Aristakês II : 1511-1521 (Aghunie)
Aristakês III : 1588-1593 (Aghunie)
Aristakês I *Part'e* : 325-333 (Armenia)
Aristakês II *At'orakal* : 1465-1469 (Armenia)
Aristakês : 1484-1499 [coadjutor] (Armenia)
Aristakês : 1555- [coadjutor] (Armenia)
Aristión : 70? [anti-archbishop] (Cyprus)
Arkadios I : 600? (Cyprus)
Arkadios II : 630?-641? (Cyprus)
Arnaldus Bernardus *du Pouget* : 1361?-1369 (Alexandria—Latin)
Arnulphus : 1275?-1280 (Cyprus—Latin)
Arnulphus : 1099-1100, 1111-1118 (Jerusalem—Latin)
Arsakios : 404-405 (Constantinople—Greek)
Arsaniyus I : 1285-1293 (Antioch—Greek)
Arsaniyus II *Haddad* : 1930-1933 (Antioch—Greek)
Arsaniyus : 1284?-1290? (Antioch—Greek Melkite)
Arsen I : 860-887 (Georgia)
Arsen II : 995-980 (Georgia)
Arsen III : 1222-1225 (Georgia)
Arsen IV : 1230-1240 (Georgia)
Arsen *Tsakawa* : 1940-1941 [locum tenens] (Japan)
Arsen : 1006-1038 (Jerusalem—Armenian)
Arseni : 1390 (Georgia—Abkhazia)
Arseniî I : 1662-1663? (Bulgaria)
Arseniî II : 1763-1767 (Bulgaria)
Arseniî I *Mohylians'kyî* : 1757-1770 (Ukraine)
Arseniî II *Moskvin* : 1860- (Ukraine)
Arsenij I : 1656-1657, 1658-1659?, 1659 (Macedonia)
Arsenij II : 1764-1767 (Macedonia)
Arsenije I *Sremac* : 1233-1263 (Serbia)
Arsenije II : 1457-1463 (Serbia)
Arsenije III *Crnojevic* : 1674-1690 (Serbia)
Arsenije IV *Jovanovic Shakabenda* : 1725?-1737 (Serbia)
Arsenije I *Crnojevic* : 1690-1706 (Austria—Karlovci)
Arsenije II *Jovanovic Shakabent* : 1741-1748 (Austria—Karlovci)
Arsenije (III) *Stojkovic* : 1870-1872 [locum tenens], 1874 [unconsecrated],
   1881 [unconsecrated] (Austria—Karlovci)
Arsenije I *Plamenac* : 1767-1773 [anti-vladika], 1781-1784 (Serbia—Monte-
   negro)
Arsenije II *Bradvarevic* : 1947-1960 (Serbia—Montenegro)
Arsenios : 1000-1010 (Alexandria—Greek)
Arsenios *Autóreianos* : 1254-1260, 1261-1265 (Constantinople—Greek)
Arsenios I : 1687-1688 (Crete)
Arsenios II : 1699-1701 (Crete)
Arsenios : 1344 (Jerusalem—Greek)
Arsenios I : 1290-1299? (Sinai)
Arsenios II : 1338? (Sinai)
Arshalawus : 311-312 (Alexandria—Coptic)
Arshalawus : 310-311 (Alexandria—Coptic Catholic)
Artemios : 1845-1847 (Alexandria—Greek)
Asbiridun *of Cyprus* : 1892-1898 (Antioch—Greek)
Ascanius *Gesualdi* : 1618-1640 (Constantinople—Latin)

INDEX OF PRIMATES

Asiz, Baselios Mar : 1471-1487 (India—Malankara Orthodox)
Aspurakês : 381-386 (Armenia)
Asqlibiyad : 211-223 (Antioch—Syrian Catholic)
Asqlibiyadhis: 212-218 (Antioch—Greek and Antioch—Greek Melkite)
Asqlibiyadis: 211-220 (Antioch—Syrian Orthodox)
Astuatsatur : 1715-1725 (Armenia)
Astuatsatur : 1693-1694? (Cilicia—Armenian Apostolic)
Astuatsatur I : 1537-1550 (Constantinople—Armenian)
Astuatsatur II : 1841-1844 (Constantinople—Armenian)
Astuatsatur I : 1313-1316 (Jerusalem—Armenian)
Astuatsatur II *of Melitene* : 1522-1542, 1550-1551 (Jerusalem—Armenian)
Astuatsatur III *of Daron* : 1645-1664, 1665-1666, 1668-1670 (Jerusalem— Armenian)
Atanasie *Anghel* : 1697-1701 (Austria—Sibiu)
Atanasiî I : 1593-1596, 1604-1614 (Bulgaria)
Atanasiî II : 1653-1660 (Bulgaria)
Atanasij I : 1593-1596, 1606- , 1614-1615 (Macedonia)
Atanasij II : 1657 (Macedonia)
Atanasije I *Ljubojevic* : 1711-1712 (Serbia)
Atanasije II *Gavrilovic* : 1746-1752 (Serbia)
Atanasije *Ljubojevic* : 1711-1712 [locum tenens] (Austria—Karlovci)
At'anasios : 1440-1441 (Aghunie)
Athanasie *Mironescu* : 1909-1911 (Romania)
Athanasios I : 328-373 (Alexandria—Greek)
Athanasios II : 1276-1316 (Alexandria—Greek)
Athanasios III : 1417-1425 (Alexandria—Greek)
Athanasios IV : 1500? (Alexandria—Greek)
Athanasios I : 1289-1293, 1303-1309 (Constantinople—Greek)
Athanasios II : 1451-1453 [locum tenens] (Constantinople—Greek)
Athanasios III *Patellarios apo Thessalonikés* : 1634, 1652 (Constantinople— Greek)
Athanasios IV *apo Rhaidestou* : 1679 (Constantinople—Greek)
Athanasios V *Krés apo Adrianoupoleós* : 1709-1711 (Constantinople—Greek)
Athanasios *Kalliopolités* : 1688-1697 (Crete)
Athanasios I : 1592-1600 (Cyprus)
Athanasios II *al-Dabbas* : 1705-1708 (Cyprus)
Athanasios I : 451-458 (Greece)
Athanasios II : 1686-1689 (Greece)
Athanasios III : 1756-1760 (Greece)
Athanasios IV *Taklikartés* : 1785-1787, 1796-1799 (Greece)
Athanasios, Paulose Mar : 1917-1935 [locum tenens], 1935-1953 (India— Malankara Jacobite)
Athanasios *Palakunnath*, Mathews Mar : 1842-1852 [suffragan], 1852-1875 (India—Malankara Syrian)
Athanasios I : 887-904 (India—Malankara Orthodox)
Athanasios II *of Edessa* : 1027-1041 (India—Malankara Orthodox)
Athanasios *Palakunnath*, Mathews Mar : 1843-1877 (India—Mar Thoma Syrian)
Athanasios, Thomas Mar : 1868-1877 [suffragan], 1877-1893 (India—Mar Thoma Syrian)
Athanasios, Thomas Mar : 1982- [suffragan] (India—Mar Thoma Syrian)
Athanasios I, Joseph Mar : 1883-1888 [suffragan], 1888-1898 (India—Thozhiyoor)

Athanasios II *Panakal*, Paulose Mar : 1917-1927 [suffragan] (India—Thozh-iyoor)
Athanasios I : 929-937 (Jerusalem—Greek)
Athanasios II : 1224-1236 (Jerusalem—Greek)
Athanasios III : 1313?-1334 (Jerusalem—Greek)
Athanasios IV : 1452-1460 (Jerusalem—Greek)
Athanasios V : 1827-1845 (Jerusalem—Greek)
Athanasios I : 1410? (Sinai)
Athanasios II *apo Naousés tés Makedonias* : 1708-1720 (Sinai)
Athanasios Mar Abraham III : 1365-1379 (India—Malankara Orthodox)
Athanasius *de Clermont* : 1219- (Alexandria—Latin)
Athanasiyus I : 326-373 (Alexandria—Coptic)
Athanasiyus II : 488-494 (Alexandria—Coptic)
Athanasiyus III *ibn Kalil* : 1250-1261 (Alexandria—Coptic)
Athanasiyus : 1945-1946, 1954-1959 [locum tenens] (Alexandria—Coptic)
Athanasiyus I : 328-373 (Alexandria—Coptic Catholic)
Athanasiyus (II) : 1741-1781 (Alexandria—Coptic Catholic)
Athanasiyus (III) *Khuzam* : 1854-1864 (Alexandria—Coptic Catholic)
Athanasiyus I *al-Jama'il* : 631 (Antioch—Greek)
Athanasiyus II : 1166-1180 (Antioch—Greek)
Athanasiyus III *al-Dabbas* : 1611-1619 (Antioch—Greek)
Athanasiyus IV *al-Dabbas* : 1686-1694 [anti-patriarch], 1720-1724 (Antioch—Greek)
Athanasiyus I : 1157?-1171 (Antioch—Greek Melkite)
Athanasiyus II *al-Dabbas* : 1612-1620 (Antioch—Greek Melkite)
Athanasiyus III *al-Dabbas* : 1685-1694, 1720-1724 (Antioch—Greek Melkite)
Athanasiyus IV *Jawhar* : 1759-1760, 1765-1768 [anti-patriarch], 1794-1794 (Antioch—Greek Melkite)
Athanasiyus V *Matar* : 1813-1814 (Antioch—Greek Melkite)
Athanasiyus I *Gammala* : 595-631 (Antioch—Syrian Catholic)
Athanasiyus II *of Baladh* : 684-688 (Antioch—Syrian Catholic)
Athanasiyus III : 724-740 (Antioch—Syrian Catholic)
Athanasiyus IV *Sandaliyus* : 756-758 (Antioch—Syrian Catholic)
Athanasiyus V *Salikha* : 987-1003 (Antioch—Syrian Catholic)
Athanasiyus VI *Khayya* : 1058-1063 (Antioch—Syrian Catholic)
Athanasiyus VII *Abu'l-Faraj* : 1091-1129 (Antioch—Syrian Catholic)
Athanasiyus VIII *Ishu' ibn Qatrah* : 1139-1166 (Antioch—Syrian Catholic)
Athanasiyus IX *Saliba Qarakha* : 1200-1207 (Antioch—Syrian Catholic)
Athanasiyus I *Gammala* : 595-631 (Antioch—Syrian Orthodox)
Athanasiyus II *of Baladh* : 684-687 (Antioch—Syrian Orthodox)
Athanasiyus III *Sandaliyus* : 724-740 (Antioch—Syrian Orthodox)
Athanasiyus IV *Salikha* : 986-1002 (Antioch—Syrian Orthodox)
Athanasiyus V *Hajji* : 1057-1063 (Antioch—Syrian Orthodox)
Athanasiyus VI *Abu'l-Faraj* : 1090-1129 (Antioch—Syrian Orthodox)
Athanasiyus VII *Ishu' ibn Qatrah* : 1137-1166 (Antioch—Syrian Orthodox)
Athanasiyus VIII *Saliba Qarakha* : 1199-1207 (Antioch—Syrian Orthodox)
Athénagoras *Spyrou* : 1930-1949 (America—Greek)
Athénagoras *Spyrou* : 1948-1972 (Constantinople—Greek)
Athénagoras I *Kabbadas* : 1954-1956, 1961-1962 [locum tenens] (Estonia)
Athénagoras II *Kokkinakés* : 1964-1973 [locum tenens] (Estonia)
Athénagoras I *Kabbadas* : 1955-1962 [locum tenens] (Latvia)
Athénagoras II *Kokkinakés* : 1964-1979 [locum tenens] (Latvia)
Athénodóros : 144-148 (Constantinople—Greek)
Atnatewos : 1869-1876 (Ethiopia—Historical)

Atnatewos : 1869-1876 (Ethiopia—Official)
Atom : 1496-1510 (Aght'amar)
Atrnerseh : 77-92 (Armenia)
Attikos : 406-425 (Constantinople—Greek)
Augen *Turuthi*, Baselios Mar : 1962-1964 [suffragan], 1964-1975 (India—Malankara Orthodox and Malankara Jacobite)
Augustins *Petersons* : 1936-1955 (Latvia)
Augustus *Foscolo* : 1830-1847 (Jerusalem—Latin)
Avgustin *Vinogradskiĭ* : 1818-1819 (Russia—Moscow)
Avraamiî *Mesapsa* : 1629?-1634? (Bulgaria)
Avram : 1629-1634 (Macedonia)
Awdiyus : 42-68 (Antioch—Syrian Catholic)
Awduksiyus : 357-360 (Antioch—Syrian Catholic)
Awduksiyus : 358-359 (Antioch—Syrian Orthodox)
Awetik' : 1702-1703, 1704-1706 (Constantinople—Armenian)
Awetik' : 1704-1706 (Jerusalem—Armenian)
Awetis : 1697 (Aght'amar)
Awetis Petros XIV *Arpiarian* : 1931-1937 (Cilicia—Armenian Catholic)
Awfruniyus : 332-333 (Antioch—Syrian Orthodox)
Awghris : 404 (Antioch—Syrian Catholic)
Awighriyus : 388-393 (Antioch—Syrian Orthodox)
Awlaliyus : 337-338 (Antioch—Syrian Catholic)
Awlaliyus : 331-333 (Antioch—Syrian Orthodox)
Awminiyus : 130-142 (Alexandria—Coptic)
Awminiyus : 129-141 (Alexandria—Coptic Catholic)
Awrus : 154-169 (Antioch—Syrian Orthodox)
Awsabiyus : unknown (Antioch—Maronite)
Awstathiyus : 320-332 (Antioch—Syrian Catholic)
Awstathiyus : 323-330 (Antioch—Syrian Orthodox)
Ayliya—SEE ALSO: Ilyas
Ayliya : 709-723 (Antioch—Syrian Catholic)
Ayliya I : 709-723 (Antioch—Syrian Orthodox)
Aymericus *de Limoges* : 1142-1187 (Antioch—Latin)
Ayrus : 154-169 (Antioch—Syrian Orthodox)
Ayruthiyus *Hagiotaphités* : 1850-1885 (Antioch—Greek)
Ayyub I : 811-826 (Antioch—Greek)
Ayyub II : 917-939 (Antioch—Greek)
Ayyub : 813?-845? (Antioch—Greek Melkite)
Azaria I : 1584-1601 (Cilicia—Armenian Apostolic)
Azaria II : 1683?-1686? (Cilicia—Armenian Apostolic)
Azaria : 1591-1592 (Constantinople—Armenian)
Azibina : 226-236 (Antioch—Syrian Catholic)
'Aziz *ibn Shabhta*, Ighnatiyus : 1466-1488 (Antioch—Syrian Orthodox—Tur Abhdin)
Babai I : 457-484 (Assyria)
Babai II : 496-502 (Assyria)
Babai : 497-503? (Babylon)
Babi : 499-502 (India—Malankara Orthodox)
Babila : 619-629 (Georgia)
Babilas : 238-250 (Antioch—Greek)
Babilas : 240-250 (Antioch—Greek Melkite)
Babkên : 1147? (Aghunie)
Babkên : 516-526 (Armenia)
Babkên *Giwlêserian* : 1931-1936 [coadjutor] (Cilicia—Armenian Apostolic)

Babula : 236-244 (Antioch—Syrian Catholic)
Babula : 237-251 (Antioch—Syrian Catholic)
Babuya : 457-484 (India—Malankara Orthodox)
Babwi : 457-484 (Babylon)
Baflinus *of Tyre* : 330-331 (Antioch—Greek)
Baflinus (I) *of Tyre* : 331 (Antioch—Greek Melkite)
Baflinus (II) : 371-376 [anti-patriarch] (Antioch—Greek Melkite)
Baghdasar : 1630? [anti-catholicos] (Aght'amar)
Baghdasar : 1735?-1736 (Aght'amar)
Bahnam I, Baselios Mar : 1404-1412 (India—Malankara Orthodox)
Bahnam II, Dioscoros Mar : 1415-1417 (India—Malankara Orthodox)
Bahnam III, Baselios Mar : 1850-1860 (India—Malankara Orthodox)
Bakhumiyus I : 1376-1393 (Antioch—Greek)
Bakhumiyus II *al-Hawrani* : 1410-1411 (Antioch—Greek)
Bakhumiyus I : 1359?-1368, 1375-1377, 1378-1386 (Antioch—Greek Melkite)
Bakhumiyus II *al-Hawrani* : 1412 (Antioch—Greek Melkite)
Baladhiyus : 490-498 (Antioch—Greek)
Baladiyun : 488-498 (Antioch—Syrian Orthodox)
Baladiyus : 488-495 (Antioch—Syrian Catholic)
Baladus : 488?-498 (Antioch—Greek Melkite)
Banyamin I : 622-662 (Alexandria—Coptic)
Banyamin II : 1327-1339 (Alexandria—Coptic)
Bar Ba'shmin : 350-358 (Assyria)
Bar Ba'shmin : 342?-348 (Babylon)
Bar Bosomin : 352-360 (India—Malankara Orthodox)
Bar Gabbara : 1135-1136 (Assyria)
Bar Suma *d'Subi* : 1133-1135 (Assyria)
Bar Suma *d'Subi* : 1134-1136 (Babylon)
Bar T'ulmai : 33 (Assyria)
Bar Yesu : 669-684 (India—Malankara Orthodox)
Bardas : 407- [anti-patriarch] (Constantinople—Greek)
Barmeya : unknown (Ethiopia—Official)
Barnabas I *Apostolos* : 45? (Cyprus)
Barnabas II : 1175- (Cyprus)
Barsauma, Baselios Mar : 1422-1455 (India—Malankara Orthodox)
Barsegh : 1105-1113 (Armenia)
Barsegh (II) : 1195-1206? [anti-catholicos] (Armenia)
Barsegh : 1549-1552 [coadjutor] (Armenia)
Barsegh : 1341-1356 (Jerusalem—Armenian)
Barsegh Petros IV *Avkadian* : 1780-1788 (Cilicia—Armenian Catholic)
Bartalomewos I : 950? (Ethiopia—Historical)
Bartalomewos II : 1398?-1436 (Ethiopia—Historical)
Bartalomewos : unknown (Ethiopia—Official)
Bartholomæus *de Braganza* : 1261- (Jerusalem—Latin)
Bartholomaios *Archondonés* : 1991- (Constantinople—Greek)
Bartholomaios *apo Drystras* : 1764-1780 (Greece)
Bart'lome : 591-595 (Georgia)
Bart'oghimêos : 60-68 (Armenia)
Baselios I *Bar Baldoyo* : 828-838 (India—Malankara Orthodox)
Baselios II : 938-962 (India—Malankara Orthodox)
Baselios III *of Tigris* : 1046-1069 (India—Malankara Orthodox)
Baselios IV : 1560-1589 (India—Malankara Orthodox)
Baselios (I), Mar : 1685 (India—Malankara Syrian)
Baselios (II), Mar : 1751-1763 (India—Malankara Syrian)

Baselios Mar Abraham IV : 1494-1496 (India—Malankara Orthodox)
Baselios Mar Asiz : 1471-1487 (India—Malankara Orthodox)
Baselios Mar Augen *Turuthi* : 1962-1964 [suffragan], 1964-1975 (India—Malankara Orthodox and Malankara Jacobite)
Baselios Mar Bahnam I : 1404-1412 (India—Malankara Orthodox)
Baselios Mar Bahnam III : 1850-1860 (India—Malankara Orthodox)
Baselios Mar Barsauma : 1422-1455 (India—Malankara Orthodox)
Baselios Mar Elias : 1838-1840 (India—Malankara Orthodox)
Baselios Mar Geevarghese I *Karnchira* : 1925-1928 (India—Malankara Orthodox)
Baselios Mar Geevarghese II *Kallacheril* : 1929-1964 (India—Malankara Orthodox)
Baselios Mar Ougen *Turuthi* : 1962-1964 [suffragan], 1964-1975 (India—Malankara Orthodox and Malankara Jacobite)
Baselios Mar Paulose I *Kathanar* : 1912-1914 (India—Malankara Orthodox)
Baselios Mar Paulose II : 1975- (India—Malankara Jacobite)
Baselios Mar Shakrulla : 1751-1764 (India—Malankara Orthodox)
Baselios Mar Thoma Mathews I *Vattakunnel* : 1970-1975 [suffragan], 1975-1991 (India—Malankara Orthodox)
Baselios Mar Thoma Mathews II : 1980-1991 [suffragan], 1991- (India—Malankara Orthodox)
Baselios Mar Yalda : 1634-1685 (India—Malankara Orthodox)
Basil—SEE ALSO: Basili
Basil I : 434-436 (Georgia)
Basil II : 914-930 (Georgia)
Basil III : 1090-1100 (Georgia)
Basil V : 1330-1350 (Georgia)
Basil VI : 1517-1528 (Georgia)
Basileios *Kompopoulos* : 1924-1930 (America—Greek)
Basileios I *Skamandrénos* : 970-974 (Constantinople—Greek)
Basileios II *Kamatéros Phylakopoulos* : 1183-1186 (Constantinople—Greek)
Basileios III *Geórgiadés* : 1925-1929 (Constantinople—Greek)
Basileios I : 680?-692? (Crete)
Basileios II : 879? (Crete)
Basileios III : 11th cent. (Crete)
Basileios IV : 12th cent. (Crete)
Basileios V : 1941-1950 (Crete)
Basileios : 1080? (Cyprus)
Basileios : 820-838 (Jerusalem—Greek)
Basili—SEE ALSO: Basil
Basili IV : 1206-1208 (Georgia)
Basiliyus I : 457-458 (Antioch—Greek)
Basiliyus II : 1042-1052 (Antioch—Greek)
Basiliyus I : 456-458 (Antioch—Greek Melkite)
Basiliyus II : 1041?-1051? (Antioch—Greek Melkite)
Basiliyus I : 456-458 (Antioch—Syrian Catholic)
Basiliyus II : 923-935 (Antioch—Syrian Catholic)
Basiliyus III *Sinnadus* : 1074-1075 (Antioch—Syrian Catholic)
Basiliyus I : 456-458 (Antioch—Syrian Orthodox)
Basiliyus II : 923-935 (Antioch—Syrian Orthodox)
Basiliyus III *Sinnadus* : 1074-1075 (Antioch—Syrian Orthodox)
Basiliyus IV *Ghubriyal* : 1349-1382 (Antioch—Syrian Orthodox)
Basiliyus V *Shim'un Man'Amaya* : 1421-1444 (Antioch—Syrian Orthodox)
Basilyos : 1951-1970 (Ethiopia—Historical)

Basilyos : 1951-1970 (Ethiopia—Official)
Bazyli *Doroszkiewicz* : 1970- (Poland)
Benedict *Troadas* : 1822, 1822 [locum tenens] (Romania)
Benedictus *Fenoja* : 1805-1812 (Constantinople—Latin)
Benedictus *Soranzo* : 1484- (Cyprus—Latin)
Benedictus I : 575-579 (Rome)
Benedictus II : 684-685 (Rome)
Benedictus III : 855-858 (Rome)
Benedictus IV : 900-903 (Rome)
Benedictus V : 964-966 (Rome)
Benedictus VI : 973-974 (Rome)
Benedictus VII : 974-983 (Rome)
Benedictus VIII : 1012-1024 (Rome)
Benedictus IX : 1032-1044, 1045, 1047-1048 (Rome)
Benedictus X *Mincius* : 1058-1059 [anti-pope] (Rome)
Benedictus XI *Boccasini* : 1303-1304 (Rome)
Benedictus XII *Fournier* : 1334-1342 (Rome)
Benedictus XIII *de Luna* : 1394-1423 [anti-pope] (Rome)
Benedictus XIII *Orsini* : 1724-1730 (Rome)
Benedictus XIV *Garnier* : 1425-1430 [anti-pope] (Rome)
Benedictus XIV *Lambertini* : 1740-1758 (Rome)
Benedictus XV *della Chiesa* : 1914-1922 (Rome)
Benediktos *apo Pisidias* : 1781-1785, 1787-1796 (Greece)
Benediktos *Papadopoulos* : 1957-1980 (Jerusalem—Greek)
Beniamin : 1600-1605 (Cyprus)
Beniamin *Philippos* : 2nd cent. (Jerusalem—Greek)
Beniaminos *Christodoulos* : 1936-1946 (Constantinople—Greek)
Bernardinus *Caraffa* : 1505? (Alexandria—Latin)
Bernardus : 1100-1134 (Antioch—Latin)
Besarion *Xhuvani* : 1929-1936 (Albania)
Besarioni : 1725-1737 (Georgia)
Besarioni : 1755-1769 (Georgia—Abkhazia)
Bessarion : 1463-1472 (Constantinople—Latin)
Bihnam *Hajlaya*, Ighnatiyus : 1412-1454 (Antioch—Syrian Orthodox)
Bihnam I *Hajlaya*, Ighnatiyus : 1412-1455 (Antioch—Syrian Catholic)
Bihnam II *Banni*, Ighnatiyus : 1893-1897 (Antioch—Syrian Catholic)
Bilatus, Ighnatiyus : 1591-1597 (Antioch—Syrian Catholic)
Bilatus, Ighnatiyus : 1591-1597 (Antioch—Syrian Orthodox)
Bilujin : 315-320 (Antioch—Syrian Catholic)
Binyamin Shim'un XXI : 1903-1918 (Assyria)
Bitalis : 313-315 (Antioch—Syrian Catholic)
Bohdan *Shpylka* : 1937-1965 (Ukraine—America and Canada)
Bonifacius *Bevilacqua* : 1598-1599 (Constantinople—Latin)
Bonifacius I : 418-422 (Rome)
Bonifacius II : 530-532 (Rome)
Bonifacius III : 607 (Rome)
Bonifacius IV : 608-615 (Rome)
Bonifacius V : 619-625 (Rome)
Bonifacius VI : 896 [unconsecrated] (Rome)
Bonifacius VII : 974, 984-985 [anti-pope] (Rome)
Bonifacius VIII *Caetani* : 1294-1303 (Rome)
Bonifacius IX *Tomacelli* : 1389-1404 (Rome)
Bonaventurus Secusius *de Caltagirone* : 1599-1618? (Constantinople—Latin)
Brguisho : 429-432 [anti-catholicos] (Armenia)

Bulinus I *of Tyre* : 323 (Antioch—Syrian Orthodox)
Bulinus II : 362-388 (Antioch—Syrian Orthodox)
Bulus I *Samasateus* : 260-268 (Antioch—Greek)
Bulus II *Xénodokos* : 519-521 (Antioch—Greek)
Bulus I *Samasateus* : 253-260 (Antioch—Greek Melkite)
Bulus II *Xénodokos* : 519-521 (Antioch—Greek Melkite)
Bulus I Butrus *Mas'ad al-Tarsi* : 1854-1890 (Antioch—Maronite)
Bulus II Butrus *al-Ma'ushi* : 1955-1975 (Antioch—Maronite)
Bulus I *Samasateus* : 263-271 (Antioch—Syrian Catholic)
Bulus II *Xénodokos* : 518-521 (Antioch—Syrian Catholic)
Bulus III *"The Black"* : 541-571 (Antioch—Syrian Catholic)
Bulus I *Samasateus* : 260-268 (Antioch—Syrian Orthodox)
Bulus II *"The Black"* : 552-578? (Antioch—Syrian Orthodox)
Burfirus : 404-414 (Antioch—Greek)
Burfirus : 404-416 (Antioch—Greek Melkite)
Burfuriyus : 404-414 (Antioch—Syrian Catholic)
Burfuriyus : 404-412 (Antioch—Syrian Orthodox)
Butrus I : 300-311 (Alexandria—Coptic)
Butrus II : 373-380 (Alexandria—Coptic)
Butrus III *Mongos* : 480-488 (Alexandria—Coptic)
Butrus IV : 567-569 (Alexandria—Coptic)
Butrus V : 1340-1348 (Alexandria—Coptic)
Butrus VI : 1718-1726 (Alexandria—Coptic)
Butrus VII *al-Gawli* : 1809-1852 (Alexandria—Coptic)
Butrus I : 300-310 (Alexandria—Coptic Catholic)
Butrus II : 373-378 (Alexandria—Coptic Catholic)
Butrus I *Apostolos* : 36-53 (Antioch—Greek)
Butrus II *Knapeus* : 464-467, 475-476, 485-490 (Antioch—Greek)
Butrus III : 1052-1056 (Antioch—Greek)
Butrus I *Apostolos* : 36-43 (Antioch—Greek Melkite)
Butrus II *Knapeus* : 470?-471?, 476?-477?, 485-488 (Antioch—Greek Melkite)
Butrus III : 1052-1057 (Antioch—Greek Melkite)
Butrus IV *Jirayjiri* : 1898-1902 (Antioch—Greek Melkite)
Butrus I : 1121? (Antioch—Maronite)
Butrus II : 1179? (Antioch—Maronite)
Butrus III : 1188? (Antioch—Maronite)
Butrus IV : 1199? (Antioch—Maronite)
Butrus V : 1269? (Antioch—Maronite)
Butrus VI *ibn Yusuf al-Hadathi* : 1458-1492 (Antioch—Maronite)
Butrus I : 35-42 (Antioch—Syrian Catholic)
Butrus II *Knapheus* : 470-471, 477-480, 483-484, 485-488 (Antioch—Syrian Catholic)
Butrus III *of Kallinikos* : 571-591 (Antioch—Syrian Catholic)
Butrus IV *Dawud*, Ighnatiyus : 1577-1591 (Antioch—Syrian Catholic)
Butrus V, Ighnatiyus : 1598-1639 (Antioch—Syrian Catholic)
Butrus VI *Shahbadin*, Ighnatiyus : 1677-1702 (Antioch—Syrian Catholic)
Butrus VII *Jarwah*, Ighnatiyus : 1820-1851 (Antioch—Syrian Catholic)
Butrus I : 37-50 (Antioch—Syrian Orthodox)
Butrus II *Knapheus* : 468-471, 476, 485-488 (Antioch—Syrian Orthodox)
Butrus III *of Kallinikos* : 581-591 (Antioch—Syrian Orthodox)
Butrus IV *al-Ma'usili*, Ighnatiyus : 1872-1894 (Antioch—Syrian Orthodox)
Cæsar *Monti* : 1629?-1650 (Antioch—Latin)
Cæsar *Podocator* : 1553- (Cyprus—Latin)
Calinic *Miclescu* : 1875-1886 (Romania)

Calistru : 1708-1728 (Austria—Cernovci)
Calixtus I : 217-222 (Rome)
Calixtus II *di Borgogna* : 1119-1124 (Rome)
Calixtus III : 1168-1178 [anti-pope] (Rome)
Calixtus III *de Borja* : 1455-1458 (Rome)
Camillus *Cybò* : 1718-1729 (Constantinople—Latin)
Cardinalis : 1332-1335 (Constantinople—Latin)
Carolus Ambrosius *Mezzabarba* : 1719? (Alexandria—Latin)
Carolus I Thomas *Maillard de Tournon* : 1701-1710 (Antioch—Latin)
Carolus II *Camuzio* : 1781- (Antioch—Latin)
Carolus III *Belgrado* : 1862-1866 (Antioch—Latin)
Carolus IV *Nocella* : 1899-1901 (Antioch—Latin)
Carolus Antonius *Nocella* : 1901-1903 (Constantinople—Latin)
Charitón *Eugeneiótés* : 1178-1179 (Constantinople—Greek)
Cheepat Mar Dionysios IV *Kattanar* : 1829-1852 (India—Malankara Syrian)
Chesarie : 1833-1840 [locum tenens] (Romania)
Ch'irmagi : 516-523 (Georgia)
Chmavon I : 1481- (Aghunie)
Chmavon II : 1586-1611 (Aghunie)
Christianus : 1256-1268 (Antioch—Latin)
Christodoulos : 907-932 (Alexandria—Greek)
Christodoulos I : 1606-1638? (Cyprus)
Christodoulos (II) : 1637-1638 [anti-archbishop] (Cyprus)
Christodoulos II : 1682-1685? (Cyprus)
Christodoulos I : 937- (Jerusalem—Greek)
Christodoulos II : 966-969 (Jerusalem—Greek)
Christophoros I : 817-841 (Alexandria—Greek)
Christophoros II *Daniélidés* : 1939-1966 (Alexandria—Greek)
Christophorus *del Monte* : 1550? (Alexandria—Latin)
Christophorus : 903-904 [anti-pope] (Rome)
Chrysanthos *apo Serrón* : 1824-1826 (Constantinople—Greek)
Chrysanthos *Lesbos* : 1843-1850 (Crete)
Chrysanthos : 1767-1783, 1783-1810 (Cyprus)
Chrysanthos *Philippidés* : 1938-1941 (Greece)
Chrysanthos *Notaras* : 1707-1731 (Jerusalem—Greek)
Chrysostom, Philipose Mar : unknown [suffragan] (India—Mar Thoma Syrian)
Chrysostomos *Kykkotés* : 1977- (Cyprus)
Chrysostomos I *Papadapoulos* : 1923-1938 (Greece)
Chrysostomos II *Chatzéstaurou* : 1962-1967 (Greece)
Cirilo—SEE ALSO: Kiril
Cirilo I : 1407-1419 (Serbia)
Clemens I : 88?-97? (Rome)
Clemens II : 1046-1047 (Rome)
Clemens III : 1080, 1084-1100 [anti-pope] (Rome)
Clemens III *Scolari* : 1187-1191 (Rome)
Clemens IV *Foulques* : 1265-1268 (Rome)
Clemens V *de Got* : 1305-1314 (Rome)
Clemens VI *Roger* : 1342-1352 (Rome)
Clemens VII *de Boulogne* : 1378-1394 [anti-pope] (Rome)
Clemens VII *de' Medici* : 1523-1534 (Rome)
Clemens VIII *Sánchez Muñoz* : 1423-1429 [anti-pope] (Rome)
Clemens VIII *Aldobrandini* : 1592-1605 (Rome)
Clemens IX *Rospigliosi* : 1667-1669 (Rome)
Clemens X *Altieri* : 1670-1676 (Rome)

Clemens XI *Albani* : 1700-1721 (Rome)
Clemens XII *Corsini* : 1730-1740 (Rome)
Clemens XIII *della Torre Rezzonico* : 1758-1769 (Rome)
Clemens XIV *Ganganelli* : 1769-1774 (Rome)
Clemens XV *Collin* : 1963-1974 (Rome—Renovated Church)
Cletus : 76?-88? (Rome)
Climis, Abraham Mar : 1957-1958 (India—Malankara Jacobite)
Coelestinus I : 422-423 (Rome)
Coelestinus II *Buccapecus* : 1124 [anti-pope] (Rome)
Coelestinus II : 1142-1144 (Rome)
Coelestinus III *Bobone* : 1191-1198 (Rome)
Coelestinus IV *da Castiglione* : 1241 [unconsecrated] (Rome)
Coelestinus V *del Morrone* : 1294 (Rome)
Conon *Aramescu-Donici* : 1912-1919 (Romania)
Conon : 686-687 (Rome)
Conradus I : 1396- (Cyprus—Latin)
Conradus II *Caraccioli* : 1402-1405 (Cyprus—Latin)
Constantinus (I) : 708-715 (Rome)
Constantinus II : 767-769 [anti-pope] (Rome)
Cornelius : 251-253 (Rome)
Cosma *Popescu* : 1787-1792 (Romania)
Dadishu' : 421-456 (Assyria)
Dadishu' : 421?-456 (Babylon)
Dagobertus *of Pisa* : 1100-1107 (Jerusalem—Latin)
Daimbertus *of Pisa* : 1100-1107 (Jerusalem—Latin)
Damaskénos : 1824-1827 (Cyprus)
Damaskénos *Papandreou* : 1938, 1941-1949 (Greece)
Damasus I : 366-384 (Rome)
Damasus II : 1048 (Rome)
Damian *Kokonesi* : 1966-1973 (Albania)
Damian : 927?-972? (Bulgaria)
Damianos : 530? (Cyprus)
Damianos *Kassiótés* : 1897-1931 (Jerusalem—Greek)
Damianos *Samartsés* : 1973- (Sinai)
Damiyanus : 569-605 (Alexandria—Coptic)
Danciu : 1516-1534 (Austria—Sibiu)
Daniêl : 347 [unconsecrated] (Armenia)
Daniêl : 1807-1808 (Armenia)
Daniêl : 1799-1800 (Constantinople—Armenian)
Daniél *apo Pethymnés* : 1722-1725 (Crete)
Daniél *apo Talantiou* : 1636-1655 (Greece)
Daniel : 838-847 (India—Malankara Orthodox)
Daniél : 1507? (Sinai)
Danieli : 1375? (Georgia—Abkhazia)
Daniil *Vlahovic* : 1789-1822 (Austria—Cernovci)
Daniil I : 1488-1500? (Austria—Sibiu)
Daniil II : 1660?-1662 (Austria—Sibiu)
Daniil : 1647?-1650 (Bulgaria)
Daniil I : 1566?-1568 (Romania)
Daniil II : 1719-1731 (Romania)
Daniil : 1522-1539 (Russia—Moscow)
Danil I *Biblesis* : 1230-1236 (Antioch—Maronite)
Danil II *al-Amshiti* : 1270?-1272? (Antioch—Maronite)
Danil : 1650? (Macedonia)

Danilo I : 1271-1272 (Serbia)
Danilo II : 1324-1337 (Serbia)
Danilo III : 1389 (Serbia)
Danilo IV : 1406 (Serbia)
Danilo V : 18th cent. (Serbia)
Danilo I *Petrovic-Njegos* : 1697-1735 (Serbia—Montenegro)
Danilo II *Petrovic-Njegos* : 1851-1852 (Serbia—Montenegro)
Danilo III *Dajkovic* : 1961-1990 (Serbia—Montenegro)
Daniyal *of Chios and Damaskus* : 1767-1791 (Antioch—Greek)
Da'ud : 1285? (India—Chaldean)
Daudesh : 421-456 (India—Malankara Orthodox)
David : 1015?-1018 (Bulgaria)
David : 1663-1679 [anti-catholicos] (Cilicia—Armenian Apostolic)
David : 687 (India—Malankara Orthodox)
David : 1015-1018 (Macedonia)
Davit' I : 944-955 (Georgia)
Davit' II : 1426-1430 (Georgia)
Davit' III : 1435-1439, 1443-1459 (Georgia)
Davit' IV : 1466-1479 (Georgia)
Davit' V *Devdariani* : 1972-1977 (Georgia)
Davit'i : 1673-1696 (Georgia—Abkhazia)
Dawit' I *T'ornikian* : 1113-1165? (Aght'amar)
Dawit' II *Sefedinian* : 1326?, 1346-1368? (Aght'amar)
Dawit' III : 1393-1433 (Aght'amar)
Dawit' I : -399 (Aghunie)
Dawit' II : 762-766 (Aghunie)
Dawit' III : 766-775 (Aghunie)
Dawit' IV : 822-849 (Aghunie)
Dawit' V : 923-929 (Aghunie)
Dawit' VI : 961-968 (Aghunie)
Dawit' VII : 968-974 (Aghunie)
Dawit' VIII : 1411 (Aghunie)
Dawit' IX : 1573-1574 (Aghunie)
Dawit' I : 728-741 (Armenia)
Dawit' II : 806-833 (Armenia)
Dawit' (III) *T'ornikian* : 1114- [anti-catholicos] (Armenia)
Dawit' : 1204-1207 [coadjutor] (Armenia)
Dawit' III : 1590-1629 (Armenia)
Dawit' IV *Gorghanian* : 1801-1807 (Armenia)
Dawit' : 1640-1641, 1643-1644, 1644-1649, 1650-1651 (Constantinople—Armenian)
Dawit' I : 1316-1321 (Jerusalem—Armenian)
Dawit' II *of Melitene* : 1583-1613 (Jerusalem—Armenian)
Dawud : 1242?-1247? (Antioch—Greek Melkite)
Dawud I : unknown (Antioch—Maronite)
Dawud II *Yuhanna* : 1367?-1402 (Antioch—Maronite)
Dawud, Ighnatiyus : 763- [anti-patriarch] (Antioch—Syrian Catholic)
Dawud, Ighnatiyus : 1519-1520 (Antioch—Syrian Catholic)
Dawud : 763- [anti-patriarch] (Antioch—Syrian Orthodox)
Dawud I, Ighnatiyus : 1517-1519 (Antioch—Syrian Orthodox)
Dawud Shah II *Butrus ibn Nur ad-Din*, Ighnatiyus : 1576-1591 (Antioch—Syrian Orthodox)
Démétrios : 189-232 (Alexandria—Greek)
Démétrios *Papadopoulos* : 1972-1991 (Constantinople—Greek)

260

Démétrios I : 835? (Greece)
Démétrios II : 846-857 (Greece)
Démophilos : 369-379, 379-386 (Constantinople—Greek)
Dengel : 969? (Ethiopia—Historical)
Denha I : 650-659 (India—Malankara Orthodox)
Denha II : 688-728 (India—Malankara Orthodox)
Denha III : 915-935 (India—Malankara Orthodox)
Deusdedit (I) : 615-618 (Rome)
Dhiyunisiyus : 1293-1308 (Antioch—Greek)
Dhumniyunus : 545-559 (Antioch—Greek)
Dhuruthiyus—SEE ALSO: Duruthiyus
Dhuruthiyus II *ibn al-Sabbuni* : 1436-1454 (Antioch—Greek)
Dhuruthiyus III *ibn al-Sabbuni* : 1497-1523 (Antioch—Greek)
Dimitri : 1080-1090 (Georgia)
Dimitrie : 1561?-1564? (Austria—Cernovci)
Dimitriî I : 923? (Bulgaria)
Dimitriî II *Khomatian* : 1216?-1234? (Bulgaria)
Dimitrij *Homatian* : 1216-1235 (Macedonia)
Dimitrije *Pavlovic* : 1905-1930 (Serbia)
Dimitriyanus : 252-260 (Antioch—Greek)
Dimitriyanus : 253 (Antioch—Greek Melkite)
Dimitriyanus : 254-260 (Antioch—Syrian Orthodox)
Dimitriyus I : 189-231 (Alexandria—Coptic)
Dimitriyus II : 1862-1870 (Alexandria—Coptic)
Dimitriyus : 188-230 (Alexandria—Coptic Catholic)
Dimitriyus *Qadi* : 1919-1925 (Antioch—Greek Melkite)
Dimitriyus : 255-263 (Antioch—Syrian Catholic)
Dinkha I *Arbilaya* : 1265-1281 (Assyria)
Dinkha II : 1329-1359 (Assyria)
Dinkha III : 1359-1368 (Assyria)
Dinkha IV *Khnanishu'* : 1976- (Assyria)
Dinkha I *Arbilaya* : 1265-1281 (Babylon)
Dinkha II : 1332-1364 (Babylon)
Dinkha : 1503? (India—Chaldean)
Dinkha Iliya XII *bar Mama* : 1722-1778 (Babylon)
Dinkha Shim'un IX *bar Mama* : 1552-1558 (Assyria)
Dinkha Shim'un XI : 1580-1600 (Assyria)
Dinkha Shim'un XV : 1692-1700 (Assyria)
Dinkha Shim'un VIII *bar Mama* : 1551-1558 (Babylon)
Diodóros *Karibalés* : 1981- (Jerusalem—Greek)
Diogenés : 114-129 (Constantinople—Greek)
Dionise : 1510-1511 (Georgia)
Dionisie : 1627-1629 (Austria—Cernovci)
Dionisie *Novacovic* : 1761-1767 (Austria—Sibiu)
Dionisie I : 1672 (Romania)
Dionisie II *Lupu* : 1819-1821 (Romania)
Dionisie : 1821-1822 [locum tenens] (Romania)
Dionisiî I : 1652-1653 (Bulgaria)
Dionisiî II *apo Chiou* : 1703-1706, 1709-1714 (Bulgaria)
Dionisiî III : 1751-1756 (Bulgaria)
Dionisiî : 1582-1587 (Russia—Moscow)
Dionisij I : 1467- (Macedonia)
Dionisij II : 1651-1656 (Macedonia)
Dionisij III *apo Chiou* : 1706-1707, 1710-1714 (Macedonia)

Dionisij IV : 1752-1757 (Macedonia)
Dionisije I : 1786-1793 (Serbia)
Dionisije II : 1813-1815 (Serbia)
Dionizus *Waledynski* : 1923-1948 (Poland)
Dionysiî I : 14th cent. (Ukraine)
Dionysiî II *Balaban* : 1657-1663 (Ukraine)
Dionysios : 248-264 (Alexandria—Greek)
Dionysios I *Symeónés apo Philippoupoleós* : 1467-1471, 1488-1490 (Constantinople—Greek)
Dionysios II : 1537, 1546-1555 (Constantinople—Greek)
Dionysios : 1586? [locum tenens] (Constantinople—Greek)
Dionysios III *Bardalis Spanos* : 1662-1665 (Constantinople—Greek)
Dionysios IV *Mouselimés Komnénos* : 1671-1673, 1676-1679, 1682-1684, 1686-1687, 1693-1694 (Constantinople—Greek)
Dionysios V : 1887-1891 (Constantinople—Greek)
Dionysios I *Byzantios* : 1850-1856 (Crete)
Dionysios II *Charitóniadés* : 1858-1868 (Crete)
Dionysios I *Areopagités* : 93? (Greece)
Dionysios II : 1820-1823 (Greece)
Dionysios I *Moosa* : 1112-1142 (India—Malankara Orthodox)
Dionysios II *Bar Msah* : 1188-1204 (India—Malankara Orthodox)
Dionysios III *Sleeba* : 1222-1231 (India—Malankara Orthodox)
Dionysios I, Thomas Mar : 1765-1808 (India—Malankara Syrian)
Dionysios II, Pulikkottil Mar : 1815-1816 (India—Malankara Syrian)
Dionysios III *Ittoop*, Punnathra Mar : 1817-1825 (India—Malankara Syrian)
Dionysios IV *Kattanar*, Cheepat Mar : 1829-1852 (India—Malankara Syrian)
Dionysios V *Putikkottil*, Joseph Mar : 1865-1909 (India—Malankara Syrian)
Dionysios VI *Vattasseril*, Geevarghese Mar : 1908-1909 [suffragan], 1909-1934 (India—Malankara Syrian)
Dionysius *du Moulin* : 1439-1447 (Antioch—Latin)
Dionysius : 259-268 (Rome)
Dios : 213 (Jerusalem—Greek)
Dioscoros Mar Bahnam II : 1415-1417 (India—Malankara Orthodox)
Dioscorus : 530 [anti-pope] (Rome)
Dioskoros : 444-451 [anti-patriarch] (Alexandria—Greek)
Dioskoros : 1036-1038 [anti-catholicos] (Armenia)
Dioskoros : 3rd cent. (Crete)
Disqurus I : 444-458 (Alexandria—Coptic)
Disqurus II : 515-517 (Alexandria—Coptic)
Diyunisiyus : 247-264 (Alexandria—Coptic)
Diyunisiyus : 246-264 (Alexandria—Coptic Catholic)
Diyunisiyus I : 1308?-1316? (Antioch—Greek Melkite)
Diyunisiyus II : 1325? (Antioch—Greek Melkite)
Diyunisiyus I *of Tell Mahar* : 818-845 (Antioch—Syrian Catholic)
Diyunisiyus II : 896-909 (Antioch—Syrian Catholic)
Diyunisiyus III : 958-961 (Antioch—Syrian Catholic)
Diyunisiyus IV *Khihi* : 1032-1042 (Antioch—Syrian Catholic)
Diyunisiyus V *Lazarus* : 1077-1079 (Antioch—Syrian Catholic)
Diyunisiyus VI : 1088-1090 (Antioch—Syrian Catholic)
Diyunisiyus VII *Aharon Angur* : 1252-1253 (Antioch—Syrian Catholic)
Diyunisiyus I *of Tell Mahar* : 818-845 (Antioch—Syrian Orthodox)
Diyunisiyus II : 896-909 (Antioch—Syrian Orthodox)
Diyunisiyus III : 958-961 (Antioch—Syrian Orthodox)
Diyunisiyus IV *Khihi* : 1033-1044 (Antioch—Syrian Orthodox)

Diyunisiyus V *Lazarus* : 1077-1078? (Antioch—Syrian Orthodox)
Diyunisiyus VI : 1088-1090 (Antioch—Syrian Orthodox)
Diyunisiyus VII *Aharon Angur* : 1252-1261 (Antioch—Syrian Orthodox)
Dolichianos : -185? (Jerusalem—Greek)
Domenicus *Marinangeli* : 1898-1912+ (Alexandria—Latin)
Domenicus *Giordani* : 1766-1780 (Antioch—Latin)
Domenicus *Lucciardi* : 1851 (Constantinople—Latin)
Domenti I : 1599-1603 (Georgia)
Domenti II : 1660-1676 (Georgia)
Domenti III : 1705-1725, 1739-1741 (Georgia)
Dometios : 272-303 (Constantinople—Greek)
Donus : 676-678 (Rome)
Dorot'eos—SEE ALSO: Dorot'eoz
Dorot'eos II : 1503-1510, 1511-1516 (Georgia)
Dorot'eoz—SEE ALSO: Dorot'eos
Dorot'eoz I : 1350-1356 (Georgia)
Dorot'eoz III : 1592-1599 (Georgia)
Doroteî I : 1320? (Bulgaria)
Doroteî II : 1466? (Bulgaria)
Dorotej *Filipp* : 1964- (Czechoslovakia)
Dorotej : 1456-1466 (Macedonia)
Dórotheos : 567- (Alexandria—Coptic—Gaianite)
Dórotheos : -407 [anti-patriarch] (Constantinople—Greek)
Dórotheos *apo Prousés* : 1918-1921 [locum tenens] (Constantinople—Greek)
Dórotheos I : 1387-1393? (Greece)
Dórotheos II : -1472 (Greece)
Dórotheos III *Kottaras* : 1956-1957 (Greece)
Dórotheos I : 1376-1417 (Jerusalem—Greek)
Dórotheos II : 1506-1537 (Jerusalem—Greek)
Dórotheos I : 1324-1333 (Sinai)
Dórotheos II *Byzantios* : 1794-1797 (Sinai)
Dositei *Filitti* : 1793-1810 (Romania)
Dositej I : 1466 (Macedonia)
Dositej II *Stojkovic* : 1958-1981 (Macedonia)
Dositheos *Hierosolymités* : 1189, 1189-1191 (Constantinople—Greek)
Dositheos I : 1191 (Jerusalem—Greek)
Dositheos II : 1669-1707 (Jerusalem—Greek)
Dosoftei *Herescu* : 1750-1789 (Austria—Cernovci)
Dosoftei : 1624-1627 (Austria—Sibiu)
Dumitiyus : unknown (Antioch—Maronite)
Dumnus I : 268-271 (Antioch—Greek)
Dumnus II : 441-449 (Antioch—Greek)
Dumnus I : 260-266 (Antioch—Greek Melkite)
Dumnus II : 442?-449 (Antioch—Greek Melkite)
Dumnus III : 545-559 (Antioch—Greek Melkite)
Dumnus I : 271-274 (Antioch—Syrian Catholic)
Dumnus II : 440-449 (Antioch—Syrian Catholic)
Dumnus I : 268-273 (Antioch—Syrian Orthodox)
Dumnus II : 442-449 (Antioch—Syrian Orthodox)
Durandus : 1212-1213 [unconsecrated] (Cyprus—Latin)
Duruthiyus—SEE ALSO: Dhuruthiyus
Duruthiyus I : 1219-1245 (Antioch—Greek)
Duruthiyus IV : 1541-1543 (Antioch—Greek)
Duruthiyus V *ibn al-Ahmar* : 1604-1611 (Antioch—Greek)

Duruthiyus (I) : 370-371 [anti-patriarch] (Antioch—Greek Melkite)
Duruthiyus I *ibn al-Sabbuni* : 1434?-1451 (Antioch—Greek Melkite)
Duruthiyus II *ibn al-Sabbuni* : 1484?-1500? (Antioch—Greek Melkite)
Duruthiyus III : 1529?-1531 (Antioch—Greek Melkite)
Duruthiyus IV *ibn al-Ahmar* : 1604-1612 (Antioch—Greek Melkite)
Dymytrii *IArema* : 1993- (Ukraine—Autocephalous)
Efrem : 1608-1613, 1616?-1623? (Austria—Cernovci)
Efrem : 1558?-1566? (Romania)
Eftim I *Karachissaridés* : 1926-1962 (Constantinople—Greek—Turkey)
Eftim II *Erenerol* : 1962- (Constantinople—Greek—Turkey)
Eftimie : 1558-1561? (Austria—Cernovci)
Eftimie : 1571?-1574 (Austria—Sibiu)
Eftimie I : 1568-1576 (Romania)
Eftimie II : 1594-1602 (Romania)
Eghia : 703-717 (Armenia)
Eghia : 774-797 (Jerusalem—Armenian)
Eghiazar : 681?-687? (Aghunie)
Eghiazar : 1663-1682 [anti-catholicos], 1682-1691 (Armenia)
Eghiazar *Adshapahian* : 1780? [coadjutor] (Cilicia—Armenian Apostolic)
Eghiazar : 1651-1652 (Constantinople—Armenian)
Eghiazar *of Hromkla* : 1664-1665, 1666-1668, 1670-1677 (Jerusalem—Armenian)
Eghishê : 1292-1300 [anti-catholicos] (Aght'amar)
Eghishê : -79 (Aghunie)
Eghishê *Rshtuni* : 941-946 (Armenia)
Eghishê : 1504-1505 [coadjutor] (Armenia)
Eghishê *Durian* : 1909-1911 (Constantinople—Armenian)
Eghishê I *Durian* : 1921-1930 (Jerusalem—Armenian)
Eghishê II *Derderian* : 1949-1957, 1958-1960 [locum tenens], 1960-1990 (Jerusalem—Armenian)
Ehremarus : 1105? [anti-patriarch] (Jerusalem—Latin)
Ek'vt'ime I : 1049-1055 (Georgia)
Ek'vt'ime II : 1220-1222 (Georgia)
Ek'vt'ime III : 1310-1325 (Georgia)
Ek'vt'ime I : 1578-1605 (Georgia—Abkhazia)
Ek'vt'ime II : 1669-1673 (Georgia—Abkhazia)
Eleutherios : 1175-1180 (Alexandria—Greek)
Eleutherios : 129-136 (Constantinople—Greek)
Eleutherius : 175?-189 (Rome)
Elia—SEE ALSO: Ilia
Elia I : 390-400 (Georgia)
Elias—SEE ALSO: Helias
Élias I : 963-1000 (Alexandria—Greek)
Élias II *Alphtheras* : 1171-1175 (Alexandria—Greek)
Elias : 1246?-1250 (Antioch—Latin)
Élias I : 787? (Crete)
Élias II : 1081-1092 (Crete)
Élias III : 14th cent. (Crete)
Elias I : 1240-1251 (Cyprus—Latin)
Elias III : 1460-1463? (Cyprus—Latin)
Elias I : 1279-1287 (Jerusalem—Latin)
Elias II *de Nabinallis* : 1342- (Jerusalem—Latin)
Élias I : 494-516 (Jerusalem—Greek)
Élias II : 770-797 (Jerusalem—Greek)

Élias III : 878-907 (Jerusalem—Greek)
Elias, Baselios Mar : 1838-1840 (India—Malankara Orthodox)
Élias : 900 (Sinai)
Eliozi : 1399-1411 (Georgia)
Elisho : 504-536 (India—Malankara Orthodox)
Elpidios : 565-567 (Alexandria—Coptic—Gaianite)
Emilian *Antal Tîrgovisteanul* : 1945-1948 [locum tenens] (Austria—Cernovci)
Ephraim : 1715 [anti-archbishop] (Cyprus)
Ephraim I : unknown (Jerusalem—Greek)
Ephraim II : 1766-1771 (Jerusalem—Greek)
Epip'ane : 1210-1220 (Georgia)
Epiphanios : 520-535 (Constantinople—Greek)
Epiphanios I : 368-403 (Cyprus)
Epiphanios II : 681?-685? (Cyprus)
Epiphanios III : 870? (Cyprus)
Ep'rem : 1809-1830 (Armenia)
Ep'rem I : 1771-1784 (Cilicia—Armenian Apostolic)
Ep'rem II : 1823-1831 (Cilicia—Armenian Apostolic)
Ep'rem : 1684-1686, 1694-1698, 1701-1702 (Constantinople—Armenian)
Ep'rem I : 1497-1500 (Georgia)
Ep'rem II *Sidamonidze* : 1960-1972 (Georgia)
Eraclius : 1180-1191 (Jerusalem—Latin)
Eremia I : -552 (Aghunie)
Eremia II : 1676-1700 (Aghunie)
Eremia *Sahagian* : 1885-1889 [locum tenens] (Jerusalem—Armenian)
Eremij : 1761-1763 (Macedonia)
Ermenus : 1709-1710 (Macedonia)
Esayi : 1701-1727 (Aghunie)
Esayi : 775-788 (Armenia)
Esayi I : 1133-1152 (Jerusalem—Armenian)
Esayi II : 1391-1394 (Jerusalem—Armenian)
Esayi III : 1430-1431 (Jerusalem—Armenian)
Esayi IV *Karapetian* : 1864-1885 (Jerusalem—Armenian)
Euagrios : 379 (Constantinople—Greek)
Eudoxios : 360-369 (Constantinople—Greek)
Eugenie *Hacman* : 1835-1873 (Austria—Cernovci)
Eugenios I : 237-242 (Constantinople—Greek)
Eugenios II *apo Pissideias* : 1821-1822 (Constantinople—Greek)
Eugenios *Psallidakés* : 1950-1978 (Crete)
Eugenios : 1567-1583 (Sinai)
Eugenius I : 654-657 (Rome)
Eugenius II : 824-827 (Rome)
Eugenius III *Pignatelli* : 1145-1153 (Rome)
Eugenius IV *Condulmaro* : 1431-1447 (Rome)
Eulalius : 418-419 [anti-pope] (Rome)
Eulogios I : 581-608 (Alexandria—Greek)
Eulogios II : 1130? (Alexandria—Greek)
Eumenés : 129-141 (Alexandria—Greek)
Eumenios I *Thaumatourgos* : 668 (Crete)
Eumenios II *Xéroudakés* : 1897-1920 (Crete)
Euphémios : 490-496 (Constantinople—Greek)
Eusebios *Nikomédeias* : 341-342? (Constantinople—Greek)
Eusebius : 309 (Rome)
Eustathios : 813-817 (Alexandria—Greek)

Eustathios *apo Palatiou* : 1019-1025 (Constantinople—Greek)
Eustathios : 890? (Cyprus)
Eustochios : 552-564 (Jerusalem—Greek)
Eustorgius *de Montaigu* : 1217?-1239 (Cyprus—Latin)
Eustratios *Garidas* : 1081-1084 (Constantinople—Greek)
Euthymios I : 907-912 (Constantinople—Greek)
Euthymios II : 1410-1416 (Constantinople—Greek)
Euthymios : 1223-1224 (Sinai)
Euthymios I : -1084 (Jerusalem—Greek)
Euthymios II : -1223 (Jerusalem—Greek)
Eutychianus : 275-283 (Rome)
Eutychios : 933-940 (Alexandria—Greek)
Eutychios : 552-565, 577-582 (Constantinople—Greek)
Euzóïos : 148-154 (Constantinople—Greek)
Evagre : 1480-1492, 1500-1503 (Georgia)
Evaristus : 97?-105? (Rome)-
Evdemoz I : 1630-1637 (Georgia)
Evdemoz II : 1701-1705 (Georgia)
Evdemoz I : 1557-1578 (Georgia—Abkhazia)
Evdemoz II : 1666-1669 (Georgia—Abkhazia)
Evdokim *Meshcherskiĭ* : 1914-1917 (America—Orthodox Church)
Evgeniĭ *Baenov* : 1834-1844 [exarch] (Georgia)
Evlale : 664-668 (Georgia)
Evlavi : 533-544 (Georgia)
Evlogie : 1623-1627, 1628-1639? (Austria—Cernovci)
Evnoni : 640-649 (Georgia)
Evsebiĭ *Ilinskiĭ* : 1858-1877 [exarch] (Georgia)
Evstatiî : 1159? (Bulgaria)
Evsuk'i : 887-908 (Georgia)
Evtimiî : 1375-1393 (Bulgaria)
Ewostatewos : unknown (Ethiopia—Official)
Ezr : 630-641 (Armenia)
Ezra : 1215? (Ethiopia—Historical)
Fabianus : 236-250 (Rome)
Fabius I *Colonna* : 1550-1554 (Constantinople—Latin)
Fabius II Maria *Asquini* : 1844-1845 (Constantinople—Latin)
Fabiyus : 250-252 (Antioch—Greek)
Fabiyus : 250-253 (Antioch—Greek Melkite)
Fabiyus : 244-255 (Antioch—Syrian Catholic)
Fabiyus : 251-254 (Antioch—Syrian Catholic)
Fabricius : 1464- (Cyprus—Latin)
Felix I : 269-274 (Rome)
Felix II : 355-365 [anti-pope] (Rome)
Felix III : 483-492 (Rome)
Felix IV : 526-530 (Rome)
Felix V *di Savoia* : 1439-1449 [anti-pope] (Rome)
Feodor : 1462-1467 (Russia—Moscow)
Feodor : 1160-1163 (Ukraine)
Feodor : 1337-1347 (Ukraine—Halych)
Feofil *Pashkovskiĭ* : 1934-1950 (America—Orthodox Church)
Feognost : 1328-1352 (Russia—Moscow)
Feognost : 1328-1353 (Ukraine)
Feofilakt *Rusanov* : 1817-1821 [exarch] (Georgia)
Feopempt : 1039- (Ukraine)

Ferdinandus *de Loazes* : 1566? (Alexandria—Latin)
Ferdinandus *de Loazes* : 1566-1568 (Antioch—Latin)
Ferdinandus Maria *de Rossi* : 1751-1759 (Constantinople—Latin)
Filaqas : 342-346 (Antioch—Syrian Catholic)
Filaqilus : 333-343 (Antioch—Syrian Orthodox)
Filaret *Vakhromeev* : 1978- (Belarus)
Filaret I *Mihalitzis* : 1753-1760 (Romania)
Filaret II : 1792-1793 (Romania)
Filaret *Romanov* : 1619-1633 (Russia)
Filaret *Drozdoz* : 1821-1867 (Russia—Moscow)
Filaret *Voznesenskiĭ* : 1964-1985 (Russia—Synodal Church)
Filaret I *Amfiteatrov* : 1837-1857 (Ukraine)
Filaret II *Denisenko* : 1966-1992 (Ukraine)
Filatawos I : unknown (Ethiopia—Official)
Filatawos II : unknown (Ethiopia—Official)
Filibbus Butrus *al-Jumayyil* : 1795-1796 (Antioch—Maronite)
Filibbus *Arkus*, Ighnatiyus : 1866-1874 (Antioch—Syrian Catholic)
Filimun *of Aleppo* : 1766-1767 (Antioch—Greek)
Filip : 1000?-1015? (Bulgaria)
Filip : 1000?-1015 (Macedonia)
Filip : 1591-1592 (Serbia)
Filipp I : 1467-1472 (Russia—Moscow)
Filipp II : 1568-1572 (Russia—Moscow)
Filippos *Berhan* : 1991- (Eritrea)
Filitus : 218-231 (Antioch—Greek and Antioch—Greek Melkite)
Filitus : 223-226 (Antioch—Syrian Catholic)
Filitus : 220-231 (Antioch—Syrian Orthodox)
Filoteî : 1714-1718 (Bulgaria)
Filotej : 1968-1970 (Czechoslovakia)
Filughunus : 319-324 (Antioch—Greek)
Filughunus : 320-325 (Antioch—Greek Melkite)
Filujuniyus : 319-323 (Antioch—Syrian Orthodox)
Filuksinus *Nimrud*, Ighnatiyus : 1283-1292 (Antioch—Syrian Catholic)
Filuksinus I *Nimrud* : 1283-1292 (Antioch—Syrian Orthodox)
Filuksinus II *"The Scribe"* : 1382-1421 (Antioch—Syrian Orthodox)
Filuthawus : 979-1003 (Alexandria—Coptic)
Fiqtor : 1050?-1077 (Ethiopia—Historical)
Fiqtor I : unknown (Ethiopia—Official)
Fiqtor II : unknown (Ethiopia—Official)
Fitalis : 306-314 (Antioch—Greek Melkite)
Fitaliyus : 314-319 (Antioch—Greek)
Fitaliyus : 313-319 (Antioch—Syrian Orthodox)
Flabiyanus I : 381-404 (Antioch—Syrian Catholic)
Flabiyanus II : 495-512 (Antioch—Syrian Catholic)
Flabiyanus I : 381-404 (Antioch—Syrian Orthodox)
Flabiyanus II : 498-512 (Antioch—Syrian Orthodox)
Flafiyanus I : 381-404 (Antioch—Greek and Antioch—Greek Melkite)
Flafiyanus II : 498-512 (Antioch—Greek and Antioch—Greek Melkite)
Flakilus : 333-342 (Antioch—Greek)
Flakilus : 334-343 (Antioch—Greek Melkite)
Flavian *Gorodetskiĭ* : 1898-1903 [exarch] (Georgia)
Formosus : 891-896 (Rome)
Fotiî : 1410-1436 (Russia—Moscow)
Fotiî : 1408-1431 (Ukraine)

Franciscus de Pauli *Cassetta* : 1895-1899 (Antioch—Latin)
Franciscus I *Landus* : 1409 (Constantinople—Latin)
Franciscus II *de Conzié* : 1430- (Constantinople—Latin)
Franciscus III *Condulmer* : 1438- (Constantinople—Latin)
Franciscus IV *de Lorris* : 1503-1506 (Constantinople—Latin)
Franciscus V *Pesaro* : 1530-1544 (Constantinople—Latin)
Franciscus VI Maria *Machiavelli* : 1640-1641 (Constantinople—Latin)
Franciscus VII Antonius *Marcucci* : 1781-1799 (Constantinople—Latin)
Fredericus *Borromée* : 1655? (Alexandria—Latin)
Fredericus *Borromée* : 1670-1673 (Constantinople—Latin)
Fulcherus : 1146-1157 (Jerusalem—Latin)
Fulin : 332-337 (Antioch—Syrian Catholic)
Gabra Krestos : 1344?-1348? (Ethiopia—Historical)
Gabr'el *Iyasu* : 1980-1985 (Eritrea)
Gabr'el : 1438-1458? (Ethiopia—Historical)
Gabr'el I : unknown (Ethiopia—Official)
Gabr'el II : unknown (Ethiopia—Official)
Gabr'el III : unknown (Ethiopia—Official)
Gabr'el IV : unknown (Ethiopia—Official)
Gabr'el V : unknown (Ethiopia—Official)
Gabr'el VI : unknown (Ethiopia—Official)
Gabr'el VII : unknown (Ethiopia—Official)
Gabr'el VIII : unknown (Ethiopia—Official)
Gabr'el IX : unknown (Ethiopia—Official)
Gabr'el X : 1438-1458? (Ethiopia—Official)
Gabriêl *Shiroyan* : 1851-1857 (Aght'amar)
Gabriêl : 1757-1770 (Cilicia—Armenian Apostolic)
Gabriél I : 1596 (Constantinople—Greek)
Gabriél II *apo Ganou kai Chóras* : 1657 (Constantinople—Greek)
Gabriél III *Smyrnaios apo Chalkédonos* : 1702-1707 (Constantinople—Greek)
Gabriél IV *apo Palaión Patrón* : 1780-1785 (Constantinople—Greek)
Gabriel I : 502-510 (Georgia)
Gabriel II : 838-860 (Georgia)
Gabriel III : 1065-1080 (Georgia)
Gabriél I : 858-860 (Greece)
Gabriél II : 1781 (Greece)
Gabriêl : 1818-1840 (Jerusalem—Armenian)
Gabriél I : 1154-1160 (Sinai)
Gabriél II : 1445? (Sinai)
Gagik I : 947-961 (Aghunie)
Gagik II : 1139- (Aghunie)
Gaïanos : 536-565 (Alexandria—Coptic)
Gaïanos : unknown (Jerusalem—Greek)
Gaïnos : 536-565 (Alexandria—Coptic)
Gaïos I : unknown (Jerusalem—Greek)
Gaïos II : unknown (Jerusalem—Greek)
Gaius : 283-296 (Rome)
Galesius *de Montolif* : 1445-1447 (Cyprus—Latin)
Galust *Vayzhavk* : 1703-1704 (Constantinople—Armenian)
Galust : 1697-1704 [coadjutor] (Jerusalem—Armenian)
Garegin *Sargisian* : 1995- (Armenia)
Garegin I *Hovespian* : 1943-1952 (Cilicia—Armenian Apostolic)
Garegin II *Sargisian* : 1977-1983 [coadjutor], 1983-1995 (Cilicia—Armenian Apostolic)

Garegin I *Khach'aturian* : 1951-1961 (Constantinople—Armenian)
Garegin II Petros *Kazanjian* : 1990- (Constantinople—Armenian)
Gavriil : 1572-1587 (Bulgaria)
Gavriil *Banulescu* : 1808-1812 (Romania)
Gavril I : 1572?-1588, 1593 (Macedonia)
Gavril II *Miloshevski* : 1986-1993 (Macedonia)
Gavrilo *Zmajevic* : 1908 [unconsecrated] (Austria—Karlovci)
Gavrilo I *Rajic* : 1648-1655 (Serbia)
Gavrilo II *Mihailovic Sarajevac* : 1752 (Serbia)
Gavrilo III : 1752- (Serbia)
Gavrilo IV : 1757?-1758 (Serbia)
Gavrilo V *Dozhic* : 1937-1950 (Serbia)
Gavrilo *Dozhic* : 1920-1938 (Serbia—Montenegro)
Geevarghese *Kallacheril*, Baselios Mar : 1958-1964 (India—Malankara Jacobite)
Geevarghese I *Karnchira*, Baselios Mar : 1925-1928 (India—Malankara Orthodox)
Geevarghese II *Kallacheril*, Baselios Mar : 1929-1964 (India—Malankara Orthodox)
Geevarghese Mar Dionysios VI *Vattasseril* : 1908-1909 [suffragan], 1909-1934 (India—Malankara Syrian)
Geevarghese Mar Koorilose II : 1794-1802 [suffragan], 1802-1808 (India—Thozhiyoor)
Geevarghese Mar Koorilose III *Koothoor* : 1829-1856 (India—Thozhiyoor)
Geevarghese Mar Koorilose V *Pulikottil* : 1892-1898 [suffragan], 1898-1935 (India—Thozhiyoor)
Geevarghese Mar Koorilose VII *Kasseesa* : 1948-1967 (India—Thozhiyoor)
Geevarghese Mar Phileksinose : 1816-1817, 1825-1829 (India—Malankara Syrian)
Geevarghese Mar Phileksinose II : 1811-1829 (India—Thozhiyoor)
Gelasios : 325? (Cyprus)
Gelasius I : 492-496 (Rome)
Gelasius II *Caetani* : 1118-1119 (Rome)
Genadiî : 1285? (Bulgaria)
Genadij : 1289? (Macedonia)
Gennadios I : 458-471 (Constantinople—Greek)
Gennadios II *Scholarios Kourtesés* : 1454-1456, 1462-1463, 1464 (Constantinople—Greek)
Gennadios : 1973 [anti-archbishop] (Cyprus)
Gêorg I *Hailorbuk* : 792-795 (Armenia)
Gêorg II : 877-897 (Armenia)
Gêorg : 1067-1072 [coadjutor] (Armenia)
Gêorg III *Jalalbêgiants'* : 1443-1465 (Armenia)
Gêorg IV *K'erest'echian* : 1866-1882 (Armenia)
Gêorg V *Surenian(ts')* : 1911-1930 (Armenia)
Gêorg VI *Ch'êôrêk'chian* : 1938-1945 [locum tenens], 1945-1954 (Armenia)
Gêorg I : 1751-1752 (Constantinople—Armenian)
Gêorg II *K'erest'echian* : 1858-1860 (Constantinople—Armenian)
Gêorg *Arslanian* : 1922-1927, 1944-1950 [locum tenens] (Constantinople—Armenian)
Gêorg : 696-708 (Jerusalem—Armenian)
Georgi I : 878?-919? (Bulgaria)
Georgi II : 1616-1617 (Bulgaria)
Georgij : 1627? (Macedonia)

Georgije (I) *Hranislav* : 1841-1842 [locum tenens] (Austria—Karlovci)
Georgije (II) *Brankovic* : 1890-1907 (Austria—Karlovci)
Georgije (III) *Letic* : 1919-1920 [locum tenens] (Austria—Karlovci)
Geórgios I : 621-630 (Alexandria—Greek)
Geórgios II : 1021-1052 (Alexandria—Greek)
Geórgios : 357-361 (Alexandria—Greek—Arian)
Geórgios I : 679-686 (Constantinople—Greek)
Geórgios II *Xiphilinos* : 1191-1198 (Constantinople—Greek)
Geórgios I : 753? (Cyprus)
Geórgios II : 1254? (Cyprus)
Geórgios I : 914-922 (Greece)
Geórgios II : 1145-1160 (Greece)
Geórgios III *Xéros* : 1175-1179 (Greece)
Geórgios IV *Bourtzés* : 1180 (Greece)
Geórgios : 797-807 (Jerusalem—Greek)
Geórgios I : unknown (Sinai)
Geórgios II : 1130-1149 (Sinai)
Geraldus Odo *de Camboulit* : 1342-1348 (Antioch—Latin)
Geraldus : 1225-1239 (Jerusalem—Latin)
Gerardus *de Crussol* : 1471-1472 (Antioch—Latin)
Gerardus *de Langres* : 1295-1312? (Cyprus—Latin)
Gerasim *Sokolovic* : 1575-1586 (Serbia)
Gerasimos I *Spartaliótés* : 1621-1636 (Alexandria—Greek)
Gerasimos II *Palidas* : 1688-1710 (Alexandria—Greek)
Gerasimos III *Gémarés Kaliklas* : 1783-1788 (Alexandria—Greek)
Gerasimos I : 1320-1321 (Constantinople—Greek)
Gerasimos II *apo Tornobou* : 1673-1674 (Constantinople—Greek)
Gerasimos III *apo Derkón* : 1794-1797 (Constantinople—Greek)
Gerasimos I *Letitzés Gerontas* : 1725-1755? (Crete)
Gerasimos II *apo Chiou* : 1756-1769 (Crete)
Gerasimos III *Pardalés* : 1800-1821 (Crete)
Gerasimos : 1127? (Greece)
Gerasimos : 1334?-1349 [anti-patriarch] (Jerusalem—Greek)
Gerasimos *Propapas* : 1891-1896 (Jerusalem—Greek)
Gerbasios I : 1432? (Greece)
Gerbasios II : 1462? (Greece)
Gerlos—SEE ALSO: Qerlos
Gerlos I : unknown (Ethiopia—Official)
German *Andjelic* : 1880-1882 [locum tenens], 1882-1888 (Austria—Karlovci)
German I : 972?-1000? (Bulgaria)
German II : 1688-1690, 1702-1703 (Bulgaria)
German I *of Voden* : 1688-1691, 1702-1703 (Macedonia)
German II : 1758-1759 (Macedonia)
German : 1563-1565 (Russia—Moscow)
German *Djoric* : 1958-1990 (Serbia)
German : 1520- (Serbia—Montenegro)
Germane : 1541-1547 (Georgia)
Germane : 1742-1750? (Georgia—Abkhazia)
Germanión : 213 (Jerusalem—Greek)
Germanos I : 715-730 (Constantinople—Greek)
Germanos II : 1223-1240 (Constantinople—Greek)
Germanos III : 1265-1266 (Constantinople—Greek)
Germanos IV *apo Derkón* : 1842-1845, 1852-1853 (Constantinople—Greek)
Germanos V : 1913-1918 (Constantinople—Greek)

Germanos I *Pésimandros* : 1260?-1275 (Cyprus)
Germanos II : 1695?-1705 (Cyprus)
Germanos I : -841 (Greece)
Germanos II *Kalligas* : 1889-1896 (Greece)
Germanos *Peloponnesios* : 1537-1579 (Jerusalem—Greek)
Germanos *Mamaladés* : 1980-1981 [locum tenens] (Jerusalem—Greek)
Germanos I : 1177? (Sinai)
Germanos II : 1228? (Sinai)
Germanos III : 1333-   (Sinai)
Germogen : 1606-1612 (Russia)
Gerontiî : 1472-1491 (Russia—Moscow)
Gervasius : 1215-1219 (Constantinople—Latin)
Ghazar : 1723? [locum tenens] (Aght'amar)
Ghazar : 4th cent. (Aghunie)
Ghazar : 1737-1748, 1748-1751 (Armenia)
Ghazar : 1545-1547 (Cilicia—Armenian Apostolic)
Ghazar : 1660-1663 (Constantinople—Armenian)
Ghedeon I : 1588-1591? (Austria—Cernovci)
Ghedeon II : 1701?-1708 (Austria—Cernovci)
Ghedeon *Nichitic* : 1783-1788 (Austria—Sibiu)
Ghelasie : unknown (Austria—Cernovci)
Ghelasie : 1376? (Austria—Sibiu)
Ghenadie I : 1579-1585 (Austria—Sibiu)
Ghenadie II : 1627-1640 (Austria—Sibiu)
Ghenadie III : 1659-1660 (Austria—Sibiu)
Ghenadie *Petrescu* : 1893-1896 (Romania)
Gheorghe I : 1552-1558 (Austria—Cernovci)
Gheorghe II *Moghila* : 1577-1588 (Austria—Cernovci)
Gheorghe : 1561?-1562 (Austria—Sibiu)
Gherasim *Adamovic* : 1789-1796 (Austria—Sibiu)
Gherasim *al Buzaului* : 1822 [locum tenens] (Romania)
Gherasim *Timus* : 1893, 1896 [locum tenens] (Romania)
Ghewond : 545-548 (Armenia)
Ghewondios : 172-190 (Armenia)
Ghrighuriyus I *al-Sinaïtah* : 570-593 (Antioch—Greek)
Ghrighuriyus II : 610-620 (Antioch—Greek)
Ghrighuriyus III : 1483-1497 (Antioch—Greek)
Ghrighuriyus IV *Haddad* : 1906-1928 (Antioch—Greek)
Ghrighuriyus I *al-Sinaïtah* : 570-593 (Antioch—Greek Melkite)
Ghrighuriyus II *Yusuf-Sayur* : 1864-1897 (Antioch—Greek Melkite)
Ghrighuriyus I : unknown (Antioch—Maronite)
Ghrighuriyus II : unknown (Antioch—Maronite)
Ghrighuriyus III *of Halat* : 1130?-1141 (Antioch—Maronite)
Ghubriyal I : 909-920 (Alexandria—Coptic)
Ghubriyal II *ibn Turaik* : 1131-1145 (Alexandria—Coptic)
Ghubriyal III : 1268-1271 (Alexandria—Coptic)
Ghubriyal IV : 1370-1378 (Alexandria—Coptic)
Ghubriyal V : 1409-1427 (Alexandria—Coptic)
Ghubriyal VI : 1466-1475 (Alexandria—Coptic)
Ghubriyal VII : 1525-1568 (Alexandria—Coptic)
Ghubriyal VIII : 1586-1601 (Alexandria—Coptic)
Ghukas : 1780-1799 (Armenia)
Ghukas : 1733-1737 (Cilicia—Armenian Apostolic)
Gibelinus *of Arles* : 1107-1111 (Jerusalem—Latin)

Gilbertus *Borromeo* : 1711-1717 (Antioch—Latin)
Gillus *Caninio* : 1524-1530 (Constantinople—Latin)
Giorgi I : 677-678 (Georgia)
Giorgi II : 826-838 (Georgia)
Giorgi III : 1055-1065 (Georgia)
Giorgi IV : 1225-1230 (Georgia)
Giorgi V : 1380-1397 (Georgia)
Giroldus : 1225-1239 (Jerusalem—Latin)
Giwargis I : 661-680 (Assyria)
Giwargis II : 825-832 (Assyria)
Giwargis I : 661-681? (Babylon)
Giwargis II : 828-831? (Babylon)
Giwargis 'Abdishu' V *Khayyat'* : 1895-1899 (Babylon)
Giwt : 461-478 (Armenia)
Giyorgis I : 1102? (Ethiopia—Historical)
Giyorgis II : 1225 (Ethiopia—Historical)
Gorazd *Pavlík* : 1921-1942 (Czechoslovakia)
Gordios : 213 (Jerusalem—Greek)
Gormundus : 1118-1128 (Jerusalem—Latin)
Gotius *Battaglia* : 1335-1339 (Constantinople—Latin)
Grégorios I : 1243-1263 (Alexandria—Greek)
Grégorios II : 1316-1354 (Alexandria—Greek)
Grégorios III : 1354-1366 (Alexandria—Greek)
Grégorios IV : 1398-1412 (Alexandria—Greek)
Grégorios V : 1484-1486 (Alexandria—Greek)
Grégorios : 339-341, 344-348 (Alexandria—Greek—Arian)
Grégorios I *Nazianzénos Theologos* : 380-381 (Constantinople—Greek)
Grégorios II *Kyprios* : 1283-1289 (Constantinople—Greek)
Grégorios III *Mammas* : 1443-1451? (Constantinople—Greek)
Grégorios IV *Straboamaseias* : 1623 (Constantinople—Greek)
Grégorios V *Angelopoulos apo Smyrnés* : 1797-1798, 1806-1808, 1818-1821
    (Constantinople—Greek)
Grégorios VI *Phourtouniados apo Serrón* : 1835-1840, 1867-1871 (Constantin-
    ople—Greek)
Grégorios VII *Serbydakés* : 1923-1924 (Constantinople—Greek)
Grégorios I : 570? (Cyprus)
Grégorios II : 1254? (Cyprus)
Grégorios I : 600? (Greece)
Grégorios II : 780? (Greece)
Grégorios III : 860-867 (Greece)
Grégorios IV : 1799-1820 (Greece)
Grégorios V *Argyrokastrités apo Euripou* : 1827-1828 (Greece)
Gregorios I *Yakoub* : 1204-1215 (India—Malankara Orthodox)
Gregorios II *Bar Hebraeus* : 1266-1286 (India—Malankara Orthodox)
Gregorios III *Bar Sauma* : 1289-1308 (India—Malankara Orthodox)
Gregorios IV *Mathai* : 1317-1360 (India—Malankara Orthodox)
Gregorios (I), Mar : 1665-1672 (India—Malankara Syrian)
Gregorios (II), Mar : 1751-1772 (India—Malankara Syrian)
Grégorios I : -1298 (Jerusalem—Greek)
Grégorios II : 1332 (Jerusalem—Greek)
Grégorios III : 1468-1493 (Jerusalem—Greek)
Grégorios *Hadgitophés* : 1988-1993 [locum tenens] (Latvia)
Grégorios : 1969-1973 (Sinai)
Gregorius *Mammas* : 1454?-1459 (Constantinople—Latin)

Gregorius I *Magnus "The Great"* : 590-604 (Rome)
Gregorius II : 715-731 (Rome)
Gregorius III : 731-741 (Rome)
Gregorius IV : 827-844 (Rome)
Gregorius V : 996-999 (Rome)
Gregorius VI : 1012 [anti-pope] (Rome)
Gregorius VI *Gratianus* : 1045-1046 (Rome)
Gregorius VII : 1073-1085 (Rome)
Gregorius VIII *Burdinus* : 1118-1121 [anti-pope] (Rome)
Gregorius VIII *de Morra* : 1187 (Rome)
Gregorius IX *di Segni* : 1227-1241 (Rome)
Gregorius X *Visconti* : 1271-1276 (Rome)
Gregorius XI *de Beaufort* : 1370-1378 (Rome)
Gregorius XII *Correr* : 1406-1415 (Rome)
Gregorius XIII *Boncompagni* : 1572-1585 (Rome)
Gregorius XIV *Sfondrati* : 1590-1591 (Rome)
Gregorius XV *Ludovisi* : 1621-1623 (Rome)
Gregorius XVI *Cappellari* : 1831-1846 (Rome)
Gregorius XVII *Tremblay* : 1968- (Rome—Renovated Church)
Grigol—SEE ALSO: Grigoli
Grigol I : 433-434 (Georgia)
Grigol II : 760-767 (Georgia)
Grigol III : 802-814 (Georgia)
Grigol I : 1612-1616? (Georgia—Abkhazia)
Grigoli—SEE ALSO: Grigol
Grigoli II : 1696-1742 (Georgia—Abkhazia)
Grigor—SEE ALSO: Grigoris
Grigor : 1140? (coadjutor) (Aght'amar)
Grigor IV *Gawahets'i* : 1707-1711 (Aght'amar)
Grigor V *Hizants'i* : 1725 (Aght'amar)
Grigor VI : 1751-1761 (Aght'amar)
Grigor III : 1441- (Aghunie)
Grigor IV : 1556-1563 (Aghunie)
Grigor V : 1634-1653 (Aghunie)
Grigor I *Lusaworich' "The Illuminator"* : 302-325 (Armenia)
Grigor II *Vkayasêr* : 1066-1105 (Armenia)
Grigor III *Pahlawuni* : 1113-1166 (Armenia)
Grigor IV *Tghay* : 1173-1193 (Armenia)
Grigor V *K'aravêzh* : 1193-1194 (Armenia)
Grigor VI *Apirat* : 1194-1203 (Armenia)
Grigor VII : 1293-1307 (Armenia)
Grigor VIII *K'antsoghat* : 1411-1418 (Armenia)
Grigor IX *Musabêgiants'* : 1439-1141 (Armenia)
Grigor X : 1536-1545 (Armenia)
Grigor XI : 1576-1590 (Armenia)
Grigor *Serapion* : 1603-1624 [coadjutor] (Armenia)
Grigor I *Musabêgiants'* : 1441-1451 (Cilicia—Armenian Apostolic)
Grigor II : 1686-1693? (Cilicia—Armenian Apostolic)
Grigor III : 1721?-1729 (Cilicia—Armenian Apostolic)
Grigor *Aleadjian* : 1895 [locum tenens] (Cilicia—Armenian Apostolic)
Grigor I : 1526-1537 (Constantinople—Armenian)
Grigor II : 1601-1608, 1611-1621, 1623-1626 (Constantinople—Armenian)
Grigor III *Pasmachian* : 1764-1773 (Constantinople—Armenian)
Grigor IV *Khamsets'i* : 1801-1802 (Constantinople—Armenian)

Grigor I *Ezekielian* : 669-696 (Jerusalem—Armenian)
Grigor II : 981-1006 (Jerusalem—Armenian)
Grigor III : 1356-1363 (Jerusalem—Armenian)
Grigor IV *of Egypt* : 1386-1391 (Jerusalem—Armenian)
Grigor V *Baron-Ter* : 1613-1645 (Jerusalem—Armenian)
Grigor VI : 1697-1704 [coadjutor] (Jerusalem—Armenian)
Grigor VII *"The Chain-Bearer"* : 1715-1749 (Jerusalem—Armenian)
Grigor Petros V *Kupelian* : 1788-1812 (Cilicia—Armenian Catholic)
Grigor Petros VI : 1815-1841 (Cilicia—Armenian Catholic)
Grigor Petros VIII *Astuatsaturian* : 1844-1866 (Cilicia—Armenian Catholic)
Grigor Petros XV *Aghajanian* : 1937-1962 (Cilicia—Armenian Catholic)
Grigorie : unknown (Austria—Cernovci)
Grigorie I : 1629-1636 (Romania)
Grigorie II : 1760-1787 (Romania)
Grigorie III *Socoteanu* : 1770-1771 [locum tenens] (Romania)
Grigorie IV *Dascalul* : 1823-1829, 1833-1834 (Romania)
Grigorii I : -927 (Bulgaria)
Grigorii II : 1317? (Bulgaria)
Grigorii III : 1364?-1378? (Bulgaria)
Grigorii IV : 1551- (Bulgaria)
Grigorii V : 1675-1676, 1683-1688 (Bulgaria)
Grigorii VI : 1691-1693 (Bulgaria)
Grigorij I : 1316? (Macedonia)
Grigorij II : 1348-1378 (Macedonia)
Grigorij III : 1553? (Macedonia)
Grigorij IV : 1669-1670 (Macedonia)
Grigorij V : 1683-1687, 1691-1693 (Macedonia)
Grigoris—SEE ALSO: Grigor
Grigoris I : 1512-1544? (Aght'amar)
Grigoris II : 1544?-1586? (Aght'amar)
Grigoris III : 1586?-1612? (Aght'amar)
Grigoris I : 340-342 (Aghunie)
Grigoris II : 1139- (Aghunie)
Grigur *Partaya* : 605-608 (Assyria)
Grigur *Partaya* : 605-609 (Babylon)
Gualterus : 1214?- (Jerusalem—Latin)
Guido *Brunelli* : 1530? (Cyprus—Latin)
Guillelmus—SEE ALSO: Willelmus
Guillelmus *de Chanac* : 1342-1348 (Alexandria—Latin)
Guillelmus I *de la Tour* : 1457?-1470 (Antioch—Latin)
Guillelmus II : 1471 (Antioch—Latin)
Guillelmus I *de Castello* : 1346-1361 (Constantinople—Latin)
Guillelmus II : 1379 (Constantinople—Latin)
Guillelmus *Gonème* : 1467- (Cyprus—Latin)
Guillelmus II : 1263-1270 (Jerusalem—Latin)
Guillelmus III : 1351- (Jerusalem—Latin)
Guillelmus IV : 1369-1374 (Jerusalem—Latin)
Habib *al-Mazziyati*, Ighnatiyus : 1674-1686 [anti-patriarch] (Antioch—Syrian Catholic)
Habib *al-Mazziyati*, Ighnatiyus : 1674-1686 [anti-patriarch] (Antioch—Syrian Orthodox)
Hakob—SEE ALSO: Hakobus
Hakob : 1736 [anti-catholicos] (Aght'amar)
Hakob I *Guitnakan* : 1268-1286 (Armenia)

INDEX OF PRIMATES

Hakob II : 1327-1341, 1355-1359 (Armenia)
Hakob III : 1404-1411 (Armenia)
Hakob IV : 1655-1680 (Armenia)
Hakob V : 1759-1763 (Armenia)
Hakob I : 1563-1573 (Constantinople—Armenian)
Hakob II *Nalian Zmarats'i* : 1741-1748, 1752-1764 (Constantinople—Armenian)
Hakob II *Nalian Zmarats'i* : 1749-1752 (Jerusalem—Armenian)
Hakob Petros II *Hovsêp'ian* : 1749-1753 (Cilicia—Armenian Catholic)
Hakob Petros VII *Holasian* : 1842-1843 (Cilicia—Armenian Catholic)
Hakob Petros IX *Bak'darian* : 1870-1880? [anti-catholicos] (Cilicia—Armenian Catholic)
Hakobus—SEE ALSO: Hakob
Hakobus III *Serobian* : 1839-1840, 1848-1858 (Constantinople—Armenian)
Hakobus I : 1254-1281 (Jerusalem—Armenian)
Hariton : 1641-1646 (Macedonia)
Hariton : 1372-1380? (Romania)
Harut'iwn : 1816?-1823 (Aght'amar)
Harut'iwn *Vehapetian* : 1885-1888 (Constantinople—Armenian)
Harut'iwn *Vehapetian* : 1889-1910 (Jerusalem—Armenian)
Havryïl I *Kremianets'kyî* : 1770-1783 (Ukraine)
Havryïl II *Banulesko-Bodoni* : 1799-1803 (Ukraine)
Havryïl : 1331? (Ukraine—Halych)
Hayrapet *P'aykhets'i* : 1705-1707 (Aght'amar)
Hedeon *Sviatopolk-Chetveryns'kyî* : 1685-1690 (Ukraine)
Hefajst : 1265? (Macedonia)
Helias—SEE ALSO: Elias
Helias II *de Nabinaux* : 1332-1342 (Cyprus—Latin)
Hemayag Petros XVII *Ghedighian* : 1976-1982 (Cilicia—Armenian Catholic)
Henricus *Cajétan* : 1585? (Alexandria—Latin)
Héraklas : 232-248 (Alexandria—Greek)
Hérakleidés : 90? [anti-archbishop] (Cyprus)
Herasym : 1431-1435 (Ukraine)
Hercules *Tassoni* : 1596-1597 (Constantinople—Latin)
Herman *Aava* : 1925-1960 (Finland)
Herman : 1918-1924 (Ukraine—Canada)
Hermón : 300-314 (Jerusalem—Greek)
Hésaïas : 1323-1332 (Constantinople—Greek)
Hésaïas : 1209?-1218? (Cyprus)
Hidayat Allah, Ighnatiyus : 1597-1639 (Antioch—Syrian Orthodox)
Hieremias I *apo Sophias* : 1520-1522, 1523-1537, 1537-1546 (Constantinople—Greek)
Hieremias II *Tranos apo Larissés* : 1572-1579, 1580-1584, 1589-1595 (Constantinople—Greek)
Hieremias III *apo Kaisareias Kappadokias* : 1716-1726, 1732-1733 (Constantinople—Greek)
Hieremias IV *apo Mitylénés* : 1809-1813 (Constantinople—Greek)
Hieremias : 983-1005 (Jerusalem—Greek)
Hieronymos *Kotsónés* : 1967-1973 (Greece)
Hieronymus *Crispi* : 1740? (Alexandria—Latin)
Hieronymus *Lando* : 1474-1497 (Constantinople—Latin)
Hierotheos : 1924-1929 (Albania)
Hierotheos I : 1825-1845 (Alexandria—Greek)
Hierotheos II *Staphylopatés* : 1847-1858 (Alexandria—Greek)

Hierotheos : 1875-1882 (Jerusalem—Greek)
Hilarión (I) : 1218?-1220 [anti-archbishop] (Cyprus)
Hilarión (II) *Tzigalas* : 1674-1682 (Cyprus)
Hilarius : 461-468 (Rome)
Hinukh *Inwardaya*, Ighnatiyus : 1421-145 (Antioch—Syrian Orthodox—Tur Abhdin)
Hippolytus : 217-235 [anti-pope] (Rome)
Hirun : 107?-130? (Antioch—Greek Melkite)
Hirun : 107-127 (Antioch—Syrian Orthodox)
Hirus I : 104-126 (Antioch—Greek)
Hirus II : 151-169 (Antioch—Greek)
Hirus : 150?-170? (Antioch—Greek Melkite)
Honorius I : 625-638 (Rome)
Honorius II *Cadalus* : 1061-1072 [anti-pope] (Rome)
Honorius II : 1124-1130 (Rome)
Honorius III *Savelli* : 1216-1227 (Rome)
Honorius IV *Savelli* : 1285-1287 (Rome)
Honoriwos : 1315? (Ethiopia—Historical)
Hormisdas : 514-523 (Rome)
Hovab : 790-791 (Armenia)
Hovakim : 1461-1478 (Constantinople—Armenian)
Hovakim *of Kanaker* : 1775-1793 (Jerusalem—Armenian)
Hovhan—SEE ALSO: Hovhannês
Hovhan IV : 892-901 (Aghunie)
Hovhannês—SEE ALSO: Hovhan
Hovhannês : 1155? (coadjutor) (Aght'amar)
Hovhannês I : 1510-1512 (Aght'amar)
Hovhannês II *T'iwt'iwnji* : 1679-1681? (Aght'amar)
Hovhannês III *Kêtsuk* : 1699-1704 (Aght'amar)
Hovhannês IV *Hayots'-Zobets'i* : 1720 (Aght'amar)
Hovhannês V : 1791? [anti-catholicos] (Aght'amar)
Hovhannês V *Shatakhets'i* : 1823-1843 (Aght'amar)
Hovhannês I : 400- (Aghunie)
Hovhannês II : 646-670 (Aghunie)
Hovhannês III : 797-822 (Aghunie)
Hovhannês V : 1103-1130 (Aghunie)
Hovhannês VI : 1195-1235 (Aghunie)
Hovhannês VII : 14th cent. (Aghunie)
Hovhannês VIII : 14th cent. (Aghunie)
Hovhannês IX : -1470 (Aghunie)
Hovhannês X : -1586 (Aghunie)
Hovhannês XI : 1633-1634 (Aghunie)
Hovhannês XII : 1763-1786 (Aghunie)
Hovhannês I *Mandakuni* : 478-490 (Armenia)
Hovhannês II : 557-574 (Armenia)
Hovhannês (III) : 590-611 [anti-catholicos] (Armenia)
Hovhannês III *Imastaser* : 717-728 (Armenia)
Hovhannês IV : 833-855 (Armenia)
Hovhannês V *Patmaban "The Historian"* : 898-929 (Armenia)
Hovhannês VI *Medzabaro* : 1203-1221 (Armenia)
Hovhannês VII *Ajakir* : 1474-1484 (Armenia)
Hovhannês : 1505-1506 [coadjutor] (Armenia)
Hovhannês (VIII) : 1740- [anti-catholicos] (Armenia)
Hovhannês VIII : 1831-1842 (Armenia)

INDEX OF PRIMATES

Hovhannês I : 1488-1489 (Cilicia—Armenian Apostolic)
Hovhannês II : 1489-1525 (Cilicia—Armenian Apostolic)
Hovhannês III : 1525-1539 (Cilicia—Armenian Apostolic)
Hovhannês IV : 1602-1621 (Cilicia—Armenian Apostolic)
Hovhannês V : 1705-1721 (Cilicia—Armenian Apostolic)
Hovhannês VI : 1729-1733 (Cilicia—Armenian Apostolic)
Hovhannês : 1831-1833 [coadjutor] (Cilicia—Armenian Apostolic)
Hovhannês I : 1573-1581 (Constantinople—Armenian)
Hovhannês II : 1590-1591 (Constantinople—Armenian)
Hovhannês III : 1600-1601, 1609-1611, 1621-1623, 1631-1636 (Constantinople—Armenian)
Hovhannês IV : 1652-1655 (Constantinople—Armenian)
Hovhannês V : 1663-1664, 1665-1667 (Constantinople—Armenian)
Hovhannês VI : 1674-1675 (Constantinople—Armenian)
Hovhannês VII : 1707-1708 (Constantinople—Armenian)
Hovhannês VIII: 1714-1715 (Constantinople—Armenian)
Hovhannês IX *Kolot* : 1715-1741 (Constantinople—Armenian)
Hovhannês X : 1781-1782 (Constantinople—Armenian)
Hovhannês XI *Zamach'erchian* : 1800-1801, 1802-1813 (Constantinople—Armenian)
Hovhannês XII *Arsharuni* : 1912-1913 (Constantinople—Armenian)
Hovhannês I : 730-758 (Jerusalem—Armenian)
Hovhannês II *of Garin* : 1230-1238 (Jerusalem—Armenian)
Hovhannês III *Joslin* : 1332-1341 (Jerusalem—Armenian)
Hovhannês IV : 1378-1386 (Jerusalem—Armenian)
Hovhannês V : 1431-1441 (Jerusalem—Armenian)
Hovhannês VI *of Egypt* : 1485-1491 (Jerusalem—Armenian)
Hovhannês VII : 1517-1522 (Jerusalem—Armenian)
Hovhannês VIII *of Amasia* : 1680-1681 (Jerusalem—Armenian)
Hovhannês IX *of Constantinople* : 1684-1697 (Jerusalem—Armenian)
Hovhannês X : 1707-1708 (Jerusalem—Armenian)
Hovhannês XI : 1714-1715 (Jerusalem—Armenian)
Hovhannês XII *Movsêsian of Zmurnia* : 1850-1860
Hovhannês Petros XVIII *Gasparian* : 1982- (Cilicia—Armenian Catholic)
Hovsêp' I : 745-762 (Aghunie)
Hovsêp' II : 849-874 (Aghunie)
Hovsêp' III : 1038? (Aghunie)
Hovsêp' I : 444-452 (Armenia)
Hovsêp' II *Karidj* : 795-806 (Armenia)
Hovsêp' (III) : 1430? [anti-catholicos] (Armenia)
Hovsêp' *Arghutian* : 1800-1801 [unconsecrated] (Armenia)
Hristofor I : 1557-1559? (Austria—Sibiu)
Hristofor II : 1574-1579 (Austria—Sibiu)
Hryhoriî I : 1072-1073 (Ukraine)
Hryhoriî II *Bolharyn* : 1458-1475 (Ukraine)
Hryhoriî *Ohiîchuk* : 1947-1985 (Ukraine—Autocephous Church in USA)
Hryhorij *Ohiîchuk* : 1980-1982 (Czechoslovakia—Slavonic)
Hugo—SEE ALSO: Ugo
Hugo I *de Pise* : 1251-1260 (Cyprus—Latin)
Hugolinus *de Malabranca* : 1371-1375? (Constantinople—Latin)
Humbertus *de Vienne* : 1351-1355 (Alexandria—Latin)
Humbertus *de Romanis* : 1262? (Jerusalem—Latin)
Husik I *Part'e* : 341-347 (Armenia)
Husik II : 373-377 (Armenia)

Hyginus : 136?-140? (Rome)
Hymenaios : 260-298 (Jerusalem—Greek)
Hypatios : 827? (Greece)
Iachint : 1359-1372 (Romania)
Iacob *Putneanul* : 1745-1750 (Austria—Cernovci)
Iacobus Juvenalis *des Ursins* : 1449-1457 (Antioch—Latin)
Iacobus I *d'Itri* : 1376-1378 (Constantinople—Latin)
Iacobus II *Sinibaldi* : 1843-1844? (Constantinople—Latin)
Iacobus III Gregorius *Gallo* : 1878-1881 (Constantinople—Latin)
Iacobus I *Benoît* : 1442 [locum tenens] (Cyprus—Latin)
Iacobus II *de Lusignan* : 1459 (Cyprus—Latin)
Iacobus I *Pantaléon* : 1255-1261 (Jerusalem—Latin)
Iacobus II *Beltritti* : 1965-1970 [coadjutor], 1970-1987 (Jerusalem—Latin)
Iakobi : 363-375 (Georgia)
Iakóbos I : 954-960 (Alexandria—Greek)
Iakóbos II *Pankóstas* : 1861-1865 (Alexandria—Greek)
Iakóbos *Kykysés* : 1958- (America—Greek)
Iakóbos *apo Larissés* : 1679-1682, 1685-1686, 1687-1688 (Constantinople—
    Greek)
Iakóbos I : 1691?-1692? (Cyprus)
Iakóbos II : 1709-1718 (Cyprus)
Iakóbos I *apo Mytilénés* : 1676-1686 (Greece)
Iakóbos II : 1713-1734 (Greece)
Iakóbos III *Babanatsos* : 1962 (Greece)
Iakóbos I *Adelphotheos* : 50?-62 (Jerusalem—Greek)
Iakóbos II : 1460- (Jerusalem—Greek)
IAkov *Proarkhiî* : 1265? (Bulgaria)
Ibrahim I : 962-963 (Antioch—Syrian Catholic)
Ibrahim II *ibn Gharib*, Ighnatiyus : 1381-1412 (Antioch—Syrian Catholic)
Ibrahim I : 962-963 (Antioch—Syrian Orthodox)
Ibrahim II *ibn Gharib*, Ighnatiyus : 1381-1412 (Antioch—Syrian Orthodox)
IEfrem I : 1055- (Ukraine)
IEfrem II : 1090-1096 (Ukraine)
Ieremia : 429-433 (Georgia)
Ieremiia : 1762-1763 (Bulgaria)
IErofei *Malits'kyî* : 1796-1799 (Ukraine)
IEvgeniî *Bolkhovytnyov* : 1822-1837 (Ukraine)
Ighnatiyus I : 68-104 (Antioch—Greek)
Ighnatiyus II : 1342-1353 (Antioch—Greek)
Ighnatiyus III *'Atiyah* : 1619-1634 (Antioch—Greek)
Ighnatiyus IV *Hazim* : 1979- (Antioch—Greek)
Ighnatiyus I : 70?-107 (Antioch—Greek Melkite)
Ighnatiyus II : 1344?-1359? (Antioch—Greek Melkite)
Ighnatiyus III *'Atiyah* : 1620-1634 (Antioch—Greek Melkite)
Ighnatiyus IV *Sarruf* : 1812 (Antioch—Greek Melkite)
Ighnatiyus V *Qattan* : 1816-1833 (Antioch—Greek Melkite)
Ighnatiyus I : 68-107 (Antioch—Syrian Catholic)
Ighnatiyus II : 878-883 (Antioch—Syrian Catholic)
Ighnatiyus III *Dawud* : 1222-1252 (Antioch—Syrian Catholic)
Ighnatiyus IV *Ishu'* : 1264-1283 (Antioch—Syrian Catholic)
Ighnatiyus V *ibn Wahib ibn Zakha* : 1293-1333 (Antioch—Syrian Catholic)
Ighnatiyus I : 68-107 (Antioch—Syrian Orthodox)
Ighnatiyus II : 878-883 (Antioch—Syrian Orthodox)
Ighnatiyus III *Dawud* : 1222-1252 (Antioch—Syrian Orthodox)

Ighnatiyus IV *Ishu'* : 1264-1283 (Antioch—Syrian Orthodox)
Ighnatiyus V *ibn Wahib ibn Zakha* : 1313-1333 (Antioch—Syrian Orthodox)
Ighnatiyus 'Abd al-Ghani : 1597-1598 (Antioch—Syrian Catholic)
Ighnatiyus 'Abd Allah : 1520-1557 (Antioch—Syrian Catholic)
Ighnatiyus 'Abd Allah I : 1520-1556 (Antioch—Syrian Orthodox)
Ighnatiyus 'Abd Allah II *al-Saddi* : 1906-1915 (Antioch—Syrian Orthodox)
Ighnatiyus 'Abd al-Masih I *al-Rawhi* : 1662-1686 (Antioch—Syrian Orthodox)
Ighnatiyus 'Abd al-Masih II : 1895-1905 (Antioch—Syrian Orthodox)
Ighnatiyus Afram II *Rahmani* : 1898-1929 (Antioch—Syrian Catholic)
Ighnatiyus Afram *Barsum* : 1933-1957 (Antioch—Syrian Orthodox)
Ighnatiyus Andrawus *Akhijan Murabbi* : 1662-1677 (Antioch—Syrian Catholic)
Ighnatiyus Antun I *Samhiri* : 1853-1864 (Antioch—Syrian Catholic)
Ighnatiyus Antun II *Huwayyik* : 1968- (Antioch—Syrian Catholic)
Ighnatiyus 'Aziz *ibn Shabhta* : 1466-1488 (Antioch—Syrian Orthodox—Tur Abhdin)
Ighnatiyus Bihnam I *Hajlaya* : 1412-1455 (Antioch—Syrian Catholic)
Ighnatiyus Bihnam II *Banni* : 1893-1897 (Antioch—Syrian Catholic)
Ighnatiyus Bihnam *Hajlaya* : 1412-1454 (Antioch—Syrian Orthodox)
Ighnatiyus Bilatus : 1591-1597 (Antioch—Syrian Catholic)
Ighnatiyus Bilatus : 1591-1597 (Antioch—Syrian Orthodox)
Ighnatiyus Butrus IV *Dawud* : 1577-1591 (Antioch—Syrian Catholic)
Ighnatiyus Butrus V : 1598-1639 (Antioch—Syrian Catholic)
Ighnatiyus Butrus VI *Shahbadin* : 1677-1702 (Antioch—Syrian Catholic)
Ighnatiyus Butrus VII *Jarwah* : 1820-1851 (Antioch—Syrian Catholic)
Ighnatiyus Butrus IV *al-Ma'usili* : 1872-1894 (Antioch—Syrian Orthodox)
Ighnatiyus Dawud : 1519-1520 (Antioch—Syrian Catholic)
Ighnatiyus Dawud I : 1517-1519 (Antioch—Syrian Orthodox)
Ighnatiyus Dawud Shah II *Butrus ibn Nur ad-Din* : 1576-1591 (Antioch—Syrian Orthodox)
Ighnatiyus Filibbus *Arkus* : 1866-1874 (Antioch—Syrian Catholic)
Ighnatiyus Filuksinus *Nimrud* : 1283-1292 (Antioch—Syrian Catholic)
Ighnatiyus Habib *al-Mazziyati* : 1674-1686 [anti-patriarch] (Antioch—Syrian Catholic)
Ighnatiyus Habib *al-Mazziyati* : 1674-1686 [anti-patriarch] (Antioch—Syrian Orthodox)
Ighnatiyus Hidayat Allah : 1597-1639 (Antioch—Syrian Orthodox)
Ighnatiyus Hinukh *Inwardaya* : 1421-145 (Antioch—Syrian Orthodox—Tur Abhdin)
Ighnatiyus Ibrahim II *ibn Gharib* : 1381-1412 (Antioch—Syrian Catholic)
Ighnatiyus Ibrahim II *ibn Gharib* : 1381-1412 (Antioch—Syrian Orthodox)
Ighnatiyus Ilyas II *Ankaz* : 1838-1847 (Antioch—Syrian Orthodox)
Ighnatiyus Ilyas III *Shakar* : 1917-1932 (Antioch—Syrian Orthodox)
Ighnatiyus Ishaq II : 1709-1723 (Antioch—Syrian Catholic)
Ighnatiyus Ishaq : 1709-1723 (Antioch—Syrian Orthodox)
Ighnatiyus Ishu' I : 1509-1510 (Antioch—Syrian Catholic)
Ighnatiyus Ishu' II *Qamah* : 1655-1661 (Antioch—Syrian Catholic)
Ighnatiyus Ishu' I : 1509-1512 (Antioch—Syrian Orthodox)
Ighnatiyus Ishu' II *Qamah* : 1659-1662 (Antioch—Syrian Orthodox)
Ighnatiyus Ishu' I *ibn Muta* : 1390-1418? (Antioch—Syrian Orthodox—Tur Abhdin)
Ighnatiyus Ishu' II *Inwardaya* : 1455-1466 (Antioch—Syrian Orthodox—Tur Abhdin)
Ighnatiyus Isma'il *Yuhanna* : 1333-1365 (Antioch—Syrian Orthodox)
Ighnatiyus Ismil *Yuhanna* : 1333-1366 (Antioch—Syrian Catholic)

Ighnatiyus Jibra'il *Tabbuni* : 1929-1968 (Antioch—Syrian Catholic)
Ighnatiyus Jirjis II : 1690-1709 (Antioch—Syrian Catholic)
Ighnatiyus Jirjis III : 1746-1768 (Antioch—Syrian Catholic)
Ighnatiyus Jirjis IV : 1768-1781 (Antioch—Syrian Catholic)
Ighnatiyus Jirjis V *Shilhut* : 1874-1891 (Antioch—Syrian Catholic)
Ighnatiyus Jirjis II : 1687-1708 (Antioch—Syrian Orthodox)
Ighnatiyus Jirjis III : 1745-1768 (Antioch—Syrian Orthodox)
Ighnatiyus Jirjis IV : 1768-1781 (Antioch—Syrian Orthodox)
Ighnatiyus Jirjis V *Sayyar* : 1819-1836 (Antioch—Syrian Orthodox)
Ighnatiyus Khalaf : 1455-1484 (Antioch—Syrian Catholic)
Ighnatiyus Khalaf : 1455-1483 (Antioch—Syrian Orthodox)
Ighnatiyus Mas'ud I *Slakhaya* : 1418-1420 (Antioch—Syrian Orthodox—Tur Abhdin)
Ighnatiyus Mas'ud II : 1490?-1495 (Antioch—Syrian Orthodox—Tur Abhdin)
Ighnatiyus Matiyus *ibn 'Abd Allah* : 1782-1817 (Antioch—Syrian Orthodox)
Ighnatiyus Mikha'il III *Jarwah* : 1782-1800 (Antioch—Syrian Catholic)
Ighnatiyus Mikha'il IV *Dahir* : 1802-1810 (Antioch—Syrian Catholic)
Ighnatiyus Ni'mat Allah : 1557-1576 (Antioch—Syrian Catholic)
Ighnatiyus Ni'mat Allah : 1557-1576 (Antioch—Syrian Orthodox)
Ighnatiyus Nuh : 1494-1509 (Antioch—Syrian Catholic)
Ighnatiyus Nuh : 1493-1509 (Antioch—Syrian Orthodox)
Ighnatiyus Quma *ibn Gafil* : 1446-1455 (Antioch—Syrian Orthodox—Tur Abhdin)
Ighnatiyus Qustantinus (II) : 1312-1313 [anti-patriarch] (Antioch—Syrian Orthodox)
Ighnatiyus Sabbas *ibn Wahib* : 1364-1389 (Antioch—Syrian Orthodox—Tur Abhdin)
Ighnatiyus Shaba *Arbaya* : 1488- [anti-patriarch] (Antioch—Syrian Orthodox—Tur Abhdin)
Ighnatiyus Shihab : 1366-1381 (Antioch—Syrian Catholic)
Ighnatiyus Shihab : 1365-1381 (Antioch—Syrian Orthodox)
Ighnatiyus Shim'un I *of Tur-Abdin* : 1640-1659 (Antioch—Syrian Catholic)
Ighnatiyus Shim'un I *of Tur-Abdin* : 1640-1659 (Antioch—Syrian Orthodox)
Ighnatiyus Shukr Allah I : 1640- (Antioch—Syrian Catholic)
Ighnatiyus Shukr Allah II : 1723-1745 (Antioch—Syrian Catholic)
Ighnatiyus Shukr Allah : 1723-1745 (Antioch—Syrian Orthodox)
Ighnatiyus Sim'an II *Hindi Zora* : 1814-1818 (Antioch—Syrian Catholic)
Ighnatiyus Ya'qub : 1510-1519 (Antioch—Syrian Catholic)
Ighnatiyus Ya'qub I : 1509-1512 (Antioch—Syrian Orthodox)
Ighnatiyus Ya'qub II : 1847-1871 (Antioch—Syrian Orthodox)
Ighnatiyus Ya'qub III *Tuma* : 1957-1980 (Antioch—Syrian Orthodox)
Ighnatiyus Yuhanna XVIII *Akhsinaya Bar Shilla* : 1484-1494 (Antioch—Syrian Catholic)
Ighnatiyus Yuhanna XIV *Akhsinaya Bar Shilla* : 1483-1493 (Antioch—Syrian Orthodox)
Ighnatiyus Yuhanna (XV) *ibn Qufar* : 1488-1493 (Antioch—Syrian Orthodox—Tur Abhdin)
Ighnatiyus Yunan : 1817-1819 (Antioch—Syrian Orthodox)
Ighnatiyus Zakka *'Iwas* : 1980- (Antioch—Syrian Orthodox)
Ignatie I : 1653-1655 (Romania)
Ignatie II : 1810-1812 (Romania)
Ignatiî I : 1272?-1277? (Bulgaria)
Ignatiî II : 1660-1662 (Bulgaria)
Ignatiî III : 1673-1675? (Bulgaria)

Ignatiî IV : 1693-1695 (Bulgaria)
Ignatiî : 1605-1606 [anti-patriarch] (Russia)
Ignatij I : 1659, 1659-1662 (Macedonia)
Ignatij II : 1673? (Macedonia)
Ignatij III : 1693-1695, 1703?- (Macedonia)
Ignatios *Gagmachian* : 1869 (Constantinople—Armenian)
Ignatios *Rhangabe* : 847-858, 867-877 (Constantinople—Greek)
Ignatios : 1634- [anti-archbishop] (Cyprus)
Ignatios I *Barkiki* : 997-1022 (India—Malankara Orthodox)
Ignatios II *Lo Asar* : 1143-1164 (India—Malankara Orthodox)
Ignatios III *David* : 1215-1222 (India—Malankara Orthodox)
Ignatios IV *Sleeba of Edessa* : 1253-1258 (India—Malankara Orthodox)
Ignatios Mar Nuh *of Homs* : 1490-1494 (India—Malankara Orthodox)
Ignatios Petros XVI *Batanian* : 1962-1976 (Cilicia—Armenian Catholic)
Ilarijon—SEE: Ilarion
Ilarion I : -1838 (Bulgaria)
Ilarion II : 1872 (Bulgaria)
Ilarion I : 1487?-1502? (Romania)
Ilarion II : 1523-1526? (Romania)
Ilarion : 1833-1840 [locum tenens] (Romania)
Ilari(j)on *Roganovic* : 1863-1882 (Serbia—Montenegro)
Ilarion : 1051-1054 (Ukraine)
Ilarion *Ohiîenko* : 1951-1972 (Ukraine—Canada)
Ilia—SEE ALSO: Elia
Ilia II *Shiolashvili* : 1977- (Georgia)
Ilie *Iorest* : 1640-1643 (Austria—Sibiu)
Iliia *Kucha* : 1577-1579 (Ukraine)
Ilisha' : 524-538 (Assyria)
Ilisha' : 524-537? (Babylon)
Iliya I : 1028-1049 (Assyria)
Iliya II *bar Mulki* : 1111-1132 (Assyria)
Iliya III *Abu Khalim* : 1176-1190 (Assyria)
Iliya IV : 1407-1420 (Assyria)
Iliya V : 1491-1504 (Assyria)
Iliya I : 1028-1049 (Babylon)
Iliya II *bar Mulki* : 1111-1132 (Babylon)
Iliya III *Abu Khalim* : 1176-1190 (Babylon)
Iliya IV : -1437 (Babylon)
Iliya V : 1502-1503 (Babylon)
Iliya VI *bar Mama* : 1558-1576 (Babylon)
Iliya VII *bar Mama*, Shim'un : 1576-1591 (Babylon)
Iliya VIII *bar Mama* : 1591-1617 (Babylon)
Iliya IX *bar Mama*, Shim'un : 1617-1660 (Babylon)
Iliya X *bar Mama*, Yukhannan : 1660-1700 (Babylon)
Iliya XI *bar Mama*, Marugin : 1700-1722 (Babylon)
Iliya XII *bar Mama*, Dinkha : 1722-1778 (Babylon)
Iliya XIII *bar Mama*, Ishu'yabh : 1778-1804 (Babylon)
Iliya XIV *Abulyunan*, Pitrus : 1879-1894 (Babylon)
Iliya Shim'un XII : 1600-1653 (Assyria)
Ilyas—SEE ALSO: Ayliya
Ilyas I : 840-852 (Antioch—Greek)
Ilyas II : 1032-1033 (Antioch—Greek)
Ilyas III : 1182-1184 (Antioch—Greek)
Ilyas IV *Muawad* : 1970-1979 (Antioch—Greek)

Ilyas I : 907-934 (Antioch—Greek Melkite)
Ilyas II : 1031-1032 (Antioch—Greek Melkite)
Ilyas Butrus *al-Huwayyik* : 1899-1931 (Antioch—Maronite)
Ilyas II *Ankaz*, Ighnatiyus : 1838-1847 (Antioch—Syrian Orthodox)
Ilyas III *Shakar*, Ighnatiyus : 1917-1932 (Antioch—Syrian Orthodox)
Indriyas : 1841 (Ethiopia—Historical)
Innocentius I : 401-417 (Rome)
Innocentius II *Papareschi* : 1130-1143 (Rome)
Innocentius III : 1179-1180 [anti-pope] (Rome)
Innocentius III *di Segni* : 1198-1216 (Rome)
Innocentius IV *Fieschi* : 1243-1254 (Rome)
Innocentius V *de Tarentaise* : 1276 (Rome)
Innocentius VI *Aubert* : 1352-1362 (Rome)
Innocentius VII *de' Migliorati* : 1404-1406 (Rome)
Innocentius VIII *Cibò* : 1484-1492 (Rome)
Innocentius IX *Facchinetti* : 1591 (Rome)
Innocentius X *Pamphili* : 1644-1655 (Rome)
Innocentius XI *Odescalchi* : 1676-1689 (Rome)
Innocentius XII *Pignatelli* : 1691-1700 (Rome)
Innocentius XIII *dei Conti* : 1721-1724 (Rome)
Innokentiî *Veniaminov* : 1840-1858 (America—Orthodox Church)
Innokentiî : 1910-1913 [exarch] (Georgia)
Innokentiî *Veniaminov* : 1868-1879 (Russia—Moscow)
Inochentie *Moisiu* : 1886 [locum tenens] (Romania)
Inokentije *Pavlovic* : 1898-1905 (Serbia)
Ióakeim I *Panu* : -1567 (Alexandria—Greek)
Ióakeim II *Kos* : 1665?-1671 (Alexandria—Greek)
Ióakeim I : 1498-1502, 1504 (Constantinople—Greek)
Ióakeim II *Kokkodés apo Kyzikou* : 1860-1863, 1873-1878 (Constantinople—
    Greek)
Ióakeim III *apo Thessalonikés* : 1878-1884, 1901-1912 (Constantinople—
    Greek)
Ióakeim IV : 1884-1886 (Constantinople—Greek)
Ióakeim : 1821-1824 (Cyprus)
Ióakeim : 1431-1450 (Jerusalem—Greek)
Ioakim I : 1233?-1246 (Bulgaria)
Ioakim II : -1272 (Bulgaria)
Ioakim III : 1291-1300 (Bulgaria)
Ioakim IV : 1590-1593 (Bulgaria)
Ioakim *Savelov* : 1674-1690 (Russia)
Ioan—SEE ALSO: Ioane
Ioan : 1605-1608 (Austria—Cernovci)
Ioan I : 1456? (Austria—Sibiu)
Ioan II : 1553-1557? (Austria—Sibiu)
Ioan III : 1585-1605? (Austria—Sibiu)
Ioan IV *Gheorghievic* : 1768-1769 (Austria—Sibiu)
Ioan *Popovic* : 1774-1784, 1788-1789, 1796-1805 [locum tenens] (Austria—
    Sibiu)
Ioan *Popasu* : 1874 [unconsecrated] (Austria—Sibiu)
Ioan V *Metianu* : 1898-1916 (Austria—Sibiu)
Ioan *Papp* : 1918-1920 [locum tenens] (Austria—Sibiu)
Ioan I : 1018-1037 (Bulgaria)
Ioan II *Lakapin* : 1065-1078? (Bulgaria)
Ioan III *Ainos* : 1079?-1084 (Bulgaria)

Ioan IV *Komnin* : 1143?-1157? (Bulgaria)
Ioan V *Kamatir* : 1183?-1215? (Bulgaria)
Ioan II : 610-619 (Georgia)
Ioane—SEE ALSO: Ioan
Ioane I : 335-363 (Georgia)
Ioane III : 744-760 (Georgia)
Ioane IV : 1100-1142 (Georgia)
Ioane V : 1208-1210 (Georgia)
Ioane VI : 1610-1613 (Georgia)
Ioane VII : 1688-1691, 1696-1700 (Georgia)
Ioane : 1455-1474 (Georgia—Abkhazia)
Ioanichie : 1472-1504 (Austria—Cernovci)
Ioanichie : 1479? (Austria—Sibiu)
Ioanikiî I : 1240? (Bulgaria)
Ioanikiî II : 1340? (Bulgaria)
Ioanikiî III : 1370? (Bulgaria)
Ioann : 1870-1876 (America—Orthodox Church)
Ioann I : 1004-1038 (Ukraine)
Ioann II : 1077-1089 (Ukraine)
Ioann III : 1089-1090 (Ukraine)
Ioann IV : 1164-1165 (Ukraine)
Ioann V *Sokolov* : 1944-1964 (Ukraine)
Ioann *Teodorovych* : 1924-1947 (Ukraine—Canada)
Ioann *Teodorovych* : 1924-1971 (Ukraine—Church of the USA)
Ióannés III : 567- (Alexandria—Coptic—Gaianite)
Ióannés I *Talaïas* : 482-489 (Alexandria—Greek)
Ióannés II *Theopeithés* : 569-579 (Alexandria—Greek)
Ióannés III *Eleémón* : 610-621 (Alexandria—Greek)
Ióannés IV *Kódónatos* : 1062-1100 (Alexandria—Greek)
Ioannes I *de Aragón* : 1328-1334 (Alexandria—Latin)
Ioannes II *de Cardaillac* : 1372- (Alexandria—Latin)
Ioannes III *Vitelleschi* : 1435? (Alexandria—Latin)
Ioannes IV *d'Harcourt* : 1451? (Alexandria—Latin)
Ioannes I *de Maguellone* : 1408- (Antioch—Latin)
Ioannes II *de Vico* : 1410? (Antioch—Latin)
Ioannes III *de Ribera* : 1568-1611 (Antioch—Latin)
Ioannes IV Baptistus *Pamfili* : 1626?-1629 (Antioch—Latin)
Ioannes V Franciscus Guidus *di Bagno dei Talenti* : 1795-1796 (Antioch—
    Latin)
Ióannés I *Chrysostomos* : 398-404 (Constantinople—Greek)
Ióannés II *Kappadokés* : 518-520 (Constantinople—Greek)
Ióannés III *Scholastikos* : 565-577 (Constantinople—Greek)
Ióannés IV *Nésteutés* : 582-595 (Constantinople—Greek)
Ióannés V : 669-675 (Constantinople—Greek)
Ióannés VI : 712-715 (Constantinople—Greek)
Ióannés VII *Grammatikos Pankratiou* : 837?-843 (Constantinople—Greek)
Ióannés VIII *Xiphilinos* : 1064-1075 (Constantinople—Greek)
Ióannés IX *Agapétos Hieromnémón* : 1111-1134 (Constantinople—Greek)
Ióannés X *Kamatéros* : 1198-1206 (Constantinople—Greek)
Ióannés XI *Bekkos* : 1275-1282 (Constantinople—Greek)
Ióannés XII *Kosmas* : 1294-1303 (Constantinople—Greek)
Ióannés XIII *Glykys* : 1315-1319 (Constantinople—Greek)
Ióannés XIV *Kalekas* : 1334-1347 (Constantinople—Greek)
Ioannes I *Halegrin* : 1226 [unconsecrated] (Constantinople—Latin)

Ioannes II *Contarini* : 1409- , 1424- (Constantinople—Latin)
Ioannes III *de la Rochetaillée* : 1412-1423 (Constantinople—Latin)
Ioannes IV *Michele* : 1497-1503 (Constantinople—Latin)
Ioannes V *Borgia* : 1503 (Constantinople—Latin)
Ioannes VI Iacobus *Panciroli* : 1641-1643 (Constantinople—Latin)
Ioannes VII Baptistus *Spada* : 1643-1658 (Constantinople—Latin)
Ioannes VIII *de la Puebla* : 1771-1779 (Constantinople—Latin)
Ioannes IX *Soglia-Ceroni* : 1835-1839 (Constantinople—Latin)
Ioannes X Ludovicus *Canali* : 1845-1851 (Constantinople—Latin)
Ioannes XI Baptistus *Casali del Drago* : 1895-1899 (Constantinople—Latin)
Ióannés I : 597 (Crete)
Ióannés II : 10th cent. (Crete)
Ióannés III : 1106? (Crete)
Ióannés IV : 1166-1177 (Crete)
Ióannés I : 691? (Cyprus)
Ióannés II *Krétikos* : 1151?-1174 (Cyprus)
Ioannes I *d'Ancone* : 1288-1295 (Cyprus—Latin)
Ioannes II *de Polo* : 1312-1332 (Cyprus—Latin)
Ioannes III : 1400? (Cyprus—Latin)
Ioannes IV Franciscus *Brusato* : 1464? (Cyprus—Latin)
Ióannés I : 550? (Greece)
Ióannés II : 680? (Greece)
Ióannés III : 704-714 (Greece)
Ióannés IV : 810-819 (Greece)
Ióannés V *Blachernités* : 1069-1087 (Greece)
Ióannés VI : 1180-1181 (Greece)
Ióannés I : unknown (Jerusalem—Greek)
Ióannés II : 386-417 (Jerusalem—Greek)
Ióannés III : 516-524 (Jerusalem—Greek)
Ióannés IV : 575-594 (Jerusalem—Greek)
Ióannés V : 706-735 (Jerusalem—Greek)
Ióannés VI : 838-842 (Jerusalem—Greek)
Ióannés VII : 964-966 (Jerusalem—Greek)
Ióannés VIII *Chrysostomités Merkouropólos* : 1098?-1107? (Jerusalem—
    Greek)
Ióannés IX : 1156-1166 (Jerusalem—Greek)
Ioannes *de Vercellis* : 1278- (Jerusalem—Latin)
Ioannes I : 523-526 (Rome)
Ioannes II : 533-535 (Rome)
Ioannes III : 561-574 (Rome)
Ioannes IV : 640-642 (Rome)
Ioannes V : 685-686 (Rome)
Ioannes VI : 701-705 (Rome)
Ioannes VII : 705-707 (Rome)
Ioannes VIII : 844 [anti-pope] (Rome)
Ioannes VIII : 872-882 (Rome)
Ioannes IX : 898-900 (Rome)
Ioannes X : 914-928 (Rome)
Ioannes XI : 931-935 (Rome)
Ioannes XII : 955-964 (Rome)
Ioannes XIII : 965-972 (Rome)
Ioannes XIV *Canepanova* : 983-984 (Rome)
Ioannes XV : 985-996 (Rome)
Ioannes XVI *Philagathos* : 997-998 [anti-pope] (Rome)

Ioannes XVII *Sicco* : 1003 (Rome)
Ioannes XVIII *Fasanus* : 1004-1009 (Rome)
Ioannes XIX : 1024-1032 (Rome)
Ioannes XX [there is no pope of this name] (Rome)
Ioannes XXI *Juliao* : 1276-1277 (Rome)
Ioannes XXII *Duèse* : 1316-1334 (Rome)
Ioannes XXIII *Cossa* : 1410-1415 [anti-pope] (Rome)
Ioannes XXIII *Roncalli* : 1958-1963 (Rome)
Ióannés I *Athénaios* : 1081-1091 (Sinai)
Ióannés II : 1164? (Sinai)
Ióannés III : 1265-1290 (Sinai)
Ióannés IV : 1299?- (Sinai)
Ioannes Paulus I *Luciani* : 1978 (Rome)
Ioannes Paulus II *Wojtyla* : 1978- (Rome)
Ioannikiî *Rudnev* : 1877-1882 [exarch] (Georgia)
Ioannikiî *Rudnev* : 1882-1891 (Russia—Moscow)
Ióannikios *Diodios Berrhoias* : 1645-1664 (Alexandria—Greek)
Ióannikios I *apo Sózopoleós* : 1522-1523 (Constantinople—Greek)
Ióannikios II *Lindios apo Hérakleias* : 1646-1648, 1651-1652, 1653-1654, 1655-1656 (Constantinople—Greek)
Ióannikios III *Karatzas apo Chalkédonos* : 1761-1763 (Constantinople—Greek)
Ióannikios *Zagorésios* : 1856-1858 (Crete)
Ióannikios : 1783 [anti-archbishop] (Cyprus)
Ióannikios : 1840-1849 (Cyprus)
Ióannikios : 1020-1040 (Jerusalem—Greek)
Ióannikios I *Laskaris* : 1671-1702 (Sinai)
Ióannikios II *Lesbios* : 1721-1728 (Sinai)
Ioaquim Fernandus *Puerto Carrero* : 1735-1743 (Antioch—Latin)
Ioasaf : 1798-1799 (America—Orthodox Church)
Ioasaf : 1682-1683 (Austria—Sibiu)
Ioasaf I : 1628? (Bulgaria)
Ioasaf II : 1719-1745 (Bulgaria)
Ioasaf I : 1634-1641 (Russia)
Ioasaf II : 1667-1672 (Russia)
Ioasaf *Leluchyn* : 1964-1966 (Ukraine)
Ióasaph I *Kokkas* : 1464-1466? (Constantinople—Greek)
Ióasaph II *Megaloprepés apo Adrianoupoleós* : 1555-1565 (Constantinople—Greek)
Ióasaph : 1701?-1710 (Crete)
Ióasaph *apo Rhodou* : 1617-1660 (Sinai)
Iób : 954-960 (Alexandria—Greek)
Iób : 1395? (Sinai)
Iobi : 375-390 (Georgia)
Iona : 425-429 (Georgia)
Iona *Vasil'evskiî* : 1821-1832 [exarch] (Georgia)
Iona : 1448-1462 (Russia—Moscow)
Iona I : 1448-1458 (Ukraine)
Iona II *Hlezna* : 1492-1494 (Ukraine)
Iona III : 1502-1507 (Ukraine)
Iona IV *Protasevych-Ostrovskiî* : 1568-1577 (Ukraine)
Ionafan *Kopolovich* : 1972-1986 (Moldova)
Iordanus *de' Caetani* : 1485- (Antioch—Latin)
Iorest : 1651?-1656 (Austria—Cernovci)
Iórios : 1035- (Sinai)

Iosebi : 1755-1764 (Georgia)
Iosebi : 1769-1776 (Georgia—Abkhazia)
Ióséph I : 1266-1275, 1282-1283 (Constantinople—Greek)
Ióséph II *apo Ephesou* : 1416-1439 (Constantinople—Greek)
Ióséph I : unknown (Jerusalem—Greek)
Ióséph II : 980-983 (Jerusalem—Greek)
Iosephus Antonius *Davanzati* : 1746? (Alexandria—Latin)
Iosephus Melchiades *Ferlisi* : 1858-1860 (Antioch—Latin)
Iosephus I *della Porta Rodiani* : 1823-1835 (Constantinople—Latin)
Iosephus II Melchiades *Ferlisi* : 1860-1865 (Constantinople—Latin)
Iosephus III *Capetelli* : 1903-1921? (Constantinople—Latin)
Iosephus *Valerga* : 1847-1872 (Jerusalem—Latin)
Iosif : unknown (Austria—Cernovci)
Iosif *Budal* : 1680-1682 (Austria—Sibiu)
Iosif I : 870-878? (Bulgaria)
Iosif II : 1746-1751 (Bulgaria)
Iosif III : 1877-1915 (Bulgaria)
Iosif I : 1464-1477? (Romania)
Iosif *al Argesului* : 1812 [locum tenens] (Romania)
Iosif II *Gheorghian* : 1886-1893, 1896-1909 (Romania)
Iosif *Naniescu* : 1896 [locum tenens] (Romania)
Iosif : 1642-1652 (Russia)
Iosif *Volchanskiĭ* : 1742-1745 (Russia—Moscow)
Iosyf I : 1237-1240? (Ukraine)
Iosyf II *Bolharynovych* : 1498-1501 (Ukraine)
Iosyf III *Soltan* : 1507-1522 (Ukraine)
Iosyf IV : 1522-1534 (Ukraine)
Iosyf V *Neliubovych-Tukals'kyĭ* : 1663-1675 (Ukraine)
Iosyf VI *Krokovs'kyĭ* : 1708-1718 (Ukraine)
Iosyf *Zuk* : 1931-1934 (Ukraine—America and Canada)
Ioubenalios : 422-458 (Jerusalem—Greek)
Ioudas I : 107?-111 (Jerusalem—Greek)
Ioudas I : -134 (Jerusalem—Greek)
Ioulianos : 178-189 (Alexandria—Greek)
Ioulianos I : unknown (Jerusalem—Greek)
Ioulianos II : unknown (Jerusalem—Greek)
Ioustos : 118-129 (Alexandria—Greek)
Ioustos I : 107?-111 (Jerusalem—Greek)
Ioustos II : unknown (Jerusalem—Greek)
Iov *Tirca* : 1706?-1707 (Austria—Sibiu)
Iov : 1587-1589 (metropolitan), 1589-1605 (patriarch) (Russia)
Iov *Bortes'kiĭ* : 1620-1631 (Ukraine)
Iovel I : 448-452 (Georgia)
Ioveli II : 668-670 (Georgia)
Ipatiĭ *Potsifi* : 1599-1613 (Ukraine)
Ireney *Bekish* : 1965-1977 (America—Orthodox Church)
Ireney *Bekish* : 1953-1960 (Japan)
Irun : 107-127 (Antioch—Syrian Catholic)
Irus : 154-170 (Antioch—Syrian Catholic)
Isaak : 941-954 (Alexandria—Greek)
Isaak : 1630 (Constantinople—Greek)
Isaak *Boryshevych* : 1633 (Ukraine)
Isaakios : 601-609 (Jerusalem—Greek)
Isaaq : 686-689 (Alexandria—Coptic)

Isaaq : 755-756 [anti-patriarch] (Antioch—Syrian Orthodox)
Isaia I : 1564?-1577 (Austria—Cernovci)
Isaia II *Balosescu* : 1823-1834 (Austria—Cernovci)
Isaiia *Kopynskiî* : 1631-1632 (Ukraine)
Isaija I *Djakovic* : 1708 (Austria—Karlovci)
Isaija II *Antonovic* : 1748-1749 (Austria—Karlovci)
Ishai Shim'un XXIII : 1920-1975 (Assyria)
Ishaq : unknown (Antioch—Maronite)
Ishaq I : 755-756 (Antioch—Syrian Catholic)
Ishaq II, Ighnatiyus : 1709-1723 (Antioch—Syrian Catholic)
Ishaq, Ighnatiyus : 1709-1723 (Antioch—Syrian Orthodox)
Ishaq : 375-386 (India—Malankara Orthodox)
Ishu' I : unknown (Antioch—Maronite)
Ishu' II : unknown (Antioch—Maronite)
Ishu' I, Ighnatiyus : 1509-1510 (Antioch—Syrian Catholic)
Ishu' II *Qamah*, Ighnatiyus : 1655-1661 (Antioch—Syrian Catholic)
Ishu' I, Ighnatiyus : 1509-1512 (Antioch—Syrian Orthodox)
Ishu' II *Qamah*, Ighnatiyus : 1659-1662 (Antioch—Syrian Orthodox)
Ishu' I *ibn Muta*, Ighnatiyus : 1390-1418? (Antioch—Syrian Orthodox—Tur Abhdin)
Ishu' II *Inwardaya*, Ighnatiyus : 1455-1466 (Antioch—Syrian Orthodox—Tur Abhdin)
Ishu' *bar Nun* : 820-824 (Assyria)
Ishu' *bar Nun* : 823-828 (Babylon)
Ishu'yabh I *Arzunaya* : 581-595 (Assyria)
Ishu'yabh II *Gdalaya* : 628-644 (Assyria)
Ishu'yabh III *Khdayabaya* : 650-660 (Assyria)
Ishu'yabh IV *bar Khazqi'il* : 1023-1027 (Assyria)
Ishu'yabh V *Baladaya* : 1148-1175 (Assyria)
Ishu'yabh I *Arzunaya* : 582-595 (Babylon)
Ishu'yabh II *Gdalaya* : 628-646? (Babylon)
Ishu'yabh III *Khdayabaya* : 650-658? (Babylon)
Ishu'yabh IV *bar Khazqi'il* : 1020-1025 (Babylon)
Ishu'yabh V *Baladaya* : 1149-1175 (Babylon)
Ishu'yabh Iliya XIII *bar Mama* : 1778-1804 (Babylon)
Ishu'yabh Shim'un VIII *bar Mama* : 1538-1551 (Assyria)
Ishu'yabh Shim'un XIII : 1653-1690 (Assyria)
Ishu'yabh Shim'un VII *bar Mama* : 1538-1551 (Babylon)
Isidor *Nikolskiî* : 1844-1858 (Georgia)
Isidor : 1436-1448 (Russia—Moscow)
Isidóros I *Boucheiras apo Monembasias* : 1347-1350 (Constantinople—Greek)
Isidóros II *Xanthopoulos* : 1456-1462 (Constantinople—Greek)
Isidóros : 1456? (Greece)
Isidorus *of Kiev* : 1459-1463 (Constantinople—Latin)
Isidorus : 1463?- (Cyprus—Latin)
Iskandar : 414-424 (Antioch—Syrian Catholic)
Iskhaq : 399-411 (Assyria)
Iskhaq : 399-410 (Babylon)
Isma'il *Yuhanna*, Ighnatiyus : 1333-1365 (Antioch—Syrian Orthodox)
Ismil *Yuhanna*, Ighnatiyus : 1333-1366 (Antioch—Syrian Catholic)
Isnardus *Tacconi* : 1311-1329 (Antioch—Latin)
Israyêl : 1763-1765 [anti-patriarch] (Aghunie)
Israyêl : 667-677 (Armenia)
Israyil *Karkaya* : 961-962 [unconsecrated] (Assyria)

Israyil I *of Kashkar* : 877 [unconsecrated] (Assyria)
Israyil II *Karkaya* : 961 (Assyria)
Istifan—SEE ALSO: Istifanus
Istifan I : 346-351 (Antioch—Syrian Catholic)
Istifan II : 480-481 (Antioch—Syrian Catholic)
Istifan III : 481-482 (Antioch—Syrian Catholic)
Istifanus—SEE ALSO: Istifan
Istifanus I *Sidarus* : 1958-1986 (Alexandria—Coptic Catholic)
Istifanus II *Ghattas* : 1986- (Alexandria—Coptic Catholic)
Istifanus I : 342-344 (Antioch—Greek)
Istifanus II : 477-481 (Antioch—Greek)
Istifanus III : 687-690 (Antioch—Greek)
Istifanus IV : 742-748 (Antioch—Greek)
Istifanus V : 871 (Antioch—Greek)
Istifanus I : 343-344 (Antioch—Greek Melkite)
Istifanus II : 478-481 (Antioch—Greek Melkite)
Istifanus III : 742?-745? (Antioch—Greek Melkite)
Istifanus IV : 866-870 (Antioch—Greek Melkite)
Istifanus I : unknown (Antioch—Maronite)
Istifanus II *ibn Mikha'il al-Duwayhi* : 1670-1704 (Antioch—Maronite)
Istifanus I : 343-344 (Antioch—Syrian Orthodox)
Istifanus II : 478-481 (Antioch—Syrian Orthodox)
Istifanus III : 481-482 (Antioch—Syrian Orthodox)
Isydor I : 1437 (Ukraine)
Isydor II *Nikol's'kyî* : 1858-1860 (Ukraine)
Iulianus : 1571-1577 (Cyprus—Latin)
Iulius Maria *della Somaglia* : 1788-1795 (Antioch—Latin)
Iulius *Lenti* : 1887-1894 (Constantinople—Latin)
Iulius I : 337-352 (Rome)
Iulius II *della Rovere* : 1503-1513 (Rome)
Iulius III *Ciocchi del Monte* : 1550-1555 (Rome)
Iustin *Moïsescu* : 1956-1957 (Austria—Sibiu)
Iustin *Moïsescu* : 1977 [locum tenens], 1977-1986 (Romania)
Ivanios, Mar : 1751-1794 (India—Malankara Syrian)
Ivanios, Joseph Mar *Kasseesa* : 1807 [suffragan] (India—Thozhiyoor)
Iyunnis I : 740-754 (Antioch—Syrian Orthodox)
Iyunnis II : 956-958 (Antioch—Syrian Orthodox)
Iyunnis III : 1080-1082 (Antioch—Syrian Orthodox)
Izid-Bozidi : 683-685 (Georgia)
Jakov *Proarhij* : 1275? (Macedonia)
Jakov : 1286-1292 (Serbia)
Jan *Kuchtin* : 1956-1964 (Czechoslovakia)
Janis *Pommers* : 1920-1934 (Latvia)
Jawrji—SEE ALSO: Jirjis
Jawrji I : 758-790 (Antioch—Syrian Orthodox)
Jawrjiyus I : 640-655 (Antioch—Greek)
Jawrjiyus II : 690-695 (Antioch—Greek)
Jawrjiyus III : 902-917 (Antioch—Greek)
Jawrjiyus IV *Laskaris* : 1034-1042 (Antioch—Greek)
Jawrjiyus I : 649?-660? (Antioch—Greek Melkite)
Jawrjiyus II : 685?-702? (Antioch—Greek Melkite)
Jefrem : 1375-1379, 1782-1387 (Serbia)
Jelevferij *Voronzov* : 1946-1955 (Czechoslovakia)
Jeremije : -1786 (Serbia)

Jerotej : 1589-1591 (Serbia)
Jerzy *Jaroszewski* : 1921-1923 (Poland)
Jerzy *Korenistow* : 1962-1964 [locum tenens] (Poland)
Jevstatij : 1134? (Macedonia)
Jevstatije I : 1279-1286 (Serbia)
Jevstatije II : 1292-1309 (Serbia)
Jibra'il I : unknown (Antioch—Maronite)
Jibra'il II *al-Hajjula* : 1357?-1367? (Antioch—Maronite)
Jibra'il III *al-Blawzawi* : 1704-1705 (Antioch—Maronite)
Jibra'il *Tabbuni*, Ighnatiyus : 1929-1968 (Antioch—Syrian Catholic)
Jirasimus *Propapas* : 1885-1891 (Antioch—Greek)
Jirjis—SEE ALSO: Jawrji
Jirjis I *ibn 'Amayrah* : 1633-1644 (Antioch—Maronite)
Jirjis II *Habakuk al-Bashalani* : 1657-1670 (Antioch—Maronite)
Jirjis I : 758-790 (Antioch—Syrian Catholic)
Jirjis II, Ighnatiyus : 1690-1709 (Antioch—Syrian Catholic)
Jirjis III, Ighnatiyus : 1746-1768 (Antioch—Syrian Catholic)
Jirjis IV, Ighnatiyus : 1768-1781 (Antioch—Syrian Catholic)
Jirjis V *Shilhut*, Ighnatiyus : 1874-1891 (Antioch—Syrian Catholic)
Jirjis II, Ighnatiyus : 1687-1708 (Antioch—Syrian Orthodox)
Jirjis III, Ighnatiyus : 1745-1768 (Antioch—Syrian Orthodox)
Jirjis IV, Ighnatiyus : 1768-1781 (Antioch—Syrian Orthodox)
Jirjis V *Sayyar*, Ighnatiyus : 1819-1836 (Antioch—Syrian Orthodox)
Joahim : 1588?-1593 (Macedonia)
Joanikij : 1238? (Macedonia)
Joanikije I : 1272-1276 (Serbia)
Joanikije II : 1338-1354 (Serbia)
Joanikije III : 1506? (Serbia)
Joanikije IV *Karadza* : 1737-1746 (Serbia)
Joanikije *Lipovac* : 1940-1945 (Serbia—Montenegro)
Joasav I : 1628? (Macedonia)
Joasav II : 1719-1745 (Macedonia)
Johannes *Rinne* : 1987- (Finland)
Joseph I : 552-556 (India—Malankara Orthodox)
Joseph II : 789-793 (India—Malankara Orthodox)
Joseph Mar Athanasios I : 1883-1888 [suffragan], 1888-1898 (India—Thozhiyoor)
Joseph Mar Dionysios V *Putikkottil* : 1865-1909 (India—Malankara Syrian)
Joseph Mar Ivanios *Kasseesa* : 1807 [suffragan] (India—Thozhiyoor)
Joseph Mar Koorilose IV *Kassesa* : 1856-1888 (India—Thozhiyoor)
Joseph Mar Koorilose IX *Panakal* : 1981-1986 [suffragan], 1986- (India—Thozhiyoor)
Josif *Rajacic* : 1842-1861 (Austria—Karlovci)
Josif : 1746-1752 (Macedonia)
Josif : 1544? (Serbia)
Josif *Zvijanovic* : 1941-1946 [locum tenens] (Serbia)
Jovan *Djordjevic* : 1768-1769 [locum tenens], 1769-1773 (Austria—Karlovci)
Jovan I : 1018-1027 (Macedonia)
Jovan II *Lampin* : 1065-1078 (Macedonia)
Jovan III *Aoinos "The Sober"* : 1079-1081? (Macedonia)
Jovan IV *Komnen* : 1143-1157 (Macedonia)
Jovan V *Kamatir* : 1183-1215 (Macedonia)
Jovan *Mladenovic* : 1993-1994 (Macedonia—Serbian Administration)
Jovan I : 1508?-1509? (Serbia)

Jovan II *Kantul* : 1592-1614 (Serbia)
Jovan *Pavlovic* : 1989-1990 [locum tenens] (Serbia)
Juhanon *Mar Thoma* : 1937-1947 [suffragan], 1947-1976 (India—Mar Thoma Syrian)
Jüri *Välbe* : 1956-1961 (Estonia)
Justinian *Marina* : 1955-1956 [locum tenens] (Austria—Sibiu)
Justinian *Marina* : 1948 [locum tenens], 1948-1977 (Romania)
Kaladyanu : unknown (Ethiopia—Official)
Kalandhiyun : 481-485 (Antioch—Greek and Antioch—Greek Melkite)
Kalinik I *Skopljanac* : 1691-1710 (Serbia)
Kalinik II : 1765-1766 (Serbia)
Kalistrate *Tsintsadze* : 1924-1927 [locum tenens], 1932-1952 (Georgia)
Kallawtiyanus : 157-167 (Alexandria—Coptic)
Kallawtiyanus : 152-166 (Alexandria—Coptic Catholic)
Kallinikos *Olympios* : 1858-1861 (Alexandria—Greek)
Kallinikos I : 694-706 (Constantinople—Greek)
Kallinikos II *Akarnan apo Prousés* : 1688, 1689-1693, 1694-1702 (Constantinople—Greek)
Kallinikos III *apo Hérakleias* : 1726 (Constantinople—Greek)
Kallinikos IV *apo Proïlabou* : 1757 (Constantinople—Greek)
Kallinikos V *apo Nikaias* : 1801-1806, 1808-1809 (Constantinople—Greek)
Kallinikos I : 1683-1687 (Crete)
Kallinikos II : 1697-1699? (Crete)
Kallinikos III *ex Ankialou* : 1823-1831 (Crete)
Kallinikos IV *Gargalados* : 1839-1842 (Crete)
Kallinikos V *Chougias* : 1842-1843 (Crete)
Kallistos I : 1350-1353, 1355-1363 (Constantinople—Greek)
Kallistos II *Xanthopoulos* : 1397 (Constantinople—Greek)
Kallistos : 1550-1564 (Greece)
Kallistratos : 1867-1884 (Sinai)
Kapión : unknown (Jerusalem—Greek)
Karapet *Krdshadz* : 1661? [anti-catholicos] (Aght'amar)
Karapet I : 1677-1679? (Aght'amar)
Karapet II : 1783-1787 (Aght'amar)
Karapet III : 1810?-1813? (Aght'amar)
Karapet IV : 1814?-1816? (Aght'amar)
Karapet : 1406-1411 (Aghunie)
Karapet I *Bobik* : 1392-1404 (Armenia)
Karapet (II) : 1446- [anti-catholicos] (Armenia)
Karapet II : 1726-1729 (Armenia)
Karapet : 1446-1478 (Cilicia—Armenian Apostolic)
Karapet I : 1478-1489 (Constantinople—Armenian)
Karapet II : 1676-1679, 1680-1681, 1681-1684, 1686-1687, 1688-1689 (Constantinople—Armenian)
Karapet III *Palat'ts'i* : 1823-1831 (Constantinople—Armenian)
Karapet I *of Jerusalem* : 1238-1254 (Jerusalem—Armenian)
Karapet II : 1356 [locum tenens] (Jerusalem—Armenian)
Karapet III *of Kantsag* : 1761-1768 (Jerusalem—Armenian)
Kassianos : unknown (Jerusalem—Greek)
Kastinos : 230-237 (Constantinople—Greek)
Kayanus : 536-565 (Alexandria—Coptic—Gaianite)
Keladión : 152-166 (Alexandria—Greek)
Keladión : 1931-1935 [locum tenens] (Jerusalem—Greek)
Kerdón : 96-106 (Alexandria—Greek)

Khach'atur : 1287? (coadjutor?) (Aght'amar)
Khach'atur I : 1813-1814 (Aght'amar)
Khach'atur II *Mokats'i* : 1844-1851 (Aght'amar)
Khach'atur III *Shiroyan* : 1864-1895 (Aght'amar)
Khach'atur I *Chorik* : 1550?-1560 (Cilicia—Armenian Apostolic)
Khach'atur II *"The Musician"* : 1560-1584 (Cilicia—Armenian Apostolic)
Khach'atur III : 1657-1674 (Cilicia—Armenian Apostolic)
Khach'atur I : 1642-1643 (Constantinople—Armenian)
Khach'atur II : 1688 (Constantinople—Armenian)
Khach'ik I *Arsharuni* : 973-992 (Armenia)
Khach'ik II : 1058-1065 (Armenia)
Kha'il I : 744-767 (Alexandria—Coptic)
Kha'il II : 849-851 (Alexandria—Coptic)
Khalaf, Ighnatiyus : 1455-1484 (Antioch—Syrian Catholic)
Khalaf, Ighnatiyus : 1455-1483 (Antioch—Syrian Orthodox)
Khariton : 1643-1647?, 1651-1652 (Bulgaria)
Khat *Adjapahian* : 1952-1955 [locum tenens] (Cilicia—Armenian Apostolic)
Khazqi'il : 570-581 (Assyria)
Khazqi'il : 567-581 (Babylon)
Khnanishu' I *"The Lame"* : 686-693 (Assyria)
Khnanishu' II : 774-778 (Assyria)
Khnanishu' I *"The Lame"* : 685?-700? (Babylon)
Khnanishu' II : 773-780 (Babylon)
Khorên *Muradbêgian* : 1930-1932 [locum tenens], 1932-1938 (Armenia)
Khorên *Baroyan* : 1955-1956 [locum tenens], 1963-1983 (Cilicia—Armenian Apostolic)
Khorên *Ashegian* : 1888-1894 (Constantinople—Armenian)
Khristufurus I : 960-966 (Antioch—Greek)
Khristufurus II : 1184-1185 (Antioch—Greek)
Khristufurus : 960-969 (Antioch—Greek Melkite)
Kiprian : 1378-1410 (Russia—Moscow)
Kirakos : 1441-1443 (Armenia)
Kirakos I *"The Great"* : 1797-1822 (Cilicia—Armenian Apostolic)
Kirakos II : 1855-1865 (Cilicia—Armenian Apostolic)
Kirakos : 1866-1871 [locum tenens] (Cilicia—Armenian Apostolic)
Kirakos : 1641-1642 (Constantinople—Armenian)
Kirakos I : 1363 [locum tenens] (Jerusalem—Armenian)
Kirakos II *Mnatsakanian of Jerusalem* : 1847-1850 (Jerusalem—Armenian)
Kiril—SEE ALSO: Cirilo, Kirilo
Kiril I : 1759-1762 (Bulgaria)
Kiril II *Markov* : 1951-1953 [locum tenens], 1953-1971 (Bulgaria)
Kiril : 1759-1762 (Macedonia)
Kiril II : 1758-1763 (Serbia)
Kirile I : 791-802 (Georgia)
Kirile II : 1737-1739 (Georgia)
Kirillus I : 412-444 (Alexandria—Coptic)
Kirillus II : 1078-1092 (Alexandria—Coptic)
Kirillus III *Dawud ibn Laqlaq* : 1235-1243 (Alexandria—Coptic)
Kirillus IV *Dawud Tuma Bashut* : 1854-1861 (Alexandria—Coptic)
Kirillus V *ibn Ibraham Sa'ad Matar al-Nasikh* : 1874-1927 (Alexandria—Coptic)
Kirillus VI *Azir Yusuf 'Ata* : 1959-1971 (Alexandria—Coptic)
Kirillus I : 412-444 (Alexandria—Coptic Catholic)
Kirillus II *Makariyus* : 1895-1908 (Alexandria—Coptic Catholic)

Kirillus I : 279-303 (Antioch—Greek)
Kirillus II : 1287-1308? [anti-patriarch] (Antioch—Greek)
Kirillus III *al-Za'im* : 1694-1720 (Antioch—Greek)
Kirillus I : 271-306 (Antioch—Greek Melkite)
Kirillus II : 1290?-1308? (Antioch—Greek Melkite)
Kirillus III : 1316- (Antioch—Greek Melkite)
Kirillus IV *al-Dabbas* : 1620-1627 [anti-patriarch] (Antioch—Greek Melkite)
Kirillus V *al-Za'im* : 1672, 1682-1720 (Antioch—Greek Melkite)
Kirillus VI *al-Tanas* : 1724-1759 (Antioch—Greek Melkite)
Kirillus VII *Siyaj* : 1794-1796 (Antioch—Greek Melkite)
Kirillus VIII *Jiha* : 1902-1916 (Antioch—Greek Melkite)
Kirillus IX *Mughabghab* : 1925-1947 (Antioch—Greek Melkite)
Kirilo—SEE ALSO: Kiril
Kirilo I : 1407-1419 (Serbia)
Kirilo III : 1826-1827 (Serbia)
Kirion I : 595-610 (Georgia)
Kirion II : 678-683 (Georgia)
Kirion III *Sadzaglishvili* : 1917-1918 (Georgia)
Klématios : 400? (Greece)
Klémés *apo Ikoniou* : 1667 (Constantinople—Greek)
Klémés : 1514? (Sinai)
Klimentos : 908-914 (Georgia)
Klyment : 1147-1154 (Ukraine)
Kodratos : 200? (Greece)
Komitas : 615-628 (Armenia)
Konstantin I : 1160?-1170? (Bulgaria)
Konstantin II *Kavasila* : 1254?-1259? (Bulgaria)
Konstantin I : 1157-1166 (Macedonia)
Konstantin II *Kabasilas* : 1250-1261 (Macedonia)
Kónstantinos *Katsarakés* : 1966-1968 [locum tenens] (Alexandria—Greek)
Kónstantinos I : 675-677 (Constantinople—Greek)
Kónstantinos II : 754-766 (Constantinople—Greek)
Kónstantinos III *Leichoudés* : 1059-1063 (Constantinople—Greek)
Kónstantinos IV *Chliarénos* : 1154-1157 (Constantinople—Greek)
Kónstantinos V : 1897-1901 (Constantinople—Greek)
Kónstantinos VI *Araboglou* : 1924-1925 (Constantinople—Greek)
Kónstantinos I : 11th cent. (Crete)
Kónstantinos II : 12th cent. (Crete)
Kónstantinos : 783?-787? (Cyprus)
Kónstantinos : 965? (Greece)
Kónstantinos : -869? (Sinai)
Kónstantios I : 1830-1834 (Constantinople—Greek)
Kónstantios II *apo Tornobou* : 1834-1835 (Constantinople—Greek)
Kónstantios *Chalkiopoulos* : 1716-1722? (Crete)
Kónstantios I : 1748-1759 (Sinai)
Kónstantios II *apo Tornobou* : 1804-1859 (Sinai)
Konstantyn I : 1154-1158 (Ukraine)
Konstantyn II : 1167-1183? (Ukraine)
Konstantyn III *Dzhakov* : 1929-1937 (Ukraine)
Konstantyn *Buggan* : 1993- (Ukraine—Orthodox Church of the USA)
Kooriakose : 964-982 (India—Malankara Orthodox)
Kooriakose Mar Koorilose VI : 1936-1947 (India—Thozhiyoor)
Koorilose, Paulose Mar : 1911-1917 (India—Malankara Jacobite)
Koorilose, Yoyakin Mar : 1846-1852 (India—Malankara Syrian)

Koorilose I *Kattamangat*, Abraham Mar : 1771-1802 (India—Thozhiyoor)
Koorilose II, Geevarghese Mar : 1794-1802 [suffragan], 1802-1808 (India—Thozhiyoor)
Koorilose III *Koothoor*, Geevarghese Mar : 1829-1856 (India—Thozhiyoor)
Koorilose IV *Kasseesa*, Joseph Mar : 1856-1888 (India—Thozhiyoor)
Koorilose V *Pulikottil*, Geevarghese Mar : 1892-1898 [suffragan], 1898-1935 (India—Thozhiyoor)
Koorilose VI, Kooriakose Mar : 1936-1947 (India—Thozhiyoor)
Koorilose VII *Kasseesa*, Geevarghese Mar : 1948-1967 (India—Thozhiyoor)
Koorilose VIII, Mathews Mar : 1978-1986 (India—Thozhiyoor)
Koorilose IX *Panakal*, Joseph Mar : 1981-1986 [suffragan], 1986- (India—Thozhiyoor)
Kornelius *Jakobs* : 1990- (Estonia)
Kosmas I *"The Needle-Maker"* : 727-768 (Alexandria—Greek)
Kosmas II *Byzantios* : 1723-1736 (Alexandria—Greek)
Kosmas III *Kalokagathos* : 1737-1746 (Alexandria—Greek)
Kosmas I *Hierosolymités* : 1075-1081 (Constantinople—Greek)
Kosmas II *Attikos* : 1146-1147 (Constantinople—Greek)
Kosmas III *Chalkédonios* : 1714-1716 (Constantinople—Greek)
Kosmas I : 867 (Greece)
Kosmas II : 1339 (Greece)
Kosmas *Byzantios* : 1703-1706 (Sinai)
Kostandin I : 1221-1267 (Armenia)
Kostandin II *Pronogordz* : 1286-1289 (Armenia)
Kostandin III : 1307-1322 (Armenia)
Kostandin IV : 1323-1326 (Armenia)
Kostandin V : 1372-1374 (Armenia)
Kostandin VI : 1430-1439 (Armenia)
Krestodolo I : 1588?- (Ethiopia—Historical)
Krestodolo II : 1663?-1671? (Ethiopia—Historical)
Krestodolo III : 1720-1735 (Ethiopia—Historical)
Krestodolo I : unknown (Ethiopia—Official)
Krestodolo II : 1663?-1671 (Ethiopia—Official)
Krestodolo III : 1720-1735 (Ethiopia—Official)
Kriskés : 256 (Crete)
K'ristap'or *Ardzuni* : 478 [anti-catholicos] (Armenia)
K'ristap'or I : 539-545 (Armenia)
K'ristap'or II : 628-630 (Armenia)
K'ristep'ore I : 1616-1622 (Georgia)
K'ristep'ore II : 1638-1660 (Georgia)
K'ristep'ore III *Tsitskishvili* : 1927-1932 (Georgia)
Kristofor *Kissi* : 1937-1949 (Albania)
Kurdunus : 98-109 (Alexandria—Coptic)
Kurdunus : 95-106 (Alexandria—Coptic Catholic)
Kuregh *Israelian* : 1944-1949 (Jerusalem—Armenian)
Kurniliyus : 126-151 (Antioch—Greek)
Kurniliyus : 130?-150? (Antioch—Greek Melkite)
Kurush : 707- (Antioch—Maronite)
Kuz'ma : 1156? (Ukraine—Halych)
Kyprian : 1389-1406 (Ukraine)
Kyprianos : 1766-1783 (Alexandria—Greek)
Kyprianos *apo Kaisareias Kappadokias* : 1707-1709, 1713-1714 (Constantinople—Greek)
Kyprianos : 1761 [anti-archbishop] (Cyprus)

Kyprianos : 1810-1821 (Cyprus)
Kyriakos I : 214-230 (Constantinople—Greek)
Kyriakos II : 595?-606 (Constantinople—Greek)
Kyrillianos : 214-230 (Constantinople—Greek)
Kyrillos I : 412-444 (Alexandria—Greek)
Kyrillos II : 1110? (Alexandria—Greek)
Kyrillos III *Loukaris* : 1601-1621 (Alexandria—Greek)
Kyrillos I *Loukaris* : 1612 [locum tenens], 1620-1623, 1623-1630, 1630-1633, 1633-1634, 1634-1635, 1637-1638 (Constantinople—Greek)
Kyrillos II *Kontarés apo Borrhoias* : 1633, 1635-1636, 1638-1639 (Constantinople—Greek)
Kyrillos III *Spanos apo Tornobou* : 1652, 1654 (Constantinople—Greek)
Kyrillos IV *apo Kyzikou* : 1711-1713 (Constantinople—Greek)
Kyrillos (V) *apo Prousés* : 1720 [anti-patriarch] (Constantinople—Greek)
Kyrillos V *Karakalos apo Nikomédeias* : 1748-1751, 1752-1757 (Constantinople—Greek)
Kyrillos VI *Serbetsoglous apo Adrianoupoleós* : 1813-1818 (Constantinople—Greek)
Kyrillos VII *apo Amaseias* : 1855-1860 (Constantinople—Greek)
Kyrillos I : 393 (Crete)
Kyrillos II : 824? (Crete)
Kyrillos I : 1849-1854 (Cyprus)
Kyrillos II *Papadopoulos* : 1900-1909 [locum tenens], 1909-1916 (Cyprus)
Kyrillos III *Basileiou* : 1916-1933 (Cyprus)
Kyrillos I : -1611 (Greece)
Kyrillos II : 1699-1703 (Greece)
Kyrillos I : 348?-357, 358-360, 362-367, 378-386? (Jerusalem—Greek)
Kyrillos II : 1845-1872 (Jerusalem—Greek)
Kyrillos I : 1470? (Sinai)
Kyrillos II *Krés* : 1759-1790 (Sinai)
Kyrillos III *Byzantios* : 1859-1867 (Sinai)
Kyros *of Phasis* : 642-651 (Alexandria—Greek)
Kyros : 706-712 (Constantinople—Greek)
Kyryl I : 1073-1077 (Ukraine)
Kyryl II : 1224-1233 (Ukraine)
Kyryl III : 1243-1281 (Ukraine)
Ladislaus Michael *Zaleski* : 1916-1925? (Antioch—Latin)
Lando : 913-914 (Rome)
Landus : 913-914 (Rome)
Laurentios : 154-166 (Constantinople—Greek)
Laurentios : 1588? (Cyprus)
Laurentios : 1528-1550 (Greece)
Laurentios : 1592-1617 (Sinai)
Laurentius I *Zane* : 1473-1485 (Antioch—Latin)
Laurentius II *Mattei* : 1822-1833 (Antioch—Latin)
Laurentius III *Passerini* : 1901-1915 (Antioch—Latin)
Laurentius : 498, 501-505 [anti-pope] (Rome)
Lavrentie I : unknown (Austria—Cernovci)
Lavrentie II : 1689-1702 (Austria—Cernovci)
Lawndiyus *"The Eunuch"* : 344-358 (Antioch—Greek)
Lawndiyus *"The Eunuch"* : 344-358 (Antioch—Greek Melkite)
Lawntiyus *"The Eunuch"* : 344-358 (Antioch—Syrian Orthodox)
Lazar Yusip V *Khindi* : 1757-1781 (Babylon)
Lazaros *apo Sina* : 1300? (Greece)

Lazaros : 1491? (Sinai)
Lazaros : 1334?-1368 (Jerusalem—Greek)
Leo I *Magnus "The Great"* : 440-461 (Rome)
Leo II : 682-683 (Rome)
Leo III : 795-816 (Rome)
Leo IV : 847-855 (Rome)
Leo V : 903 (Rome)
Leo VI : 928 (Rome)
Leo VII : 936-939 (Rome)
Leo VIII : 963-965 (Rome)
Leo IX *von Egisheim* : 1049-1054 (Rome)
Leo X *de' Medici* : 1513-1521 (Rome)
Leo XI *de' Medici* : 1605 (Rome)
Leo XII *della Genga* : 1823-1829 (Rome)
Leo XIII *Pecci* : 1878-1903 (Rome)
León *Styppés* : 1134-1143 (Constantinople—Greek)
León : 11th cent. (Crete)
León I *Synkellos* : 1054?-1061? (Greece)
León II *Synkellos* : 1061?-1069? (Greece)
Leonardus *Delfino* : 1401-1402? (Alexandria—Latin)
Leonardus *Faliero* : 1302-1305? (Constantinople—Latin)
Leonid *Poliakov* : 1966-1989 (Latvia)
Leonide *Okropiridze* : 1917 [locum tenens], 1918-1921 (Georgia)
Leónidés : 250? (Greece)
Leontiî : 919- (Bulgaria)
Leontiî *Lebedinskiî* : 1891-1893 (Russia—Moscow)
Leontiî : 991-1004 (Ukraine)
Leontije *Lambrovic* : 1801-1809, 1811-1813 (Serbia)
Leontios : 1052-1059 (Alexandria—Greek)
Leontios *Theotokités* : 1189 (Constantinople—Greek)
Leontios *Leontiou* : 1933-1947 [locum tenens], 1947 (Cyprus)
Leontios I : 912-929 (Jerusalem—Greek)
Leontios II : 1170-1190 (Jerusalem—Greek)
Leonty *Turkevich* : (America—Orthodox Church)
Leuis : unknown (Jerusalem—Greek)
Lev I *ek Rómaión* : 1027-1056 (Macedonia)
Lev II *Boungos* : -1120 (Macedonia)
Liberius : 352-366 (Rome)
Linus : 67?-76 (Rome)
Livius *Podocator* : 1524- (Cyprus—Latin)
Lo Asar : 856-869 (India—Malankara Orthodox)
Lotharius : 1214?- (Jerusalem—Latin)
Loukas : 365-378 (Alexandria—Greek—Arian)
Loukas *Chrysobergés* : 1157-1169? (Constantinople—Greek)
Luca : 1602-1629 (Romania)
Lucas Ermenegildus *Pasetto* : 1950-1953? (Alexandria—Latin)
Lucius I : 253-254 (Rome)
Lucius II *Caccianemici* : 1144-1145 (Rome)
Lucius III *Allucingoli* : 1181-1185 (Rome)
Ludovicus I Caetanus *di Sermoneta* : 1622-1626? (Antioch—Latin)
Ludovicus II *Calini* : 1751-1766 (Antioch—Latin)
Ludovicus I : 1405 (Constantinople—Latin)
Ludovicus II *Pic de la Mirandole* : 1706-1712 (Constantinople—Latin)
Ludovicus *Perez Fabrice* : 1471-1483 (Cyprus—Latin)

Lukijan *Bogdanovic* : 1907-1908 [locum tenens], 1908-1913 (Austria—Karlovci)
Luqa : 1137-1155 (Antioch—Greek)
Luqa *al-Banhrani* : 1272-1300 (Antioch—Maronite)
Luv I *ek Rómaión* : 1037?-1054? (Bulgaria)
Luv II *Mung* : 1108?-1120? (Bulgaria)
Macarie I : 1477-1487? (Romania)
Macarie II : 1512-1521? (Romania)
Maghak'ia *Örmanian* : 1896-1908 (Constantinople—Armenian)
Magina : 398-400 (India—Malankara Orthodox)
Makar *Ter-Petrosian* : 1885-1891 (Armenia)
Makari : 553-569 (Georgia)
Makariî I : -1291 (Bulgaria)
Makariî II : 1295?-1299? (Bulgaria)
Makariî I : 1542-1563 (Russia—Moscow)
Makariî II *Bulgakov* : 1879-1882 (Russia—Moscow)
Makariî III *Nevskiî* : 1912-1917 (Russia—Moscow)
Makariî I : 1495-1497 (Ukraine)
Makariî II : 1534-1556 (Ukraine)
Makarij : 1294-1299 (Macedonia)
Makarije *Sokolovic* : 1557-1574 (Serbia)
Makarije *Korneciani* : 1659-1675 (Serbia—Montenegro)
Makarios : 1376?-1379, 1390-1391 (Constantinople—Greek)
Makarios : 1357? (Crete)
Makarios I : 1854-1865 (Cyprus)
Makarios II *Myriantheus* : 1947-1950 (Cyprus)
Makarios III *Mouskos* : 1950-1973, 1973-1977 (Cyprus)
Makarios I : 1394-1404 (Greece)
Makarios II *Pelekanos* : 1689-1693 (Greece)
Makarios I : 478-486 (Jerusalem—Greek)
Makarios II : 552, 564-575 (Jerusalem—Greek)
Makarios I : 454? (Sinai)
Makarios II : 967? (Sinai)
Makarios III : 1224- (Sinai)
Makarios IV : 1486? (Sinai)
Makarios V *Kyprios* : 1547- (Sinai)
Makariusz *Oksijuk* : 1951-1961 (Poland)
Makariyus I : 932-952 (Alexandria—Coptic)
Makariyus II : 1102-1128 (Alexandria—Coptic)
Makariyus III : 1944-1945 (Alexandria—Coptic)
Makariyus I : 656-681 (Antioch—Greek)
Makariyus II : 1164-1166 (Antioch—Greek)
Makariyus III *al-Za'im* : 1648-1672 (Antioch—Greek)
Makariyus I : 660?-681 (Antioch—Greek Melkite)
Makariyus II *ibn Khilal* : 1543?-1550? [anti-patriarch] (Antioch—Greek Melkite)
Makariyus III *al-Za'im* : 1647-1672 (Antioch—Greek Melkite)
Makariyus IV *Tawil* : 1814-1815 (Antioch—Greek Melkite)
Makaryos : 1804-1808? (Ethiopia—Historical)
Makaryos : 1804-1808? (Ethiopia—Official)
Makedonios I : 344-346, 350-360 (Constantinople—Greek)
Makedonios II : 496-511 (Constantinople—Greek)
Makkikha I *bar Shlimun* : 1092-1109 (Assyria)
Makkikha II : 1257-1265 (Assyria)

Makkikha I *bar Shlimun* : 1092-1110 (Babylon)
Makkikha II : 1257-1265 (Babylon)
Maksim *Minkov* : 1971- (Bulgaria)
Maksim : 1477-1481 (Macedonia)
Maksim *Skopljanac* : 1655-1674 (Serbia)
Mak'sime I : 1639-1657 (Georgia—Abkhazia)
Mak'sime II : 1776-1795 (Georgia—Abkhazia)
Maksiminus : 188-191 (Antioch—Greek)
Maksimiyanus : 182-191 (Antioch—Greek Melkite)
Maksimiyanus : 182-190 (Antioch—Syrian Orthodox)
Maksimus : 264-282 (Alexandria—Coptic)
Maksimus (I) : 264-282 (Alexandria—Coptic Catholic)
Maksimus (II) *Jayid* : 1824-1831 (Alexandria—Coptic Catholic)
Maksimus (III) *Sidfawi* : 1908-1926 (Alexandria—Coptic Catholic)
Maksimus : 451-455 (Antioch—Greek)
Maksimus I : 449?-455 (Antioch—Greek Melkite)
Maksimus II *Hakim* : 1760-1761 (Antioch—Greek Melkite)
Maksimus III *Mazlum* : 1833-1855 (Antioch—Greek Melkite)
Maksimus IV *al-Sa'igh* : 1947-1967 (Antioch—Greek Melkite)
Maksimus V *Hakim* : 1967- (Antioch—Greek Melkite)
Maksimus I : 172-190 (Antioch—Syrian Catholic)
Maksimus II : 449-456 (Antioch—Syrian Catholic)
Maksimus : 449-455 (Antioch—Syrian Orthodox)
Maksym *Hrek "The Greek"* : 1283-1305 (Ukraine)
Malak'ia : 1528-1538 (Georgia)
Malak'ia I : 1529-1532 (Georgia—Abkhazia)
Malak'ia II : 1616-1639 (Georgia—Abkhazia)
Malatiyus I : 360-361, 378-381 (Antioch—Greek)
Malatiyus II *Dumani* : 1899-1906 (Antioch—Greek)
Malatiyus : 359?-381 (Antioch—Greek Melkite)
Malatiyus : 362-381 (Antioch—Syrian Catholic)
Mamai : 731-744 (Georgia)
Ma'na : 420 (Assyria and Babylon)
Manouél I *Saranténos Charitopoulos* : 1216?-1222 (Constantinople—Greek)
Manouél II : 1243?-1254 (Constantinople—Greek)
Manouél I : 12th cent. (Crete)
Manouél II : 12th cent. (Crete)
Maqares : 1320? (Ethiopia—Historical)
Maqares : unknown (Ethiopia—Official)
Maqiduniyus : 628-631, 632-640 (Antioch—Greek)
Maqiduniyus : 639?-649? (Antioch—Greek Melkite)
Marcellinus : 296-304 (Rome)
Marcellus I : 308-309 (Rome)
Marcellus II *Cervini* : 1555 (Rome)
Marcu : 1516- (Austria—Sibiu)
Marcus *Condolmer* : 1445? (Alexandria—Latin)
Marcus *Cornaro* : 1506-1507, 1522-1524 (Constantinople—Latin)
Marcus : 336 (Rome)
Mardarie : 1591?-1595 (Austria—Cernovci)
Mari I : 48-81 (Assyria)
Mari II *bar Tubi At'uraya* : 987-1000 (Assyria)
Mari I : 1st cent. (Babylon)
Mari II *bar Tubi At'uraya* : 987-999 (Babylon)
Mari : 152-185 (India—Malankara Orthodox)

Mari Aba I *Raba* : 540-552 (Assyria)
Mari Aba II : 741-751 (Assyria)
Mari Immih : 647-650 (Assyria and Babylon)
Marinos : 386- [anti-patriarch] (Constantinople—Greek)
Marinos : 702-704 (Greece)
Marinus *Grimani* : 1545-1546 (Constantinople—Latin)
Marinus I : 882-884 (Rome)
Marinus II : 942-946 (Rome)
Mark *Ksilocarf* : 1466-1467 (Macedonia)
Markiyanus : 143-154 (Alexandria—Coptic)
Markiyanus : 141-152 (Alexandria—Coptic Catholic)
Marko *Ksilokarav* : 1467?- (Bulgaria)
Marko : 1524? (Serbia)
Markos : 1788-1791 (Aght'amar)
Markos I : 997- (Aghunie)
Markos II : -1077 (Aghunie)
Markos I *Euangelistés* : -61 (Alexandria—Greek)
Markos II : 142-152 (Alexandria—Greek)
Markos III : 1180-1209 (Alexandria—Greek)
Markos IV : 1385-1389 (Alexandria—Greek)
Markos V : 1425-1435 (Alexandria—Greek)
Markos VI : 1459-1484 (Alexandria—Greek)
Markos I : 198-211 (Constantinople—Greek)
Markos II *Xylokarabés Eugenikos* : 1466 (Constantinople—Greek)
Markos I : 134?- (Jerusalem—Greek)
Markos II : 1191 (Jerusalem—Greek)
Markos III : 1503 (Jerusalem—Greek)
Markos I : 869- (Sinai)
Markos II : 1100? (Sinai)
Markos III : 1181? (Sinai)
Markos IV : 1375? (Sinai)
Markos V : 1496? (Sinai)
Markozi : 1460-1466 (Georgia)
Marqos I : 1481-1530? (Ethiopia—Historical)
Marqos II : 1538-1546? (Ethiopia—Historical)
Marqos III : 1576?-1588? (Ethiopia—Historical)
Marqos IV : 1634-1648? (Ethiopia—Historical)
Marqos V : 1671? (Ethiopia—Historical)
Marqos VI : 1693?-1716 (Ethiopia—Historical)
Marqos I : unknown (Ethiopia—Official)
Marqos II : unknown (Ethiopia—Official)
Marqos III : unknown (Ethiopia—Official)
Marqos IV : unknown (Ethiopia—Official)
Marqos V : unknown (Ethiopia—Official)
Marqos VI : unknown (Ethiopia—Official)
Marqos VII : 1481-1530? (Ethiopia—Official)
Marqos VIII : 1576?-1588? (Ethiopia—Official)
Marqos IX : 1634?-1648? (Ethiopia—Official)
Marqos X : 1693?-1716 (Ethiopia—Official)
Martinus I : 649-655 (Rome)
Martinus II [there is no pope with this name] (Rome)
Martinus III [there is no pope with this name] (Rome)
Martinus IV *de Brie* : 1281-1285 (Rome)
Martinus V *Colonna* : 1417-1431 (Rome)

Martiriyus : 459-471 (Antioch—Greek)
Martiriyus : 459-470? (Antioch—Greek Melkite)
Martiros *Gurji* : 1660-1662 (Aght'amar)
Martiros I : 1509-1526 (Constantinople—Armenian)
Martiros II : 1659-1660 (Constantinople—Armenian)
Martiros III : 1706 (Constantinople—Armenian)
Martiros I : 1399 [coadjutor] (Jerusalem—Armenian)
Martiros II *of Egypt* : 1419-1430 (Jerusalem—Armenian)
Martiros III *of Broussa* : 1491-1501 (Jerusalem—Armenian)
Martiros IV : 1677-1680, 1681-1683 (Jerusalem—Armenian)
Martiros V : 1706 (Jerusalem—Armenian)
Martur : 460-470, 471-473 (Antioch—Syrian Catholic)
Marturiyus : 459-468 (Antioch—Syrian Orthodox)
Martyrios : 451 (Crete)
Martyrios : 478-486 (Jerusalem—Greek)
Martyrios : 400? (Sinai)
Ma'ruf Yusip III *Sliba* : 1696-1712 (Babylon)
Marugin Iliya XI *bar Mama* : 1700-1722 (Babylon)
Marun 'Abdishu' IV : 1555-1567 (Babylon)
Mashtots' : 897-898 (Armenia)
Mas'ud I *Slakhaya*, Ighnatiyus : 1418-1420 (Antioch—Syrian Orthodox—Tur
    Abhdin)
Mas'ud II, Ighnatiyus : 1490?-1495 (Antioch—Syrian Orthodox—Tur Abhdin)
Mateî : 1408-1411? (Bulgaria)
Matej : 1408-1410 (Macedonia)
Matewos : 1889-1926 (Ethiopia—Historical)
Matewos I : unknown (Ethiopia—Official)
Matewos II : unknown (Ethiopia—Official)
Matewos III : unknown (Ethiopia—Official)
Matewos IV : unknown (Ethiopia—Official)
Matewos V : unknown (Ethiopia—Official)
Matewos VI : unknown (Ethiopia—Official)
Matewos VII : unknown (Ethiopia—Official)
Matewos VIII : unknown (Ethiopia—Official)
Matewos IX : unknown (Ethiopia—Official)
Matewos X : unknown (Ethiopia—Official)
Matewos XI : 1889-1926 (Ethiopia—Official)
Matfeî : 1210-1220 (Ukraine)
Mathew Mar Thoma VII : 1796-1809 (India—Malankara Syrian)
Mathews I *Vattakunnel*, Baselios Mar Thoma : 1970-1975 [suffragan], 1975-
    1991 (India—Malankara Orthodox)
Mathews II, Baselios Mar Thoma : 1980-1991 [suffragan], 1991- (India—
    Malankara Orthodox)
Mathews Mar Athanasios *Palakunnath* : 1842-1852 [suffragan], 1852-1875
    (India—Malankara Syrian)
Mathews Mar Athanasios *Palakunnath* : 1843-1877 (India—Mar Thoma Syr-
    ian)
Mathews Mar Koorilose VIII : 1978-1986 (India—Thozhiyoor)
Matiyus *ibn 'Abd Allah*, Ighnatiyus : 1782-1817 (Antioch—Syrian Orthodox)
Matta—SEE ALSO: Mattawus
Matta I : 1378-1409 (Alexandria—Coptic)
Mattawus—SEE ALSO: Matta
Mattawus I : 1378-1409 (Alexandria—Coptic)
Mattawus II : 1452-1465 (Alexandria—Coptic)

Mattawus III : 1634-1649 (Alexandria—Coptic)
Mattawus IV *al-Miri* : 1660-1675 (Alexandria—Coptic)
Mattawus *Righat* : 1788-1822 (Alexandria—Coptic Catholic)
Matt'ê—SEE ALSO: Matt'êos
Matt'ê II : 775-777 (Aghunie)
Matt'êos—SEE ALSO: Matt'ê
Matt'êos I : 342- (Aghunie)
Matt'êos III : 1412-1440 (Aghunie)
Matt'êos IV : 1470- (Aghunie)
Matt'êos I *Ch'ukhachian* : 1858-1865 (Armenia)
Matt'êos II *Izmirlian* : 1908-1910 (Armenia)
Matt'êos : 1694-1705 (Cilicia—Armenian Apostolic)
Matt'êos I : 1692-1694, 1706 (Constantinople—Armenian)
Matt'êos II *Ch'ukhachian* : 1844-1848 (Constantinople—Armenian)
Matt'êos III *Izmirlian* : 1894-1896, 1908-1909 (Constantinople—Armenian)
Matt'êos : 1706 (Jerusalem—Armenian)
Matthæus : 1221-1226 (Constantinople—Latin)
Matthaios *Psaltés* : 1746-1766 (Alexandria—Greek)
Matthaios I *apo Kyzikou* : 1397-1402, 1403-1410 (Constantinople—Greek)
Matthaios II *apo Ióanninón* : 1595, 1598?-1602, 1603 (Constantinople—Greek)
Matthias : unknown (Jerusalem—Greek)
Maxim *Brancovici* : 1505-1508 (Romania)
Maximianos : 431-434 (Constantinople—Greek)
Maximos : 265-282 (Alexandria—Greek)
Maximos I *Kynikos* : 381 (Constantinople—Greek)
Maximos II *apo Akoimétón* : 1216 (Constantinople—Greek)
Maximos III *Manassés* : 1476-1482 (Constantinople—Greek)
Maximos IV *apo Serrón* : 1491-1497 (Constantinople—Greek)
Maximos V *Baportzés* : 1946-1948 (Constantinople—Greek)
Maximos *Progiannakopoulos* : 1786-1800 (Crete)
Maximos I : unknown (Jerusalem—Greek)
Maximos II : unknown (Jerusalem—Greek)
Maximos III : 333-348 (Jerusalem—Greek)
Mazabanés : 251-260 (Jerusalem—Greek)
Mehruzhan : 240-270 (Armenia)
Melchiades : 311-314 (Rome)
Melentije I *Stefanovic* : 1809-1811 (Serbia)
Melentije II *Pavlovic* : 1831-1833 (Serbia)
Meletie : unknown (Austria—Cernovci)
Meletiî I : 1637-1643 (Bulgaria)
Meletiî II : 1676-1677 (Bulgaria)
Meletij I : 1637-1641 (Macedonia)
Meletij II : 1677-1679 (Macedonia)
Meletios I *Pégas* : 1590-1601 (Alexandria—Greek)
Meletios II *Metaxakés* : 1926-1935 (Alexandria—Greek)
Meletios I *Pégas* : 1597-1598? [locum tenens] (Constantinople—Greek)
Meletios II *apo Larissés* : 1768-1769 (Constantinople—Greek)
Meletios III *Pankalos apo Kyzikou* : 1845 (Constantinople—Greek)
Meletios IV *Metaxakés* : 1921-1923 (Constantinople—Greek)
Meletios I *Nikoletakés* : 1831-1839 (Crete)
Meletios II *Kalymnios* : 1868-1873?, 1877-1882 (Crete)
Meletios I : 1275-1289 (Greece)
Meletios II *Métrou apo Naupaktou kai Artés* : 1703-1713 (Greece)
Meletios III *Metaxakés* : 1918-1920 (Greece)

Meletios *apo Kaisareias* : 1731-1737 (Jerusalem—Greek)
Melhisedek *Paieuski* : 1922-1925 (Belarus)
Melitê : 452-456 (Armenia)
Melk'isedek : 1593-1603 [coadjutor] (Armenia)
Melk'isedek I : 1599-1600 (Constantinople—Armenian)
Melk'isedek II : 1698-1699, 1700-1701 (Constantinople—Armenian)
Melk'isedek I : 1012-1045 (Georgia)
Melk'isedek II : 1538-1541 (Georgia)
Melk'isedek III *Pk'aladze* : 1952-1960 (Georgia)
Melk'iset' : 1593-1596 (Aghunie)
Ménas *Sampsón* : 536-552 (Constantinople—Greek)
Merbukhat : 401-420 (India—Malankara Orthodox)
Merkorewos *Fenta* : 1988-1991 (Ethiopia—Historical)
Merkorewos *Fenta* : 1988-1991 (Ethiopia—Official)
Mesrop : 439-440 [locum tenens] (Armenia)
Mesrop : 1359-1372 (Armenia)
Mesrop *Naroyan* : 1927-1944 (Constantinople—Armenian)
Mesrop I : 1008 [coadjutor] (Jerusalem—Armenian)
Mesrop II : 1402 [coadjutor] (Jerusalem—Armenian)
Mesrop III : 1454-1461 (Jerusalem—Armenian)
Mesrop IV *Nishanian* : 1930-1931 [locum tenens], 1939-1944 (Jerusalem—Armenian)
Methodios I : 843-847 (Constantinople—Greek)
Methodios II : 1240?-1241? (Constantinople—Greek)
Methodios III *Mórónés apo Hérakleias* : 1668-1671 (Constantinople—Greek)
Methodios *apo Karpathou* : 1823 (Crete)
Methodios *Fougas* : 1979-1988 [locum tenens] (Latvia)
Metodiî I : 1708 (Bulgaria)
Metodiî II : 1757-1758 (Bulgaria)
Metodij I : 1708 (Macedonia)
Metodij II : 1757-1758 (Macedonia)
Metodije : 1793-1801 (Serbia)
Métrophanés : 1636-1639 (Alexandria—Greek)
Métrophanés I : 315-325 (Constantinople—Greek)
Métrophanés II *apo Kyzikou* : 1440-1443 (Constantinople—Greek)
Métrophanés III *apo Kaisareias* : 1565-1572, 1579-1580 (Constantinople—Greek)
Métrophanés : -1619 (Greece)
Michaél I : 860-870 (Alexandria—Greek)
Michaél II : 870-907 (Alexandria—Greek)
Michael *Bonelli* : 1587? (Alexandria—Latin)
Michaél *Kónstantinidés* : 1949-1958 (America—Greek)
Michael Angelus *Mattei* : 1693- (Antioch—Latin)
Michaél I *Kéroularios* : 1043-1058 (Constantinople—Greek)
Michaél II *Kourkouas Oxeités* : 1143-1146 (Constantinople—Greek)
Michaél III *Anchialou* : 1170-1178 (Constantinople—Greek)
Michaél IV *Autóreianos* : 1208-1214 (Constantinople—Greek)
Michael *Zezza di Zapponeta* : 1923-1927 (Constantinople—Latin)
Michaél : 11th cent. (Crete)
Michael : 1375? (Cyprus—Latin)
Michaél I : 1007-1030 (Greece)
Michaél II : 1133? (Greece)
Michaél III *Akominatos Chóniatés* : 1182-1222 (Greece)
Michael I : 1194 (Jerusalem—Latin)

Michael II *Sabbah* : 1987- (Jerusalem—Latin)
Michaél : 1455? (Sinai)
Michael *Augustine*, Mar : 1900-1911 (India—Chaldean)
Mihail I *Maksim* : 1120- (Macedonia)
Mihail II *Gogov* : 1993- (Macedonia)
Mihail I : 1585?-1589 (Romania)
Mihail II : 1592-1594 (Romania)
Mihaïlo *Gryjic* : 1913-1914 [locum tenens] (Austria—Karlovci)
Mihaïlo *Jovanovic* : 1859-1881, 1889-1898 (Serbia)
Mika'el *Wolde Mika'el* : -1980? (Eritrea)
Mika'el I *Habib al-Atfihi* : 1105?-1153 or 1130?-1199? (Ethiopia—Historical)
Mika'el II *Kilus ibn al-Mulabbas* : 1205-1210? (Ethiopia—Historical)
Mika'el III, Yerda' : 1220? (Ethiopia—Historical)
Mika'el IV : 1438-1455? (Ethiopia—Historical)
Mika'el V : 1649? (Ethiopia—Historical)
Mika'el I : unknown (Ethiopia—Official)
Mika'el II : unknown (Ethiopia—Official)
Mika'el III : unknown (Ethiopia—Official)
Mika'el IV : unknown (Ethiopia—Official)
Mika'el V : unknown (Ethiopia—Official)
Mika'el VI : unknown (Ethiopia—Official)
Mika'el VII : unknown (Ethiopia—Official)
Mika'el VIII : unknown (Ethiopia—Official)
Mika'el IX : unknown (Ethiopia—Official)
Mika'el X : unknown (Ethiopia—Official)
Mika'el XI : 1438-1458? (Ethiopia—Official)
Mika'el XII : unknown (Ethiopia—Official)
Mika'el XIII : 1648? (Ethiopia—Official)
Mikalay *Mucukievich* : 1984- (Belarus)
Mik'ayêl : 1796-1810 (Aght'amar)
Mik'ayêl : 706-741 (Aghunie)
Mik'ayêl : 1567-1576 (Armenia)
Mik'ayêl I : 1737-1758 (Cilicia—Armenian Apostolic)
Mik'ayêl II : 1832-1855 (Cilicia—Armenian Apostolic)
Mik'ayêl : 1706-1707 (Constantinople—Armenian)
Mik'ayêl : 1706-1707 (Jerusalem—Armenian)
Mik'ayêl Petros III *Gasparian* : 1753-1780 (Cilicia—Armenian Catholic)
Mik'el I : 452-467 (Georgia)
Mik'el II : 774-780 (Georgia)
Mik'el III : 930-944 (Georgia)
Mik'el IV : 1178-1186 (Georgia)
Mik'el V : 1325-1330 (Georgia)
Mik'el VI : 1411-1426 (Georgia)
Mikha'il—SEE ALSO: Khail
Mikha'il III : 880-907 (Alexandria—Coptic)
Mikha'il IV : 1092-1102 (Alexandria—Coptic)
Mikha'il V : 1145-1146 (Alexandria—Coptic)
Mikha'il VI : 1476-1478 (Alexandria—Coptic)
Mikha'il I : 879-890 (Antioch—Greek)
Mikha'il II : 1353-1376 (Antioch—Greek)
Mikha'il III : 1401-1410 (Antioch—Greek)
Mikha'il IV *ibn al-Mawardi* : 1454-1462 (Antioch—Greek)
Mikha'il V *ibn al-Mawardi* : 1523-1541 (Antioch—Greek)
Mikha'il VI *al-Hamawi* : 1577-1581 (Antioch—Greek)

Mikha'il I : 1368-1375 (Antioch—Greek Melkite)
Mikha'il II : 1395-1412 (Antioch—Greek Melkite)
Mikha'il III *ibn al-Mawardi* : 1451?-1456? (Antioch—Greek Melkite)
Mikha'il IV : 1470?-1484? (Antioch—Greek Melkite)
Mikha'il V *ibn al-Mawardi* : 1523?-1529 (Antioch—Greek Melkite)
Mikha'il VI *Sabbagh* : 1534-1543 (Antioch—Greek Melkite)
Mikha'il VII *al-Hamawi* : 1576-1593 (Antioch—Greek Melkite)
Mikha'il I *ibn Yuhanna al-Ruzzi* : 1567-1581 (Antioch—Maronite)
Mikha'il II Butrus *Fadl* : 1793-1795 (Antioch—Maronite)
Mikha'il I *al-Kabir* : 1167-1200 (Antioch—Syrian Catholic)
Mikha'il II *Ishu' Siftana* : 1207-1208 (Antioch—Syrian Catholic)
Mikha'il III *Jarwah*, Ighnatiyus : 1782-1800 (Antioch—Syrian Catholic)
Mikha'il IV *Dahir*, Ighnatiyus : 1802-1810 (Antioch—Syrian Catholic)
Mikha'il I *al-Kabir* : 1166-1199 (Antioch—Syrian Orthodox)
Mikha'il II *ibn Sawma* : 1292-1312 (Antioch—Syrian Orthodox)
Mikha'il III *Ishu' ibn Shushan* : 1312-1349 (Antioch—Syrian Orthodox)
Mikhail *Maksim* : 1120?- (Bulgaria)
Mikhail : 1948-1949 [locum tenens] (Bulgaria)
Mikha'il Shim'un XVII : 1740?-1780? (Assyria)
Militus : 360-381 (Antioch—Syrian Orthodox)
Miliyus: 83-98 (Alexandria—Coptic)
Miltiades : 311-314 (Rome)
Mina I : 767-774 (Alexandria—Coptic)
Mina II : 956-974 (Alexandria—Coptic)
Minas : 1751-1753 (Armenia)
Minas : 1621-1632 (Cilicia—Armenian Apostolic)
Minas : 1749-1751 (Constantinople—Armenian)
Minas I : 270? (Ethiopia—Historical)
Minas II : 923? (Ethiopia—Historical)
Minas I : unknown (Ethiopia—Official)
Minas II : unknown (Ethiopia—Official)
Minas III : unknown (Ethiopia—Official)
Minas IV : unknown (Ethiopia—Official)
Minas V : unknown (Ethiopia—Official)
Minas I : 1191-1205 (Jerusalem—Armenian)
Minas II : 1426 [coadjutor] (Jerusalem—Armenian)
Minas III : 1697-1704 (Jerusalem—Armenian)
Miron *Nikolic* : 1914-1919 [locum tenens] (Austria—Karlovci)
Miron *Romanul* : 1874-1898 (Austria—Sibiu)
Miron *Cristea* : 1919-1939 (Romania)
Misaél *Apostolidés* : 1862 (Greece)
Misail I : 1685?-1689 (Austria—Cernovci)
Misail II : 1729-1735 (Austria—Cernovci)
Mithudiyus *of Naxos* : 1823-1850 (Antioch—Greek)
Mitrofan *Sevic* : 1908 [refused election] (Austria—Karlovci)
Mitrofan : 1550?-1552 (Austria—Cernovci)
Mitrofan : 1614-1616 (Bulgaria)
Mitrofan : 1610?-1614 (Macedonia)
Mitrofan I : 1526?-1534? (Romania)
Mitrofan II : 1716-1719 (Romania)
Mitrofan *Ban* : 1885-1920 (Serbia—Montenegro)
Mkhit'ar : 1341-1355 (Armenia)
Mkhit'ar : 1699-1700 (Constantinople—Armenian)
Mkrtich' *Khrimian* : 1892-1907 (Armenia)

Mkrtich' *K'êfsizian* : 1871-1894 (Cilicia—Armenian Apostolic)
Mkrtich' *Khrimian* : 1869-1873 (Constantinople—Armenian)
Mkrtich' I : 708-730 (Jerusalem—Armenian)
Mkrtich' II : 1363-1378 (Jerusalem—Armenian)
Mkrtich' III : 1476-1479 (Jerusalem—Armenian)
Mobidani : 436-448 (Georgia)
Modestos : 431? (Greece)
Modestos : 632-634 (Jerusalem—Greek)
Moiseî *Bogdanov-Platonov* : 1832-1834 [exarch] (Georgia)
Mojsej I *Petrovic* : 1726-1730 (Austria—Karlovci)
Mojsej II *Putnik* : 1781-1790 (Austria—Karlovci)
Mojsije *Rajovic* : 1712-1725? (Serbia)
Monachus : 1194- (Jerusalem—Latin)
Mondillus *Orsini* : 1729- (Constantinople—Latin)
Morooso : 628-649 (India—Malankara Orthodox)
Mose : 410-425 (Georgia)
Móüsés : unknown (Sinai)
Movsês I : 4th cent. (Aghunie)
Movsês II : 777-779 (Aghunie)
Movsês III : 822 (Aghunie)
Movsês IV : 992-997 (Aghunie)
Movsês I : 456-461 (Armenia)
Movsês II : 574-604 (Armenia)
Movsês III : 1629-1632 (Armenia)
Movsês : 1109-1133 (Jerusalem—Armenian)
Mstyslav *Skrypnyk* : 1969-1990 (metropolitan), 1990-1993 (patriarch) (Ukraine—Autocephalous)
Mstyslav *Skrypnyk* : 1947-1950 (Ukraine—Canada)
Mstyslav *Skrypnyk* : 1971-1993 (Ukraine—Orthodox Church of the USA)
Muron : 1436-1437 [coadjutor] (Jerusalem—Armenian)
Murqus I : 43?-68 (Alexandria—Coptic)
Murqus II : 799-819 (Alexandria—Coptic)
Murqus III *ibn Zur'a* : 1167-1189 (Alexandria—Coptic)
Murqus IV : 1349-1363 (Alexandria—Coptic)
Murqus V : 1602-1618 (Alexandria—Coptic)
Murqus VI : 1650-1660 (Alexandria—Coptic)
Murqus VII : 1745-1769 (Alexandria—Coptic)
Murqus VIII : 1796-1809 (Alexandria—Coptic)
Murqus : 1870-1874 [locum tenens] (Alexandria—Coptic)
Murqus I : 50?-68 (Alexandria—Coptic Catholic)
Murqus II *Khuzam* : 1926-1958 (Alexandria—Coptic Catholic)
Murqus I : 1308-1342 (Antioch—Greek)
Murqus II : 1426-1436 (Antioch—Greek)
Murqus III : 1462-1476 (Antioch—Greek)
Murqus I : 1377-1378 (Antioch—Greek Melkite)
Murqus II : 1425?-1434? (Antioch—Greek Melkite)
Murqus III : 1456?-1458? (Antioch—Greek Melkite)
Murqus : unknown (Antioch—Maronite)
Mushê I : 93-123 (Armenia)
Mushê II : 526-534 (Armenia)
Musi *ibn Sa'adi al-'Aquri* : 1524-1567 (Antioch—Maronite)
Mykhaïl I : 988-991 (Ukraine)
Mykhaïl II : 1130-1145 (Ukraine)
Mykhaïl III *Rohoza* : 1589-1596 (Ukraine)

Mykhaïl IV : 1921-1929 (Ukraine)
Mykhaïl *Horoshyî* : 1972-1975 (Ukraine—Canada)
Mykhaïl-Mitay : 1378?-1380? (Ukraine)
Mykolaî I : 1097-1101 (Ukraine)
Mykolaî II *IArushevych* : 1940-1944 (Ukraine)
Mykolaî II *Borets'kyî* : 1927-1930 (Ukraine—Autocephalous)
Mykolaî *Hrokh* : 1990-1991 [locum tenens] (Ukraine—Autocephalous)
Myrón *Thaumatourgos* : 249 (Crete)
Mysaïl : 1475-1480 (Ukraine)
Nahapet : 1691-1705 (Armenia)
Narkissos : 117-138 (Greece)
Narkissos : 185-211 (Jerusalem—Greece)
Narsai : 524-535 (Assyria)
Narsai : 524-537? (Babylon)
Nasr Allah Butrus *Sufayr* : 1986- (Antioch—Maronite)
Natéras : unknown (Sinai)
Nathanaél *Emporos* : 1602-1604 (Greece)
Nectarie *Cotlarciuc* : 1924-1935 (Austria—Cernovci)
Nectarie : 1812-1819 (Romania)
Neilos *Kerameus* : 1380-1388 (Constantinople—Greek)
Neilos *Kouerinos* : 1555? (Sinai)
Nektariî I : 1598-1604 (Bulgaria)
Nektariî II : 1617-1622? (Bulgaria)
Nektariî III : 1673? (Bulgaria)
Nektarij I : 1598- (Macedonia)
Nektarij II : 1616-1623? (Macedonia)
Nektarij III : 1671-1673 (Macedonia)
Nektarios : 381-397 (Constantinople—Greek)
Nektarios : 1660-1669 (Jerusalem—Greek)
Nektarios : 1660-1661 (Sinai)
Neofit : 1840?-1850?, 1856?-1857? (Bulgaria)
Neofit : 1934-1944 [locum tenens] (Bulgaria)
Neofit : 1551 (Macedonia)
Neofit I *Cretanul* : 1738-1753 (Romania)
Neofit II : 1829-1833, 1833-1840 [locum tenens], 1840-1849 (Romania)
Neophytos I *Enkleistos Klaustrarios* : 1153? (Constantinople—Greek)
Neophytos II *Karykés* : 1602-1603, 1607-1612 (Constantinople—Greek)
Neophytos III *apo Hérakleias* : 1636-1637 (Constantinople—Greek)
Neophytos IV *apo Adrianoupoleós* : 1688-1689 (Constantinople—Greek)
Neophytos V *apo Hérakleias* : 1707 [unconsecrated] (Constantinople—Greek)
Neophytos VI *apo Kaisareias Kappadokias* : 1734-1740, 1743-1744 (Constantinople—Greek)
Neophytos VII *apo Maróneias* : 1789-1794, 1798-1801 (Constantinople—Greek)
Neophytos VIII : 1891-1894 (Constantinople—Greek)
Neophytos *Patelaros* : 1645?-1679 (Crete)
Neophytos I : 1222?-1251 (Cyprus)
Neophytos II : -1592 (Cyprus)
Neophytos (III) : 1745 [anti-archbishop] (Cyprus)
Neophytos I : 1366 (Greece)
Neophytos II : 1492-1498 (Greece)
Neophytos III *Karykés* : 1597-1602 (Greece)
Neophytos IV : 1774-1776 (Greece)
Neophytos V *Metaxas apo Talantiou* : 1833-1861 (Greece)

Néphón : 1366-1385 (Alexandria—Greek)
Néphón I *apo Kyzikou* : 1310-1314 (Constantinople—Greek)
Néphón II *apo Thessalonikés* : 1486-1488, 1497-1498, 1502 (Constantinople—
  Greek)
Nersês (I) : 1312 (coadjutor) (Aght'amar)
Nersês (II) *Bolat* : 1368?-1369? [anti-catholicos] (Aght'amar)
Nersês (III) : 1393? [anti-catholicos] (Aght'amar)
Nersês (IV) *Kurdjibeguyan* : 1489? [anti-catholicos] (Aght'amar)
Nersês I : 687?-704 (Aghunie)
Nersês II : 1171? (Aghunie)
Nersês III : 1235-1262 (Aghunie)
Nersês IV : 1478-1481 (Aghunie)
Nersês V : 1706-1763 (Aghunie)
Nersês I *"The Great"* : 353-373 (Armenia)
Nersês II : 548-557 (Armenia)
Nersês III *Shinogh* : 641-661 (Armenia)
Nersês IV *Shnorhali* : 1166-1173 (Armenia)
Nersês : 1506-1507 [coadjutor] (Armenia)
Nersês V *Ashtaraketsi* : 1843-1857 (Armenia)
Nersês *Vartsapetian* : 1884 [unconsecrated] (Armenia)
Nersês : 1648-1654 (Cilicia—Armenian Apostolic)
Nersês I : 1704 (Constantinople—Armenian)
Nersês II *Vartsapetian* : 1874-1884 (Constantinople—Armenian)
Nestor : 1879-1882 (America—Orthodox Church)
Nestorios : 428-431 (Constantinople—Greek)
Netras : unknown (Sinai)
Nichifor : 1589-1592 (Romania)
Nicodim *Munteanu* : 1939 [locum tenens], 1939-1948 (Romania)
Nicolae (I) : unknown (Austria—Cernovci)
Nicolae (II) *Vasilevic* : 1691- [anti-archbishop] (Austria—Cernovci)
Nicolae *Hutovic* : 1805-1811 [locum tenens] (Austria—Sibiu)
Nicolae I *Balan* : 1920-1955 (Austria—Sibiu)
Nicolae II *Colan* : 1957-1967 (Austria—Sibiu)
Nicolae *Corneanu* : 1967 [locum tenens] (Austria—Sibiu)
Nicolae III *Mladin* : 1967-1981 (Austria—Sibiu)
Nicolaus *Tanara* : 1845-1853 (Antioch—Latin)
Nicolaus I *de Castro Arquato* : 1234-1251 (Constantinople—Latin)
Nicolaus II : 1308-1331? (Constantinople—Latin)
Nicolaus *de Hanapis* : 1288-1294 (Jerusalem—Latin)
Nicolaus I *Magnus "The Great"* : 858-867 (Rome)
Nicolaus II : 1059-1061 (Rome)
Nicolaus III *Orsini* : 1277-1280 (Rome)
Nicolaus IV *Masci* : 1288-1292 (Rome)
Nicolaus V *Rainalducci* : 1328-1330 [anti-pope] (Rome)
Nicolaus V *Parentucelli* : 1447-1455 (Rome)
Nifon I : 1503?-1505 (Romania)
Nifon II : 1849-1850 [locum tenens], 1850-1875 (Romania)
Nifont : 1303-1305 (Ukraine—Halych)
Nikanór : 1866-1869 (Alexandria—Greek)
Nikanor *Gryjic* : 1872-1874 [locum tenens] (Austria—Karlovci)
Nikanor : -1557 (Bulgaria)
Nikanór : 1570-1592 (Greece)
Nikanor : 1555?-1557 (Macedonia)
Nikanor : 1589? (Serbia)

Nikanor *Ivanovic-Njegus* : 1855-1860 (Serbia—Montenegro)
Nikanor *Burshak-Abramovych* : 1953-1969 (Ukraine—Autocephalous)
Niképhoros *Klarontzanés* : 1639-1645 (Alexandria—Greek)
Niképhoros I : 806-815 (Constantinople—Greek)
Niképhoros II *apo Ephesou* : 1260-1261 (Constantinople—Greek)
Niképhoros *Hierodiakonos* : 1586?, 1586?- [locum tenens] (Constantinople—
    Greek)
Niképhoros I : 1296? (Crete)
Niképhoros II : 1312?-1318? (Crete)
Niképhoros III *Skótakés* : 1679-1681? (Crete)
Niképhoros : 1640?-1674 (Cyprus)
Niképhoros : 1103-1121 (Greece)
Niképhoros I : 1020 (Jerusalem—Greek)
Niképhoros II : 1166-1170 (Jerusalem—Greek)
Niképhoros *Marthalés Glykys* : 1728-1747 (Sinai)
Nikétas I : 766-780 (Constantinople—Greek)
Nikétas II *Mountanés* : 1186-1189 (Constantinople—Greek)
Nikétas I : 11th cent. (Crete)
Nikétas II : 11th cent. (Crete)
Nikétas III : 1086? (Crete)
Nikétas I : 867-877 (Greece)
Nikétas II : 922-927 (Greece)
Nikétas III *Kourtés* : 1086-1103 (Greece)
Nikétas IV *Hagiotheodórités* : 1166-1175 (Greece)
Nikodémos : 1371? (Greece)
Nikodémos : 1883-1890 (Jerusalem—Greek)
Nikodim *Rotov* : 1963 (Belarus)
Nikodim : 1452? (Bulgaria and Macedonia)
Nikodim I : 1317-1324 (Serbia)
Nikodim II : 1446-1452 (Serbia)
Nikodim : -1551 (Serbia—Montenegro)
Nikodimos *Abebe* : 1988-1991 (Eritrea)
Nikoghayos : 1736-1751 (Aght'amar)
Nikoghayos : 1478-1489 (Constantinople—Armenian)
Nikolaî : 1891-1898 (America—Orthodox Church)
Nikolaî I : 1347? (Bulgaria)
Nikolaî II : 1486-1502? (Bulgaria)
Nikolaî : 1898-1905 (Finland)
Nikolaî : 1905-1906 [exarch] (Georgia)
Nikolaî I *Kassatkin* : 1880-1912 (Japan)
Nikolaî II *Ono* : 1941-1967? (Japan)
Nikolaî III *Sayama* : 1967-1970 (Japan)
Nikolaj *Dmitrijevic* : 1730-1731 [locum tenens] (Austria—Karlovci)
Nikolaj *Kocvar* : 1993- (Czechoslovakia—Slovakia)
Nikolaj I : 1345-1348? (Macedonia)
Nikolaj II : 1481?-1487? (Macedonia)
Nikolaos I : 1210-1243 (Alexandria—Greek)
Nikolaos II : 1263-1276 (Alexandria—Greek)
Nikolaos III : 1389-1398 (Alexandria—Greek)
Nikolaos IV : 1412-1417 (Alexandria—Greek)
Nikolaos V *Euangelidés* : 1936-1939 (Alexandria—Greek)
Nikolaos VI *Barelopoulos* : 1968-1986 (Alexandria—Greek)
Nikolaos I *Mystikos* : 901-907, 912-925 (Constantinople—Greek)
Nikolaos II *Chrysobergios* : 979-991 (Constantinople—Greek)

Nikolaos III *Grammatikos Kyrdiniatés* : 1084-1111 (Constantinople—Greek)
Nikolaos IV *Mouzalón* : 1147-1151 (Constantinople—Greek)
Nikolaos I : 12th cent. (Crete)
Nikolaos II : 1195?-1221? (Crete)
Nikolaos *Mouzalón* : 1110? (Cyprus)
Nikolaos *Hagiotheodórités* : 1166-1175 (Greece)
Nikolaos : 1156 (Jerusalem—Greek)
Nikoloz I : 1150-1178 (Georgia)
Nikoloz II : 1240-1280 (Georgia)
Nikoloz III : 1364-1380 (Georgia)
Nikoloz IV : 1562-1584 (Georgia)
Nikoloz V : 1584-1591 (Georgia)
Nikoloz VI : 1678-1688, 1691-1696 (Georgia)
Nikoloz VII : 1741-1744 (Georgia)
Nikoloz : 1290? (Georgia—Abkhazia)
Nikon *Sofiĭskiĭ* : 1906-1908 [exarch] (Georgia)
Nikon *de Greve* : 1960-1962 (Japan)
Nikon *Fomichev* : 1963-1966 (Latvia)
Nikon : 1652-1658 (Russia)
Nikon : 1420-1435 (Serbia)
Nikyfor I : 1103-1121 (Ukraine)
Nikyfor II : 1183-1197 (Ukraine)
Nilus : 1393-1401 (Antioch—Greek)
Ni'mat Allah, Ighnatiyus : 1557-1576 (Antioch—Syrian Catholic)
Ni'mat Allah, Ighnatiyus : 1557-1576 (Antioch—Syrian Orthodox)
Niqifurus *"The Black"* : 1084-1088 (Antioch—Greek)
Niqifurus *"The Black"* : 1090- (Antioch—Greek Melkite)
Niqula Ishai Ya'qub *Zaya* : 1838-1847 (Babylon)
Niqulawus I : 826-834 (Antioch—Greek)
Niqulawus II : 860-871, 871-879 (Antioch—Greek)
Niqulawus III *Stoudités* : 1025-1031 (Antioch—Greek)
Niqulawus I : 847-866? (Antioch—Greek Melkite)
Niqulawus II *Stoudités* : 1022-1032 (Antioch—Greek Melkite)
Niqun : 1387?-1395 (Antioch—Greek Melkite)
Niyufutus *apo Chiou* : 1674-1684 (Antioch—Greek)
Niyufutus *apo Chiou* : 1672-1682 (Antioch—Greek Melkite)
Novatianus : 251 [anti-pope] (Rome)
Nuh, Ighnatiyus : 1494-1509 (Antioch—Syrian Catholic)
Nuh, Ighnatiyus : 1493-1509 (Antioch—Syrian Orthodox)
Nuh, Ignatios Mar *of Homs* : 1490-1494 (India—Malankara Orthodox)
Nykyta : 1122-1126 (Ukraine)
Oah : 386-393 (India—Malankara Orthodox)
Odoardus *Cybò* : 1689-1700 (Constantinople—Latin)
Ok'ropir I : 980-1001 (Georgia)
Ok'ropir II : 1045-1049 (Georgia)
Olympianos : 187-198 (Constantinople—Greek)
Olympios I : 449?-451? (Cyprus)
Olympios II : 490? (Cyprus)
Olympios : 300? (Greece)
Onésimos : 54-68 (Constantinople—Greek)
Onysyfor *Petrovych-Divochka* : 1579-1589 (Ukraine)
Opizio I : 1254-1255 (Antioch—Latin)
Opizio II *Fieschi* : 1270?-1292 (Antioch—Latin)
Orestés : 983-1005 (Jerusalem—Greek)

Otto *de Sala* : 1322-1323 (Alexandria—Latin)
Ouales I : unknown (Jerusalem—Greek)
Ouales II : unknown (Jerusalem—Greek)
Ougen *Turuthi*, Baselios Mar : 1962-1964 [suffragan], 1964-1975 (India—
  Malankara Orthodox and Malankara Jacobite)
Paavali *Olmari* : 1960-1987 (Finland)
Pachómios I *apo Zichnón* : 1503-1504, 1504-1513 (Constantinople—Greek)
Pachómios II *Patestos apo Kaisareias* : 1584-1585 (Constantinople—Greek)
Pafnutiî : 1660 (Bulgaria)
Pahomie : 1504-1522 (Austria—Cernovci)
Pahomije *Gachic* : 1994- (Macedonia—Serbian Administration)
Païsi *Vodica* : 1949-1966 (Albania)
Païsiî I : 1558-1566 (Bulgaria)
Païsiî II : 1850?-1856?, 1861- (Bulgaria)
Païsios : 1671-1678 (Alexandria—Greek)
Païsios I *apo Larissés* : 1652-1653, 1654-1655 (Constantinople—Greek)
Païsios II *Kiomourtzoglous apo Nikomédeias* : 1726-1732, 1740-1743, 1744-
  1748, 1751-1752 (Constantinople—Greek)
Païsios : 1759-1761, 1761-1767 (Cyprus)
Païsios : 1645-1660 (Jerusalem—Greek)
Pajsij : 1565-1566 (Macedonia)
Pajsije I *Janjevac* : 1614-1647 (Serbia)
Pajsije II : 1757? (Serbia)
Palladiî *Raev* : 1887-1892 [exarch] (Georgia)
Palladiî *Vydybida-Rudenko* : 1954-1971 (Ukraine—Autocephalous Church in
  Exile)
Paloungerus : 1370? (Cyprus—Latin)
Panaret I : 1671 (Bulgaria)
Panaret II : 1838-1840? (Bulgaria)
Panaret : 1671 (Macedonia)
Panaretos : 1827-1840 (Cyprus)
Pant : 4th cent. (Aghunie)
Pantaleon *Giustiniani* : 1253-1286 (Constantinople—Latin)
Panteleiman *Rozhnovskiî* : 1942-1946 (Belarus)
Paonije *Komanin* : 1568-1582 (Serbia—Montenegro)
Papa *bar Gaggai* : 247-326 (Assyria)
Papa *bar Gaggai* : 300? (Babylon)
Paphnytios : 282- [anti-patriarch] (Alexandria—Greek)
Pappa : 267-336 (India—Malankara Orthodox)
P'arhên *of Ashtishat* : 348-352 (Armenia)
Partenie *Clinceni* : 1896 [locum tenens] (Romania)
Parteniî I : 1566-1567 (Bulgaria)
Parteniî II : 1677-1683 (Bulgaria)
Partenij I : 1566?-1567? (Macedonia)
Partenij II : 1679-1683 (Macedonia)
Parthenios I *Prochoros* : 1678-1688 (Alexandria—Greek)
Parthenios II *Pankóstas* : 1788-1805 (Alexandria—Greek)
Parthenios III *Koinidés* : 1987- (Alexandria—Greek)
Parthenios I *Gerón apo Naupaktou* : 1639-1644 (Constantinople—Greek)
Parthenios II *Oxys Keskinés* : 1644-1646, 1648-1651 (Constantinople—Greek)
Parthenios III *Parthenakés apo Chiou* : 1656-1657 (Constantinople—Greek)
Parthenios IV *Mogilalos Koukoumés* : 1657-1662, 1665-1667, 1671, 1675-
  1676, 1684-1685 (Constantinople—Greek)
Parthenios : 1806 [locum tenens] (Constantinople—Greek)

Parthenios : 1737-1766 (Jerusalem—Greek)
Paschalis I : 687 [anti-pope] (Rome)
Paschalis I : 817-824 (Rome)
Paschalis II : 1099-1118 (Rome)
Paschalis III *da Crema* : 1164-1168 [anti-pope] (Rome)
Paul *Menebisoglou* : 1974- [locum tenens] (Estonia)
Paulos : 537-542 (Alexandria—Greek)
Paulos I : 337?-339, 342-344, 346-351 (Constantinople—Greek)
Paulos II : 641-653 (Constantinople—Greek)
Paulos III : 688-694 (Constantinople—Greek)
Paulos IV : 780-784 (Constantinople—Greek)
Paulos I : 64? (Crete)
Paulos II : 667 (Crete)
Paulos *Gebre-Yohannes* : 1992- (Ethiopia—Historical)
Paulos *Gebre-Yohannes* : 1992- (Ethiopia—Official)
Paulose I : 537-539 (India—Malankara Orthodox)
Paulose II : 728-757 (India—Malankara Orthodox)
Paulose I *Kathanar*, Baselios Mar : 1912-1914 (India—Malankara Orthodox)
Paulose II, Baselios Mar : 1975- (India—Malankara Jacobite)
Paulose Mar Athanasios : 1917-1935 [locum tenens], 1935-1953 (India—Malankara Jacobite)
Paulose Mar Koorilose : 1911-1917 (India—Malankara Jacobite)
Paulose Mar Phileksenose III : 1967 [suffragan], 1967-1977 (India—Thozhiyoor)
Paulus I Augustus *Foscolo* : 1847-1867 (Alexandria—Latin)
Paulus II *Ballerini* : 1867-1897 (Alexandria—Latin)
Paulus III *de Huyn* : 1921-1949? (Alexandria—Latin)
Paulus *Brunoni* : 1869-1877 (Antioch—Latin)
Paulus I *Guillelmus* : 1366-1370 (Constantinople—Latin)
Paulus II : 1379?- (Constantinople—Latin)
Paulus I : 757-767 (Rome)
Paulus II *Barbo* : 1464-1471 (Rome)
Paulus III *Farnese* : 1534-1549 (Rome)
Paulus IV *Carafa* : 1555-1559 (Rome)
Paulus V *Borghese* : 1605-1621 (Rome)
Paulus VI *Montini* : 1963-1978 (Rome)
Pavel : 1867-1870 (America—Orthodox Church)
Pavel *Lebedev* : 1882-1887 [exarch] (Georgia)
Pavel : 16th cent. (Serbia—Montenegro)
Pavle *Nenadovic* : 1749-1768 (Austria—Karlovci)
Pavle I : 1530?-1541? (Serbia)
Pavle II *Stojchevic* : 1990- (Serbia)
Pelagius I : 556-561 (Rome)
Pelagius II : 579-590 (Rome)
Pertinax : 169-187 (Constantinople—Greek)
Petar *Jovanovic* : 1833-1858 (Serbia)
Petar I *Petrovic-Njegos* : 1784-1830 (Serbia—Montenegro)
Petar II *Petrovic-Njegos* : 1830-1851 (Serbia—Montenegro)
Petr : 1859-1867 (America—Orthodox Church)
Petr : 1305-1325 (Russia—Moscow)
Petr *Polianskiĭ* : 1925 [locum tenens] (Russia)
Petr I : 1308-1326 (Ukraine)
Petr II *Mohyla* : 1633-1647 (Ukraine)
Petre I : 467-474 (Georgia)

Petre II : 689-720 (Georgia)
Petro I : 1308-1326 (Ukraine)
Petros I : 1662?-1670 (Aght'amar)
Petros II *Pilpilian* : 1858-1864 (Aght'amar)
Petros I : 974-992 (Aghunie)
Petros II : 1323- (Aghunie)
Petros III : -1406 (Aghunie)
Petros IV : 1653-1675 (Aghunie)
Petros I : 300-311 (Alexandria—Greek)
Petros II : 373-381 (Alexandria—Greek)
Petros III : 631-641 (Alexandria—Greek)
Petros *Getadardz* : 1019-1058 (Armenia)
Petros *Kutur* : 1048 [locum tenens] (Armenia)
Petros I : 1601-1608 [coadjutor] (Cilicia—Armenian Apostolic)
Petros (II) : 1708-1710 [anti-catholicos] (Cilicia—Armenian Apostolic)
Petros II *Sarachian* : 1939-1941 (Cilicia—Armenian Apostolic)
Petros I *Ardzivian*, Abraham : 1740-1749 (Cilicia—Armenian Catholic)
Petros II *Hovsêp'ian*, Hakob : 1749-1753 (Cilicia—Armenian Catholic)
Petros III *Gasparian*, Mik'ayêl : 1753-1780 (Cilicia—Armenian Catholic)
Petros IV *Avkadian*, Barsegh : 1780-1788 (Cilicia—Armenian Catholic)
Petros V *Kupelian*, Grigor : 1788-1812 (Cilicia—Armenian Catholic)
Petros VI, Grigor : 1815-1841 (Cilicia—Armenian Catholic)
Petros VII *Holasian*, Hakob : 1842-1843 (Cilicia—Armenian Catholic)
Petros VIII *Astuatsaturian*, Grigor : 1844-1866 (Cilicia—Armenian Catholic)
Petros IX *Hassun*, Anton : 1866-1879 (Cilicia—Armenian Catholic)
Petros IX *Bak'darian*, Hakob : 1870-1880? [anti-catholicos] (Cilicia—Armenian Catholic)
Petros X *Azarian*, Step'anos : 1881-1899 (Cilicia—Armenian Catholic)
Petros XI *Emmanuelian*, Poghos : 1899-1904 (Cilicia—Armenian Catholic)
Petros XII *Sabbaghian*, Poghos : 1904-1910 (Cilicia—Armenian Catholic)
Petros XIII *Terzian*, Poghos : 1910-1931 (Cilicia—Armenian Catholic)
Petros XIV *Arpiarian*, Awetis : 1931-1937 (Cilicia—Armenian Catholic)
Petros XV *Aghajanian*, Grigor : 1937-1962 (Cilicia—Armenian Catholic)
Petros XVI *Batanian*, Ignatios : 1962-1976 (Cilicia—Armenian Catholic)
Petros XVII *Ghedighian*, Hemayag : 1976-1982 (Cilicia—Armenian Catholic)
Petros XVIII *Gasparian*, Hovhannês : 1982- (Cilicia—Armenian Catholic)
Petros : 654-666 (Constantinople—Greek)
Petros I *Eikonios* : 431 (Crete)
Petros II *Kolybités* : 761 (Crete)
Petros I : 923? (Ethiopia—Historical)
Petros II : 1559?-1570 (Ethiopia—Historical)
Petros III : 1600?-1607 (Ethiopia—Historical)
Petros IV : 1881-1889 (Ethiopia—Historical)
Petros I : unknown (Ethiopia—Official)
Petros II : unknown (Ethiopia—Official)
Petros III : unknown (Ethiopia—Official)
Petros IV : unknown (Ethiopia—Official)
Petros V : unknown (Ethiopia—Official)
Petros VI : 1600?-1607 (Ethiopia—Official)
Petros VII : 1881-1889 (Ethiopia—Official)
Petros I : 1461-1476 (Jerusalem—Armenian)
Petros II : 1501-1507 (Jerusalem—Armenian)
Petros III : 1794-1800 (Jerusalem—Armenian)
Petros : 524-552 (Jerusalem—Greek)

Petros : 985? (Sinai)
Petru : 1538-1550 (Austria—Sibiu)
Petru *Peduraru* : 1992- [locum tenens] (Moldova—Bessarabia)
Petrus I *Amiel de Brenac* : 1388?- (Alexandria—Latin)
Petrus II Amaury *de Lordat* : 1409? (Alexandria—Latin)
Petrus I *d'Angoulême* : 1201-1208 (Antioch—Latin)
Petrus II *d'Amalfi* : 1209-1217 (Antioch—Latin)
Petrus III *de Capoue* : 1219 (Antioch—Latin)
Petrus IV *Clasquerin* : 1375- (Antioch—Latin)
Petrus V *Villanova Castellacci* : 1879-1881 (Antioch—Latin)
Petrus I *Correr* : 1286-1302 (Constantinople—Latin)
Petrus II *de Bolonesio* : 1331?- (Constantinople—Latin)
Petrus III *Thomas* : 1364-1366 (Constantinople—Latin)
Petrus IV *Riario* : 1472-1474 (Constantinople—Latin)
Petrus I *de Plana-Cassano* : 1314-1322 (Jerusalem—Latin)
Petrus II *Nicosiensis* : 1322-1324 (Jerusalem—Latin)
Petrus III *de Palude* : 1329-1342 (Jerusalem—Latin)
Petrus : 40?-67? (Rome)
Phélix : 136-141 (Constantinople—Greek)
Philadelphos : 211-214 (Constantinople—Greek)
Phileksinose, Geevarghese Mar : 1816-1817, 1825-1829 (India—Malankara Syrian)
Phileksinose I *Kasseesa*, Skaria Mar : 1807-1808 [suffragan], 1808-1811 (India—Thozhiyoor)
Phileksinose II, Geevarghese Mar : 1811-1829 (India—Thozhiyoor)
Phileksinose III, Paulose Mar : 1967-1977 (India—Thozhiyoor)
Philipose Mar Chrysostom : unknown [suffragan] (India—Mar Thoma Syrian)
Philippos : 2nd cent. (Crete)
Philippos : 981? (Greece)
Philippos : unknown (Jerusalem—Greek)
Philippus *Anastasi* : 1724-1735 (Antioch—Latin)
Philippus Ioshua *Caucci* : 1760-1771 (Constantinople—Latin)
Philippus I *de Chambarlhac* : 1344-1360 (Cyprus—Latin)
Philippus II *Mocenigo* : 1560-1571? (Cyprus—Latin)
Philippus I *de Cabassole* : 1361-1368 (Jerusalem—Latin)
Philippus II *Camassei* : 1906-1919 (Jerusalem—Latin)
Philippus : 768 [anti-pope] (Rome)
Philotheos I : 1435-1459 (Alexandria—Greek)
Philotheos II : 1523- (Alexandria—Greek)
Philotheos *Kokkinos apo Hérakleias* : 1353-1354?, 1364-1376 (Constantinople—Greek)
Philotheos : 1734-1745, 1745-1759 (Cyprus)
Philoxenos : 510? (Cyprus)
Phlabianos : 446-449 (Constantinople—Greek)
Phótios : 1900-1925 (Alexandria—Greek)
Phótios I : 858-867, 877-886 (Constantinople—Greek)
Phótios II *Maniatés* : 1929-1935 (Constantinople—Greek)
Phótios : 544?-546? (Sinai)
Phrabitas : 489-490 (Constantinople—Greek)
P'ilippos : 1671? (Aght'amar)
P'ilippos : 1563- (Aghunie)
P'ilippos : 1632-1655 (Armenia)
P'ilippos : 1542-1550 (Jerusalem—Armenian)
Pimen *Izvekov* : 1970-1971 [locum tenens], 1971-1990 (Russia)

Pimen : 14th cent. (Ukraine)
Piruz : 880? (India—Chaldean)
Pistos : 336-338? (Alexandria—Greek—Arian)
Pistos : 325? (Greece)
Pitirim : 1672-1673 (Russia)
Pit'iun : 731-740 (Assyria and Babylon)
Pitrus Iliya XIV *Abulyunan* : 1879-1894 (Babylon)
Pius I : 140?-155? (Rome)
Pius II *Piccolomini* : 1458-1464 (Rome)
Pius III *Todeschini-Piccolomini* : 1503 (Rome)
Pius IV *de' Medici* : 1559-1565 (Rome)
Pius V *Ghislieri* : 1566-1572 (Rome)
Pius VI *Braschi* : 1775-1799 (Rome)
Pius VII *Chiaramonti* : 1800-1823 (Rome)
Pius VIII *Castiglione* : 1829-1830 (Rome)
Pius IX *Mastai-Ferretti* : 1846-1878 (Rome)
Pius X *Sarto* : 1903-1914 (Rome)
Pius XI *Ratti* : 1922-1939 (Rome)
Pius XII *Pacelli* : 1939-1958 (Rome)
Placidus *Ralli* : 1882-1884 (Antioch—Latin)
Platon *Rozhdestvenskiî* : 1907-1914, 1922-1934 (America—Orthodox Church)
Platon *Kulbusch* : 1917-1919 (Estonia)
Platon *Ciosu* : 1919 [locum tenens] (Romania)
Platon I *Malinovskiî* : 1748-1754 (Russia—Moscow)
Platon II *Levshin* : 1775-1812 (Russia—Moscow)
Ploutarchos : 89-105 (Constantinople—Greek)
Ploutarchos : 620?-625? (Cyprus)
Poghos : 1086-1087 [anti-catholicos] (Armenia)
Poghos I : 1374-1382 (Armenia)
Poghos II : 1418-1430 (Armenia)
Poghos I *Grigorian* : 1815-1823 (Constantinople—Armenian)
Poghos II *T'agt'agian* : 1863-1869 (Constantinople—Armenian)
Poghos I : 1321-1323 (Jerusalem—Armenian)
Poghos II *of Karni* : 1415-1419 (Jerusalem—Armenian)
Poghos III *of Van* : 1768-1775 (Jerusalem—Armenian)
Poghos IV : 1824-1847 [vicar general] (Jerusalem—Armenian)
Poghos Petros XI *Emmanuelian* : 1899-1904 (Cilicia—Armenian Catholic)
Poghos Petros XII *Sabbaghian* : 1904-1910 (Cilicia—Armenian Catholic)
Poghos Petros XIII *Terzian* : 1910-1931 (Cilicia—Armenian Catholic)
Politianos : 768-813 (Alexandria—Greek)
Polyeuktos : 956-970 (Constantinople—Greek)
Polykarp *Sikors'kyî* : (Ukraine—Autocephalous Church)
Polykarpos I : 71-89 (Constantinople—Greek)
Polykarpos II : 141-144 (Constantinople—Greek)
Polykarpos : 1808-1827 (Jerusalem—Greek)
Pontianus : 230-235 (Rome)
Porfiriî *Paleolog* : 1624? (Bulgaria)
Porfirij *Paleolog* : 1623-1624 (Macedonia)
Porfyryî : 1521-1522 (Russia—Moscow)
Porphyrios *Phótiadés* : 1839 (Crete)
Porphyrios I *apo Zakynthou* : 1885-1904 (Sinai)
Porphyrios II *Logothetés* : 1904-1926 (Sinai)
Porphyrios III *Paulinos* : 1926-1968 (Sinai)
Poulos *Konikara* : 1945-1952 [locum tenens] (India—Chaldean)

Pouplios : 161-180 (Greece)
Pouplios : unknown (Jerusalem—Greek)
Praulios : 417-422 (Jerusalem—Greek)
Primos : 106-118 (Alexandria—Greek)
Probos : 303-315 (Constantinople—Greek)
Procopie *Ivascovic* : 1873-1874 (Austria—Sibiu)
Prohor : 1523-1550 (Macedonia)
Prokhor : 1528?-1550 (Bulgaria)
Prokhoron : 1749 (Constantinople—Armenian)
Proklos : 434-446 (Constantinople—Greek)
Prokopije *Ivachkovic* : 1874-1880 (Austria—Karlovci)
Prokopios *apo Smyrnés* : 1785-1789 (Constantinople—Greek)
Prokopios I *Geórgiadés* : 1874-1889 (Greece)
Prokopios II *Oikonomidés* : 1896-1901 (Greece)
Prokopios I : 1787-1788 (Jerusalem—Greek)
Prokopios II : 1873-1875 (Jerusalem—Greek)
Prosperus *Rebiba* : 1573-1594 (Constantinople—Latin)
Proterios : 451-457 (Alexandria—Greek)
Pulikkottil Mar Dionysios II : 1815-1816 (India—Malankara Syrian)
Pulus : 539-540 (Assyria)
Pulus I : 537?-539? (Babylon)
Pulus II *Shaikhu* : 1958-1989 (Babylon)
Pulus : 1295? (India—Chaldean)
Pulus Shim'un XXII : 1918-1920 (Assyria)
Punnathra Mar Dionysios III *Ittoop* : 1817-1825 (India—Malankara Syrian)
Pyrrhos : 638-641, 654 (Constantinople—Greek)
Qalandiyun : 482-485 (Antioch—Syrian Orthodox)
Qalandun : 482-483 (Antioch—Syrian Catholic)
Qarabukt : 421 (Assyria)
Qarabukt : 420 (Babylon)
Qayuma : 393-399 (Assyria)
Qayuma : -399 (Babylon)
Qerlos—SEE ALSO: Gerlos
Qerlos I : 623? (Ethiopia—Historical)
Qerlos II *Abdon* : 1077- (Ethiopia—Historical)
Qerlos III : 1144? [anti-abuna] (Ethiopia—Historical)
Qerlos IV : 1260?-1273 (Ethiopia—Historical)
Qerlos V : 1815?-1828? (Ethiopia—Historical)
Qerlos VI : 1929-1936, 1941-1950 (Ethiopia—Historical)
Qerlos II : unknown (Ethiopia—Official)
Qerlos III : unknown (Ethiopia—Official)
Qerlos IV : 1815?-1828? (Ethiopia—Official)
Qerlos V : 1929-1936, 1941-1950 (Ethiopia—Official)
Qozmos I : unknown (Ethiopia—Official)
Qozmos II : unknown (Ethiopia—Official)
Quma *ibn Gafil*, Ighnatiyus : 1446-1455 (Antioch—Syrian Orthodox—Tur Ab-
    hdin)
Quom Yesu : 578-579 (India—Malankara Orthodox)
Quoyumo : 370-375 (India—Malankara Orthodox)
Qurillus : 283-299 (Antioch—Syrian Catholic)
Qurillus : 283-303 (Antioch—Syrian Orthodox)
Quriyaqus : 793-817 (Antioch—Syrian Catholic)
Quriyaqus : 793-817 (Antioch—Syrian Orthodox)
Qurnil : 127-154 (Antioch—Syrian Catholic)

Sabrishu' II : 832-836 (Assyria)
Sabrishu' III *bar Zanbur* : 1057-1072 (Assyria)
Sabrishu' IV *bar Qayyuma* : 1222-1226 (Assyria)
Sabrishu' V *bar Masikh* : 1226-1256 (Assyria)
Sabrishu' I *Garmaqaya* : 596-604 (Babylon)
Sabrishu' II : 831-835 (Babylon)
Sabrishu' III *bar Zanbur* : 1064-1072 (Babylon)
Sabrishu' IV *bar Qayyuma* : 1222-1224 (Babylon)
Sabrishu' V *bar Masikh* : 1226-1256 (Babylon)
Sabrishu' : 880? (India—Chaldean)
Sahak (I) *Artskets'i* : 1698 (Aght'amar)
Sahak (II) : 1736 [anti-catholicos] (Aght'amar)
Sahak I : 4th cent. (Aghunie)
Sahak II : 929-947 (Aghunie)
Sahak I *Part'e "The Great"* : 387-436 (Armenia)
Sahak II : 534-539 (Armenia)
Sahak III : 677-703 (Armenia)
Sahak : 1624-1629? [coadjutor] (Armenia)
Sahak *Ahagwin* : 1755-1760 [unconsecrated] (Armenia)
Sahak I *Mêykhachêchi* : 1674-1686 (Cilicia—Armenian Apostolic)
Sahak II *Khapayan* : 1902-1939 (Cilicia—Armenian Apostolic)
Sahak : 1707, 1708-1714 (Constantinople—Armenian)
Sahak I : 1152-1180 (Jerusalem—Armenian)
Sahak II : 1707, 1708-1714 (Jerusalem—Armenian)
Sahan *Sivakian* : 1990 [locum tenens] (Constantinople—Armenian)
Salama I *Fremenatos* : 245? (Ethiopia—Historical)
Salama II : 870? (Ethiopia—Historical)
Salama III : 1285? (Ethiopia—Historical)
Salama IV : 1348-1388 (Ethiopia—Historical)
Salama V : 1762-1770? (Ethiopia—Historical)
Salama VI : 1841-1867 (Ethiopia—Historical)
Salama I *Fremenatos* : 245? (Ethiopia—Official)
Salama II *Minas* : unknown (Ethiopia—Official)
Salama III : unknown (Ethiopia—Official)
Salama IV *Andreyas* : 1841-1867 (Ethiopia—Official)
Salloustios : 486-494 (Jerusalem—Greek)
Samoel I : 474-502 (Georgia)
Samoel II : 544-553 (Georgia)
Samoel III : 575-582 (Georgia)
Samoel IV : 582-591 (Georgia)
Samoel V : 634-640 (Georgia)
Samoel VI : 670-677 (Georgia)
Samoel VII : 780-790 (Georgia)
Samoel VIII : 814-826 (Georgia)
Samouél *Kapasoulés* : 1710-1723 (Alexandria—Greek)
Samouél *Chantzerés apo Derkón* : 1763-1768, 1773-1774 (Constantinople—Greek)
Samouél *Primpetos* : 1602 (Greece)
Samuêl : 874-891 (Aghunie)
Samuêl : 516-526 (Armenia)
Samu'el : 1223? (Ethiopia—Historical)
Samuel : 614-624 (India—Malankara Orthodox)
Samuïl *Myslavs'kyî* : 1783-1796 (Ukraine)

316

Samuïlo *Mashirevic* : 1861-1864 [locum tenens], 1864-1870 (Austria—Karlovci)
Sanutiyus—SEE ALSO: Shanudah
Sanutiyus I : 858-880 (Alexandria—Coptic)
Sanutiyus II : 1032-1046 (Alexandria—Coptic)
Sargis I : 1521-1555 (Aghunie)
Sargis II *Hassan-Jalaliants'* : 1794-1815 (Aghunie)
Sargis I : 992-1019 (Armenia)
Sargis (II) : 1076-1077 [anti-catholicos] (Armenia)
Sargis II *Ajatar* : 1469-1474 (Armenia)
Sargis III *Miwsayl* : 1484-1515 (Armenia)
Sargis IV : 1520-1536 (Armenia)
Sargis *Subaya* : 860-872 (Assyria and Babylon)
Sargis I : 1587-1590 (Constantinople—Armenian)
Sargis II : 1592-1596 (Constantinople—Armenian)
Sargis III : 1664-1665, 1667-1670 (Constantinople—Armenian)
Sargis IV : 1679-1680 (Constantinople—Armenian)
Sargis V *Guyumchian* : 1860-1861 (Constantinople—Armenian)
Sargis : 872-883 (India—Malankara Orthodox)
Sargis I : 1281-1313 (Jerusalem—Armenian)
Sargis II : 1394-1415 (Jerusalem—Armenian)
Sargis III : 1507-1517 (Jerusalem—Armenian)
Sarkis *al-Ruzzi* : 1581-1596 (Antioch—Maronite)
Sarmeane : 767-774 (Georgia)
Sava I : unknown (Austria—Cernovci)
Sava II : 1656-1658 (Austria—Cernovci)
Sava I : 1559- , 1562-1570 (Austria—Sibiu)
Sava II *Brancovic* : 1656, 1662-1680 (Austria—Sibiu)
Sava III : 1684-1685 (Austria—Sibiu)
Sava I *Nemanjic* : 1219-1233 (Serbia)
Sava II *Nemanjic* : 1263-1271 (Serbia)
Sava III : 1309-1316 (Serbia)
Sava IV : 1354-1375 (Serbia)
Sava V : 1389-1404 (Serbia)
Sava I *Kalugericic* : 1695-1697 (Serbia—Montenegro)
Sava II *Petrovic-Njegos* : 1719-1735 [coadjutor], 1735-1750, 1766-1767, 1773-1781 (Serbia—Montenegro)
Savatije *Sokolovic* : 1587 (Serbia)
Sawira I *al-Antakhah* : 512-518 (Antioch—Syrian Catholic)
Sawira II *ibn Mashqa* : 667-680 (Antioch—Syrian Catholic)
Sawiriyus I *al-Antakhah* : 512-538 (Antioch—Syrian Orthodox)
Sawiriyus II *ibn Mashqa* : 667-683 (Antioch—Syrian Orthodox)
Sawiros : 1078? (Ethiopia—Historical)
Scipio *Rebiba* : 1565-1573 (Constantinople—Latin)
Sebastian *Rusan* : 1948-1950 [titular] (Austria—Cernovci)
Sebastianus : 1495? (Antioch—Latin)
Sebastianus *Priuli* : 1496-1498? (Cyprus—Latin)
Sedekión : 105-114 (Constantinople—Greek)
Se'la Krestos : 1617?-1633 (Ethiopia—Official)
Se'la Krestos : 1617?-1633? [anti-abuna] (Ethiopia—Official)
Sem'on : 1600?-1617 (Ethiopia—Historical)
Sem'on I : unknown (Ethiopia—Official)
Sem'on II : unknown (Ethiopia—Official)
Sem'on III : unknown (Ethiopia—Official)

Sem'on IV : unknown (Ethiopia—Official)
Sem'on V : 1600?-1617 (Ethiopia—Official)
Senekas : 2nd cent. (Jerusalem—Greek)
Serafim : 1667-1669, 1671-1685? (Austria—Cernovci)
Serafim : 1576-1585 (Romania)
Serafim *Glagolevskiĭ* : 1819-1821 (Russia—Moscow)
Serapheim I *apo Nikomédeias* : 1733-1734 (Constantinople—Greek)
Serapheim II *apo Philippoupoleós* : 1757-1761 (Constantinople—Greek)
Serapheim *Tikas* : 1974- (Greece)
Seraphim *Lukianov* : 1918-1924 (Finland)
Seraphinus Oliverus *Razalio* : 1602? (Alexandria—Latin)
Serapion *Fadeev* : 1986-1989 (Moldova)
Serapion *Aleksandrovych* : 1803-1822 (Ukraine)
Sergej : 1241? (Macedonia)
Sergi *Stragorodskiĭ* : 1906-1917 (Finland)
Sergiĭ *Petrov* : 1963-1965 (Belarus)
Sergiĭ I : 925? (Bulgaria)
Sergiĭ II : 1250? (Bulgaria)
Sergiĭ *Tykhomirov* : 1912-1940 (Japan)
Sergiĭ *Liapidevskiĭ* : 1893-1898 (Russia—Moscow)
Sergiĭ *Stragorodskiĭ* : 1925-1937 [deputy locum tenens], 1937-1943 [locum
    tenens], 1943-1944 (Russia)
Sergios I : 610-638 (Constantinople—Greek)
Sergios II : 1001-1019 (Constantinople—Greek)
Sergios : 643? (Cyprus)
Sergios I : 842-844 (Jerusalem—Greek)
Sergios II : 908-911 (Jerusalem—Greek)
Sergius *Samon* : 1973-1974 [unconsecrated] (Estonia)
Sergius I : 687-701 (Rome)
Sergius II : 844-847 (Rome)
Sergius III : 904-911 (Rome)
Sergius IV : 1009-1012 (Rome)
Severinus : 640 (Rome)
Shaba *Arbaya*, Ighnatiyus : 1488- [anti-patriarch] (Antioch—Syrian Ortho-
    dox—Tur Abhdin)
Shahak : 352-353, 359-363 [locum tenens], 373-377 (Armenia)
Shahdust : 345-347 (Assyria)
Shahdust : 341?-342 (Babylon)
Shahên : 124-150 (Armenia)
Shahluppa : 246-266 (India—Malankara Orthodox)
Shahoudoth : 350-352 (India—Malankara Orthodox)
Shakhlupa *of Kashkar* : 224-244 (Assyria)
Shakhlupa *of Kashkar* : 3rd cent. (Babylon)
Shakrulla, Baselios Mar : 1751-1764 (India—Malankara Orthodox)
Shanudah—SEE ALSO: Sanutiyus
Shanudah III *Gayid Rafail* : 1971- (Alexandria—Coptic)
Sharbeel : 794-810 (India—Malankara Orthodox)
Shawarsh : 151-171 (Armenia)
Shihab, Ighnatiyus : 1366-1381 (Antioch—Syrian Catholic)
Shihab, Ighnatiyus : 1365-1381 (Antioch—Syrian Orthodox)
Shila : 505-523 (Assyria)
Shila : 505-522? (Babylon)
Shilo : 502-504 (India—Malankara Orthodox)
Shim'un—SEE ALSO: Sim'an

Shim'un I *of Tur-Abdin*, Ighnatiyus : 1640-1659 (Antioch—Syrian Catholic)
Shim'un *of Tur-Abdin*, Ighnatiyus : 1640-1659 (Antioch—Syrian Orthodox)
Shim'un I *Kipa* : 33 (Assyria)
Shim'un II *bar Sabba'i* : 328-341 (Assyria)
Shim'un III : 1369-1392 (Assyria)
Shim'un IV : 1403-1407 (Assyria)
Shim'un V : 1420-1447 (Assyria)
Shim'un VI *d'Bat' Sadi* : 1448-1490 (Assyria)
Shim'un VII : 1505-1538 (Assyria)
Shim'un VIII *bar Mama*, Ishu'yabh : 1538-1551 (Assyria)
Shim'un IX *bar Mama*, Dinkha : 1552-1558 (Assyria)
Shim'un X, Yabhalaha : 1558-1580 (Assyria)
Shim'un XI, Dinkha : 1580-1600 (Assyria)
Shim'un XII, Iliya : 1600-1653 (Assyria)
Shim'un XIII, Ishu'yabh : 1653-1690 (Assyria)
Shim'un XIV, Yabhalaha : 1690-1692 (Assyria)
Shim'un XV, Dinkha : 1692-1700 (Assyria)
Shim'un XVI, Shlimun : 1700-1740? (Assyria)
Shim'un XVII, Mikha'il *Mukhatas* : 1740?-1780? (Assyria)
Shim'un XVIII, Yunan : 1780?-1820? (Assyria)
Shim'un XIX, Abraham : 1820?-1860? (Assyria)
Shim'un XX, Rubil : 1860-1903 (Assyria)
Shim'un XXI, Binyamin : 1903-1918 (Assyria)
Shim'un XXII, Pulus : 1918-1920 (Assyria)
Shim'un XXIII, Ishai : 1920-1975 (Assyria)
Shim'un I *bar Sabba'i* : -341 (Babylon)
Shim'un II : 1364- (Babylon)
Shim'un III : 1400? (Babylon)
Shim'un IV *d'Bat' Sadi* : 1437-1497 (Babylon)
Shim'un V : 1497-1502? (Babylon)
Shim'un VI : 1504-1538 (Babylon)
Shim'un VII *bar Mama*, Ishu'yabh : 1538-1551 (Babylon)
Shim'un VIII *bar Mama*, Dinkha : 1551-1558 (Babylon)
Shim'un IX *Sulaqa*, Yukhannan : 1551-1555 [rival patriarch] (Babylon)
Shim'un Iliya VII *bar Mama* : 1576-1591 (Babylon)
Shim'un Iliya IX *bar Mama* : 1617-1660 (Babylon)
Shio I : 1356-1364 (Georgia)
Shio II : 1440-1443 (Georgia)
Shlimun Shim'un XVI : 1700-1740? (Assyria)
Shmuel : 432-437 [anti-catholicos] (Armenia)
Shnorhk' *Galustian* : 1961-1990 (Constantinople—Armenian)
Shukr Allah I, Ighnatiyus : 1640- (Antioch—Syrian Catholic)
Shukr Allah II, Ighnatiyus : 1723-1745 (Antioch—Syrian Catholic)
Shukr Allah, Ighnatiyus : 1723-1745 (Antioch—Syrian Orthodox)
Shup'aghishoy : 500- (Aghunie)
Silbestros : 1569-1590 (Alexandria—Greek)
Silbestros : 1718-1733 (Cyprus)
Silfistrus *of Cyprus* : 1724-1766 (Antioch—Greek)
Silouanos : 1465? (Sinai)
Silverius : 536-537 (Rome)
Silvestru *Moraru-Andrievic* : 1880-1895 (Austria—Cernovci)
Silvius *Savelli* : 1594-1596 (Constantinople—Latin)
Sim'an—SEE ALSO: Shim'un
Sim'an I : 834-840 (Antioch—Greek)

Sim'an II *ibn Abu Sa'ib* : 1245-1260 (Antioch—Greek)
Sim'an I *ibn Zarnaq* : 892-907 (Antioch—Greek Melkite)
Sim'an II *ibn Abu Sa'ib* : 1206?-1235? (Antioch—Greek Melkite)
Sim'an I : unknown (Antioch—Maronite)
Sim'an II : unknown (Antioch—Maronite)
Sim'an III : unknown (Antioch—Maronite)
Sim'an IV : 1244?-1268? (Antioch—Maronite)
Sim'an V : 1300?-1322? (Antioch—Maronite)
Sim'an VI *ibn Dawud al-Hadathi* : 1492-1524 (Antioch—Maronite)
Sim'an VII Butrus *Awwad* : 1743-1756 (Antioch—Maronite)
Sim'an II *Hindi Zora*, Ighnatiyus : 1814-1818 (Antioch—Syrian Catholic)
Simawun I : 689-701 (Alexandria—Coptic)
Simawun II : 830 (Alexandria—Coptic)
Simêon I : 704-706 (Aghunie)
Simêon II : 902-923 (Aghunie)
Simêon III : 1596- (Aghunie)
Simêon IV : 1675-1701 [anti-patriarch] (Aghunie)
Simêon V : 1794-1810 (Aghunie)
Simêon : 1763-1780 (Armenia)
Simeon I : 1346? (Bulgaria)
Simeon II : 1550 (Bulgaria)
Simêon I : 1539-1545 (Cilicia—Armenian Apostolic)
Simêon II : 1633-1648 (Cilicia—Armenian Apostolic)
Simêon I : 1090-1109 (Jerusalem—Armenian)
Simêon II : 1688-1691 [coadjutor] (Jerusalem—Armenian)
Simeon I : 1550 (Macedonia)
Simeon II : 1634- (Macedonia)
Simeon : 1496-1511 (Russia—Moscow)
Simeon : 1528-1532? (Serbia)
Simion *Stefan* : 1643-1656 (Austria—Sibiu)
Simon *de Cramaud* : 1391? (Alexandria—Latin)
Simon : 1227-1232 (Constantinople—Latin)
Simun I *Bar Sheba* : 337-350 (India—Malankara Orthodox)
Simun II : 812-828 (India—Malankara Orthodox)
Simplicius : 468-483 (Rome)
Sinoda : 1671?-1693? (Ethiopia—Historical)
Sinoda : 1671?-1693? (Ethiopia—Official)
Sion : 767-775 (Armenia)
Sirabiyun : 191-212 (Antioch—Greek)
Sirabiyun : 191-212 (Antioch—Greek Melkite)
Sirabiyun : 190-211 (Antioch—Syrian Catholic)
Sirabiyun : 190-211 (Antioch—Syrian Orthodox)
Sirafim *of Constantinople* : 1813-1823 (Antioch—Greek)
Siricius : 384-399 (Rome)
Sirjiyus *of Tella* : 544-547 (Antioch—Syrian Orthodox)
Sirkis *of Tella* : 539-541 (Antioch—Syrian Catholic)
Sisinnios I : 426-427 (Constantinople—Greek)
Sisinnios II : 996-998 (Constantinople—Greek)
Sisinnius : 708 (Rome)
Sixtus I : 115?-125? (Rome)
Sixtus II : 257-258 (Rome)
Sixtus III : 432-440 (Rome)
Sixtus IV *della Rovere* : 1471-1484 (Rome)
Sixtus V *Peretti* : 1585-1590 (Rome)

Step'anos II : -1272 (Aght'amar)
Step'anos III *Sefedinian* : 1272-1296? (Aght'amar)
Step'anos (IV) *Tghay* : 1288-1292 [anti-catholicos?] (Aght'amar)
Step'anos IV *Ardzruni* : 1336?-1346 (Aght'amar)
Step'anos V *Kurdjibeguyan* : 1464-1489 (Aght'amar)
Step'anos VI : 1612? [anti-catholicos] (Aght'amar)
Step'anos VI : 1671? (Aght'amar)
Step'anos I : 1077-1103 (Aghunie)
Step'anos II : 1130-1132 (Aghunie)
Step'anos III : 1155?-1195 (Aghunie)
Step'anos IV : 1262-1323 (Aghunie)
Step'anos I : 788-790 (Armenia)
Step'anos II *Rshtuni* : 929-930 (Armenia)
Step'anos III : 969-972 (Armenia)
Step'anos IV : 1290-1293 (Armenia)
Step'anos V : 1545-1567 (Armenia)
Step'anos : 1567- [coadjutor] (Armenia)
Step'anos : 1477?-1483 (Cilicia—Armenian Apostolic)
Step'anos I : 1550-1561 (Constantinople—Armenian)
Step'anos II : 1670-1674 (Constantinople—Armenian)
Step'anos III *Zak'arian* : 1831-1839, 1840-1841 (Constantinople—Armenian)
Step'anos : 758-774 (Jerusalem—Armenian)
Step'anos Petros X *Azarian* : 1881-1899 (Cilicia—Armenian Catholic)
Stephanos I : 886-893 (Constantinople—Greek)
Stephanos II *apo Amaseias* : 925-927 (Constantinople—Greek)
Stephanos : 1027?-1030? (Crete)
Stephanus I : 1339-1345 (Constantinople—Latin)
Stephanus II : 1346 (Constantinople—Latin)
Stephanus III *Ugolini* : 1667-1670 (Constantinople—Latin)
Stephanus *de Carrare* : 1406-1412 (Cyprus—Latin)
Stephanus : 1128-1130 (Jerusalem—Latin)
Stephanus I : 254-257 (Rome)
Stephanus (II) : 752 [unconsecrated] (Rome)
Stephanus II : 752-757 (Rome)
Stephanus III : 768-772 (Rome)
Stephanus IV : 816-817 (Rome)
Stephanus V : 885-891 (Rome)
Stephanus VI : 896-897 (Rome)
Stephanus VII : 928-931 (Rome)
Stephanus VIII : 939-942 (Rome)
Stephanus IX : 1057-1058 (Rome)
Stevan I *Metohijac* : 1708-1709 (Austria—Karlovci)
Stevan II *Stratimirovic* : 1790-1836 (Austria—Karlovci)
Stevan III *Stankovic* : 1837-1841 (Austria—Karlovci)
Subrus *al-Antakhah* : 512-518 (Antioch—Greek and Antioch—Greek Melkite)
Sufruniyus : 1335? (Antioch—Greek Melkite)
Suk'ias : 1323- (Aghunie)
Sulpitius : 1191- (Jerusalem—Latin)
Suntyos : unknown (Ethiopia—Official)
Surin : 752-754 (Assyria)
Surin : 754 (Babylon)
Surmak : 428-429, 437-444 [anti-catholicos] (Armenia)
Svimeon—SEE ALSO: Svimon
Svimeon I : 400-410 (Georgia)

Svimeon IV : 1142-1146 (Georgia)
Svimon—SEE ALSO: Svimeon
Svimon II : 569-575 (Georgia)
Svimon III : 1001-1012 (Georgia)
Svimon V : 1547-1550 (Georgia)
Svimon : 1660-1666 (Georgia—Abkhazia)
Svimon Petre : 595-610 (Georgia)
Sylvester I : 314-335 (Rome)
Sylvester II : 999-1003 (Rome)
Sylvester III *of Sabina* : 1045 (Rome)
Sylvester IV : 1105-1111 [anti-pope] (Rome)
Syl'vestr I *Belkvych* : 1556-1567
Syl'vestr II *Kosiv* : 1647-1653 (Ukraine)
Symeón *Trapezountios* : 1466?-1467, 1471-1475, 1482-1486 (Constantinople—
    Greek)
Symeón : 1218?-1220 (Cyprus)
Symeón I *Kleópa* : 62?-107? (Jerusalem—Greek)
Symeón II : 1084-1098 (Jerusalem—Greek)
Symeón I : 1003-1035 (Sinai)
Symeón II : 1203-1223 (Sinai)
Symeón III : 1258? (Sinai)
Symeón IV : 1306-1324 (Sinai)
Symeon : 1480-1488 (Ukraine)
Symmachos : 2nd cent. (Jerusalem—Greek)
Symmachus : 498-514 (Rome)
Syrhiey *Okhotsenko* : 1948-1971 (Belarus)
T'abori : 629-634 (Georgia)
T'addai—SEE ALSO: Addai
T'addai I *Shlikha* : 33-45 (Assyria)
T'adêos : 43-66 (Armenia)
T'adêos : 1499-1504 [coadjutor] (Armenia)
T'adêos : 1577- [coadjutor] (Armenia)
Tadewos *Biwonegin* : 1985-1988 (Eritrea)
Takla Haymanot I : 1280 (Ethiopia—Historical)
Takla Haymanot II *Wolde Mika'el* : 1976-1988 (Ethiopia—Historical)
Takla Haymanot I : unknown (Ethiopia—Official)
Takla Haymanot II *Wolde Mika'el* : 1976-1988 (Ethiopia—Official)
T'alale : 720-731 (Georgia)
Tarasios : 784-806 (Constantinople—Greek)
T'avp'ech'agh I : 510-516 (Georgia)
T'avp'ech'agh II : 649-664 (Georgia)
Telesphorus : 125?-136? (Rome)
Teoctist *Blajevic* : 1877-1879 (Austria—Cernovci)
Teoctist : 1606-1622 (Austria—Sibiu)
Teoctist *Arapasu* : 1980-1982 [locum tenens] (Austria—Sibiu)
Teoctist *Arapasu* : 1986- (Romania)
Teodor I : 15th cent. (Romania)
Teodor II : 1521?-1523 (Romania)
T'eodore I : 685-689 (Georgia)
T'eodore II : 1186-1206 (Georgia)
T'eodore III : 1430-1435 (Georgia)
T'êodoros : 1792-1794 (Aght'amar)
T'êodoros : 782-786 (Aghunie)
T'êodoros I *Rshtuni* : 930-941 (Armenia)

T'êodoros (II) *Alakhosik* : 1077-1090 [anti-catholicos] (Armenia)
T'êodoros II : 1382-1392 (Armenia)
T'êodoros I *of Khorên* : 1752-1761 (Jerusalem—Armenian)
T'êodoros II *of Van* : 1800-1818 (Jerusalem—Armenian)
Teodosie I : 1530-1550? (Austria—Cernovci)
Teodosie II *Barbovschi* : 1598-1600, 1600-1605 (Austria—Cernovci)
Teodosie III : 1669?-1671 (Austria—Cernovci)
Teodosie : 1668-1672, 1679-1708 (Romania)
Teodosie *Atanasiu* : 1911-1912 [locum tenens] (Romania)
Teodosiî I : 1337? (Bulgaria)
Teodosiî II : 1363? (Bulgaria)
Teodosije I : 1520? (Serbia)
Teodosije II *Mraovic* : 1883-1889 (Serbia)
Teodul I *apo Mókiou* : 1056?-1065 (Bulgaria)
Teodul II : 1588-1590 (Bulgaria)
Teodul I *apo Mókiou* : 1056-1065 (Macedonia)
Teodul II : 1588 (Macedonia)
Teofan I : 1528-1530 (Austria—Cernovci)
Teofan II : 1646?-1651 (Austria—Cernovci)
Teofan III : 1658-1666 (Austria—Cernovci)
Teofan *Zhivkovic* : 1880 [locum tenens], 1881 [unconsecrated] (Austria—Karlovci)
Teofan : 1676 (Bulgaria)
Teofan : 1675?-1676 (Macedonia)
Teofan I : 1446 (Serbia)
Teofan II : 1544? (Serbia)
Teofil *Bendela* : 1873-1875 (Austria—Cernovci)
Teofil : 1692-1697 (Austria—Sibiu)
Teofil : 1636-1648 (Romania)
Teofilakt *ex Euripou* : 1085?-1108? (Bulgaria)
Teofilakt *ex Euripou* : 1081-1112? (Macedonia)
Terrius : 1206-1211 (Cyprus—Latin)
Tewoflos *Melaktu* : 1971-1976 (Ethiopia—Historical)
Tewoflos *Melaktu* : 1971-1976 (Ethiopia—Official)
Thaddaios : 1298 (Jerusalem—Greek)
Thawdurus : 731-743 (Alexandria—Coptic)
Thawdurus *Abu Karim* : 1832-1854 (Alexandria—Coptic Catholic)
Thawdusiyus I : 535-567 (Alexandria—Coptic)
Thawdusiyus II : 1294-1300 (Alexandria—Coptic)
Thawdusiyus : 887-896 (Antioch—Syrian Orthodox)
Thawdutus : 417?-428 (Antioch—Syrian Orthodox)
Thawfaniyus : 952-956 (Alexandria—Coptic)
Thawfilus : 385-412 (Alexandria—Coptic)
Thawfilus : 384-412 (Alexandria—Coptic Catholic)
Thawfilus : 169-182 (Antioch—Syrian Orthodox)
Thawna : 282-300 (Alexandria—Coptic)
Thawna : 282-300 (Alexandria—Coptic Catholic)
Theocharistos : 694-702 (Greece)
Theodégios : 985-1007 (Greece)
Theodoricus : 1100 [anti-pope] (Rome)
Theodóros : 700? (Alexandria—Coptic—Gaianite)
Theodóros *Skribón* : 608-610 (Alexandria—Greek)
Theodóros I : 677-679, 686-687 (Constantinople—Greek)
Theodóros II *Eirénikos Kópas* : 1214-1216 (Constantinople—Greek)

Theodóros : 553 (Crete)
Theodóros : 431? [anti-archbishop] (Cyprus)
Theodóros : 1438-1453? (Greece)
Theodóros : 735-770 (Jerusalem—Greek)
Theodóros : 649?-680? (Sinai)
Theodorus I : 642-649 (Rome)
Theodorus II : 687 [anti-pope] (Rome)
Theodorus II : 897 (Rome)
Theodosios : 1100?- (Alexandria—Greek)
Theodosios I *Borrhadiotés* : 1179-1183 (Constantinople—Greek)
Theodosios II *Maridakés apo Thessalonikés* : 1769-1773 (Constantinople—Greek)
Theodosios I : 800? (Greece)
Theodosios II : 820? (Greece)
Theodosios : 862-878 (Jerusalem—Greek)
Theodosios : 1239? (Sinai)
Theodosius *Lazor* : 1977- (America—Orthodox Church)
Theodosius *Nagashima* : 1972- (Japan)
Theodotos I *Kassitéras Melissénos* : 815-821 (Constantinople—Greek)
Theodotos II : 1151?-1153? (Constantinople—Greek)
Theoklétos I *Ménopoulos* : 1902-1917, 1920-1922 (Greece)
Theoklétos II *Panagiótopoulos* : 1957-1962 (Greece)
Theoleptos I *apo Ióanninón* : 1513-1522 (Constantinople—Greek)
Theoleptos II *apo Philippoupoleós* : 1585-1586? (Constantinople—Greek)
Theónas : 282-300 (Alexandria—Greek)
Theophanés I *Karykés* : 1596-1597 (Constantinople—Greek)
Theophanés II *apo Melekinou* : 1657 (Constantinople—Greek)
Theophanés I : 1458? (Greece)
Theophanés II *Karykés* : 1592-1597 (Greece)
Theophanés III : 1620-1633 (Greece)
Theophanés I : 1424-1431 (Jerusalem—Greek)
Theophanés II : 1450-1452 (Jerusalem—Greek)
Theophanés III : 1608-1644 (Jerusalem—Greek)
Theophilos I : 385-412 (Alexandria—Greek)
Theophilos II : 1010-1020 (Alexandria—Greek)
Theophilos III *Pankóstas* : 1805-1825 (Alexandria—Greek)
Theophilos *Blachopapadopoulos* : 1862-1873 (Greece)
Theophilos I : 1012-1020 (Jerusalem—Greek)
Theophilos II : 1417-1424 (Jerusalem—Greek)
Theophilus *Pashkovskiĭ* : 1934-1950 (America—Orthodox Church)
Theophylaktos *Lekapénos* : 933-956 (Constantinople—Greek)
Theophylaktos : 1140? (Greece)
Thiyudhurus I : 767-787 (Antioch—Greek)
Thiyudhurus II : 966-977 (Antioch—Greek)
Thiyudhurus III *Laskaris* : 1034-1042 (Antioch—Greek)
Thiyudhurus IV *Balsamón* : 1185-1199 (Antioch—Greek)
Thiyudur : 649-667 (Antioch—Syrian Catholic)
Thiyuduritus : 787? (Antioch—Greek Melkite)
Thiyudurus I : 970-976 (Antioch—Greek Melkite)
Thiyudurus II *Laskaris* : 1033-1041 (Antioch—Greek Melkite)
Thiyudurus III *Balsamón* : 1185?-1195? (Antioch—Greek Melkite)
Thiyudusiyus I : 852-860 (Antioch—Greek)
Thiyudusiyus II *Chrysobergés* : 1075-1084 (Antioch—Greek)
Thiyudusiyus III : 1180-1182 (Antioch—Greek)

Thiyudusiyus IV : 1269-1276 (Antioch—Greek)
Thiyudusiyus V *de Villehardouin* : 1276-1285 (Antioch—Greek)
Thiyudusiyus VI *Abu Rajaili* : 1958-1970 (Antioch—Greek)
Thiyudusiyus I : 870-890 (Antioch—Greek Melkite)
Thiyudusiyus II : 936-943 (Antioch—Greek Melkite)
Thiyudusiyus III *Chrysobergés* : 1057?- (Antioch—Greek Melkite)
Thiyudusiyus IV *de Villehardouin* : 1275-1284? (Antioch—Greek Melkite)
Thiyudusiyus V *Dahan* : 1761-1788 (Antioch—Greek Melkite)
Thiyudusiyus : 887-895 (Antioch—Greek Melkite)
Thiyudusiyus : 887-895 (Antioch—Syrian Catholic)
Thiyudusiyus : 649-667 (Antioch—Syrian Orthodox)
Thiyudut : 424-427 (Antioch—Syrian Catholic)
Thiyudutus : 424-428 (Antioch—Greek)
Thiyudutus : 417-429? (Antioch—Greek Melkite)
Thiyufanis : 681-687 (Antioch—Greek)
Thiyufanis : 681-683? (Antioch—Greek Melkite)
Thiyufilaktus *ibn Qanbara* : 748- (Antioch—Greek)
Thiyufilaktus *ibn Qanbara* : 745?-768? (Antioch—Greek Melkite)
Thiyufilus : 169-188 (Antioch—Greek)
Thiyufilus : 170?-182 (Antioch—Greek Melkite)
Thiyufilus : 170-172 (Antioch—Syrian Catholic)
Thiyukharistus : 944-948 (Antioch—Greek Melkite)
Thoma—SEE ALSO: Thomas, T'uma
Thoma II *of Tigris* : 848-856 (India—Malankara Orthodox)
Thoma III *Asthunoro* : 912-913 (India—Malankara Orthodox)
Thoma I *Pakalomarram*, Mar : 1652-1670 (India—Malankara Syrian)
Thoma II, Mar : 1670-1686 (India—Malankara Syrian)
Thoma, Mar : 1674 (India—Malankara Syrian)
Thoma III, Mar : 1686-1688 (India—Malankara Syrian)
Thoma IV, Mar : 1688-1728 (India—Malankara Syrian)
Thoma V, Mar : 1728-1765 (India—Malankara Syrian)
Thoma VI, Mar : 1761-1765 [suffragan], 1765-1808 (India—Malankara Syrian)
Thoma VII, Mathew Mar : 1796 [suffragan], 1796-1809 (India—Malankara Syrian)
Thoma VIII, Mar : 1806-1816 (India—Malankara Syrian)
Thoma IX, Mar : 1816 (India—Malankara Syrian)
Thoma (IV) *Rocos* : 1861-1862 (India—Chaldean)
Thoma (V) *Darmo* : 1952-1968 (India—Chaldean)
Thomas—SEE ALSO: Thoma
Thómas I : 607-610 (Constantinople—Greek)
Thómas II : 667-669 (Constantinople—Greek)
Thomas I *Morosini* : 1204-1211 (Constantinople—Latin)
Thomas II *Palaiologos Tagaris* : 1379?-1384? (Constantinople—Latin)
Thomas III *Bakócz de Erdoed* : 1507-1521 (Constantinople—Latin)
Thómas I : 807-820 (Jerusalem—Greek)
Thómas II : 969-977 (Jerusalem—Greek)
Thomas I : 35-72 (India—Malankara Orthodox)
Thomas *Angi de Lentino* : 1272-1277 (Jerusalem—Latin)
Thomas Mar Athanasios : 1877-1893 (India—Mar Thoma Syrian)
Thomas Mar Athanasios : 1982- [suffragan] (India—Mar Thoma Syrian)
Thomas Mar Timotheos : 1992- [suffragan] (India—Malankara Orthodox)
Thomuso : 360-368 (India—Malankara Orthodox)
Tikhon *Belavin* : 1899-1907 (America—Orthodox Church)

INDEX OF PRIMATES

Tikhon *Belavin* : 1917-1925 (Russia)
Tilotej : 1714-1718 (Macedonia)
Timathiyus : 274-283 (Antioch—Syrian Catholic)
Timat'ius I : 780-820 (Assyria)
Timat'ius II : 1318-1328 (Assyria)
Timat'ius I : 780-823 (Babylon)
Timat'ius II : 1318-1332 (Babylon)
Timat'ius Yusip IV *Mushi* : 1713-1757 (Babylon)
Timayus : 271-279 (Antioch—Greek)
Timayus : 266-271 (Antioch—Greek Melkite)
Timiyus : 273-282 (Antioch—Syrian Orthodox)
Timofeî *Sacherbatskiî* : 1764-1767 (Russia—Moscow)
Timotheos I *Aktémón* : 381-385 (Alexandria—Greek)
Timotheos (II) *Ailouros* : 457-460, 475-477 [anti-pope] (Alexandria—Greek)
Timotheos II *Salophakialos* : 460-475, 477-482 (Alexandria—Greek)
Timotheos *Euangelidés* : 1949 (America—Greek)
Timotheos I *Kélón* : 511-518 (Constantinople—Greek)
Timotheos II *apo Palaión Patrón* : 1612-1620 (Constantinople—Greek)
Timotheos I *Kastrinogiannakés* : 1882-1897 (Crete)
Timotheos II *Benerés* : 1933-1941 (Crete)
Timotheos III *Papoutsakés* : 1978- (Crete)
Timotheos (I) : 1572-1588? (Cyprus)
Timotheos (II) : 1622- [anti-archbishop] (Cyprus)
Timotheos, Thomas Mar : 1992- [suffragan] (India—Malankara Orthodox)
Timotheos *Themelés* : 1935-1955 (Jerusalem—Greek)
Timuthawus I : 380-385 (Alexandria—Coptic)
Timuthawus II *Ailouros* : 458-460?, 475-480 (Alexandria—Coptic)
Timuthawus (III) *Salophakialos* : 460-475 [anti-pope] (Alexandria—Coptic)
Timuthawus III : 517-535 (Alexandria—Coptic)
Timuthawus : 378-384 (Alexandria—Coptic Catholic)
Tiran *Nersoyan* : 1957-1958 (Jerusalem—Armenian)
Tiranus : 304-314 (Antioch—Greek)
Tiranus : 306-314 (Antioch—Greek Melkite)
Tiratur : 1586-1592 [anti-catholicos] (Cilicia—Armenian Apostolic)
Tiratur : 1561-1563, 1596-1599 (Constantinople—Armenian)
Tit *Simedrea* : 1940-1945 (Austria—Cernovci)
Titos : 242-272 (Constantinople—Greek)
Titos I *Apostolos* : 64? (Crete)
Titos II *Zógraphidés* : 1922-1933 (Crete)
Titos I *Mar Thoma* : 1894-1910 (India—Mar Thoma Syrian)
Titos II *Mar Thoma* : 1899-1910 [suffragan], 1910-1944 (India—Mar Thoma Syrian)
T'iyaduris : 850-852 (Assyria)
T'iyadusis I : 850-852 (Assyria)
T'iyadusis II : 1257-1265 (Assyria)
T'iyadusis : 853-858 (Babylon)
Tiyufilaqtus : unknown (Antioch—Maronite)
Tóbias : 2nd cent. (Jerusalem—Greek)
Tomas : 1237 (Ethiopia—Historical)
T'orgom *Manugian* : 1994-1995 [locum tenens] (Armenia)
T'orgom I *Gushakian* : 1931-1939 (Jerusalem—Armenian)
T'orgom II *Manugian* : 1990- (Jerusalem—Armenian)
T'oros I : 1548-1550? (Cilicia—Armenian Apostolic)
T'oros II : 1654-1657 (Cilicia—Armenian Apostolic)

T'oros III *Adshapahian* : 1784-1796 (Cilicia—Armenian Apostolic)
T'oros : 1681, 1687-1688 (Constantinople—Armenian)
T'ovma—SEE ALSO: T'ovmas
T'ovma I *Toghlabeghian* : 1681-1698 (Aght'amar)
T'ovma : 1722? [locum tenens] (Aght'amar)
T'ovma II : 1761-1783 (Aght'amar)
T'ovma : -1495 (Aghunie)
T'ovma II : 1644, 1657-1659 (Constantinople—Armenian)
T'ovmas—SEE ALSO: T'ovma
T'ovmas I : 1581-1587 (Constantinople—Armenian)
Trdat I : 741-764 (Armenia)
Trdat II : 764-767 (Armenia)
Tróïlos : -431 (Cyprus)
Tryphón : 927-931 (Constantinople—Greek)
Tubiyya Butrus *al-Khazin* : 1733, 1756-1766 (Antioch—Maronite)
Tuma : 683?-685? (Antioch—Greek Melkite)
T'uma—SEE ALSO: Thoma
T'uma I *Shlikha* : 33 (Assyria)
T'uma II *Darmu* : 1968-1969 (Assyria—Old Apostolic Church of the East)
T'uma *Shlikha* : -33 (Babylon)
T'uma I : 795?-824? (India—Chaldean)
T'uma II : 1056? (India—Chaldean)
T'uma III : 1490? (India—Chaldean)
T'uma IV *Rocos* : 1861-1862 (India—Chaldean)
T'uma V *Darmu* : 1952-1968 (India—Chaldean)
T'umarsa : 383-393 (Assyria)
T'umarsa : 388?- (Babylon)
Turanniyus : 304-313 (Antioch—Syrian Orthodox)
Turanus : 299-313 (Antioch—Syrian Catholic)
Tymofiî *Shcherbants'kiî* : 1748-1757 (Ukraine)
Tymoteusz *Szretter* : 1948-1951, 1959-1961 [locum tenens], 1961-1962 (Poland)
Ugo—SEE ALSO: Hugo
Ugo *de Robertis* : 1402- (Alexandria—Latin)
Ugo II *de Lusignan* : 1413-1442 (Cyprus—Latin)
Ukhtanês : 670-681? (Aghunie)
'Ummanu'il : 937-949 (Assyria)
'Ummanu'il I : 937-960 (Babylon)
'Ummanu'il II *T'uma*, Yusip : 1900-1947 (Babylon)
Urbanus I : 222-230 (Rome)
Urbanus II : 1088-1099 (Rome)
Urbanus III *Crivelli* : 1185-1187 (Rome)
Urbanus IV *Pantaléon* : 1261-1264 (Rome)
Urbanus V *de Grimoard* : 1362-1370 (Rome)
Urbanus VI *Prignano* : 1378-1389 (Rome)
Urbanus VII *Castagna* : 1590 (Rome)
Urbanus VIII *Barberini* : 1623-1644 (Rome)
Ursinus : 366-367 [anti-pope] (Rome)
Vahan *Siuni* : 968-969 (Armenia)
Vahan *Kostanian* : 1954-1955 [locum tenens] (Armenia)
Valaam : 1596-1598 (Bulgaria)
Valaam : 1597-1598 (Macedonia)
Valentinus : 827 (Rome)
Varfolomeî *Gondarovskiî* : 1969-1972 (Moldova)

Varlaam : 1735-1745 (Austria—Cernovci)
Varlaam : 1685-1692 (Austria—Sibiu)
Varlaam *Eristavi* : 1811-1817 [exarch] (Georgia)
Varlaam I : 1534?-1544 (Romania)
Varlaam II : 1672-1679 (Romania)
Varlaam : 1511-1521 (Russia—Moscow)
Varlaam I *IAsyns'kyî* : 1690-1707 (Ukraine)
Varlaam II *Vonatovych* : 1722-1730 (Ukraine)
Varnava *Rosic* : 1930-1937 (Serbia)
Vasile I *Moga* : 1810-1845 (Austria—Sibiu)
Vasile II *Mangra* : 1916-1918 (Austria—Sibiu)
Vasiliî I : 1185-1233 (Bulgaria)
Vasiliî II : 1246- (Bulgaria)
Vasilije *Jovanovic-Brkic* : 1763-1765, 1772 (Serbia)
Vasilije I : 16th cent. (Serbia—Montenegro)
Vasilije II *Veljekraïski* : -1689 (Serbia—Montenegro)
Vasilije III : 1744-1750 [coadjutor], 1750-1766 (Serbia—Montenegro)
Vasyl' *Lypkisv'kyî* : 1921-1927 (Ukraine—Autocephalous)
Vasyl' *Fedak* : 1985- (Ukraine—Canada)
Vasyl'ii *Lypkisv'kyî* : 1921-1927 (Ukraine—Autocephalous)
Vavyla : 1491-1520 (Serbia—Montenegro)
Vazgên *Palchian* : 1955-1994 (Armenia)
Venceslaus *Králik* : 1397-1416 (Antioch—Latin)
Veniamin *Babalich* : 1946-1953 (Japan)
Venijamin : 1582-1631 (Serbia—Montenegro)
Vicentije I *Popovic* : 1713-1725 (Austria—Karlovci)
Vicentije II *Jovanovic* : 1731-1737 (Austria—Karlovci)
Vicentije III *Jovanovic-Vidak* : 1774-1780 (Austria—Karlovci)
Victor *Marcello* : 1477- (Cyprus—Latin)
Victor I : 189-199 (Rome)
Victor II *von Dollnstein-Hirschberg* : 1055-1057 (Rome)
Victor III : 1086-1087 (Rome)
Victor IV *Conti* : 1138 [anti-pope] (Rome)
Victor IV *de Monticelli* : 1159-1164 [anti-pope] (Rome)
Vigilius : 537-555 (Rome)
Vikentije I *Stefanovic* : 1756? (Serbia)
Vikentije II *Prodanov* : 1950-1958 (Serbia)
Vincentius *Tizzani* : 1886-1892 (Antioch—Latin)
Vincentius *Bracco* : 1873-1889 (Jerusalem—Latin)
Viroy : 596-630 (Aghunie)
Visarion *Puiu* : 1935-1940 (Austria—Cernovci)
Visarion : 1310? (Bulgaria)
Visarion I *Baïca* : 1689-1695 (Serbia—Montenegro)
Visarion II *Ljubisha* : 1882-1884 (Serbia—Montenegro)
Vissarion *Xhuvani* : 1929-1937 (Albania)
Vitalianus : 657-672 (Rome)
Vitaliî *Ustinov* : 1985-1986 [locum tenens], 1986- (Russia—Synodal Church)
Vladimir : 1888-1891 (America—Orthodox Church)
Vladimir *Repta* : 1902-1924 (Austria—Cernovci)
Vladimir *Bogoiavlens'kyî* : 1892-1898 [exarch] (Georgia)
Vladimir *Nagoskiî* : 1962-1972 (Japan)
Vladimir *Cantarian* : 1989- (Moldova)
Vollunius *Bandinelli* : 1658-1667 (Constantinople—Latin)
Volodymyr I *Bogoiavlens'kyî* : 1915-1918 (Ukraine)

Volodymyr II *Slobodan* : 1992- (Ukraine—Moscow)
Volodymyr II *Romaniuk* : 1993- (Ukraine—Kiev)
Vrt'anês *Part'e* : 333-341 (Armenia)
Vrt'anês *Kert'ogh* : 604-607 [locum tenens] (Armenia)
Vrt'anês I : 1323-1332 (Jerusalem—Armenian)
Vrt'anês II : 1860-1864 [locum tenens] (Jerusalem—Armenian)
Vsevolod *Maîdanskiî* : 1987- (Ukraine—America)
Willelmus—SEE ALSO: Guillelmus
Willelmus I : 1130-1145 (Jerusalem—Latin)
Yabhalaha I : 415-420 (Assyria)
Yabhalaha II *bar Qayyuma* : 1191-1222 (Assyria)
Yabhalaha III *bar Turkaya* : 1281-1318 (Assyria)
Yabhalaha IV Shim'un X : 1558-1580 (Assyria)
Yabhalaha I : 415-420 (Babylon)
Yabhalaha II *bar Qayyuma* : 1190-1220 (Babylon)
Yabhalaha III *bar Turkaya* : 1283-1318 (Babylon)
Yabhalaha IV, Shim'un : 1578-1580 (Babylon)
Yabhalaha I : 1407? (India—Chaldean)
Yabhalaha II : 1503? (India—Chaldean)
Yabhalaha Shim'un XIV : 1690-1692 (Assyria)
Ya'eqob I : 848? (Ethiopia—Historical)
Ya'eqob II : 1250? (Ethiopia—Historical)
Ya'eqob III *Madhinana Egzie* : 1337-1344 (Ethiopia—Historical)
Ya'eqob : unknown (Ethiopia—Official)
Yahb Allaho : 393-398 (India—Malankara Orthodox)
Yakoub : 213-231 (India—Malankara Orthodox)
Yalda, Baselios Mar : 1634-1685 (India—Malankara Orthodox)
Ya'qub : 819-830 (Alexandria—Coptic)
Ya'qub I *Butrus of Ramat* : 1141?-1154 (Antioch—Maronite)
Ya'qub II : 1268?- (Antioch—Maronite)
Ya'qub III *ibn Hid al-Hadathi* : 1445-1458 (Antioch—Maronite)
Ya'qub IV Butrus *Awwad* : 1705-1733 (Antioch—Maronite)
Ya'qub, Ighnatiyus : 1510-1519 (Antioch—Syrian Catholic)
Ya'qub I, Ighnatiyus : 1512-1517 (Antioch—Syrian Orthodox)
Ya'qub II, Ighnatiyus : 1847-1871 (Antioch—Syrian Orthodox)
Ya'qub III *Tuma*, Ighnatiyus : 1957-1980 (Antioch—Syrian Orthodox)
Ya'qub I : 172-190 (Assyria)
Ya'qub II : 754-773 (Assyria)
Ya'qub I : 2nd cent. (Babylon)
Ya'qub II : 754-773 (Babylon)
Ya'qub I : 1328? (India—Chaldean)
Ya'qub II : 1503-1549? (India—Chaldean)
Yaraklas : 231-247 (Alexandria—Coptic)
Yaraklas : 230-246 (Alexandria—Coptic Catholic)
Yerda' Mika'el III : 1220? (Ethiopia—Historical)
Yes'aq—SEE ALSO: Yeshaq
Yes'aq I : 1210?- (Ethiopia—Historical)
Yes'aq I : unknown (Ethiopia—Official)
Yeshaq—SEE ALSO: Yes'aq
Yeshaq II : 1481-1505? (Ethiopia—Historical)
Yeshaq II : 1481-1510? (Ethiopia—Official)
Yoakim Mar Koorilose : 1846-1852 (India—Malankara Syrian)
Yohannes I : 820?-840? (Ethiopia—Historical)
Yohannes II : 1310? (Ethiopia—Historical)

Yohannes III : 1437? (Ethiopia—Historical)
Yohannes IV : 1530? (Ethiopia—Historical)
Yohannes V : 1649?- (Ethiopia—Historical)
Yohannes VI : 1743-1761 (Ethiopia—Historical)
Yohannes VII : 1939-1941 [anti-abuna] (Ethiopia—Historical)
Yohannes : 1976 [locum tenens] (Ethiopia—Historical)
Yohannes I : unknown (Ethiopia—Official)
Yohannes II : unknown (Ethiopia—Official)
Yohannes III : unknown (Ethiopia—Official)
Yohannes IV : unknown (Ethiopia—Official)
Yohannes V : unknown (Ethiopia—Official)
Yohannes VI : unknown (Ethiopia—Official)
Yohannes VII : unknown (Ethiopia—Official)
Yohannes VIII : unknown (Ethiopia—Official)
Yohannes IX : unknown (Ethiopia—Official)
Yohannes X : unknown (Ethiopia—Official)
Yohannes XI : unknown (Ethiopia—Official)
Yohannes XII : unknown (Ethiopia—Official)
Yohannes XIII : 1648?- (Ethiopia—Official)
Yohannes XIV : 1743-1761 (Ethiopia—Official)
Yohannes XV : 1939-1941 [anti-abuna] (Ethiopia—Official)
Yohannes : 1976 [locum tenens] (Ethiopia—Official)
Yohannon (V) Elia *Mellus* : 1874-1882 (India—Chaldean)
Yosab I : unknown (Ethiopia—Official)
Yosab II : 1539?-1559? (Ethiopia—Official)
Yosab III : 1770-1803 (Ethiopia—Official)
Yosef : unknown (Ethiopia—Official)
Yostos I : unknown (Ethiopia—Official)
Yostos II : unknown (Ethiopia—Official)
Youhanon I *Soubo* : 687-688 (India—Malankara Orthodox)
Youhanon II *Keeyunoyo* : 758-788 (India—Malankara Orthodox)
Youhanon III *of Damascus* : 991-997 (India—Malankara Orthodox)
Youhanon IV *Sleeba* : 1075-1106 (India—Malankara Orthodox)
Youhanon V *Srugayo* : 1165-1188 (India—Malankara Orthodox)
Youhanon VI *Bar Madan* : 1232-1253 (India—Malankara Orthodox)
Yoyakin Mar Koorilose : 1846-1852 (India—Malankara Syrian)
Yuhanna I : 428-441 (Antioch—Greek)
Yuhanna II *Kódónatos* : 477 (Antioch—Greek)
Yuhanna III : 798-811 (Antioch—Greek)
Yuhanna IV *Polités* : 995-1022 (Antioch—Greek)
Yuhanna V : 1057-1062 (Antioch—Greek)
Yuhanna VI *Oxeités* : 1088-1106 (Antioch—Greek)
Yuhanna VII : 1106-1137 (Antioch—Greek)
Yuhanna VIII : 1155-1159 (Antioch—Greek)
Yuhanna I : 429?-442? (Antioch—Greek Melkite)
Yuhanna II *Kódónatos* : 477?-478? (Antioch—Greek Melkite)
Yuhanna III *Polités* : 997-1022 (Antioch—Greek Melkite)
Yuhanna IV *Oxeités* : 1098-1100 (Antioch—Greek Melkite)
Yuhanna I *Marun* : 681-707 (Antioch—Maronite)
Yuhanna II *Marun* : 8th cent. (Antioch—Maronite)
Yuhanna III : 8th cent. (Antioch—Maronite)
Yuhanna IV : unknown (Antioch—Maronite)
Yuhanna V : unknown (Antioch—Maronite)
Yuhanna VI : unknown (Antioch—Maronite)

Yuhanna VII *of Lahfad* : 1160? (Antioch—Maronite)
Yuhanna VIII Butrus *of Giag* : 1239? (Antioch—Maronite)
Yuhanna IX : 1322?-1357? (Antioch—Maronite)
Yuhanna X *al-Jaji* : 1404-1445 (Antioch—Maronite)
Yuhanna XI *ibn Makhluf* : 1608-1633 (Antioch—Maronite)
Yuhanna XII *al-Safrawi* : 1648-1656 (Antioch—Maronite)
Yuhanna XIII Butrus *al-Hilu* : 1809-1823 (Antioch—Maronite)
Yuhanna XIV Butrus *Hajj* : 1890-1899 (Antioch—Maronite)
Yuhanna I : 427-440 (Antioch—Syrian Catholic)
Yuhanna II *Kódónatos* : 480, 484-485 (Antioch—Syrian Catholic)
Yuhanna III : 631-649 (Antioch—Syrian Catholic)
Yuhanna IV : 740-755 (Antioch—Syrian Catholic)
Yuhanna (V) : 758-763? [anti-patriarch] (Antioch—Syrian Catholic)
Yuhanna V : 847-874 (Antioch—Syrian Catholic)
Yuhanna VI : 910-922 (Antioch—Syrian Catholic)
Yuhanna VII : 936-953 (Antioch—Syrian Catholic)
Yuhanna VIII : 954-957 (Antioch—Syrian Catholic)
Yuhanna IX *Sarighta* : 965-986 (Antioch—Syrian Catholic)
Yuhanna X *of Abhdun* : 1004-1030 (Antioch—Syrian Catholic)
Yuhanna XI : 1042-1057 (Antioch—Syrian Catholic)
Yuhanna XII *Ishu' ibn Shushan* : 1063-1073 (Antioch—Syrian Catholic)
Yuhanna XIII *Shinudah* : 1075-1077 (Antioch—Syrian Catholic)
Yuhanna XIV : 1079-1087 (Antioch—Syrian Catholic)
Yuhanna XV *Mawdyani* : 1129-1137 (Antioch—Syrian Catholic)
Yuhanna XVI *Ishu'* : 1208-1220 (Antioch—Syrian Catholic)
Yuhanna XVII *ibn Ma'dani* : 1253-1263 (Antioch—Syrian Catholic)
Yuhanna XVIII *Akhsinaya Bar Shilla*, Ighnatiyus : 1484-1494 (Antioch—Syrian Catholic)
Yuhanna I : 428-442 (Antioch—Syrian Orthodox)
Yuhanna II *Kódónatos* : 476-478 (Antioch—Syrian Orthodox)
Yuhanna III : 631-648 (Antioch—Syrian Orthodox)
Yuhanna (IV) : 758-763? [anti-patriarch] (Antioch—Syrian Orthodox)
Yuhanna IV : 849-873 (Antioch—Syrian Orthodox)
Yuhanna V : 910-922 (Antioch—Syrian Orthodox)
Yuhanna VI : 936-956 (Antioch—Syrian Orthodox)
Yuhanna VII *Sarighta al-Ma'tuk* : 965-985 (Antioch—Syrian Orthodox)
Yuhanna VIII *ibn Abhduni* : 1004-1033 (Antioch—Syrian Orthodox)
Yuhanna IX : 1044-1057 (Antioch—Syrian Orthodox)
Yuhanna X *Ishu' ibn Shushan* : 1063-1072 (Antioch—Syrian Orthodox)
Yuhanna XI *Mawdyani* : 1129-1137 (Antioch—Syrian Orthodox)
Yuhanna XII *Ishu'* : 1208-1220 (Antioch—Syrian Orthodox)
Yuhanna XIII *ibn al-Ma'dani* : 1261-1263 (Antioch—Syrian Orthodox)
Yuhanna XIV *Akhsinaya Bar Shilla*, Ighnatiyus : 1483-1493 (Antioch—Syrian Orthodox)
Yuhanna (XV) *ibn Qufar*, Ighnatiyus : 1488-1493 (Antioch—Syrian Orthodox—Tur Abhdin)
Yuhanna, Mar : 1685-1693 (India—Malankara Syrian)
Yuhannis I *Hemula* : 495-503 (Alexandria—Coptic)
Yuhannis II *Nikiotés* : 503-515 (Alexandria—Coptic)
Yuhannis III : 677-686 (Alexandria—Coptic)
Yuhannis IV : 775-799 (Alexandria—Coptic)
Yuhannis V *ibn Abi'l-Fath* : 1147-1167 (Alexandria—Coptic)
Yuhannis VI *ibn Abi Ghali* : 1189-1216 (Alexandria—Coptic)
Yuhannis VII *ibn Abi Sa'id* : 1262-1268, 1271-1293 (Alexandria—Coptic)

Yuhannis VIII : 1300-1320 (Alexandria—Coptic)
Yuhannis IX : 1320-1327 (Alexandria—Coptic)
Yuhannis X *al-Mu'taman* : 1363-1369 (Alexandria—Coptic)
Yuhannis XI *Abu'l-Farag* : 1427-1452 (Alexandria—Coptic)
Yuhannis XII : 1479-1482 (Alexandria—Coptic)
Yuhannis XIII : 1484-1524 (Alexandria—Coptic)
Yuhannis XIV *al-Manfulati* : 1570-1585 (Alexandria—Coptic)
Yuhannis XV : 1619-1634 (Alexandria—Coptic)
Yuhannis XVI *al-Maghribi* : 1676-1718 (Alexandria—Coptic)
Yuhannis XVII *al-Malawi* : 1726-1745 (Alexandria—Coptic)
Yuhannis XVIII *al-Fayumi* : 1769-1796 (Alexandria—Coptic)
Yuhannis XIX : 1928-1942 (Alexandria—Coptic)
Yuhannis *Faragi* : 1781-1788 (Alexandria—Coptic Catholic)
Yukhannan I *bar Marta* : 680-682 (Assyria)
Yukhannan II *Garba "The Leper"* : 693-694 (Assyria)
Yukhannan III *bar Narsai* : 884-892 (Assyria)
Yukhannan IV *bar Akhiha* : 892-898 (Assyria)
Yukhannan V *bar Abgara* : 900-905 (Assyria)
Yukhannan VI *bar Ishu'* : 1001-1012 (Assyria)
Yukhannan VII *Nazuk* : 1013-1022 (Assyria)
Yukhannan VIII *bar Targali* : 1049-1057 (Assyria)
Yukhannan I *bar Marta* : 681?-683 (Babylon)
Yukhannan (II) *Garba "The Leper"* : 691-693? [anti-patriarch] (Babylon)
Yukhannan II *bar Akhiha* : 884-891 (Babylon)
Yukhannan III *bar Narsai* : 893-899 (Babylon)
Yukhannan IV *bar Abgara* : 900-905 (Babylon)
Yukhannan V *bar Ishu'* : 1000-1011 (Babylon)
Yukhannan VI *Nazuk* : 1012-1016 (Babylon)
Yukhannan VII *bar Tarbali* : 1049-1057 (Babylon)
Yukhannan VIII *Khurmiz* : 1804-1830 [locum tenens], 1830-1838 (Babylon)
Yukhannan I : 1000? (India—Chaldean)
Yukhannan II : 1110? (India—Chaldean)
Yukhannan III : 1122?-1129? (India—Chaldean)
Yukhannan IV : 1490? (India—Chaldean)
Yukhannan V Elia *Mellus* : 1874-1882 (India—Chaldean)
Yukhannan Iliya X *bar Mama* : 1660-1700 [locum tenens], 1830-1838 (Babylon)
Yukhannan Shim'un *Sulaqa* : 1551-1555 (Babylon)
Yuliyanus—SEE ALSO: Yulyan
Yuliyanus : 180-189 (Alexandria—Coptic)
Yuliyanus : 178-188 (Alexandria—Coptic Catholic)
Yuliyanus : 471 (Antioch—Greek)
Yuliyanus : 471-476? (Antioch—Greek Melkite)
Yuliyanus I : 471-476 (Antioch—Syrian Orthodox)
Yulyan—SEE ALSO: Yuliyanus
Yulyan I : 473-477 (Antioch—Syrian Catholic)
Yulyan II : 592-595 (Antioch—Syrian Catholic)
Yulyan III *"The Roman"* : 688-709 (Antioch—Syrian Catholic)
Yulyan II : 591-595 (Antioch—Syrian Orthodox)
Yulyan III *"The Roman"* : 687-708 (Antioch—Syrian Orthodox)
Yunan, Ighnatiyus : 1817-1819 (Antioch—Syrian Orthodox)
Yunan Shim'un XVIII : 1780?-1820? (Assyria)
Yusab I : 830-849 (Alexandria—Coptic)
Yusab II *Filibbus* : 1942-1944 [locum tenens], 1946-1954 (Alexandria—Coptic)

Yusab I : 1547?-1559? (Ethiopia—Historical)
Yusab II : 1770-1803 (Ethiopia—Historical)
Yusip : 552-567 (Assyria)
Yusip I : 551-567? (Babylon)
Yusip II : 1681-1695 (Babylon)
Yusip III *Sliba*, Ma'ruf : 1696-1712 (Babylon)
Yusip IV *Mushi*, Timat'ius : 1713-1757 (Babylon)
Yusip V *Khindi*, Lazar : 1757-1781 (Babylon)
Yusip (VI) *Khindi*, Agustinus : 1804-1828 [unconsecrated] (Babylon)
Yusip VI *Audu* : 1848-1878 (Babylon)
Yusip VII *Ghanima* : 1947-1958 (Babylon)
Yusip I *of Edessa* : 345? (India—Chaldean)
Yusip II :. 1231 (India—Chaldean)
Yusip III : 1556-1569 (India—Chaldean)
Yusip 'Ummanu'il II *T'uma* : 1900-1947 (Babylon)
Yustus : 122-130 (Alexandria—Coptic)
Yustus : 118-129 (Alexandria—Coptic Catholic)
Yusuf I *al-Jirjisi* : 1100? (Antioch—Maronite)
Yusuf II *ibn Musa al-Ruzzi* : 1599-1608 (Antioch—Maronite)
Yusuf III *ibn Halib al-'Aquri* : 1644-1647 (Antioch—Maronite)
Yusuf IV Butrus *Dirgham al-Khazin* : 1733-1742 (Antioch—Maronite)
Yusuf V Butrus *Istifan* : 1766-1793 (Antioch—Maronite)
Yusuf VI Butrus *al-Tiyyan* : 1796-1808 (Antioch—Maronite)
Yusuf VII Butrus *Hubaysh* : 1823-1845 (Antioch—Maronite)
Yusuf VIII Butrus *al-Khazin* : 1846-1854 (Antioch—Maronite)
Yusuf : 790-792 (Antioch—Syrian Catholic)
Yusuf : 791-792 (Antioch—Syrian Orthodox)
Yuwakim I : 1199-1219 (Antioch—Greek)
Yuwakim II : 1411-1426 (Antioch—Greek)
Yuwakim III : 1476-1483 (Antioch—Greek)
Yuwakim IV *ibn Jumma* : 1543-1576 (Antioch—Greek)
Yuwakim V *ibn Daww* : 1581-1592 (Antioch—Greek)
Yuwakim VI *Ziyada* : 1593-1604 (Antioch—Greek)
Yuwakim VII : 1724 [anti-patriarch] (Antioch—Greek)
Yuwakim I : 1412?-1425? (Antioch—Greek Melkite)
Yuwakim II : 1458?-1459? (Antioch—Greek Melkite)
Yuwakim III : 1527 [anti-patriarch], 1531-1534? (Antioch—Greek Melkite)
Yuwakim IV *ibn Jumma* : 1540 [anti-patriarch], 1543?-1575 (Antioch—Greek Melkite)
Yuwakim V *ibn Daww* : 1581-1592 [anti-patriarch] (Antioch—Greek Melkite)
Yuwakim VI *Ziyada* : 1593-1604 (Antioch—Greek Melkite)
Yuwakim VII : 1724 [anti-patriarch] (Antioch—Greek Melkite)
Zabina : 231-237 (Antioch—Syrian Orthodox)
Zacharias *Moridakés* : 1769-1786 (Crete)
Zacharias : 1734-1741 (Greece)
Zacharias : 609-632 (Jerusalem—Greek)
Zacharias : 1103-1114 (Sinai)
Zacharias : 741-752 (Rome)
Zaharij : 1487?- (Macedonia)
Zak'aria I *Sefedinian* : 1296-1336 (Aght'amar)
Zak'aria II *Nahatak* : 1369-1393 (Aght'amar)
Zak'aria III : 1434-1464 (Aght'amar)
Zak'aria IV : 1489-1496 (Aght'amar)
Zak'aria I : 4th cent. (Aghunie)

ABOUT THE AUTHOR

MICHAEL BURGESS has been a professor at California State University, San Bernardino since 1970, which was also the year his first book was published. His previous works include a history of the Falkland Islands War, a dictionary of arms control and disarmament, two film guides, and several dozen annotated subject and personal bibliographies, among many others. He has also edited several journals and over 650 other volumes.